*Far Eastern and Russian Institute
Publications on Asia
Number 19*

THIS BOOK IS SPONSORED BY THE
MODERN CHINESE HISTORY PROJECT OF THE
FAR EASTERN AND RUSSIAN INSTITUTE

# Chinese Intellectuals and the Revolution of 1911

## THE BIRTH OF MODERN CHINESE RADICALISM

*By Michael Gasster*

UNIVERSITY OF WASHINGTON PRESS

*Seattle and London*

*This book is dedicated*
*to the memory of*
*Shelley Hsien Cheng, 1924–66*

"He only harbored a
vague dream, and its very
refusal to become a reality
made his longing the keener."

— Junichiro Tanizaki
in *Some Prefer Nettles*

# *Preface*

This book is devoted to discussing the ideas of a few Chinese revolutionaries in a brief period. The period studied most intensively is 1905–7, but I also include 1903–5 and 1907–8 at modest length, 1898–1903 and 1908–1911 much less, and pre–1898 and post–1911 hardly at all. The men discussed were intellectuals who participated in a movement to overthrow the Ch'ing dynasty (1644–1912) and establish a republic. Of the many revolutionaries who wrote in this period I have selected a small number for discussion. I chose them because taken together they represent the dominant trends in the thinking of the time; that thinking is important, in turn, because it represents the emergence of a new intelligentsia. This group had been taking shape for decades, but it began to dominate Chinese intellectual and political life around 1905. I discuss those members of the group who I think best reveal both its diversity and its unity.

The decline of the traditional Chinese intellectual elite may conveniently be marked by the years 1898 and 1905. In 1898 the most brilliant Confucianist of his time, K'ang Yu-wei, lost his battle to rejuvenate Confucian thought and institutions and equip them for the modern age; in 1905 the abolition of the examination system guaranteed that the old scholar-gentry would soon pass into history. Indeed within a few years after 1898 there hardly existed in China any conservatism worthy of the name, at least by traditional Chinese standards.[1]

[1] For a discussion of conservatism with particular reference to nineteenth-

Conservatives, someone once remarked only partly in jest, are people who believe that nothing should be done for the first time. If there were many such men in China at the turn of the century, few others were paying much attention to them. There were many persons who held to the more respectable conservative view that innovation must be justified more powerfully than the retention of the tried and familiar before it can become state policy; among them were doubtless some who applied stricter standards of performance to innovation than to retention, mainly because the new usually meant something foreign. But by the early 1900's even the most conservative elements in Chinese society, including those at court and in the bureaucracy, were abandoning this sort of conservatism and turning increasingly toward reform. The empress dowager, whose coup ended the 1898 reforms, was seeing things quite differently when she sent a mission abroad to study foreign constitutions in 1905. Traditional conservatives were becoming fewer and also more disorganized, even isolated. Organized conservatism by 1905 looked conservative mainly in contrast to the growing radicalism.

Like most other sizable movements, modern Chinese radicalism had a long prenatal period, perhaps forty years or more. But it was born and acquired some of its adult characteristics during the period 1903–8. It came to life with the appearance of a new intelligentsia, persons dedicated to the overthrow of the Manchu dynasty, the establishment of a republic, and the initiation of a vast program of rapid and thoroughgoing social, economic, and political change, or what we would today call modernization. This group became an organized movement and began to spell out its program between about 1903 and 1905. By 1905 no group that can be considered a serious contender for political power in China denied that there was a need for substantial change; the issue had become less whether to modernize than how. This issue was threshed out chiefly between 1905 and 1907; the contending parties were "reformers"[2] led by Liang

century China see Mary C. Wright, *The Last Stand of Chinese Conservatism*, pp. 1–5 and *passim*. A refreshing and more general discussion of conservatism is in the essay by Michael Oakeshott, "On Being Conservative," in a collection of his essays titled *Rationalism in Politics*, pp. 168–96.

[2] The term "reformers" is generally used in this book to designate Liang Ch'i-ch'ao and his followers. Where it has another meaning, the context should make it clear; in Chapter 1 it includes all those who wished to accelerate change but keep it comfortably short of revolutionary change.

Ch'i-ch'ao, speaking for the Manchu reform program but also for his own, and members of the T'ung-meng-hui led by Sun Yat-sen, Wang Ching-wei, and a number of other revolutionaries whose writings are the main subject of this book. By 1908 most of the revolutionaries' opponents had either joined them, disengaged, lost their following, or in some other way acknowledged the end of the contest; a contest continued after the fall of 1908, but the parties to it were so differently aligned, the issues between them so altered, the arena in which they struggled so unlike the earlier one, and the methods of the contest so different, that the story is too dissimilar from that of 1905–8 for much of it to be told here. The turning point was marked by a deep rift that opened between the Manchus and Liang Ch'i-ch'ao in the summer and fall of 1908 and by a split among the revolutionaries which occurred about the same time. After the split the most traditionalistic components broke away from the T'ung-meng-hui. Mainly for these reasons I concentrate here on the 1903–8 period.

Victory in the struggle within the new Chinese intelligentsia went to a particular kind of radicalism, one that was closely related to, and possibly paved the way for, the radicalism of the New Culture Movement and of the Communists. The radicalism that has dominated Chinese thought and politics in the twentieth century first saw the light of day and won its first victory between 1903 and 1908. The character of the nascent radicalism and of its victory is the main subject of this book. The relationship of early radicalism to subsequent radicalism, which can only be hypothesized and hinted at here, awaits further research.

As the remarks above suggest, many of the questions with which this book deals go beyond my immediate aims and far beyond most of the material I have studied. I have chosen to view China's new intelligentsia from two angles. First, I am concerned with the role they played in the revolution of 1911. Second, I am concerned with their place in the history of revolution, particularly intellectual revolution, in modern China. Thus on the one hand my subject is the role of intellectuals and their ideas in a political-military movement, a movement directed at the violent overthrow of existing government and the acquisition of political power; on the other, my subject is the ideas developed in the course of the 1911 revolution and how they

compare with those held by leading intellectuals before and especially after the period I am studying. Viewed narrowly, therefore, the
book focuses upon the nature of the revolutionaries' dissatisfaction
with the existing regime and their thoughts about what should replace it. This was the original focus of the doctoral dissertation out
of which the book has grown, and it still occupies a large part of the
study; such firm conclusions as may be drawn also refer to this
limited subject. But while no one is more aware than I that this is
too slight a book to warrant far-reaching conclusions on much
broader problems, I cannot resist the temptation to set down such
scattered ideas as I have about wider issues. I do this, quite frankly,
partly because the only way to stop them from buzzing around in
my head is to try to express them in an orderly fashion, and partly
because the best way to learn if these ideas have any value is to solicit
readers' comments on them. Finally and more fundamentally, it is
my belief that the purpose of scholarship is to raise questions as well
as suggest answers; I hope not to end discussion of my subject but
to encourage it.

In this immodest hope I offer some tentative conclusions and speculations about such immense subjects as the nature of nationalism,
democracy, revolution, and modernization in twentieth-century
China, the relationships among these four great forces, the roles of
Chinese intellectuals in twentieth-century politics, and the relationship between political thought and political action. The questions
interested me. I hope they interest the reader.

Before I express still another hope I should like to insert a few
words of explanation for it. We historians, like other scholars, are
required to examine our assumptions and biases; our professional
code stipulates that we beware of allowing present perspectives and
values to seep into our reading of the past and warp our understanding. This obligation weighs particularly heavily upon students of
revolution and most of all upon those of us who find ourselves in
sympathy with many of the goals of contemporary revolutionaries.
Much of the revolutionary ferment that has gripped and shaken the
modern world stems from a growing realization by more and more
people that a better life is possible. As human beings come to believe
that change is desirable, possible, and necessary, and as such belief
is matched by a growing control over their physical environment that

seems to promise them greater control of their entire destiny, the pace of change quickens and the demand for change intensifies. We live in a world of accelerating change, a revolutionary world. We begin to accept the likelihood that such changes will continue; reluctant to predict, the historian cannot escape a feeling that the general trend is not likely to be reversed in the near future. But more than this, I would not wish it to be reversed. My assumption and bias, in brief, is that revolutionary changes will and should be prominent in our lives for a long time.

Students of revolution also learn very quickly that past revolutions have often frustrated, defeated, and even cruelly devoured their progenitors. I wonder how the balance sheet would look if we could measure the degree to which revolutions have achieved their goals as against the degree of failure, to say nothing of the revolutions that have produced unforeseen evils matching or exceeding those they were directed against. However the balance would tip, there is reason to be sobered by the knowledge of those revolutions which have added to human misery.

A historian in the 1960's finds it difficult to study revolution without some hope that what little he learns about it will help others. May we carry out the profound and rapid changes that are necessary to realize human potential to the fullest; may we learn not how to prevent revolution but how to control it, channel it, and guide it as constructively as possible.

A few of the mechanics of the book also require some explanation. I have not consistently given names of organizations and publications in translation. Some, such as "T'ung-meng-hui," occur frequently enough that they should not trouble even the reader who is not used to Chinese. Many names translate only clumsily or misleadingly, and even in translation they are often so similar to each other that the reader is not rescued from confusion. Thus I translate some and not others, perhaps haphazardly, but with the intention of helping the reader as much as possible. Characters for names and terms may be found in the Glossary.

I have attempted by the organization of Parts Two and Three to distinguish the body of revolutionary ideology from its wings and at the same time show the range of revolutionary thinking. For example,

I treat Chang Ping-lin in a separate chapter even at the risk of magnifying his part in the story. Wang Ching-wei contributed much more to the core of revolutionary thought than Chang, but Wang is included in Part Two with Hu Han-min and other close followers of Sun Yat-sen as well as Sun himself; none of these key figures receives the individual examination I reserve for Chang. I have done this because even though Chang wrote a great deal at a crucial time on important topics, he operated largely on the fringes of the revolutionary movement and shared few of the others' values, assumptions, and beliefs. My treatment of him is also in part a confession of how difficult I found it to study him. The quality of his writing, his erudition, the diverse sources of his ideas, and his wide range of interests and concerns made his thinking hard for me to grasp, particularly since I was able to treat only a small segment of his highly unusual life and career. I hope others who are better equipped than I to study Chang in a broader time span and in a context more suitable to his major lifelong interests will some day give him the attention he deserves.

Finally, I regret my inability to make use of the vast body of scholarly literature in Japanese that bears on the subject matter of this book. I shall be grateful if readers will bring to my attention any material I have failed to take into account, but most of all I would appreciate knowing of data in Japanese that suggest interpretations other than mine.

I am delighted at last to have an opportunity to thank in print the many teachers, friends, and colleagues who have helped me. The original topic out of which this book grew was worked out in 1957 with the advice of the members of my dissertation reading committee, Professors Kung-chuan Hsiao, Franz Michael, and Hellmut Wilhelm. All three gave most generously of their time, learning, and wisdom; I owe them the unmeasurable debt a student owes to superlative teachers. And in subsequent years, as a colleague, I have been privileged to continue to learn from them.

Of the many others who helped me I must particularly thank Professor Mary C. Wright for her advice and encouragement and for her leadership in organizing the 1965 conference on the revolution of 1911, which led me to re-examine a dissertation that had gathered dust for three years and decide to revise it for publication.

The study resulting in this publication was made under a fellowship granted by the Ford Foundation and benefited by field training in Chinese made possible by an Inter-University Fellowship for Field Training in Chinese awarded by Cornell University and supported by the Ford Foundation. However, the conclusions, opinions, and other statements in this publication are those of the author and not necessarily those of the Ford Foundation or of any member of Cornell University. I wish to express my deep gratitude for the generous help I received from 1957 to 1961.

Much of my research was done in 1958–59 in Taiwan, where I was helped a great deal by Dr. Lo Chia-lun and by his courteous and efficient staff at the Kuomintang archives. I also wish to acknowledge my debt to Dr. Hsü Dau-lin, Professor Kuo Ting-yee of the Institute of Modern History at the Academia Sinica, Professor Wu Hsiang-hsiang, Mr. Ch'en Chieh-hsien, Mr. Chang Heng, and especially to Miss Yeh Leng-pin, who helped me with the difficult reading of Chang Ping-lin. Professor Leon Hurvitz also helped me to interpret some of Chang's Buddhist terms and concepts. Mr. Young-tsu Wong checked many of my footnotes, saved me from several errors of translation, discovered a number of source materials and biographical data which had escaped my attention, and suggested several clarifications and other improvements in the text for which I am very grateful. Mr. Richard C. Howard gave me a number of leads for biographical information, and he and Professor Lloyd Eastman allowed me to see some of their unpublished research which was very helpful. Mrs. Margaret Karzmar provided secretarial assistance with unique graciousness and efficiency, sharing my administrative responsibilities at the same time that she managed to type the manuscript, prepare it for the Press, and cheerfully perform countless other duties; I express to her my deepest thanks. I am equally grateful to Miss Gladys M. Greenwood, Editor of Far Eastern publications at the University of Washington, for her rigorous attention to content and style. For his many specific suggestions as well as general intellectual stimulation I thank my good friend John Fincher.

Finally, substantial portions of this book were discussed at meetings of the Modern Chinese History Project colloquium at the University of Washington. To all participants I owe more than I can express. But of one former member, the man to whose memory this book is dedicated, I must speak. Shelley Cheng was the most devoted student of the 1911 revolution I have known. When I began my research Shelley, who had recently begun work on his dissertation dealing with the T'ung-meng-hui, led me to the basic sources. In later years he was an inexhaustible source of information himself. But far more than that, his gaiety, wit, and sheer humanity enlivened the years of graduate study, and his abiding dedication to accuracy, thoroughness, and learning set standards for us all. I mourn his death, and I offer this book in homage to his life.

M.G.

*Seattle, Washington*
*November, 1968*

# Contents

# Introduction

## *From Traditional Conservatism to Modern Radicalism by Way of Revolution: Some Problems of Interpretation*

When does modern, as opposed to traditional, Chinese history begin? Questions of periodization are not so idle as they sometimes seem. For scholars, periodization provides an indispensable framework of analysis. Historians of Western civilization, for example, have relied upon general categories such as ancient, medieval, and modern to help them identify the main transitions Western society has undergone; and the identification of these transitions is inseparable from the evaluation of the chief features of each stage. A decision to date the beginning of modern European history at about 1500 might begin with a judgment about what distinguishes modern European society from the premodern; the historian then examines the historical record to determine at what point in time the modern characteristics began to outweigh the premodern. This examination often leads in turn to a revision of what is meant by modern characteristics. Some Western historians are pushing the Renaissance so far into the past that the medieval period may one day be in danger of being removed from the history books; on the other hand, this same tendency inclines other historians to abandon the "Renaissance" as an indicator of incipient modernity and begin their study of modern European history with the French and industrial revolutions.

Historians of China face special challenges in attempting this sort of periodization. It is no accident that the beginning of modern Chinese history is dated as variously as 1200, or even earlier, and 1840, or even later. This extraordinary range of disagreement may of course reflect only the great continuity of Chinese history; since China changed so much less than Europe, it might be thought more difficult to periodize Chinese than European history. On the other hand, it might also be thought less necessary to periodize Chinese history precisely because continuity was so great. Furthermore, China was far more a unity than Europe; thus there should not be the disagreements among historians of China that there are among those who study English, French, Spanish, and Italian history.

It is obvious that the periodization of Chinese history poses special problems if only because Chinese culture was more homogeneous than Europe's and also had greater staying power (or inertia); it maintained itself with fewer sharp turns or breaks. China's modern period seems much shorter than Europe's, much less clearly marked off from her premodern period, and thus much less clearly a historical entity than Europe's modern period. In brief, change in China has not yet been so sharp and so extensive as in Europe. The new in China has not yet been sufficiently assimilated to permit us to say with any confidence which new features are going to last and which are not. Far more persistently than historians of Europe, historians of China disagree about how the new is different from the old. These uncertainties are reflected in the widely varying opinions on when modern Chinese history began.

Plainly, there have been vast changes in China in recent times, and for that matter, in earlier times as well; indeed, if there had not been great change there would be no need to raise the issue. It is even possible that the rate of change in China during the last twenty, forty, sixty, or even one hundred years exceeds or nearly matches that of Europe for equivalent periods; we have no way accurately to measure rates of this sort. But the qualitative changes in Chinese society are less discernible than they are in Europe, partly because the process of "modernization" has been under way for a shorter time in China and partly because Chinese tradition resisted the process more powerfully.

The issue of when modern Chinese history began needs airing, because discussion of it will dispel the shadows cast by European (and Japanese) history. Comparison with Europe and Japan can make China seem to have changed rather little in the century or so following the Opium War. But no matter how the pace of change in China compares with the pace elsewhere, it is obvious that it has been accelerating rapidly for a long time. At some point in the recent past, change achieved a speed which, if ever before reached in China, was reached only briefly and probably millennia ago; far more significant, recent change has been in a totally new direction. It was propelled by foreign might and guided by foreign influence. Change in earlier periods may have rivaled the speed of recent change, and there may have been times (such as Ch'in-Han) when China shifted direction as sharply, but never before had change in China been so fast, so sharp, and at the same time so much directed toward borrowing from foreigners as in the last century. It is the concurrence of all three factors — speed of change, sharpness of change, and the degree of foreign influence — that is unprecedented in Chinese history. The third factor, of course, is crucially important. Never before recent times did Chinese leaders feel forced to import foreign ideas, foreign institutions, and foreign teachers, and even to take into account the reactions of foreigners to Chinese policy decisions of all sorts.

If the concurrence of these three factors is what distinguishes modern from premodern Chinese history, I would conclude that China's modern period did not clearly begin until the decade of 1895–1905. It was in this decade that men who were clearly and unequivocally more dedicated to Western-style modernization than to the preservation of traditional institutions, values, customs, and beliefs began to dominate Chinese life. It was in this period that the goals of revolutionaries such as Sun Yat-sen began to become national goals. Henceforth, those who made national policy and guided China's course, those who made the decisions that affected the lives of most of their countrymen, and those who represented China abroad were men whose goals were shaped more by what they considered to be modern and by related considerations than they were by traditional considerations.

The origins of the transition can be seen at least as early as 1860, and the transition itself can be seen most dramatically in the person of K'ang Yu-wei. K'ang, whose personal and direct influence on the course of history probably reached its peak in the summer of 1898, contained within himself powerful tendencies in both directions. He wanted preservation — or perhaps rather rejuvenation — of tradition, but he also wanted a fully modern China. Although the majority of scholars would probably consider K'ang the last great Confucianist rather than the father of modern China, historians will probably long debate whether he was more a traditional or more a modern man. Whatever the majority view of K'ang may turn out to be, and whatever the wisdom of majorities, the issue may be debated in regard to K'ang but it cannot be debated in regard to his successors.

This book concerns some of K'ang Yu-wei's successors. Its principal themes are that almost immediately after the failure of the reform movement of 1898 there came to the fore in Chinese thought and politics a new group of men; that this group was characterized by certain radical tendencies; that these tendencies distinguish them sharply from almost all of K'ang Yu-wei's predecessors, relate them in certain ways to K'ang, Liang Ch'i-ch'ao, and some other "reformers," and give them a great deal in common with later radicals, particularly the leaders of the New Culture Movement and the Communists. In this book I attempt to show how rapidly China shifted from traditionalism to radicalism and also to analyze the significance of that rapid shift, particularly the absence of any substantial moderate current of thought.

It is evident that there are obstacles to developing themes of this sort. Some of the difficulties concern matters of historical interpretation; these I attempt to deal with in the chapters that follow. Other difficulties too, particularly conceptual ones, cannot easily be handled apart from the history in which they are rooted, but while I count heavily on the body of the book to make it clear what is meant by *radicalism, moderate, revolution, modernization, intellectuals,* and other controversial terms I have used so casually up to now, some discussion of them is appropriate at the outset, if only to clarify what the issues are that the book attempts to explore.[1]

[1] For this discussion I have drawn upon the work of more scholars than I can cite in individual footnotes. Students of revolution, modernization, and intellectual

*Modernization* and modernity, the process and the condition, continue to be as difficult for social scientists to define now as they were for Chinese intellectuals to understand sixty years ago. The problems we face as social scientists are different from the ones the Chinese faced as revolutionaries, but they are not so different as to be totally unrelated. The similarities, differences, and relationships require our attention. According to social scientists, a "modern" society is characterized by certain levels of communication, transportation, per capita production, literacy, and "participation," certain features of social and bureaucratic organization, such as "functional specificity," and certain values, beliefs, and attitudes, such as those of secular rationality, goal-orientation, and the possibility and desirability of "progress." It is well known that these and other indices of modernity raise many additional conceptual problems, but at least they begin to suggest that the "modern" is not merely a period — the present time or the most recent fifteen, twenty-five, or fifty years. It is not the most recent time — it is a condition. Defining that condition still poses enormous problems, but the very imprecision of "modernity" may be an asset in the study of modernization in China. In this book we deal with Chinese whose knowledge of the modern world was skimpy. They were groping to understand what modernity was and how modernization in China could be accelerated. It is their very groping that we are trying to understand. We may better see with

history may wish to know that among the authors I have consulted are Hannah Arendt, Crane Brinton, Samuel P. Huntington, Chalmers A. Johnson, Joseph R. Levenson, R. R. Palmer, and Benjamin Schwartz; the relevant titles may be found in the bibliography. I should also like to mention several works which came to my attention only as this study neared completion but whose interpretations I find interestingly congenial to my own; they are C. E. Black, *The Dynamics of Modernization*; J. L. Talmon, *The Origins of Totalitarian Democracy* and *Political Messianism: The Romantic Phase*, and Michael Walzer, *The Revolution of the Saints: A Study in the Origins of Radical Politics*. Other references to my sources and to these conceptual problems may be found in my article, "Reform and Revolution in China's Political Modernization," in *China in Revolution: The First Phase, 1900–1913*, ed. Mary C. Wright, pp. 67–96. I have also touched upon some related problems in a review article dealing with Joseph R. Levenson's *Confucian China and Its Modern Fate*; see "The Death and Transfiguration of Confucianism," *Philosophy East and West*, XVIII, No. 3 (July, 1968), 205–13.

I hope it is understood that an elementary discussion of this sort is solely for the purpose of promoting understanding between reader and author and is offered under no illusions of making an original contribution to theory.

their eyes if we also are groping to understand what modernity is and how the process of modernization takes place.

This is not to make an asset out of a liability. Impersonal social scientific analysis employing "models" and measures serves one set of purposes, while historical awareness of open situations serves another. A model of modernity or modernization will not meet all the needs of our inquiry. The men we are studying wanted a different China from the one they had grown up in, and most of them wanted it to be more like England, France, America, and Japan than it was; of men such as Chang Ping-lin and the anarchists who wanted China to be different from these societies too, most wanted other radical changes that do not fit so neatly into the categories of social scientists. What they wanted does not correspond to any model I know of or any that I feel capable of designing. Our view of the process of modernization in China requires an attempt to see the alternatives and choices from the standpoint of the men we are studying and not only through the lenses of abstract concepts. Further discussion of modernization therefore depends upon exposition of what being modern meant to Sun Yat-sen and his compatriots; for now I refer to them as "modernizers" only in the very general sense that almost without exception they advocated more rapid and fundamental changes than had taken place in China until that time — changes in the direction they thought Japan and the leading Western powers had taken.

There were exceptions such as Chang Ping-lin; there were also the revolutionaries' secret-society followers and many others whose support turned out to be crucial in late 1911 and early 1912. Not all of the revolutionaries were modernizers. Equally significant, not all Chinese modernizers of the time were revolutionaries, at least not revolutionaries of the T'ung-meng-hui variety. The best example, and the one to whom I turn time and again in this book, is Liang Ch'i-ch'ao.

Liang shared many of the revolutionaries' goals of modernization. For much of the 1898–1912 period, including the climactic 1911 phase of the anti-Manchu movement,[2] he was also as much a revo-

---

[2] See Ernest P. Young, "The Reformer as a Conspirator: Liang Ch'i-ch'ao and the 1911 Revolution," in *Approaches to Modern Chinese History*, ed. Albert Feuerwerker, Rhoads Murphey, and Mary C. Wright, pp. 239–67.

lutionary as anyone. In the crucial 1905–8 period, however, he not only fought against the T'ung-meng-hui revolutionaries but was their bitterest, most feared, perhaps even most hated enemy, the recipient of much of their attention and abuse. If not a determined defender of the Ch'ing from 1905 to 1908, he was at least the most valuable ideological buffer the Manchus had between them and the revolutionaries. There is much about Liang's career that is puzzling, but one certainty is that for a time he was the ablest intellectual foe of the revolution.

The dispute between Liang and his T'ung-meng-hui adversaries raises questions about the nature of revolution and the relation between revolution and modernization. In a revolutionary age change tends to be rapid, deep, and extensive everywhere, but are these characteristics even more pronounced in late-modernizing societies? It is a commonplace of current writing that in their drive to modernize, the societies of the so-called third world are trying to compress centuries into decades. Thus change in Asia tends to be revolutionary. But even the most superficial observation reveals that the pace of change varies from country to country; indeed the consensus seems to be that the pace of change is greater in the more modern countries and that therefore the gap between the rich and the poor nations widens. Even within one nation some things change more rapidly and profoundly than others. There are degrees of revolutionary change. Also, seemingly identical results in two different societies are likely to reveal two degrees of change, since it is unlikely that any two societies would have begun to change at the same time or, what is even more important, from the same base point; even two (hypothetical) societies that adopted the same educational policies in 1950 and that today have the same proportions of their population receiving elementary, high school, and college educations would be likely to have differences in student-teacher relationships and other qualitative variations that stem from their traditional backgrounds. On the other hand, one may hypothesize that societies initiating similar reforms from similar base points will differ in process and results, also owing partly to differing traditions and choices. In brief, the term "revolutionary change" blankets many shadings. Men who are equally convinced that vast changes are urgently needed can differ sharply about pace, direction, pattern, sequence, and priorities. Liang Ch'i-ch'ao and the Chinese revolutionaries remind us, therefore, that modernizers are not necessarily revolutionaries, and it is by no means certain which route to modernization was best then or is best now.

The revolutionaries differed also among themselves. They differed about priorities and about direction. Some wanted greater emphasis placed on certain social and economic goals; some cared little if at all about anything but driving the Manchus from power. Some wanted a republic and some did not. The list of differences among the revolutionaries is nearly endless. One problem for us in this book is to identify the areas of greatest and least agreement among them. But analysis of this sort leads to questions about revolution.

If revolution is defined as nothing more than a sharp and sudden break with the past, we are already faced with conceptual problems. How fast is "sudden"? We speak of an industrial revolution, but more and more we realize that as it nears the end of its second century it is still in its infancy. Cannot a revolution take place in stages, or waves, over a long period of time? If it can, how does it differ from other forms of change? Perhaps by the sharpness of each break. Thus the Chinese revolution of 1911 may be seen as one stage in a series of sharp and sudden breaks that affected different sectors of Chinese life. The end of the Manchu monarchy in 1911 was undoubtedly a sharp and sudden break with the past; but which was the more important, the fall of the Manchus or the end of the monarchy? Only if we choose the former can we conclude that the consistent and virulent anti-Manchu but otherwise rather conservative Chang Ping-lin was more a revolutionary than the modernizer Liang Ch'i-ch'ao. If it is not merely the immediate consequences of a revolutionary movement that count, not only does Liang appear to be more revolutionary than Chang but we are back to the puzzle of determining 1911's significance. Was it more than a political revolution? And if it was only a political revolution, is our estimate of its significance influenced by our estimate of how important the central government was in 1911? How is the gradual decay of imperial rule to be weighed against the sudden transfer of authority in 1911–12? Even if it is mainly the immediate consequences that determine the significance of a revolution, how does one weigh them?

Another standard by which to measure a revolution's significance is the aims of its leaders. Did the revolution accomplish its leaders' goals? Who were the leaders and what were the most sought-after goals? The earliest and the most widespread, abiding, and angry complaint the Chinese revolutionaries had was that China's position in the world was humiliating, but 1911's contribution to the solution of that problem is hard to see. China's world position grew much worse for a long time after 1911 before it improved. Can it be said that 1911 was significant mainly because it saw the achievement of its leaders' most cherished aims?

The results of the 1911 revolution are beyond the scope of this book, and knowledge of the outcome should not distort the historian's view of the contest. But the consequences of revolution were one of the things that Liang Ch'i-ch'ao and T'ung-meng-hui writers such as Wang Ching-wei argued about most heatedly. Liang, of course, predicted that the results would be dire, and Wang insisted they would be salutary. Both were partly right and partly wrong, but I have no wish to determine whose foresight was better. I am concerned with the puzzle of why these two men, whose goals overlapped so much, found themselves enemies because of what divided them instead of allies because of what united them. One crucial thing that divided them was their different expectations about the results revolution would produce.

Liang and Wang drew not only upon Chinese needs and conditions for evidence to support their predictions but also on the history of other revolutions. It is difficult to ascertain very precisely how much the early twentieth-century Chinese intellectuals knew about other revolutions, but they seemed to know a good deal about the French; they also observed the rise of the Young Turks and the Russian Revolution of 1905 very closely and excitedly, and referred to these and other revolutions frequently. It is even more difficult to ascertain what made men like Liang Ch'i-ch'ao and Wang Ching-wei react so differently to basically similar information. They knew something about the American Revolution, even though it is highly improbable that they knew anything of the interesting career of William Paterson, a revolutionary and statesman from New Jersey who detested most that "pernicious class of men called moderates" and who as a Supreme Court justice became "a terror to democrats in the days of the Alien and Sedition laws." [3] Thus even the American

[3] R. R. Palmer, *The Age of the Democratic Revolution*, I, 199.

Revolution, variously interpreted today as an anti-colonial war of independence, or as a conservative movement to regain the rights of Englishmen, or as the opening gun in a prolonged struggle for liberty, equality, and popular sovereignty, had its quota of extremism, arbitrariness, and unforeseen consequences. If these different features of the American Revolution were not well known to the Chinese, and if they could not know the similar features of the Young Turk and Russian revolutions, they did know of the terror in France. Some regarded such evils as a necessary price to pay for revolution and progress; others thought that if the Chinese were aware of the flaws in other revolutions, they could avoid similar excesses; still others brooded over the evils of revolution and decided they outweighed the good that could come of it; and finally there were those who gave no thought to such problems, out of either ignorance or impatience.

The phenomenon is as old as human history. Similar conditions do not produce the same men, and challenges tend to expose men's differences. H. G. Creel observed that the sight of a spirited horse makes one man only more anxious to ride, but it makes another all the more determined to walk. The prospect of revolution exhilarated some, inspired hope or caution in others, and made still others fearful. Many knew a revolution would have consequences few could foresee and none would intend; but the grievances were great, and the present seemed intolerable. And so to the revolutionaries, but not to all the modernizers, the risk seemed worth it.

George Bernard Shaw once said, "Please do not do unto me as you would have me do unto you; our tastes may be different." Ever since Shaw, simplistic remarks about individual human differences have seemed even more simplistic. The point to be made here is not merely that the challenge of early twentieth-century conditions revealed the personality differences and biases of revolutionaries such as Sun Yat-sen and Wang Ching-wei and reformers such as K'ang Yu-wei and Liang Ch'i-ch'ao but also that at a crucial point in history those differences so overshadowed the similarities among these men that they drove reformers and revolutionaries into bitterly contending camps. This fact is the point of departure for this book.

The men discussed here were intellectuals. Some, such as K'ang

Yu-wei, more obviously fit into this category than do others such as Sun Yat-sen. It is almost impossible for professional revolutionaries like Sun to be considered intellectuals by the most rigorous definition of that term, but Sun had his substantial intellectual side. In any case, he receives less attention in this book than some other revolutionaries, partly because he is much better known than they, even if he is not sufficiently understood, partly because other scholars are concentrating on him, partly because he wrote much less than others in the period with which I am concerned, but also because he is less easily identifiable as an intellectual. It is the role of intellectuals in politics that interests me most.

By intellectuals I mean people who are reflective, who deliberately and self-consciously apply themselves to understanding life beyond their own personal and immediate existence. An intellectual is one whose mental horizons far transcend the here and now and who accordingly devotes a considerable portion of his energies to analyzing the human condition beyond himself and beyond those who are related to him or intimately involved in his own life. In particular I am interested in those intellectuals who cared enough about their thoughts to air them, whether by writing, teaching, or any other method. This act of communication suggests a desire to solve as well as to understand, to do more than reflect; it also suggests a stronger tie with one's fellow human beings, most of all with other intellectuals. Thus men who reflect and communicate are likely to be active in joint ventures with other intellectuals and to have a feeling of identity with them.

Activist intellectuals with a feeling of group identity are particularly interesting because of several characteristics of that feeling. Intellectuals are often defined — by other intellectuals, that is, themselves — as being "ahead of their time." [4] This means that their attitudes presage attitudes that will at some later date become common; intellectuals are said to articulate views that the masses either do not have or that they have but cannot express. Intellectuals, by expressing themselves, create new climates of discussion and eventually see their pioneering rewarded with wide acceptance. By that time, of course, they have moved on to new vistas.

[4] A good brief discussion of this phenomenon may be found in Chad Walsh, *From Utopia to Nightmare*, especially pp. 17–21.

While intellectuals have doubtless fulfilled this role at times, I wonder whether history would show it to be a very common phenomenon. I suspect that partisans of this congenial interpretation have either fastened on the winners in history or sought solace in the thought of future recognition. I suspect, in other words, that as intellectuals we like to think we are ahead of our time. One characteristic of intellectuals that I find to be interesting and historically significant stems from this illusion. The faith that history will prove them right, that the times will catch up with them, that their personal vision will be seen one day by others has pushed many men, and not all of them intellectuals, to great heights. But it has also produced self-righteousness, dogmatism, and inflexibility.

Intellectuals, it is clear, are not guided solely by their intellects. Ideas and emotions mix and clash; the balance tips wildly in the mind of each man. Thus the fact that the protagonists of this story were intellectuals should not lead the reader to expect coolly rational, dispassionate, detached thinking.[5] The times were filled with the belief that China required much faster and more extensive change than she had seen for a long time, if ever before. The times fostered radicalism, by which I mean a desire for change that goes to the root of problems, thoroughgoing change, extreme change, change by direct and uncompromising methods, change propelled by a zeal that leads to violent action against those whose views the radicals reject.

The radicalism that emerged among Chinese revolutionaries in the early twentieth century was something new in China. I suggest that it had little in common with anything that went before, much in common with important movements that came later, and that the manner of its emergence contributed to the rise of subsequent radical movements. This last — the manner of its emergence — refers chiefly to the speed and ease with which the revolutionaries' radicalism swamped that of Liang Ch'i-ch'ao. For Liang too was a part of the new Chinese radicalism. The difference can be studied best in the 1903–8 period, when Liang and the revolutionaries observed the same circumstances and drew different conclusions about what they saw.

[5] See Hannah Arendt's discussion of how the compassion felt by the men of the French Revolution led to a "rebellion against reason" by Rousseau and others. *On Revolution*, pp. 74–76 and *passim*.

Circumstances create the framework within which a man thinks and acts, but what is decisive is how he reacts. And his reactions are conditioned by a multitude of forces; not all of them are environmental by any means, and many of them defy sharp definition. On the other hand, a man's acts are probably best understood in terms of his intentions. His ideas provide important clues to his intentions, and his writings, closely analyzed and compared with his actions, are the best guide to his ideas. Emerson wrote: "A man thinks. He not only thinks, but he lives on thoughts; he is the prisoner of thoughts; ideas, which in words he rejects, tyrannize over him, and dictate or modify every word of his mouth, every act of his hand. There are no walls like the invisible ones of an idea." Men's thoughts reveal the problems they face; and the problems history poses reveal the nature of history.

# PART ONE

# China's Problems and the Attempts to Solve Them, 1860–1905

# 1

## *The Reformers' Solutions*

The problems history posed to the Chinese in the nineteenth century concerned change. Never before had the Chinese been compelled to revise their way of life so rapidly and so extensively. No problems commanded the attention of modern China's leaders so insistently as those concerning the pace, scale, and direction of change. However great "traditional" China's varieties and discontinuities, the more striking features of pre-nineteenth-century China were continuity and the apparent ease of maintaining it. Leaders of modern China, on the other hand, may not have presided over as much change as is sometimes claimed,[1] but after 1860 their energies were increasingly directed to coping with problems of rapid and extensive change.

For most of the nineteenth century, problems of change were not easily recognized as novel, partly because so many of China's troubles — minority discontent, peasant unrest, secret-society uprisings, to name a few — seemed familiar. But familiarity probably made the troubles more serious by contributing to complacency and

[1] "The Chinese Revolution is for the latter half of the twentieth century what the Russian Revolution was for the first half. By transforming Chinese society, it has brought a great power into being. . . . China had its political revolution in 1911 and thus became a modern nation-state. . . . Chinese culture has not disappeared but China's traditional social system has. . . . There can be no further phase to the social revolution." Franz Schurmann, *Ideology and Organization in Communist China*, pp. xxix, xxxii, xlvi, 499.

the consequent failure to see the new elements in old problems. By the end of the century, however, awareness was spreading among China's leaders that the country was faced with needs of unprecedented magnitude and character. And with this dawning awareness the sun rose on China's revolutionary era.

It may be true that none of the problems China faced in the nineteenth century were entirely new. Even foreign onslaughts — cultural as well as military — had confronted China frequently in the past. But never before had the population increased by more than half within the space of some seventy years, exceeding by an estimated 180 million the point at which the best balance is said to exist between people and resources.[2] And never before had there been foreign invaders like the nineteenth-century Westerners, who combined military and naval might, a new technology, an unwavering belief in the right of merchants to trade freely, an evangelistic and zealous Christianity, and the confidence (already present at the end of the eighteenth century) in "that superiority which Englishmen, wherever they go, cannot conceal."[3] Most of all, never before had challenges of these dimensions interacted with each other to intensify old troubles as well as new ones.

Even after allowances are made for imprecise statistics, it seems clear that China's population, after a drop in the first part of the seventeenth century, had more than doubled in the eighteenth and may have nearly tripled between about 1700 and 1850. At the same time the amount of land under cultivation increased only slowly, until by 1800 the shortage of land began to make itself felt. China was faced with an immense problem of feeding her people. Between the latter part of the eighteenth century and the middle of the nineteenth, China became increasingly impoverished.[4] This economic pressure was intensified by the long series of costly wars in the Ch'ien-lung period (1736–95), extremely lavish spending at court, and large-scale corruption. Economic problems and corruption fed the discontent that was already present and created a revolutionary potential of immense proportions. This potential began to realize it-

[2] Ping-ti Ho, *Studies in the Population of China, 1368–1953*, p. 270.
[3] See John K. Fairbank, *Trade and Diplomacy on the China Coast*, p. 59.
[4] Ping-ti Ho, *Population*, pp. 64, 168, 277–78, and *passim*.

self in the eighteenth century and finally erupted in the nineteenth with a series of uprisings culminating in the great Taiping rebellion of 1850–64. Its suppression left the Manchu dynasty with still another critical problem, the serious weakening of central control and the rise of semiautonomous regional leaders.[5]

The forces undermining China's economic and political stability from within were further intensified by foreign pressure. As China's economy sagged, that of the West was revolutionized, releasing powerful drives that soon reached the China coast. The clash that ensued, between two fundamentally different civilizations, made relations with the West a central issue in Chinese politics. To a degree without precedent in China's history her internal affairs became enmeshed with foreign relations. The most important affairs of state became inseparable from dealings with foreigners. Hardly a decision could be made that did not have to take into account its effect upon China's relations with England. The course of those relations in turn affected every significant domestic problem.[6]

As foreign encroachment proceeded, a gradual transformation of China began. The treaty system and its manifold ramifications are well known — the creation of Western settlements in Chinese cities, extraterritoriality, tariff restrictions, missionary activity, increasing tension between Chinese and foreigners and then, as competition increased, rivalry within the foreigners' ranks. For China it meant a loss of territory, a loss of income, and a loss of dignity and confidence. She began to change, but decades passed before even a start was made, and even then change proceeded slowly. An arsenal, a shipyard, some study of Western languages, the dispatch of a small number of students abroad for a limited period — such measures were adopted on a small scale but with no central direction by the deteriorating central government, and no fundamental or far-reaching change in institutions or attitudes took place. Regional leaders showed the way, but there was no integrated national program; their own personal interests and traditionalist orientation militated against any broadly conceived or sustained effort at modernization. So too

[5] See Franz Michael, "Regionalism in Nineteenth-Century China," Introduction to Stanley Spector, *Li Hung-chang and the Huai Army*, pp. xxi–xliii.

[6] A detailed study of how China's relations with England intensified and complicated her domestic problems may be found in Frederic Wakeman, Jr., *Strangers at the Gate: Social Disorder in South China, 1839–1861*.

did China's economic weakness, aggravated by her inability to set tariffs at a level that could earn foreign exchange and protect infant industries. The result was China's growing weakness vis-à-vis the West and the now rapidly modernizing Japanese. Military, political, and economic weakness furthered psychological disorientation, and the latter in turn limited China's capacity to strengthen herself. By the end of the nineteenth century the Middle Kingdom seemed trapped in a downward spiral that would lead to an abyss not only of political subjugation but of cultural disfigurement and the loss of identity as well. In 1895 it appeared that China's stunning defeat by Japan might be the final blow.

It is against this background that the intellectual history of China in the nineteenth century must be viewed. That history may be likened to a series of Sputnik scares. One unexpected setback after another created doubts about China's superiority and ability to go her own way. A smashing and surprising defeat in 1839–42 led an occasional individual, such as Lin Tse-hsü, cautiously and fearfully to pose new questions about China's strength and position in the world. After the catastrophes of 1858 and 1860, there were others who expressed broader and more systematic criticisms and did so publicly; with the stimuli of foreign pressure and the Taiping threat, the "self-strengthening" movement got under way. After 1894–95, the even more astonishing humiliation dealt to China by her hitherto lightly regarded neighbor, Japan, had almost immediate consequences in domestic politics and the intellectual world, as evidenced by the activities and ideas of K'ang Yu-wei, Yen Fu, and Sun Yatsen. Finally, the outcome of the Boxer episode prompted the Manchu court itself to initiate a reform program which, however modest, had revolutionary implications.

Thus the interplay of foreign and domestic affairs occupied a more prominent place in Chinese politics and had important effects in Chinese intellectual life. Put briefly and simply, the period after 1840 saw a series of decreasingly tradition-bound responses by Chinese political leaders and intellectuals to intensifying foreign and domestic pressures. New political conditions, resulting from the Western incursion and costly rebellions, gave rise to new ideas and new political programs.

By the 1860's the unspeakable could be uttered; by 1898 it could be said openly to the emperor. What Lin Tse-hsü had been almost afraid to think, Feng Kuei-fen was willing to write; what Feng was unwilling to have published, the Kuang-hsü emperor circulated to all government offices. Lin confessed to a friend in 1842 that because of China's weakness he "took the risk of calling the Emperor's attention to two things: ships and guns. . . . But at this time I must strictly observe the advice to seal my lips as one corks the mouth of a bottle. . . . I cannot conceal these things from myself. I only beg you to keep them confidential." Not quite twenty years later Feng wrote as follows: "Why are they [Russia, America, France, and England] small and yet strong? Why are we large and yet weak? We must try to discover some means to become their equal. . . . What we then have to learn from the barbarians is only the one thing, solid ships and effective guns." By 1898 K'ang Yu-wei could go so far as to urge the Kuang-hsü emperor to change "all the laws and the political and social systems" and obtain his consent to "reform the institutions." K'ang emphasized that "the four barbarians are all invading us and their attempted partition is gradually being carried out: China will soon perish. . . . Unless we change the old institutions entirely and make them new again, we cannot make ourselves strong." [7] Thus he resembled his predecessors in his concern about the danger posed by the foreign powers and the need to make China strong. But in the solutions he proposed were seeds of revolution. The desire for moderate reform was giving way to radicalism.

MODERATE REFORMERS

The "moderate reformers" differed from each other a great deal. Lin Tse-hsü's cautious suggestion that China's ships and guns should be improved upon was not K'ang Yu-wei's daring proposal to renovate all Chinese institutions. A variety of reform proposals issued from men such as Wang Hsien-ch'ien, Hsüeh Fu-ch'eng, Cheng Kuan-ying, T'ang Chen, and Chang Chih-tung. These men made proposals that covered an extremely wide range but were similar in many ways: modernize the military, manufacture modern weapons, teach Western languages, translate Western books, reform or

[7] Ssu-yü Teng and John K. Fairbank, *China's Response to the West*, pp. 28, 52–53, 177.

abolish the examination system, and send students abroad; some even wanted to establish a parliament.

There were other men who had other ideas, but except for a very few, such as Ho Ch'i and Hu Li-yüan, who advocated complete westernization, they may be considered moderate reformers. They believed that a fusion of Western technology with Chinese morality would result in a synthesis of the best of both civilizations. This view found its fullest expression in Chang Chih-tung, who popularized the slogan "Chinese learning for the fundamental principles, Western learning for the practical application," the famous *t'i-yung* formula. Like other regional leaders such as Tseng Kuo-fan and Li Hung-chang, Chang pioneered in modernization; building arsenals, an iron foundry, and railways, sending students abroad, and introducing many fiscal reforms were only a few of his activities. All of these measures were aimed at preserving the Chinese substance. Even after playing a leading role in the movement to abolish the examination system, Chang sponsored a school in which only the Chinese classics, history, and literature were taught. The nineteenth century also saw the gradual broadening of the philosophical basis for reform, from "self-strengthening" and "Chinese-foundation–Western-application" (*t'i-yung*) to K'ang's exhaustive reinterpretation of the entire Confucian tradition. Terms such as "moderate reformers" obscure many other important differences. But in the longer historical perspective it can be seen that the reformers of the nineteenth century had things in common that were more significant than their differences.

First of all the reformers represented a small minority who recognized that China confronted new problems and who desired substantial changes in government policy to deal with those problems. Second, the reformers agreed that since the fundamental problems were created by the foreign powers, domestic reforms should be designed chiefly to make China strong enough to defend herself. Third, and for our purposes most important, they did not think it necessary for China to depart very far from her traditional values and traditional patterns of life to achieve this sort of reform. This attitude on the part of the reformers is what justifies their being termed "moderate." Whatever their differences, the moderate reformers envisioned change within tradition more than change departing from tradition. This attitude is also what distinguishes the moderate reformers from the revolutionaries.

One hastens to modify these sweeping judgments. The reforms of 1860 to 1898 were indeed halting, reluctant, spotty, superficial, harnessed to the preservation of traditional society, and inadequate to meet the needs of modernization. Nevertheless, they added up to something quite substantial by the end of the nineteenth century. In 1900, China was not quite where she had been in 1860. She had the beginnings of modern education, industry, and armed forces, and her concepts and techniques of diplomacy had been virtually revolutionized.[8] In many respects the country was moving toward fundamental changes. One area in which the new trends can be most plainly seen is government. Political ideas and institutions were changing more than is often realized. For example, a considerable number of men were becoming increasingly concerned about what today might be called a "communications gap" between rulers and ruled; numerous proposals were advanced to solve the problem, ranging from establishing newspapers to introducing some sort of representative government.[9] The Ch'ing administrative apparatus was also being significantly revamped from about 1850 on.[10] Although Ch'ing reform undeniably fell far short of solving China's problems, so much so that these problems may even have been further from solution in 1900 than they were in 1860, this is not in itself proof that the reforms were negligible. The growing gap between problems and solutions also testifies to how immensely China's problems grew during the nineteenth century. Much was done to deal with administrative decay, military weakness, financial insolvency, and out-

---

[8] The vast and still growing scholarly literature on reform in nineteenth-century China makes detailed discussion of the subject unnecessary here. See the listing in the bibliography of books by Banno, Biggerstaff, Chu, Feuerwerker, King, Lo, Powell, Rawlinson, Spector, and Wright, and articles by Hsiao Kung-ch'üan. The time is fast approaching when a fresh look at Ch'ing reform may conclude that it changed China a good deal.

[9] See Lloyd E. Eastman, "Political Reformism in China before the Sino-Japanese War" (unpublished manuscript, see Bibliography), and Richard C. Howard, "The Concept of Parliamentary Government in 19th Century China: A Preliminary Survey" (an unpublished paper presented to the Columbia University Seminar on Modern East Asia, Jan. 9, 1963). Both of these papers were kindly lent to me by the authors, and I am very grateful.

[10] See Esther Morrison, "The Modernization of the Confucian Bureaucracy" (unpublished Ph.D. dissertation, Radcliffe College, 1959).

moded educational practices, but China's needs grew far more rapidly than her ability to meet those needs.

Until nearly the end of the nineteenth century, there was considerable agreement among Chinese reformers about what the major problems were and how they should be approached. This agreement broke down steadily in the 1880's and early 1890's as a number of men advanced one or another radical idea — representation, constitutionalism, popular sovereignty — but almost no one yet envisioned a thoroughgoing restructuring of Chinese society. Most reformers adhered to some variant of the *t'i-yung* concept. Some came to think that more and more Western *yung* should be adopted, but their chief concern remained Chinese *t'i*, and they still viewed *yung* as consisting mainly of military and technical skills. It was only with China's defeat by Japan in 1894–95 that this informal but widespread consensus evaporated.

Before it vanished, however, this consensus had embraced men as widely separated by time and circumstances as the initiator of "self-strengthening," Feng Kuei-fen, and the "father of the Chinese republic," Sun Yat-sen. Five years before Sun was born, Feng edited a collection of essays in which he wrote:

> Regarding the present situation there are several major points: in making use of the ability of our manpower, with no one neglected, we are inferior to the barbarians; in securing the benefit of the soil, with nothing wasted, we are inferior to the barbarians; in maintaining a close relationship between the ruler and the people, with no barrier between them, we are inferior to the barbarians; and in the necessary accord of word with deed, we are also inferior to the barbarians. The way to correct these four points lies with ourselves, for they can be changed at once if only our Emperor would set the general policy right.[11]

These ideas have some striking similarities to those expressed by Sun Yat-sen more than thirty years later. In the summer of 1894, shortly before his twenty-eighth birthday, Sun abandoned his medical practice in Canton to journey all the way to Tientsin in the hope of delivering a reform proposal to Li Hung-chang.[12] Sun stated

---

[11] Teng and Fairbank, *China's Response*, p. 53.

[12] There has been disagreement on whether Sun himself wrote the letter to Li, but even those who question his authorship do not deny that it represents the ideas Sun

in his memorandum that the wealth and power of the West had a broader base than military might. Four factors, he declared, had been central to European progress. First, people were able to develop their talents to the fullest; second, the greatest possible yield was obtained from the land; third, natural resources were exploited to the utmost; fourth, goods flowed freely from place to place. If China was to employ Western methods to make herself strong, she had to focus on these four matters.[13]

The path to the first he declared to be through education. People of all classes should be encouraged to study, practical matters related to men's daily lives should occupy an important place in the curriculum, specialized training geared to specific occupations and taught by specialists should be introduced, and government employment policy should be to use people according to their individual abilities and particular training. Sun urged that the government have offices corresponding to the professions taught in the schools, so that "what one studies as a youth he will practice as an adult, and what one excels at in his studies he will be appointed to work at." Sun frequently referred to the practices adopted by Western governments in these matters, but he saw fit to add that such policies as employing people in government according to their abilities bore great resemblance to the ideas of Yao and Shun.[14]

To achieve maximum exploitation of the land, Sun pointed to three Western practices from which China could learn. Since agriculture is a basic source of a nation's wealth, Western countries maintain special agencies to administer agricultural affairs, he said. In ancient times China followed similar practices, but this effort soon deteriorated to the point where the absence of government activity in this field was considered good; in recent times, agricultural administration had virtually disappeared. Besides advocating the revival of this function of government, Sun called for a comprehensive system of agricultural education and the introduction of modern farm machinery and tools. A network of schools in which not only plant and animal husbandry but also related subjects such as zoology

held at this time. It is worth noting that an authoritative collection of his writings includes the letter. See "Shang Li Hung-chang t'ung-ch'en chiu-kuo ta-chi shu," *Kuo-fu ch'üan-chi*, V, 1–12.

[13] *Ibid.*, p. 1.      [14] *Ibid.*, p. 3.

and botany were taught would enable China to develop the great number of agricultural specialists she needed. With mechanization China could produce more with less human labor and at the same time bring new lands under cultivation. If all this could be accomplished, Sun concluded, China need not fear famine no matter how rapidly her population expanded.[15]

In his discussion of China's need to exploit her natural resources to the full, Sun emphasized the importance of science. Through science, nature becomes a source of power, and human energies can be freed to be increasingly concentrated on mental activity. He again stressed the need for mechanization. He noted too that many traditional Chinese practices, such as burning paper during holiday festivals, were wasteful and unprofitable; he recommended that these customs be prohibited by the government.[16]

Finally, Sun discussed the need for a broad expansion of trade. He called for the abolition of the restrictive *likin* tax, government protection of trade, and the creation of a far-flung network of rail and ship transportation. An interesting feature of Sun's remarks was his stress on the importance of cooperation between government and business. Western countries sent military and diplomatic missions to help those of its citizens who conducted business abroad — the businessmen who established banks and other organizations; the two worked hand-in-glove, Sun declared, pointedly noting the role played by business in England's overseas expansion.[17]

These four matters having been attended to, China could then see to her political, military, and other needs. When the foundation had been laid, Sun claimed, China could overtake and surpass Europe. His country's basic deficiency was her excessive number of ignorant people, he continued, but education would take years to show results. Although the development of "human talent" (*jen-ts'ai*) was the fundamental need, it was essential to deal with the immediate danger of overpopulation. "To build the nation we must first nourish and then teach; thus the promotion of the agricultural policy is the most urgent business of the day." Sun pointed out that agriculture had been a main concern of Chinese policy since ancient times, as was proved by the old ceremony of the emperor himself turning

[15] *Ibid.*, pp. 3–5.          [16] *Ibid.*, pp. 5–7.          [17] *Ibid.*, pp. 7–8.

the soil. "Thus to promote agriculture we need only extend our old practices and apply them together with the new ways." [18]

Sun's letter to Li shows him to have been chiefly concerned with the problems of promoting technology, improving agriculture, and expanding trade, all these efforts to be based in large part on educational reform. One discerns no hint of political revolution, nor is there any discussion of the social upheaval that would accompany the changes he advocated. Like other reformers of his time Sun Yat-sen in the summer of 1894 can be considered to have been moderate; it was only after his moderate proposals were ignored that he turned to revolution.

THE TRANSITIONAL DECADE, 1895–1905

When Sun Yat-sen left Tientsin in the late summer of 1894 he was on his way to Honolulu and the beginning of a lifelong commitment to the Chinese revolution. But eleven years passed before his efforts bore substantial fruit. In the intervening period he played a peripheral role in Chinese politics. Even among the revolutionaries his activities were not the focal point. The revolutionaries, in fact, were overshadowed during most of this decade by the Ch'ing court and by K'ang Yu-wei, Liang Ch'i-ch'ao, and their followers.

The high point of the nineteenth-century Ch'ing reform came in 1898, when both K'ang Yu-wei and the Kuang-hsü emperor "had come to a position wholly in favor of the emperor relinquishing his powers to a parliament." [19] K'ang Yu-wei is perhaps the most difficult individual to place in any categorization of reformers and revolutionaries that depends upon whether the person in question stayed largely within tradition or was more willing to depart from it. A strong case can be made that K'ang's departures from tradition were more significant than the ties he retained to it. In the longer perspective of modern Chinese history, however, it seems to me that K'ang belongs more to the nineteenth century than to the twen-

[18] *Ibid.*, p. 11.
[19] Richard C. Howard, "The Concept of Parliamentary Government in 19th Century China," p. 22. See also Hsiao Kung-ch'üan, "The Case for Constitutional Monarchy: K'ang Yu-wei's Plan for the Democratization of China," *Monumenta Serica*, XXIV, 21.

tieth.[20] In any case, a major break took place around 1898 or shortly thereafter, for however heavily one wishes to count the modernizing elements of K'ang Yu-wei's program, no subsequent reform movement took such elaborate pains to link itself to Chinese tradition. And no moderate reform movement ever again occupied the center of China's political stage. The break is not sharp. Moderate reform continued with the post-1898 Ch'ing program, but it rapidly intensified to the point of being revolutionary itself.

The failure of K'ang Yu-wei's Hundred Days Reform in the summer of 1898 has generally been attributed to his having attempted to do too much too quickly. There is of course far more to be said on this question, but at least it is clear that K'ang's opponents held this view. The coup which ended the Hundred Days also claimed the lives of six leading reformers, cast others into jail, sent K'ang and others fleeing abroad, cost the Kuang-hsü emperor his authority, and restored the empress dowager's full power at court. As a result, the reform movement was effectively checked. Two concurrent lines of development could be seen almost immediately thereafter. One was a resumption of moderate reform along the lines followed between 1860 and 1894. The other was a tendency toward radical reform. The former took place at the instigation of the court and under its leadership. Radical tendencies were several, but they are best seen in the activities of Sun Yat-sen, Liang Ch'i-ch'ao, and a group we shall call the new intelligentsia. Thus with regard to Ch'ing government reform, the immediate consequence of the Hundred Days was retrenchment.

Despite the changes that were already under way, many Chinese intellectuals were not convinced of the necessity for reform. Some

[20] We cannot begin to do justice to K'ang in this study. For his role in the reform movement see Hsiao Kung-ch'üan, "Weng T'ung-ho and the Reform Movement of 1898," *Tsinghua Journal of Chinese Studies*, N. S. I, No. 2 (Apr., 1957), pp. 111–245. On his philosophy see Hsiao, "K'ang Yu-wei and Confucianism," *Monumenta Serica*, XVIII, 96–212, and "The Philosophical Thought of K'ang Yu-wei," *Monumenta Serica*, XXI, 129–93; also, K'ang Yu-wei, *Ta T'ung Shu: The One-World Philosophy of K'ang Yu-wei*, trans. Laurence G. Thompson. For K'ang's political ideas see Hsiao, "The Case for Constitutional Monarchy: K'ang Yu-wei's Plan for the Democratization of China," *Monumenta Serica*, XXIV, 1–83. The most recent treatment of K'ang is *K'ang Yu-wei: A Biography and a Symposium*, edited with Translation by Jung-pang Lo.

remained serenely confident that Chinese values would reassert themselves.[21] Others, such as Wo-jen and Chu I-hsin, sensed that the adoption of some Western techniques or institutions would not buttress Confucian morality but would ultimately weaken and destroy it.[22] Nevertheless most intellectuals saw no alternative to some degree of modernization; the question was not whether to reform but what and how much China should change. Before long, statesmen were asking once again what the priorities, sequence, and pace of reform should be.

The court's first response was to pull back from the far-reaching measures advocated by K'ang Yu-wei and to follow the program of Chang Chih-tung.[23] But as China's predicament rapidly worsened, the government in desperation initiated wider reforms. The Boxer incident, for example, revealed that some provincial governors were independent enough to ignore an imperial edict to make war on a foreign invader. Shaken by this demonstration of her weakness at home and humbled by the international expedition's march into Peking, forced to flee Peking and remain away for more than a year, the empress dowager in 1901 grudgingly allowed an edict to say that "she is now thoroughly bent on radical reform."[24] While "her belated interest in these matters [political and social reforms] may properly be interpreted as gestures to win the approval of foreigners and the support of the governors," it is also true that "the reforms in government which she decreed were now essentially those which the Emperor had sought in 1898."[25]

Between 1901 and 1905 the court went further still. Once again crises in foreign relations stimulated Chinese action. The major crisis occurred in Manchuria, which had been the subject of tense negotiations between China and Russia ever since Russia had occupied it

[21] See, for example, the letter by Yeh Te-hui quoted by Li Chien-nung, *The Political History of China, 1840–1928,* ed. and trans. Ssu-yü Teng and Jeremy Ingalls, p. 165. One line reads: "The powerful and intangible influence of our sages can absorb cultures without the people being aware of what is happening and will influence, undoubtedly, those books which are written in illegible horizontal lines."

[22] See W. T. deBary, *et al.* (eds.), *Sources of Chinese Tradition,* pp. 738–41.

[23] See Hsiao, "Weng T'ung-ho and the Reform Movement of 1898," pp. 189–95, for details.

[24] See Meribeth E. Cameron, *The Reform Movement in China, 1898–1912,* pp. 57 ff., for this edict and subsequent reforms.

[25] Arthur W. Hummel (ed.), *Eminent Chinese of the Ch'ing Period,* I, 299.

during the Boxer incident. Japan, Britain, and the United States we soon involved, and in the spring of 1902 it appeared that Chinc diplomacy had won a major victory. About a year later, however, the Russian withdrawal, which had been agreed upon and actually even begun, was suddenly halted. Russia reoccupied the territory she had evacuated and more besides, a move exemplifying the Russian policies of 1903, which had contributed so considerably to the outbreak of the Russo-Japanese War in January, 1904.[26] During the war the Ch'ing government could do little more than stand by helplessly as Russia and Japan fought to determine which of them would be dominant in that part of China and adjacent areas. This and other humiliating demonstrations of China's weakness made the Manchus highly vulnerable to hostile criticism and spurred them to undertake some remarkable reforms.[27]

Two of those reforms, the abolition of the traditional civil service examination system and the decision to establish a constitutional and representative system of government, require special mention. The significance of the first is obviously enormous. The subject matter of the examinations had been Confucian thought; education was training in the Confucian classics. The examinations which had tested men's traditional learning were gone. No more dramatic a symbol of the passing of traditional China can be imagined. But this was far more than a symbolic event. The examination system served concrete functions in Chinese society without which that society lost much of its framework. Probably the greatest single barrier between social groups in China was the possession of a degree;[28] without the

[26] For details see Masataka Kosaka, "Ch'ing Policy Over Manchuria (1900–1903)," *Papers on China*, XVI, 126–53; also Andrew Malozemoff, *Russian Far Eastern Policy, 1881–1904*, pp. 200–249.

[27] Another major issue of the time concerned United States immigration policy. See Edward J. M. Rhoads, "Nationalism and Xenophobia in Kwangtung (1905–1906); The Canton Anti-American Boycott and the Lienchow Anti-Missionary Uprising," *Papers on China*, XVI, 154–97. For a discussion of how such incidents and hostile criticism spurred the Manchus to further reforms see E-tu Zen Sun, "The Chinese Constitutional Missions of 1905–1906," *Journal of Modern History*, XXIV, 251–53; also Wolfgang Franke, *The Reform and Abolition of the Traditional Chinese Examination System*, p. 69.

[28] For discussion of this highly complex and controversial issue see Chang Chung-li, *The Chinese Gentry*, especially Part 1; Ping-ti Ho, *The Ladder of Success in Imperial China*, especially chap. 1; T'ung-tsu Ch'ü, *Local Government in China Under the Ch'ing*, chap. 10.

examination system the old basic criterion for the division between upper and lower class no longer existed. It does not seem excessive to describe this as a social revolution. The term "revolution" seems even more apt in view of the further repercussions that the abolition of the examination system had. Educational reform, for example, which already by 1905 had made more than insignificant gains, sharply accelerated. Without the old examination system much of the incentive for the old education in the Confucian classics vanished. As so often occurs during modernization, this sharp change also made some men only more anxious to preserve what they could of the old, but the more common tendency was for young Chinese to seek modern learning more than the traditional education. The first effects of this tendency were seen chiefly in the large increase in the number of those who went abroad to study, but education in China also changed with increasing rapidity.[29] At a stroke the Ch'ing court guaranteed that study would never again be what it had been for centuries. One contemporary observer felt that "by this act the door to the past was closed to the younger generation once and for all. . . . China was now surely on the road to westernization."[30]

A watershed of these dimensions in Chinese social and educational practices and concepts inevitably marked off new boundaries in other areas of Chinese life. Without the old examinations there was no longer the reservoir from which China had drawn her government officials and military officers. New methods of recruitment had to be found. New opportunities were created, and a new type of bureaucracy and army began to grow. In the bureaucracy, the army, and throughout Chinese society, relationships between people could never again be what they had been. All those changes occurred only with time, and often they were not so drastic as might have appeared on the surface to be inevitable, but with the abolition of the traditional examination system, the traditional Chinese organism in which each part was a means and an end to every other

---

[29] Evidence for these assertions about changes in education is far from complete, but there are reasonably good indications that they are defensible. See Cameron, *The Reform Movement in China, 1898–1912*, chap. 4; more recent and detailed discussions are in Samuel C. Chu, *Reformer in Modern China*, chap. 5, especially p. 107, and Y. C. Wang, *Chinese Intellectuals and the West, 1872–1949*, pp. 52–98.

[30] Chiang Monlin, *Tides from the West*, p. 62.

received a mortal blow. The death might be lingering, but all could see that it would come.

The Ch'ing court itself could see this, and was beginning to look toward creating new institutions at almost the same time that it escorted the old into oblivion. Its decision to adopt a constitution and introduce a representative system began to crystallize in that same summer of 1905, when it took the concrete step of sending five officials abroad to study foreign constitutions. The members of the mission were appointed in July, but a September departure was forestalled by a revolutionary's attack on them at the railroad station in Peking. The mission finally set out in December, returned eight months later, and set in motion the process by which China began to inch toward parliamentary and constitutional government.[31] Students of modern Chinese history largely agree that the Manchus promoted this process chiefly to buttress their sagging authority, convince the foreign powers and the Chinese people that the Ch'ing government still had some vigor and an interest in reform, and in general to undercut the growing revolutionary movement; Ch'ing constitutionalism is not regarded as a genuine effort to promote popular sovereignty or to institutionalize a sharing of power.[32]

There is little reason at present to challenge this estimate of Ch'ing constitutionalism, but there are several reasons why this reform should be taken more seriously than it has been. One is its timing. It came after several years in which reform had been slowly moving ahead, very slowly indeed, but not without some dramatic steps such as the abolition of the examination system. All of these reforms may have been far less than adequate to meet China's needs, but they must also be measured against the possibilities for change and against the pace of change in preceding decades. These are very difficult measurements to make, but in view of the Hundred Days failure only seven years before, it may well be asked how much

---

[31] The best source on the mission is the article by E-tu Zen Sun cited above.

[32] For example, E-tu Zen Sun, *op. cit.*, pp. 255–68. A more recent study that confirms this estimate is Y. C. Wang, *Chinese Intellectuals*; for example, pp. 51–52: "By 1902 more reforms had been decreed than had even been contemplated by the Emperor in 1898. . . . Nevertheless, these changes failed to save the dynasty, for China's faith in traditionalism had disappeared." When that faith evaporated, Professor Wang observes, so did the Manchu regime, for it was "a symbol of tradition."

reform it was possible to effect in 1905. A possible answer is that China might not have been able to move toward constitutional and representative government more rapidly than she actually did between 1905 and 1910.

It can be argued that Ch'ing reform would never have led to a democratic or modern state, but this view is no less speculative. It might be helpful to consider at this point Japan's political modernization. It has been postulated by Robert E. Ward that authoritarian forms can be effective in the early stages of modernization, that they do not necessarily preclude the emergence of more democratic forms, and that some such gradual transition may be essential for modernization and democracy.[33] It is conceded that the last is the most tentative of these three hypotheses, but the first two seem particularly relevant to our discussion. For the aims of the Meiji leaders, who engineered Japan's remarkable modernization, were strikingly similar to the goals of Chinese modernizers — national unity and enough military strength to guarantee security against foreign aggression and economic exploitation. Ward points out that the Meiji leaders did not see immediately what all this would lead to, but in pursuing these goals they found themselves in a kind of "modernization spiral." The most significant point for us is that the Meiji constitution gave Japan more political change than is generally recognized; it *began* a process of democratization: "Even the concession of a very carefully restricted and seemingly impotent governmental role to a popularly elected body can, over a period of time, have consequences well nigh fatal to sustained authoritarian rule." Even limited political modernization, Ward suggests, may contribute to pluralism by, for example, promoting role specialization and professionalization.

It may be unlikely that China could have accomplished what Japan did, even under a constitution that was to be modeled on the Meiji document. The many differences between the Chinese and the Japanese tradition cannot be written off, nor can the fact that the Manchu dynasty was in an advanced state of decay by the end of the nineteenth century. But perhaps we underestimate the steps toward modernization that were taken in China under the Manchus

[33] Robert E. Ward, "Political Modernization and Political Culture in Japan," *World Politics*, XV, 588–96, is the source upon which this paragraph is based.

from 1860 to 1911, because we cannot help comparing the pace of change in China with what took place in Japan and the West. In terms of what was possible in China around 1905, the Manchus may have been very close to the limits.

Less in the realm of speculation is that Ch'ing constitutionalism was an acceleration of a many-faceted reform program which included, as Professor Morrison has shown, modernization of the bureaucracy and adoption of Western political forms. However inadequate these measures were, they represented a sharp break with the past. Changes in mood or attitude may be intangible, but the intangible can be monumental in history. For centuries China had basked in a cultural pride that was continually reinforced by her contact with foreigners. Her superiority was no illusion: One foreign visitor after another verified it, many of them in breathless astonishment at the level of Chinese civilization.[34] In the greatness of traditional Chinese culture, nothing figured more prominently than the imperial state; indeed, "the Chinese state was regarded as coterminous with Chinese culture." [35] It is difficult to imagine a sharper break with past attitudes than for imperial China's rulers to turn to the West and Japan for instruction in the art of government.

Finally, speculation and intangibles aside, Ch'ing reform was significant because modern-minded men thought it was significant. And when a man like Liang Ch'i-ch'ao took Ch'ing reform seriously, he made it more significant. Liang was probably the most influential writer of his time,[36] and there is reason to think that his support of

[34] See Derk Bodde, *China's Cultural Tradition*, pp. 4–7, for a few samples.

[35] Edwin O. Reischauer and John K. Fairbank, *East Asia: The Great Tradition*, p. 293.

[36] ". . . Students of Mao [Tse-tung]'s generation were nearly all influenced by the brilliance of Liang's books and essays." Jerome Ch'en, *Mao and the Chinese Revolution*, p. 23, note 25.

"I was one among thousands who came under his influence. I think this great scholar did more than anyone else in his time to popularize modern knowledge among the rising generation. His was the fountain of wisdom from which every young man drew to quench his thirst for the new learning." Chiang Monlin, *Tides from the West*, p. 51.

Liang himself later confessed, perhaps immodestly but in a spirit of scholarly detachment, that "his style had a clear structure and the flow of his pen was often passionate, with a rare magical kind of power for the reader." See *Intellectual Trends in the Ch'ing Period*, translated with introduction and notes by Immanuel C. Y. Hsü, p. 102. I shall return to this subject in my conclusion.

Ch'ing reform made others pay more attention to it than they would have otherwise. Some consideration of Liang's position and how he arrived at it is essential to an understanding of Ch'ing reform and the revolutionary movement.

A uniquely complex human personality such as Liang's intimidates historians even as it irresistibly draws their attention. Brilliant enough to stand out among eight grandsons even at a very early age, thereby catching his grandfather's eye, Liang was also capable of the intellectual discipline required to excel in the traditional examinations;[37] deeply and solidly grounded in the orthodox learning, Liang was also receptive to new ideas and to fresh perspectives on old ones; reverent toward his teacher K'ang Yu-wei, and excited by K'ang's ideas, Liang maintained his independence and critical faculties despite his youth and inexperience. Probably as early as 1898, but certainly no later than 1900, Liang was beginning to differ with K'ang more than he agreed with him. By 1900, Liang was a revolutionary.[38]

All the diverse currents that coursed through China's history in the tumultuous years of Liang's life, 1873–1929, may have touched him no more than many of his contemporaries, but Liang reacted differently to the touch. One of Liang's most prominent characteristics was his introspection, and one of the most revealing examples of his introspection was his effort, as he put it, to "discuss my person in a purely detached and objective spirit; . . . I have only striven to do justice to the historical Liang Ch'i-ch'ao exactly as I have striven to do justice to the other historical personages."[39] When he examined himself he pointed to contradictions produced by warring conservative and progressive instincts and decided they were "probably the result of an inherent weakness of character."[40] Many will feel that this stern judgment did not quite do justice to the historical Liang, but the severity of the judgment is as important a part of his personality as the shortcoming itself.

Among the numerous changes of viewpoint Liang underwent, two of the most important were in large part the result of extensive jour-

---

[37] Joseph R. Levenson, *Liang Ch'i-ch'ao and the Mind of Modern China*, pp. 15–16.
[38] Liang, *Intellectual Trends*, pp. 93, 99–102.
[39] *Ibid.*, p. 15.        [40] *Ibid.*, pp. 102–3.

neys abroad. His travels in Europe from February, 1919, to January, 1920, and in the United States and Canada from March to October, 1903, were chastening experiences.[41] A meeting Liang had with J. P. Morgan in 1903 indicates the effect the West had upon him. Having requested in advance a five-minute interview, Liang was ushered into the tycoon's presence only to find himself unable to say enough to use up the time.[42] (Morgan also lacked five minutes' worth of things to say to Liang, but then he had not asked for the meeting.) Liang's travels in the West show him to be perhaps more interested in the West than westerners were in him, but they also reveal that when Liang and the West confronted each other they found little common ground. After both visits Liang found himself shifting to a position that was more critical of Western society or at least less optimistic about the advisability and possibility of promoting westernization in China.

The shift that Liang made in 1903–4 is of particular interest. Liang, in the five years after the 1898 debacle, was as fully entitled as Sun to be called a revolutionary. The Manchus had put a price on his head after the Hundred Days, he had helped provide funds for T'ang Ts'ai-ch'ang's uprising in 1900, and even the Society to Protect the Emperor (Pao-Huang-hui) was an implicit challenge to the empress dowager.[43] It is also known that Liang was for some time interested in formal cooperation with Sun Yat-sen.[44]

Liang was not only a revolutionary in spirit and action from 1898 to 1903, but he may even be considered to have done more to sire the revolution than Sun, who had little influence in that period. Liang was surely the most prolific writer of the time, and the in-

---

[41] On the later trip, which we cannot discuss here, see Ting Wen-chiang (ed.), *Liang Jen-kung hsien-sheng nien-p'u ch'ang-pien ch'u-kao*, III, 554–72. For the earlier journey see II, 174–91.

[42] Levenson, *Liang Ch'i-ch'ao*, p. 70.

[43] Chang P'eng-yüan points out that Liang rarely used the phrase "protect the Emperor" (*pao-Huang*) alone; he spoke of "Emperor-protection in name, revolution in fact." Chang, *Liang Ch'i-ch'ao yü Ch'ing-chi ke-ming*, p. 182.

[44] See Yen-p'ing Hao, "The Abortive Cooperation Between Reformers and Revolutionaries (1895–1900)," *Papers on China*, XV, 91–114. Efforts to mediate between Liang and the revolutionaries continued at least into 1907; see Hidemi Onogawa, "Liu Shih-p'ei and Anarchism," *Acta Asiatica*, No. 12, pp. 71–72. This effort at mediation and many other matters in my book are also dealt with in Ch'i Ping-feng, *Ch'ing-mo ke-ming yü chün-hsien ti lun-cheng*.

fluence of essays such as the "Hsin-min shuo" ("A People Made New") probably exceeded that of any other writings. Liang at times ridiculed gradualism and demanded that "we must shatter at a blow the despotic and confused governmental system of some thousands of years; we must sweep away the corrupt and sycophantic learning of these thousands of years." [45]

Joseph Levenson has pointed out that in this period Liang's references to the classics "seem parenthetical, not central"; in a discussion of a certain economic problem, for example, a quotation from the *Ta-hsüeh* ("The Great Learning") was considered "no more than rhetorical baggage." [46] And instead of a prophet, Confucius became to Liang merely one hero among many, Chinese and Western. [47] In 1901 Liang rejected attempts others had made to portray the abdications of Yao and Shun as examples of ancient Chinese democracy; even if they really did abdicate, he noted skeptically, "that still is entirely different from modern democracy." Furthermore, democracy is a "world universal principle. Where universal principles are concerned, one must not consider as a matter of any importance whether or not the ancients previously applied it." [48]

As Levenson notes, it had now become less important that the Chinese be culturally orthodox than that what they did be useful to the nation. [49] The preservation of the nation was at stake, and in this contest "the means of survival are the ultimate national values; if adherence to tradition is incompatible with the adoption of these means, tradition will go." [50] Although he believes that they approached it by significantly different routes, Levenson affirms that Liang and the revolutionaries reached the same conclusion about tradition. [51]

Up to 1903 at least, and in fact for some time thereafter, Liang shared other views with the revolutionaries. For example, he placed great stress on the importance of making China strong; [52] he attributed Europe's progress to its tradition of popular representation; [53]

---

[45] Liang Ch'i-ch'ao, "Hsin-min shuo" (A People Made New), quoted in *Sources of Chinese Tradition*, W. T. deBary *et al.* (eds.), p. 759.

[46] Joseph R. Levenson, *Liang Ch'i-ch'ao*, pp. 88–89.

[47] *Ibid.*, p. 121.

[48] Quoted by Levenson, *ibid.*, p. 92.

[49] *Ibid.*, p. 110.        [51] *Ibid.*, p. 167.        [53] *Ibid.*, p. 138.

[50] *Ibid.*, p. 119.        [52] *Ibid.*, p. 117.

he criticized his countrymen for having a slave mentality and lacking enterprise and initiative;[54] and on occasion he became so exasperated with China's backwardness that he uncharacteristically praised revolution and permitted himself an anti-Manchu outburst.[55] For the pre-1903 period this position was not atypical of Liang; in these years his anti-Manchuism was similar to that of the revolutionaries.[56]

In 1903–4, however, Liang underwent an intellectual crisis. For about eight months during 1903 he traveled in Canada and the United States, where he was consumed by a growing sense of emptiness. For reasons that remain obscure he lost confidence in what he had been doing. As China's plight worsened and there seemed to be no time to waste, Liang was stricken with uncertainty about how to help save his country.[57] By 1905, a number of factors had combined to propel Liang along a new path. At odds with the revolutionaries for personal and intellectual reasons, under pressure from his teacher K'ang Yu-wei, and increasingly fearful that in the chaos of revolution China might be partitioned by the foreign powers, Liang abandoned his advocacy of revolution and took up the cause of peaceful reform.[58]

The principal influence upon Liang Ch'i-ch'ao during his period of indecision seems to have been exerted by Huang Tsun-hsien. Friends since 1896,[59] Liang and Huang exchanged numerous letters from 1902 until Huang's death in 1905. Huang's ideas of moderate reform were based on the conviction that destructive violence should be avoided while a kind of partnership between ruler and ruled was worked out; as the people's understanding of freedom grew, they would be guided toward democracy while maintaining respect for monarchy. Huang's view that Chinese conditions as of 1904 were not suitable for the establishment of a republic struck a responsive

---

[54] *Ibid.*, p. 140.      [55] *Ibid.*, pp. 156–59.

[56] Chang P'eng-yüan, *Liang Ch'i-ch'ao*, pp. 171–72, and Levenson, *Liang Ch'i-ch'ao*, p. 159. K'ang Yu-wei, disturbed by the anti-Manchu sentiments of Liang and others among his followers, took pains in 1902 to remind them of the dangers of revolution and the need for moderation; see Jung-pang Lo, *K'ang Yu-wei*, pp. 190–92.

[57] Chang P'eng-yüan, *Liang Ch'i-ch'ao*, pp. 177–82.

[58] *Ibid.*, pp. 167–72, 208.

[59] Teng and Fairbank, *China's Response*, p. 149.

chord in Liang and signaled his turn to support of peaceful reform leading toward constitutional monarchy under the Manchus.[60]

Several other features of Huang's thinking suited Liang's temperament particularly well. Among these were Huang's observation that patriotic spirit and universal education had been important factors in Japan's success and were also necessary for China, and his suggestion to pursue revolution without calling it revolution.[61] Huang's views may have carried extra weight because of his considerable experience abroad. From 1877 to 1882 he served in the Chinese Legation in Japan; from 1882 to 1885 he was consul-general in San Francisco; in 1890–91 he served in London and from 1891 to 1894 in Singapore. His writings about Japan and the United States indicate that he was thoughtful, critical, and devoted to reform;[62] at the very least, he was as much of a "foreign expert" as China had.

Huang's stay in the United States underlined for him the vast gulf between East and West and convinced him that China was not ready for a republic.[63] It is striking that Liang's change of heart came during and after a visit to the United States. It was then that he began to criticize republicanism and to argue, for example, that the difference between the American and French revolutions was that the colonists' greater experience with a parliamentary system and self-government facilitated a successful republican revolution; China, he maintained, was more like France than the United States in this respect, and therefore a republican revolution in China would bring results more like those in France.[64] Liang may have been particularly sensitive to the way in which Robespierre's dream of a "Republic of Virtue" yielded to the Reign of Terror, the short-lived Directory, and the coups of 1797 and 1799; for in his subsequent debates with T'ung-meng-hui writers Liang's chief argument was that revolution

[60] Chang P'eng-yüan, *Liang Ch'i-ch'ao*, pp. 174–75; also Ting Wen-chiang, *Liang Jen-kung hsien-sheng nien-p'u*, II, 195–97.

[61] Ting, *op. cit.*, II, 196, 202. See also Chang P'eng-yüan, *Liang Ch'i-ch'ao*, p. 182.

[62] See Hummel, *Eminent Chinese*, I, 350–51; also, Teng and Fairbank, *China's Response*, p. 149.

[63] Ting, *Liang Jen-kung hsien-sheng nien-p'u*, II, 195–96.

[64] Chang P'eng-yüan, *Liang Ch'i-ch'ao*, pp. 164, 173–74. It is very interesting to read Liang in the light of the differences between America and France noted by R. R. Palmer, *The Age of the Democratic Revolution*, I, 189.

would ultimately produce only chaos and a takeover by a military strong man.[65] The point is this: it was not in the United States that Liang first became acquainted with the French Revolution; in the United States he saw for the first time a modern Western society. If it is merely a coincidence that his thinking changed so radically at precisely this time,[66] it is surely a startling one. An equally plausible interpretation is that Liang's first contact with a modern Western society impressed him with how far China was behind other nations.[67] This perception would have made Liang all the more responsive to Huang Tsun-hsien's influence and, combined with the other forces we have noted, could have been decisive in persuading him to abandon revolution in favor of peaceful reform and constitutional monarchy. Whatever the reasons, in 1905 Liang Ch'i-ch'ao had cast his lot with the Manchu government.

After 1903, then, the clash between Liang and the revolutionaries crystallized. It is at this point that the differences between reformists and revolutionaries take on special significance, for an important shift in the character of the revolutionary movement also occurred after 1903.

[65] See Liang's explicit reference to the French Revolution and the dangers of republican revolution in his article, "Cheng-chih-hsüeh ta-chia Po-lun-chih-li chih hsüeh-shuo," *Yin-ping-shih wen-chi*, XIII, 83–86. I am grateful to Dr. Philip C. Huang for calling this item to my attention.

[66] Chang P'eng-yüan believes that Liang's writings before and after 1903 are so different on the question of revolution that they seem almost to represent two different men. Chang P'eng-yüan, *Liang Ch'i-ch'ao*, p. 163.

[67] Philip C. Huang, "A Confucian Liberal: Liang Ch'i-ch'ao in Action and Thought" (unpublished Ph.D. dissertation, University of Washington, 1966), pp. 125–27.

# 2

# *The Swing Toward Revolution*

In June, 1904, Liang Ch'i-ch'ao and K'ang Yu-wei were still regarded by the Ch'ing court as enemies comparable only to Sun Yat-sen.[1] But while Liang underwent the agonizing reappraisal of 1903–4 that brought him from near cooperation with Sun Yat-sen to prominence among the pro-Manchu and anti-revolutionary forces, K'ang Yu-wei embarked on a series of travels in Europe and North America that kept him on the distant fringes of events for at least the next four and a half years. Meanwhile, the revolutionaries reorganized themselves and developed new themes in their attack upon the Manchus. In brief, as Liang moderated his views, the revolutionaries hardened theirs. A somewhat desultory debate between reformers and revolutionaries that for several years had sputtered from Hong Kong to Japan to San Francisco[2] suddenly ignited. For Liang Ch'i-ch'ao posed to the revolutionaries a far more formidable challenge than the less illustrious writers who had previously argued the reformist case. At the same time the revolutionaries produced writers who could match Liang's fire and issues that were inexhaustible fuel.

[1] See Marius B. Jansen, *The Japanese and Sun Yat-sen*, p. 78. Although it declared an amnesty in 1904 for all other participants in the 1898 reform, only after the outbreak of the 1911 (Wuchang) revolt did the Manchu government rescind its order for the arrest of K'ang and Liang. See Jung-pang Lo, *K'ang Yu-wei*, p. 218, and Joseph R. Levenson, *Liang Ch'i-ch'ao and the Mind of Modern China*, p. 80.

[2] Li Chien-nung, *The Political History of China, 1840–1928*, ed. and trans. Ssu-yü Teng and Jeremy Ingalls, p. 205.

The principal changes in the revolutionary movement that took place between 1903 and 1905 were organizational and ideological. From a mélange of small groups the revolutionaries moved toward larger groupings and ultimately founded an organization, the T'ung-meng-hui, which was intended to unify their movement; simultaneously, their close affiliations with secret societies, which had largely determined their membership and strategy, became increasingly overshadowed by relations with student groups and the new army. These organizational changes were closely related to the revolutionaries' attempts to spell out new doctrines.

STIRRINGS OF REVOLUTION, 1894–1903

The efforts of Sun Yat-sen provide a convenient guide to the beginnings of revolutionary organization. Sun's chilly reception by Li Hung-chang in August, 1894, and the rapidity with which China was overwhelmed by Japan must have crystallized the anti-Manchu feelings he is said to have nourished for a decade before. Sun may have wavered between reform and revolution before the autumn of 1894, but from that time on he was a committed revolutionary until his death. The Chinese revolutionary movement thus began to take shape in November of 1894 with the establishment in Honolulu of Sun Yat-sen's Hsing-Chung-hui (Society to Revive China). This organization had only a few members and little promise of wide support. Two months later Sun returned to Hong Kong, where he and some friends joined forces with a group led by Yang Ch'ü-yün to establish a Hong Kong Hsing-Chung-hui.[3] Whether or not this was an avowedly revolutionary organization,[4]

---

[3] Chün-tu Hsüeh has pointed out the interesting similarities among all the men in these groups, particularly their travel and education abroad and their strong ties with overseas Chinese. *Huang Hsing and the Chinese Revolution,* p. 28.

[4] The issue turns partly upon the implications of the phrase *k'ai-kuo chih jih,* which was in the charter of the Hong Kong organization and can be interpreted to mean "the founding day of the new government," and also upon whether or not there existed a revolutionary oath. Cf. Shelley Cheng, "The T'ung-meng-hui: Its Organization, Leadership and Finances, 1905–1912" (unpublished Ph.D. dissertation, University of Washington, 1962), pp. 12–13, 54, note 53, and Hsüeh, *Huang Hsing,* pp. 29–30. Hsüeh doubts that an oath existed and believes that "as a revolutionary party, the organization of the Hsing Chung Hui left much to be desired." He finds its significance lay in its being "the first political society in modern China." According to Cheng, whose source was Feng Tzu-yu, there was an oath that included among its aims the establishment of a republic.

less than a month after its founding the Hong Kong Hsing-Chung-hui began to plan an uprising in Canton, and shortly before the day of rebellion arrived its members elected a "President of the Provisional Government." [5] It seems clear that in 1895 the Chinese revolutionary movement was under way.

The revolt was quickly suppressed. Sun fled to Japan, and soon continued on to Hawaii, the United States, and England. During his travels he sought support from overseas Chinese but had little success. In London, in 1896, Sun was seized by representatives of the Ch'ing government. His doom appeared certain, but he was able to escape and open a new chapter in the revolutionary movement.

Sun's experience in London deepened his hatred of the Manchus and reinforced his sense of his own destiny. He wrote a book, *Kidnapped in London*, that helped to publicize his cause and to enhance his reputation as a determined and resourceful revolutionary. Sun then spent nine months studying in England, and absorbed many of the Western ideas from which he would later try to form his own system of thought. However, the time for theories had not yet arrived. The revolutionaries' most urgent needs were arms, money, and supporters.

In August, 1897, Sun returned to Japan, where he spent the next several years trying to strengthen his organization.[6] In 1899 he was able to gain financial support for a revolt from revolutionaries in the Philippines and from his Japanese friends. The Hsing-Chung-hui, which had all but disappeared after the failure of 1895, was now re-formed with Sun at its head to lead another revolt. The Triad Society, the largest secret society in south China, also participated, but played only a minor role.[7] The uprising, in Kwangtung in October, 1900,

[5] Hsüeh, *Huang Hsing*, p. 30. Yang rather than Sun seems to have been chosen, but the circumstances are blurred by conflicting testimony. See *ibid.*, p. 196, note 19.

[6] The details of Sun's activities in these years can be found in Jansen, *The Japanese and Sun Yat-sen*, chaps. 3 and 4, and Lo Chia-lun (ed.), *Kuo-fu nien-p'u ch'u-kao*, I, 75–106. Jansen's book describes the role played by Sun's Japanese cohorts; Lo's work deals primarily with Sun and his chief lieutenants, especially Yang Ch'ü-yün, Shih Chien-ju, Ch'en Shao-pai, Pi Yung-nien, and Cheng Shih-liang. See also Shelley Cheng, "The T'ung-meng-hui," pp. 16–34.

[7] Ch'en Shao-pai, "Hsing-Chung-hui ke-ming shih-yao," in *Hsin-hai ke-ming*, ed. Chung-kuo shih-hsüeh hui (hereafter cited as *HHKM*), Vol. I. Ch'en's own entrance into the Triad Society is described on pp. 60–61; see pp. 65 ff. for the

was a failure, but the support given by the local population indicated that the revolutionary movement had a reservoir of strength that might one day bring it victory.

Sun continued his work but had little success. His Japanese friends lost their influence in Japanese politics as the government became more conservative, and they could no longer provide the help Sun needed.[8] His organization had been weakened by the failure of 1900, and four of his top assistants had died in the uprising or shortly afterward. The alliance with the Triad Society quickly collapsed. Sun stayed in Japan for three years, making only brief trips to Hong Kong, Siam, and Hanoi. He succeeded in establishing a branch of the Hsing-Chung-hui in Hanoi early in 1903 but received little other encouragement. That September Sun left Japan for Hawaii and spent the next twenty-one months seeking support in the United States and Europe.

Sun Yat-sen's nine years as a professional revolutionary had borne little fruit. The two uprisings he had tried to promote had both failed. By 1903 his organization still had only slight support and no access to funds, manpower, or military equipment. He had formulated no program other than the objective of overthrowing the Manchu dynasty and replacing it with an as yet undefined new government. The one accomplishment he could claim was the establishment of his reputation as a man of honor, vigor, and potential leadership abilities. For the time being, however, he seemed to have reached an impasse.

Before 1903 other revolutionary activity in China resembled Sun's but was even less promising. Organizations proliferated and quickly fell apart, scattered uprisings fizzled, vague programs evaporated, ambitions soared and plummeted. The most ambitious effort of the time, T'ang Ts'ai-ch'ang's in the summer of 1900, was like the rest in its mixed reformist-revolutionary ideas and leadership, its basic reliance upon secret societies, its hope of sparking a general anti-Ch'ing uprising, and the ease and rapidity with which it col-

---

Hui-chou uprising. Secret societies such as the Triad had a long history of opposition to the Manchu dynasty, and some of them had organizations that reached into far corners of the country. The ideas of their members were sometimes bizarre mixtures of religion, superstition, and political and economic grievances, but they represented a surge of popular protest that the revolutionaries were inevitably tempted to harness.

[8] Jansen, *The Japanese and Sun Yat-sen*, pp. 106–7.

lapsed.[9] Overseas the scene was similar. In Southeast Asia, for example, there came into being many organizations that were to affiliate with the T'ung-meng-hui in 1905. Among the more prominent ones were the Chung-ho-t'ang, which also had a branch in Yokohama, and the "Eighteen Saviors of the Country" (*Chiu-kuo shih-pa yu*), which worked for collaboration with local Triad leaders.[10] All of these groups lacked funds and attracted few members.

In other quarters, however, the revolutionary movement was burgeoning. Only a few Chinese students had gone abroad in the second half of the nineteenth century, but after China's disastrous defeat by Japan in 1894–95 the Manchu government began to send more students to Japan to study military and naval science. From that time on, the number of Chinese students in Japan gradually increased; some paid their own way and others were supported by provincial officials. The reforms in education instituted by the Manchus in 1901 created a need for more teachers that impelled still more students to go to Japan for training. After 1905, as the revolutionary movement accelerated, thousands more flocked to Japan, and although many returned to China to work for the overthrow of the dynasty, there was a large number of Chinese students in Japan throughout the T'ung-meng-hui period.[11]

[9] T'ang's organization, best known as the Independence Society (*Tzu-li-hui*), was originally called the Righteous Spirit Society (*Cheng-ch'i-hui*), an organization that dates at least to 1890. It was established in large part to cooperate with the Elder Brother Society (*Ko-lao-hui*), but for a time it attracted revolutionaries such as Pi Yung-nien and Chang Ping-lin. See Chung-hua min-kuo k'ai-kuo wu-shih-nien wen-hsien pien-tsuan wei-yüan-hui (Committee to Edit Documentary Collections for the 50th Anniversary of the Founding of the Chinese Republic), *Chung-hua min-kuo k'ai-kuo wu-shih-nien wen-hsien* (Documents on the 50th Anniversary of the Founding of the Chinese Republic), Sec. (*Pien*) 1, *Ke-ming yüan-liu yü ke-ming yün-tung* (Origins of the Revolution and the Revolutionary Movement) (hereafter cited *50th Anniversary Documents*), Vol. (*ts'e*) X, "Ke-ming chih ch'ang-tao yü fa-chan: Hsing-Chung-hui, hsia" (Promotion and Development of the Revolution: Hsing-Chung-hui, part 2), p. 285. T'ang was mainly supported by the reformers, however; for K'ang Yu-wei's role see Jung-pang Lo, *K'ang Yu-wei*, pp. 185–89. A general treatment is by E. Joan Smythe, "The Tzu-li-Hui," *Papers on China*, XII, 51–68.

[10] *50th Anniversary Documents*, X, 138–42, 217–22, 227. Vols. IX and X in this collection are the best introduction to the vast literature on the pre-1905 revolutionary movement. See also *HHKM*, Vol. I.

[11] One source says that in 1902 there were less than 300 Chinese students in

The Chinese students in Japan organized provincial associations, many of which sponsored publications. Organizations and publications sprouted as young Chinese breathed the heady air of new ideas in a country that was swiftly becoming a modern power. As early as 1900, organizations such as the Determination Society (*Li-chih-hui*) were founded to promote contact among the provincial groups.[12] The students' writings acquired an increasingly radical tone. In 1901 Cantonese youth in Japan formed a Kwangtung Independence Association and called on provincial officials in China to declare their areas independent. One year later a student club was established in Tokyo that included Chinese from many provinces. At its first meeting Wu Lu-chen, in a burst of revolutionary ardor, likened their meeting place to Independence Hall in Philadelphia.[13] Soon thereafter Chang Ping-lin called a meeting to commemorate the 242nd anniversary of the loss of China to the Manchus.[14] At the request of the Ch'ing government, Japanese authorities tried to prevent the meeting, but the students merely moved to another place, where they issued a declaration written by Chang. At about the same time Feng Tzu-yu and others formed the Youth Society (*Ch'ing-nien hui*), whose guiding principle was "nationalism" (*min-tsu chu-i*) and whose goal was "destruction" (*p'o-huai chu-i*).[15] Anti-

---

Japan. Their number had increased to only 2,406 by the beginning of 1905, but ten months later there were 8,620 and by 1908 about 17,000. These figures are taken from H. E. King, *The Educational System of China as Recently Reconstructed*, U.S. Bureau of Education Bulletin No. 15, pp. 92–93; see Howard S. Galt, "Oriental and Occidental Elements in China's Modern Education System," Part II, *Chinese and Political Science Review*, Vol. XII, No. 4 (Oct., 1928), pp. 643–44.

Roger F. Hackett, however, puts the figure at 1,058 in 1902. According to his source, the *Japan Weekly Mail*, the peak was reached in September, 1906, when there were 13,000 Chinese students in Japan. The number had fallen to 8,000 by July, 1907, and to about 5,000 a year later. "Chinese Students in Japan, 1900–1910," *Papers on China*, III, 141–42. Y. C. Wang, *Chinese Intellectuals and the West, 1872–1949*, p. 55, puts the peak at 15,000 in 1906.

[12] *50th Anniversary Documents*, XI, 311.

[13] See Wu's biography in *Ke-ming hsien-lieh chuan-chi*, pp. 231–52. Li Chien-nung, *Political History*, p. 193, also describes this incident.

[14] Chang dated China's demise from the date of the last Ming emperor's death; see Lo Chia-lun, *Kuo-fu nien-p'u ch'u-kao*, p. 109. According to Li Chien-nung, however, it was called a meeting to mourn the 258th anniversary of the Manchu conquest. Feng Tzu-yu is Lo's source.

[15] *50th Anniversary Documents*, XI, 312.

Manchu feeling on the part of Chinese students in Japan was intensifying, and the Manchus were increasingly concerned about the radical turn that student activities were taking.

Efforts by the Manchus to interfere with the student movement served mainly to heighten revolutionary passions. At the 1903 New Year's celebration, in the presence of the Chinese minister to Japan, two Chinese students made speeches demanding the expulsion of the Manchus and the return of sovereignty to the Chinese. A member of the minister's party who tried to object was overruled. Three months later, when Russia failed to evacuate her troops from Manchuria, Youth Society members organized a Volunteer Corps to Resist Russia (*Chü O i-yung-tui*). Ch'ing authorities succeeded in having the corps disbanded, but many of its members later returned to China and joined the Restoration Society (*Kuang-fu-hui*) and the China Arise Society (*Hua-hsing-hui*), two of the larger revolutionary groups whose members later joined the T'ung-meng-hui.

Thus by spring, 1903, the beginnings of new trends could be seen among the thousand Chinese students in Japan. These trends are most interestingly summarized in the person of the twenty-three-year-old Ch'en Tu-hsiu. A leading founder and the first secretary-general of the Chinese Communist Party less than twenty years later, the foremost exponent of "science and democracy" a few years before that, and a republican bureaucrat in 1912–13, Ch'en was nevertheless to play no significant role in the revolutionary movement before 1911. Still in 1903 he was quite typical of Chinese students in Japan. He had received a traditional education, earned the title of *sheng-yüan* in the 1896 district examinations, and after failing at the provincial level had begun to study Western subjects at a school in Hangchow. About 1900 Ch'en went to Japan for further study, and there he joined an Anhwei student group. By 1903 this group had become the Patriotic Society (*Ai-kuo-hui*), and to the cheers of an excited crowd Ch'en delivered the opening speech. Ch'en's audience was aroused most of all by China's mistreatment at the hands of foreign powers, and his group was dedicated fundamentally to promoting "patriotic thought and a military spirit" and "recovering national sovereignty" (*kuo-ch'üan*). But the organization also dedicated itself to a number of higher principles; for instance, its declaration said that patriotism included not only the preservation of the national entity but also such precepts as regarding the country as one family in which each gave and received respect and love.[16] This combination of militant patriotism, anti-imperialism, and incipient nationalism on the one hand, and a deep humanitarian impulse on the other, pervaded the early revolutionary writings. The militant patriotism predominated, and as time went on it increasingly overshadowed the ideals of love and respect, but the humanitarian ideals never totally relinquished their place in revolutionary thinking.

Between 1901 and 1905 a flood of publications issued from the various student organizations.[17] *Overseas Students Translations* (*Yu-hsüeh i-pien*), for example, published by students from Hunan, consisted almost exclusively of translations but occasionally carried an original item such as an editorial advocating self-government for Hunan, an open letter to Hunanese youth urging them to study in foreign lands, or an essay on Chinese nationalism. The translations were made from Japanese and Western sources and covered a great variety of subjects, many of which were not directly related to contemporary political problems but helped to introduce Western culture to Chinese readers. The magazine was organized under such headings as art, history, politics, economics, military affairs, and geography. The editors were not always discriminating in their choice of authors — an extract from Aristotle might be followed by a story from an obscure European newspaper, or an article by a noted Japanese historian might be sandwiched between a short story by a minor French writer and an eyewitness account of Russian atrocities in Poland — but exchanges of letters by students reveal that they were highly excited by the new worlds such journals opened to them. Gradually, too, the students' interests gave more shape to the journals' contents.

As time went on periodicals came to resemble each other more and more in form and substance. They became primarily propaganda sheets designed to stimulate anti-Manchu feeling and revolutionary

[16] *Ibid.*, X, 423–26.

[17] The best introduction to these periodicals is Chang Nan and Wang Jen-chih (eds.), *Hsin-hai ke-ming ch'ien shih-nien chien-shih-lun hsüan-chi* (Selected Essays from the Decade preceding the 1911 Revolution). Vol. I, in two parts, covers 1901–4. Vol. II covers 1905–7. On the pre-1905 period see also *50th Anniversary Documents*, X, 499–763.

activity. Numerous articles appeared describing how China had declined under the Manchus to the point where she could easily be preyed upon by foreign aggressors. Readers were urged to be conscious of China's heritage and how it had been disgraced by the Manchus. Demands were made for local self-government. The student movement was described for the benefit of the home audience. The *Hupeh Student World* (*Hupei hsüeh-sheng chieh*) paid special tribute to one of its editors, Liu Ch'eng-yü, one of the daring orators at the 1903 New Year's party. *Twentieth-Century China* (*Erh-shih shih-chi chih Chih-na*) attacked the Manchus for standing idly by while both Russia and Japan violated Chinese territory. Other articles discussed the need for constitutional government. Many writers dwelt on the Chinese people's lack of national spirit. Discussions of Western philosophers from Socrates to Mill were common, but they continued to be chosen by a seemingly random method that brought the great minds of the Western world to China together with the most obscure writers.

There were scores of these journals. Some were published for several years, others for only one or two issues. Most were run on a shoestring; a few had wealthy backers. A magazine would run out of funds or be closed by the police and then start again with new support or under a new name. Copies were circulated among the students in Japan and smuggled back into China. Some were distributed to other overseas Chinese communities. These journals had no single message and elicited no single response. But they were passionate, and they aroused passions. The students bombarded each other with ideas of all sorts until they were nearly shell-shocked. Could anything be clear in this babble of sound? Was there a point to defend, a skirmish line to defend it? Chiang Monlin, eighteen years old at the time, recalled years later:

> All the conflicting ideas, as between new and old, constitutional reforms and revolution, buzzing around in this topsy-turvy world of mine, were more than an immature mind could endure. I became restless and often had a fantasy in which, by a sort of somersault, I rocketed high into the air and then whirled down rapidly to the ground, where I burst to bits and was gone forever. . . .
> Was I crazy in this crazy world? At least one problem always re-

mained clear in my mind: how to save China from dismemberment by the foreign Powers.[18]

The revolutionary movement in Japan had mushroomed almost overnight. Within a few years thousands of students had come to study and had been caught up in a surge of political activity. In their midst was a handful of mature men, including scholar-revolutionaries such as Chang Ping-lin. The students were scattered among a host of small organizations usually representing one or two provinces, but a feeling of unity based on a growing awareness of their common interest in a strong and independent China was beginning to draw them together. In 1903–4, however, the theme of saving China from dismemberment began to be rivaled by a deeper anti-Manchuism.

FLOWERING AND FALTERING, 1903–4

As the revolutionary movement gained momentum among Chinese abroad, events in China were moving in similar directions in the few years before 1905. While secret-society activity against the Manchus also continued to grow, by 1903 students returning from Japan were becoming an even more serious threat to the dynasty. The young intellectuals founded new organizations in China, and although they persistently sought alliances with secret-society groups, sustained cooperation proved difficult to achieve. The student revolutionaries found themselves forced to act independently.

The expansion of revolutionary activity on the mainland grew directly out of the student movement in Japan. Toward the end of 1902 a group of outstanding Chinese scholars led by Ts'ai Yüan-p'ei, Chang Ping-lin, and Wu Chih-hui established in Shanghai a Chinese Education Society (*Chung-kuo chiao-yü hui*). Chang had become famous in the incident of the commemoration of the Manchu conquest, and we have seen how this incident reflected both the increasing student unrest and the growing Manchu uneasiness. The Ch'ing government ruled that only officially sponsored students could henceforth enroll in Japanese military academies. Radical students were incensed. A group of them, led by Wu Chih-hui, stormed the Chinese legation and demanded that the order be revoked. The Chi-

[18] Chiang Monlin, *Tides from the West*, p. 59.

nese minister used his influence to have Wu and one other leader deported on the grounds that they were a menace to law and order. Some of the other students decided to accompany them back to China.

The outcome of this affair was that a group of incensed students landed in Shanghai seeking an outlet for their hostility. They found it in the Chinese Education Society. At the same time, they were joined by students from Nanyang Academy in Shanghai, who had gone on strike in protest against the reading materials chosen by the school authorities. Another organization, the Patriotism Academy (*Ai-kuo hsüeh-she*), was established as an affiliate of the Chinese Education Society. The Nanyang students were the main element in the new group.[19]

The Shanghai revolutionary movement promptly acquired new life. Almost at once, however, the fledgling organizations faced financial difficulties. These were partly solved by securing aid from some overseas Chinese businessmen. According to one writer, seven teachers on the Patriotism Academy staff also began to write articles for the newspaper *Su-pao* in order to earn more money for the Society.[20] This may well not have been the chief motive for the affiliation with the *Su-pao*, since many participants affirm that there was a common desire among the members to secure a journal through which they could reach a wider audience. In any case, the *Su-pao* quickly became the most important vehicle of revolutionary propaganda in China. Within two months its editorials had so infuriated the Manchus that they determined to suppress the newspaper. Among the writings that the Manchus considered most objectionable was one by Chang Ping-lin in which he referred to the emperor as a "little clown" (*hsiao-ch'ou*) [21] and another by Tsou Jung called *The Revolutionary Army* (*Ke-ming chün*). Tsou's small pamphlet was issued through the *Su-pao* by the Patriotism Academy and is an

[19] For more information on the membership and activities of these organizations see the following: Chiang Wei-ch'iao, "Chung-kuo chiao-yü hui chih hui-i," *HHKM*, I, 485–96; Feng Tzu-yu, *Ke-ming i-shih*, I, 115–19. Both of these writers were participants in the events they describe.

[20] Chang Huang-chi, "Su-pao-an shih-lu," *HHKM*, I, 368.

[21] This term has also been translated as "low wretch." See Tsou Jung's biography in Arthur W. Hummel (ed.), *Eminent Chinese of the Ch'ing Period*, II, 769. Chang Ping-lin, at his trial, cited ancient usage in which it meant simply "little child."

excellent sample of some of the new emphases in revolutionary journalism.

Tsou Jung was only eighteen years old when he wrote *The Revolutionary Army*.[22] He had left his home in Szechwan to go to Shanghai in 1901. There he studied Japanese for several months and then went to Japan in the spring of 1902. He enrolled in Japanese language classes and also took an elementary science course. He immediately became a favorite of some of the leaders of the student movement, including Chang Chi and Feng Tzu-yu. A year later he returned to Shanghai, having already drafted *The Revolutionary Army*. Through Chang Chi he met Chang Ping-lin and other leaders and was soon in the midst of the revolutionary ferment. As he had in Japan, Tsou caught the attention of the most prominent men he met. Chang Ping-lin was so attracted by him that at Chang's suggestion they, Chang Chi, and Chang Shih-chao (Hsing-yen), who later became the editor of *Su-pao*, swore eternal brotherhood.

The opening lines of *The Revolutionary Army* set the tone of the pamphlet:

> To sweep away thousands of years of despotism, to throw off thousands of years of slavery, to wipe out the five million barbarian Manchus, to wash away the shame of two hundred and sixty years of cruelty and oppression, to make the China mainland clean once again, if every descendant of Huang Ti [becomes a] George Washington there will be a return to life from the eighteen layers of hells, and a rising to heaven . . . the most revered and exalted, the one and only, the supreme and unparalleled goal that we call revolution![23]

Tsou then lumped the English, American, and French revolutions together as revolutions that "did away with the corrupt and retained the good," that brought their countries "from barbarism to civilization," that "made masters of slaves, sacrificed the individual for the good of all and the nobility for the welfare of the common people,

[22] *Ibid.* There is also a more detailed biography by Tu Ch'eng-hsiang, *Tsou Jung chuan.*

[23] Tsou Jung, "Ke-ming chün," *HHKM*, I, 333. See pp. 331–64 for the full text, an introduction by Chang Ping-lin (which appeared originally in the *Su-pao* on June 10, 1903), and a brief biographical note on Tsou.

and brought the blessings of freedom and equality to all." Then: "What a wondrous and precious thing is revolution!"[24]

China had had more than two thousand years of despotic government, Tsou continued. Now, at last, she had the good fortune to have Western models, to be able to read Rousseau, Montesquieu, and Mill, and to have men like Washington and Napoleon to imitate. His first chapter concludes:

> Revolt! Revolt! If successful, we live; if not, we die. Do not retreat. Do not stand neutral. Do not be irresolute. Now is the time. Now is the time. . . . Let us hand in hand, comrades together, carry out this revolutionary principle. . . .[25]

Then, in a long chapter that constitutes about half the work, Tsou explained why he felt that revolution was necessary.[26] He charged that the Manchus had ruined China by weakening her so seriously that she could not defend herself against the Powers and had been reduced to the status of a semi-colony. But this point, made frequently by other writers of the time, yielded to another that was soon to become the revolutionaries' principal rallying cry.

Tsou accused the Manchus of discriminating against Chinese in a variety of ways. For example, all high official positions were held by Manchus, some of whom were illiterate; even Chinese who performed especially valuable services for the dynasty were not appointed to high positions, and were often the ones blamed when things went wrong. Chinese officeholders were kept so busy taking examinations that they had time for little else but preparing for them. Tsou reviled the Manchus for using the perquisites of gentry status as levers to bend Chinese scholars to their purposes. He denounced them for having men of great learning work at stultifying jobs such as editing dictionaries, robbing them of their ambition and eroding their vitality until they became corrupt or hopelessly ossified.

Tsou also indicted the Manchus for abusing the entire population. They maintained troop garrisons throughout the country to prevent rebellions; this, said Tsou, amounted to regarding the people as ban-

---

[24] *Ibid.*, p. 334.    [25] *Ibid.*, p. 335.

[26] *Ibid.*, pp. 335–49. It was this chapter and the introductory one that the Manchus regarded as particularly provocative. See Chang Huang-chi, "Su-pao-an . . . ," *HHKM*, I, 375.

dits. Farmers toiled in the fields from dawn until night without rest, and the Manchus rewarded them by stealing most of their earnings through excessive taxes. The Manchus also stood by, feigning ignorance, while Chinese workers in America were discriminated against and even made victims of mob violence.

Again and again Tsou returned to the issue of the Manchus' anti-Chinese bias. He charged that they sent Chinese troops to fight with old and inadequate weapons and provided no extra pay to the wounded or to families of soldiers killed in action. He flayed them for complaining that there was too little money to build more schools or send more students abroad while they built splendid palaces for the empress dowager. Finally, Tsou accused the Manchus of giving Chinese territory to foreigners solely to keep themselves in power. Even if China could become wealthy and strong under the Manchus, he concluded, it would not benefit the Chinese at all. The only solution was to overthrow the Manchu regime. Then China would regain her dignity and good name; her size, her wealth in human and material resources, and her great energy would be employed for the welfare of the Chinese people; foreign countries would no longer dare to violate Chinese territory; and there would be freedom, equality, and happiness in the land.

In the rest of his pamphlet Tsou tried to emphasize that the real purpose of the revolution was to build and that destruction was only a prelude to reconstruction. The aims were broadly stated to be freedom, equality, independence, and self-determination. Education had to play a leading role both before and after the revolution: before, to give the people new ideas and persuade them that they had to work together to carry out the revolution, to train "countless Washingtons and Napoleons"; [27] afterward, to build a new country.

Three ideas had to be spread. The first was that China belonged to the Chinese and that all violations of Chinese integrity had to be resisted at all costs. Next was the meaning of freedom and equality. Tsou claimed that in ancient times the monarch was the representative of the people and that the people were free and equal. Later, however, the emperor came to regard the country as his property and its wealth as his own; the people then lost both freedom and equality.

[27] "Ke-ming chün," *HHKM,* I, 351.

The low point had been reached in the Ch'ing dynasty, which was a disgrace to the Chinese tradition. The Chinese had to regain their "natural human rights." [28] The third point that Tsou regarded as an essential feature of the new education was inculcation of the concepts of popular participation in government and respect for law. Without these, modern civilized self-government was impossible.

Tsou concluded with a list of twenty-five aims drawn, he said, from the American Revolution and the independence it brought to the United States. These aims included killing the Manchu emperor as an example to later would-be autocrats, but Tsou also hinted at what a future Chinese government would be. He referred in general terms to the need for establishing a central government; elections of representatives at the *hsien, chou, fu,* and provincial levels; equal rights for women; inalienable rights of personal liberty, speech, thought, and publication; the obligation of the government to protect the people's rights; the right of the people to revolt if the government violated their rights. But Tsou could do no more than list these points and concluded rather lamely by calling for a constitution modeled after America's, self-government similar to America's, and finally a system that would deal with all questions concerning relations between the group and the individual, and in fact with all the problems of government, in the manner of the United States.[29]

This first and only writing of an eighteen-year-old boy who grew up in Szechwan at the close of the nineteenth century and whose contact with the outside world was limited to two years in Shanghai and Tokyo became one of the most famous and influential writings of the Chinese revolution. It remains to be seen how older men of wider experience and greater learning acquitted themselves in the years that followed. Tsou Jung, however, typified the early years of the Chinese revolutionary movement in his passion for change and improvement, his startling receptivity to new ideas, and his boundless courage and determination. Beyond this, in the breadth and intensity of his attack upon the Manchus and his emphasis upon freedom, equality, self-determination, and the need for popular participation in government and respect for law, he seemed to sum up the views of a generation.

[28] *Ibid.* The term used for natural human rights was "T'ien-fu chih jen-ch'üan."
[29] *Ibid.*, pp. 361–63.

The Manchus succeeded in closing down the *Su-pao*; Chang Ping-lin was sent to jail for three years and Tsou Jung for two. Chang went on to become a leading figure in the revolutionary movement after his release from prison in 1906. Tsou died one month before his term expired. He was then twenty years old.

When the *Su-pao* was forced to close, the Patriotism Academy was disbanded and the Chinese Education Society went underground. The leaders of these organizations went into hiding. Most of them remained in Shanghai, but Wu Chih-hui decided to forgo revolutionary activity in favor of study in England. Ts'ai Yüan-p'ei had left Shanghai for Tsingtao shortly before the *Su-pao* was closed.

The revolutionary movement had suffered another sharp setback, but it was only temporary. Like the deportation a few months before, this reversal only infuriated the students and stiffened their resolve. Anti-Manchu newspapers and magazines in Shanghai, Japan, and Hong Kong gave wide coverage to what quickly became famous as the "*Su-pao* case." The revolutionaries hailed Chang Ping-lin and Tsou Jung as martyrs and intensified their attacks on the Manchus.[30] But revolutionary journalism continued to deal as much with the threat posed by foreign powers as with the weakness of the Manchus. For one thing, while the *Su-pao* case dramatically exposed the Manchus' limited control over their own people, it also underlined Western domination.[31] At the same time the crisis in Manchuria and the subsequent outbreak of war between Russia and Japan drew everyone's attention to the foreign threat. The two issues remained inseparable; the growing anti-Manchuism was not quite yet powerful enough to overshadow anti-imperialism.

It is estimated that in 1904 and 1905 more than one hundred revolutionary publications appeared in Shanghai.[32] Among the most pop-

[30] See *HHKM*, I, 329–500, for more details on the *Su-pao* case. Note especially the articles by Chang Huang-chi, already cited above, and Chang Hsing-yen, "Su-pao-an shih-mo chi," pp. 387–90. Albert Maybon, in *La Politique Chinoise. 1898–1908*, pp. 164–65, also has some interesting notes on the *Su-pao* case, although his account contains some minor inaccuracies.

[31] See the perceptive discussion by Y. C. Wang, *Chinese Intellectuals*, p. 239.

[32] Li Chien-nung, *Political History*, p. 192. The Chinese edition of this book mentions the names of some of the leading publications. See Li Chien-nung, *Chung-kuo chin pai-nien cheng-chih shih*, I, 224. Note that one, *Su-pao-an chi-shih*, was devoted to the *Su-pao* case.

ular and influential were the *Russia Alarm* (*O-shih ching-wen*) and the *Warning Bell Daily* (*Ching-chung jih-pao*).[33] The *Russia Alarm* was established to protest Russian occupation of Manchuria and, equally important, to belabor the Manchus for permitting Chinese territory to be violated.[34] It continued to focus on the Russian question throughout its short existence, but after the Russo-Japanese War broke out there seemed to be little reason to write any more on the subject. The *Russia Alarm* then changed its name to the *Warning Bell Daily*, which, although it contained articles on a wider variety of subjects than its predecessor, concentrated on the threat posed to China's independence by the foreign powers. Its criticisms of the Manchus were overwhelmingly on the count that they were too weak to resist aggression.

Thus the new ideological trends of the early 1900's, while they flowed toward a broader and more virulent attack upon the Manchus together with an undercurrent of advocating political westernization, remained largely within the confines of a growing anti-imperialism. As the general and vague ideas became more specific and concrete, their advocates also became more numerous, their feelings more intense, and their outlets more varied. Rebuffed in Japan in 1902, the revolutionaries bobbed up in Shanghai; suppressed in Shanghai, they surfaced again there and in the interior. For in addition to the activity in Shanghai in 1904–5, many revolutionaries went inland after the *Su-pao* case to carry the struggle to the Manchus' home grounds.

One of the most important new groups was the Hua-hsing-hui, founded by Huang Hsing in the fall of 1903. Its strength was concentrated in Hunan and Hupeh, but its organization included students and soldiers from at least eight other provinces. Huang, after receiving a classical Chinese education, studied for a short time in Japan. In 1903 he returned to China, where he led his followers into

[33] The *O-shih ching-wen* was published daily from December 15, 1903, to February 25, 1904. All 73 issues may be seen in the Kuomintang archives in Taiwan. The same paper was known as the *Ching-chung jih-pao* from February 29, 1904, until it ceased publication on January 30, 1905. The Kuomintang archives possess 324 issues of the 338 that were published. The *O-shih ching-wen* was the only revolutionary publication the writer has seen that consistently used a colloquial (*pai-hua*) writing style.

[34] It was now two months after the Russian withdrawal was supposed to have been completed. Russia had not pulled back but had in fact strengthened her forces in anticipation of war with Japan.

an alliance with several secret-society groups and formed a revolutionary army. Toward the end of 1904, after intensive preparation, Huang and the secret-society leaders were prepared to launch simultaneous uprisings in six Hunan cities. The plot was discovered by the Manchu authorities, and Huang had to escape to Japan.[35]

Another important organization was the Restoration Society (*Kuang-fu-hui*), founded in 1904 in Shanghai. It was essentially an alliance between a group of Chekiang secret-society men led by T'ao Ch'eng-chang and some prominent intellectuals including Ts'ai Yüan-p'ei and Chang Ping-lin. The Restoration Society retained its name and organization even after the T'ung-meng-hui was formed, and eventually broke away entirely and resumed independent action after its leadership split with Sun Yat-sen.[36]

The organizations out of which the Restoration Society grew give us only a vague notion of what principles it stood for, if any, besides the obvious ones of opposition to the Manchus. According to Feng Tzu-yu, its roots can be traced to the 1902 meeting in Japan at which Chinese students mourned the Manchu conquest of China. After this meeting, some Chinese students including Feng established the Youth Society (*Ch'ing-nien-hui*), out of which the Volunteer Corps to Resist Russia was organized in the spring of 1903. When the Japanese government prohibited other countries from conducting military activities on Japanese soil, the students merely changed the name of their organization to the Society for the Education of a Militant Citizenry (*Chün-kuo-min chiao-yü hui*). Soon, faced with possible arrest by Manchu authorities and becoming ever more firmly convinced that the Manchus would not carry out basic reforms, the students returned to China. They were now determined to use force; some among them organized an assassination squad (*an-sha t'uan*) in Shanghai and plotted to murder several top Manchu officials. It was at this juncture that Ts'ai Yüan-p'ei returned from Tsingtao.

[35] See Hsüeh, *Huang Hsing*, pp. 13–25; *50th Anniversary Documents*, X, 429–53; *HHKM*, I, 501–12. There is some disagreement about the date and place of the Hua-hsing-hui's founding; it may have originated in Japan as late as the spring of 1904. Cf. Tso Shun-sheng, "Huang Hsing p'ing-chuan," *Chuan-chi wen-hsüeh*, Vol. X, No. 3, p. 12.

[36] See Mary Backus Rankin, "The Revolutionary Movement in Chekiang: A Study in the Tenacity of Tradition," *China in Revolution: The First Phase, 1900–1913*, ed. Mary C. Wright, pp. 319 ff.

According to Feng, Ts'ai suggested cooperation between his Chinese Education Society and the would-be assassins. The idea was warmly received and the Restoration Society was founded with Ts'ai as its head.[37]

We know, therefore, that the Restoration Society grew out of the revolutionaries' protest against the occupation of Manchuria and the Manchus' inability to prevent the Russian move. But we know little more about its organization and aims. Feng Tzu-yu tells us merely that "the regulations," presumably those of the assassination squad, were "carefully revised." He gives no hint of what the changes were or what the final version contained.

We know also that secret-society elements played an important and perhaps even a leading role in the affairs of the Restoration Society. According to Feng, Ts'ai believed that it was necessary to bring all the revolutionary groups together, and he knew that the merger was not possible without the approval of the secret-society leader T'ao Ch'eng-chang. "Consequently [Ts'ai] agreed to have [T'ao] Ch'eng-chang join the Society [Kuang-fu-hui]." From this account it appears that Ts'ai accepted secret-society support only with reluctance, feeling that without it the organization could not function.[38]

T'ao Ch'eng-chang, whose own description of the origins of the Restoration Society is almost identical to that of Feng Tzu-yu, presents the aims of the group and his own entrance into it in a strikingly different light. The original motive for establishing the society, T'ao wrote, was to organize for assassination. Ts'ai, seeking ruffians to carry out the work and knowing that T'ao had connections with all the secret societies in China, urged him to join. T'ao, who had earlier pointed out that he and Ts'ai came from the same part of Chekiang and that he had always respected Ts'ai for his virtue (*te-hsing*), then added that he could not disappoint Ts'ai. And so he joined the Restoration Society.[39]

During the first few months of its existence, the Restoration Society

[37] Feng Tzu-yu, "Kuang-fu-hui," *HHKM*, I, 515–16.

[38] *Ibid.*, p. 516.

[39] T'ao Ch'eng-chang, "Che-an chi-lüeh," *HHKM*, III, 17. T'ao's account of the origins of the Restoration Society is on pp. 14–17. From what we know of Ts'ai Yüan-p'ei, and considering the subsequent inactivity of the Restoration Society, T'ao's account of his entrance into the organization seems inaccurate. It is difficult to imagine Ts'ai deliberately organizing a band of assassins.

did little to advance the revolutionary cause. Feng Tzu-yu attributed this to Ts'ai Yüan-p'ei's weak leadership; Ts'ai was a bookish man, impatient with the details of administration and lacking the vitality and ability to recruit and organize.[40] As a result, the center of revolutionary activity on the China mainland gradually shifted away from Shanghai to other areas in the lower Yangtze basin, where sporadic uprisings were carried out by secret societies. An important new development in 1903–4 was the penetration by the revolutionaries of the New Army.[41] The revolutionaries now began to hope that future uprisings would find the government army unwilling to take action against the insurgents, but that future seemed distant.

By the beginning of 1905 the major revolutionary organizations had failed to gain any semblance of widespread popular support. The uprisings they had attempted had met with no success. The Hsing-Chung-hui was virtually inactive while its leader, Sun Yat-sen, was seeking support in Europe and America. Members of the Hua-hsing-hui had scattered to Japan and various provinces in China. The Restoration Society languished under impotent leadership. Early in 1905, the *Warning Bell Daily* was forced to close, and the Shanghai revolutionary movement was finally halted. Only among the secret societies and the overseas Chinese students and within the New Army did there seem to exist any potential for revolution. But the secret societies were unreliable and old-fashioned; the students politically and militarily inexperienced, disorganized, and preoccupied with trying to unravel a jumble of undigested new ideas; and the military closely supervised and checked by organizational controls. The revolution offered little promise for the foreseeable future.

WELDING A REVOLUTIONARY SPEARHEAD

*The Founding of the T'ung-meng-hui*

When Sun Yat-sen left Japan in September, 1903, he would seem to have had little cause for optimism, although his biographer tells us that he "felt encouraged by the indications that the number of

[40] Feng Tzu-yu, *Chung-hua min-kuo k'ai-kuo ch'ien ke-ming shih*, II, 21.

[41] See Josef Fass, "The Role of the New Style Army in the 1911 Revolution in China," *Archiv Orientalni*, XXX, 183–91, and Yoshihiro Hatano, "The New Armies," in *China in Revolution . . .*, ed. Mary C. Wright, pp. 365 ff.

revolutionary-minded Chinese was growing."[42] His spirits were doubtless buoyed up by the support he had found in Hanoi earlier that year and by the fourteen followers, including several student leaders, that he recruited just before he left Japan.[43] But elsewhere the prospects for revolution seemed dim.

The student movement, which was to be the brightest spot on the revolutionary scene before long, was only at an early stage of its development in 1903. The number of Chinese students in Japan was still growing rather slowly,[44] and they had barely begun to organize and publish at this time. Furthermore, Sun had little to do with their activities. Chang Ping-lin wrote that Sun, living in Yokohama in 1902–3, "was quite well known to the foreigners and Chinese. But, on the whole, the Chinese students in Japan thought he was an uncultured outlaw, hard to get along with, and they did not associate with him."[45] Although anti-Manchu secret societies in China were continuing their operations, it was not until the end of 1903 that they renewed and strengthened their ties with the returned students from Japan. Sun himself had nothing to do with these activities. Shortly after he left Japan he wrote to Hirayama Shu from Hawaii: "When I reached Tokyo [in July, 1903], I searched everywhere for old comrades, [but] there was not one to be seen, and I was deeply disappointed."[46]

Sun was to write in retrospect, however, that the 1895–1900 period was the most difficult time.[47] After 1895, he was regarded as an

[42] Lyon Sharman, *Sun Yat-sen: His Life and Its Meaning*, p. 76. Cf. Ch'i Ping-feng, *Ch'ing-mo ke-ming yü chün-hsien ti lun-cheng*, p. 24.

[43] Shelley Cheng, "The T'ung-meng-hui . . . ," pp. 36–37. Among the students Sun met at this time was Liao Chung-k'ai (1878–1925), later to become an important Kuomintang leader; see Lo Chia-lun, *Kuo-fu nien-p'u ch'u-kao*, I, 123, Liao's wife, Ho Hsiang-ning, provides a participant's account in "Wo te hui-i" (My Recollection), in *Hsin-hai ke-ming hui-i-lu* (Recollections of the 1911 Revolution), pp. 12–14.

[44] See above, note 11.

[45] Quoted in Hsüeh, *Huang Hsing*, p. 35. Interestingly enough, Chang himself was friendly with Sun in those years and tried, apparently without success, to bring him more actively into the students' activities. Chang seems to have shared his comrades' view of Sun, but was willing to associate with him nevertheless.

[46] Sun Yat-sen, *Kuo-fu ch'üan-chi*, V, 23. In the same letter Sun complained about inadequate funds, which indicates that the contributions he had received in Hanoi were meager.

[47] "Tzu-chuan," in *ibid.*, I, 36.

outcast, but five years later he detected a change in people's attitudes toward him, as "the last vestige of the Court's prestige was swept away . . . and the revolutionary tide streamed forth." [48]

Whatever Sun's real feelings at the time, there is no reason to doubt that in 1904 both he and the revolutionary movement were moving into a new stage of development. For Sun the path led from Hawaii to the United States, where he continued to seek money and supporters chiefly from secret-society elements, merchants, and laborers. He found reason to hope despite his meager success and his concern about the activities of the reformist Emperor Protection Society. Sun wrote that K'ang Yu-wei, Liang Ch'i-ch'ao, and their supporters were masquerading as revolutionaries and deceiving many people into making contributions to their cause. Nevertheless, he was encouraged by this demonstration of enthusiasm for revolution and confident that it would not be difficult to expose his rivals and transfer their support to his own banners. Accordingly he urged his followers in Shanghai to send more revolutionary literature for distribution in Hawaii and the United States.[49]

On December 14, 1904, Sun sailed for England, turning his thoughts more toward working with students. We are told that Sun went to England because a group of students had recently arrived there from China and Japan. Most of them had been influenced by revolutionary ideas, and Sun was now anxious to make contact with them.[50] It was not in England, however, but on the continent that Sun and the overseas Chinese students joined forces. In response to a request by Liu Ch'eng-yü, who was now editing a Chinese newspaper in San Francisco, his Hupeh comrades in Belgium, France, and Germany raised eight thousand francs to finance Sun's journey.

In the months that followed, Sun met frequently with Chinese students in Europe. In Brussels he outlined the four-point program that was later to be incorporated into that of the T'ung-meng-hui: drive out the Tartars, restore Chinese rule, establish a republic, and equalize land ownership.[51] An oath was drawn up, and some thirty stu-

[48] *Ibid.*, p. 38. Cf. Ch'i Ping-feng, *Ch'ing-mo ke-ming yü chün-hsien ti lun-cheng*, pp. 19–24, 116.

[49] See his letters to Huang Tsung-yang, *Kuo-fu ch'üan-chi*, V, 25–27.

[50] Lo Chia-lun, *Kuo-fu nien-p'u ch'u-kao*, I, 137.

[51] Feng Tzu-yu, *Ke-ming i-shih*, II, 132. Shelley Cheng, "The T'ung-meng-

dents were sworn into the cabal, but no formal organization was created, nor were officers chosen or a name selected. Similar meetings in France and Germany achieved the same results.

According to some accounts, the only differences of opinion at the Brussels meeting concerned minor matters such as whether there should be an oath sworn to Heaven (*T'ien*) and how the date should be recorded.[52] One of the participants, however, Chu Ho-chung, tells us that he himself raised another important issue. When Sun asked the others who were present what methods they thought should be adopted to promote the revolution, Chu argued that the New Army and the intellectuals had to be won over. Sun disagreed, maintaining that these groups were incapable of revolution and that reliance upon secret-society uprisings was the only course. "We debated for three days and three nights, the result being a decision to advance along both paths simultaneously." Chu argued that secret-society men were too ignorant to grasp the profundities of revolutionary theory and therefore could not be the basis for the revolutionary movement; indeed, he ascribed Sun's previous failures to his lack of support from intellectuals. Sun rejected this view, citing the learning of his old conspiratorial comrades Shih Chien-ju and Lu Hao-tung, but Chu insisted that their number was unequal to the task. "We must have the majority of intellectuals with us; then the matter will be half as difficult and the success twice as great." [53]

Sun's trip to Europe early in 1905 thus seems to have marked an important stage in the development of the Chinese revolutionary movement. Sun returned to vigorous activity after several years of relative inaction, and if Chu Ho-chung's account is correct, Sun's attitude toward the student movement changed significantly.[54] In any

hui . . . ," p. 36, states that this four-point program was first enunciated in Tokyo in 1903.

[52] Feng Tzu-yu, *Ke-ming i-shih*, II, 132. The question of the oath seems to have centered more on whether there should be an oath at all than on whether it should be sworn to Heaven.

[53] Chu Ho-chung, "Ou-chou T'ung-meng-hui chi-shih," *Ke-ming wen-hsien*, II, 256. Chu does not mention any disagreement on dating; his version of the oath gives the date as *Huang-ti* 4646. However, he mentions a discussion concerning the oath: most of those present believed that they had already fully committed themselves to the revolution and that an oath was therefore superfluous. If we are to believe this account, the tide was running heavily against Sun on this issue until Chu agreed to take the oath.

[54] According to Li Chien-nung and several other sources, when Sun left Japan

case, it is true that in 1905 Sun began to work more closely with students than he ever had in the past. It seems reasonable to ascribe this shift less to Chu Ho-chung's persuasiveness than to the sudden increase in the number of people who were leaving China to study abroad. As these students began to stream into Japan in 1905, they were becoming a force that even the unpracticed eye could recognize as potentially powerful. To Sun, who for fully a decade had been a leader so unsuccessful in his search for a following that he can scarcely be called a leader, there came into view a movement that was so loosely organized, its purposes so ill-defined, and, until now, its numbers so small that it hardly deserved to be termed a movement. Sun hurried back to Japan, prepared, no doubt, to channel the swelling tide. His comrades in Europe were no less aroused. "We excitedly sent a letter to Tokyo to report this affair [the meeting with Sun] and to ask each of our comrades to join eagerly when Sun arrived in Japan." [55]

Sun reached Yokohama on July 19, 1905, and we may guess at the exhilaration he must have felt. In sharp contrast to the situation he had left twenty-two months before, he was now enthusiastically welcomed by students whose numbers may have reached well into the hundreds. Japan, whose fleet had only a month earlier smashed the Russians at Tsushima, transmitted her vigor and confidence to the Chinese revolutionaries. Through the efforts of old friends such as Miyazaki Torazō and Ch'eng Chia-ch'eng, Sun was soon introduced to Huang Hsing, Sung Chiao-jen, Ch'en T'ien-hua, and other leading figures. Within a month a series of meetings had been held, the formation of a united revolutionary organization decided upon, and its regulations drafted. On August 20 the T'ung-meng-hui came into being.

The unity, firmness of purpose, and decisiveness with which the revolutionary leaders acted in the summer of 1905 was not to be ex-

---

in 1903 he asked Liao Chung-k'ai, Ma Chün-wu, and others to organize the Chinese students in Tokyo. See the Teng and Ingalls translation, *Political History*, p. 201. Chu's account magnifies his own role, but it seems clear that Sun only gradually came to accept the idea that young students could be important in the revolution. For further discussion of this and other aspects of Sun's role see Harold Z. Schiffrin, "The Enigma of Sun Yat-sen," in *China in Revolution*, ed. Mary C. Wright, pp. 443–74.

[55] Chu Ho-chung, "Ou-chou T'ung-meng-hui chi-shih," p. 257.

ceeded at any later time. The years that followed would see discord and disappointment, faltering and confusion. Even the great events of late 1911 and early 1912, Wuchang and the abdication, would in the one case take many of them by surprise and in the other be effected by a new and powerful rival. Nevertheless, the T'ung-meng-hui was to do much to shape those events, and for a brief moment in 1905, as well as on several occasions thereafter, it stood proudly in the mainstream of history.

## T'ung-meng-hui Personnel, Organization, and Activities[56]

A basic characteristic that distinguished the T'ung-meng-hui from the Hong Kong Hsing-Chung-hui, and also from other earlier revolutionary groups, is the varied background of its members.[57] Besides men like Sun who had spent much time abroad or in Hong Kong and the treaty ports and who had obtained most of their education in Western schools, there were now many revolutionaries who had had little or no contact with the West and whose foreign travel was limited to the short time they had spent in Japan. Many had an extensive classical Chinese education. Perhaps the most outstanding in this respect were Chang Ping-lin, Wu Chih-hui (who was a *chü-jen* of 1891 and competed unsuccessfully in the metropolitan examinations of 1895), and Liu Shih-p'ei, a *chü-jen* of 1902. In addition, to mention only a few of the most prominent, Huang Hsing was a *sheng-yüan* of 1892, and Wang Ching-wei and Ch'en T'ien-hua earned the same title in 1902. The outlook of such men was naturally affected by their deep familiarity with the Chinese written tradition. And even in the case of a man like Wu who rejected the tradition, this added dimension would both complicate his anti-traditional stand and give it deeper meaning.

The differences in the background, life experiences, ages, and personalities of T'ung-meng-hui members greatly complicate the problem of understanding the Chinese revolutionary movement. The prob-

[56] For details see *50th Anniversary Documents*, Vols. XI–XVI; *HHKM*, Vols. II–VIII; Shelley Cheng, "The T'ung-meng-hui . . . ," pp. 100–328; Hsüeh, *Huang Hsing*, pp. 38–117; and Josef Fass, "Revolutionary Activity in the Province Hu-pei and the Wu-ch'ang Uprising of 1911," *Archiv Orientalni*, XXVIII, 127–49.

[57] Hu Han-min, for example, characterized the Chinese student body in Japan as "complicated, confusing, and containing all sorts." See his "Tzu-chuan," in *Ke-ming wen-hsien*, III, 385. Cf. Chün-tu Hsüeh, *Huang Hsing*, pp. 44–45.

lem can be seen most clearly, and for this study most appropriately, in some similarities and differences among Sun Yat-sen, Wang Ching-wei, Chang Ping-lin, and their opponent Liang Ch'i-ch'ao.

Sun and Chang, very close to each other in age, represented an older generation than Wang and Liang, but in background and personality Sun had most in common with Wang, less with Liang, and perhaps even less with Chang. Sun was far too complex a man to be described briefly, but there can be little doubt that his Western orientation was one of his most important characteristics. Certainly he had more Chinese education and familiarity with Chinese conditions than many Chinese thought around the turn of the century and more than many scholars thought until recently;[58] but most of his adolescence and young manhood was spent abroad. In Sun's formative years, from the age of about thirteen to twenty-seven, he spent scarcely any time in China, and not a great deal after that. His formal education was largely in Western or Western-style schools, and he probably spent at least as much time in the company of non-Chinese people as he did with Chinese. There is ample reason for stressing Sun's identification with foreigners, especially with Japanese and Westerners.[59]

Sun had great self-assurance in all things, but was especially confident of his ability to deal with Westerners. He was ready to attribute a certain amount of good will to most Westerners, and seemed sure that any concessions he might make to them would redound to his and therefore to China's benefit. However, Chang, a great classical scholar bred in the Old Text tradition and hypersensitive (in the Ming loyalist tradition) to foreign violation of Chinese cultural integrity, remained suspicious of Westerners' intentions and resentful of Western influence in the Chinese revolutionary movement.[60] Indeed, there is reason to believe that Chang's anti-foreign predilections were so deeply reinforced by his trial in a Western court

[58] For correctives see Ch'i Ping-feng, *Ch'ing-mo ke-ming yü chün-hsien ti lun-cheng*, p. 18, and Shelley Cheng, "The T'ung-meng-hui . . . ," pp. 2–4; also Lyon Sharman, *Sun Yat-sen*, p. 23, although this one paragraph is overshadowed by the discussion of Sun's Western training.

[59] See Jansen, *The Japanese and Sun Yat-sen, passim*; and Schiffrin. "The Enigma of Sun Yat-sen," in *China in Revolution*, ed. Mary C. Wright, pp. 443–74.

[60] Cf. Schiffrin, "The Enigma of Sun Yat-sen," pp. 455–57, 468–69.

on Chinese territory in 1903 that all things Western were doubly distasteful to him from then on.[61]

Wang Ching-wei, seventeen years younger than Sun and fifteen years younger than Chang, was only twenty-two when the T'ung-meng-hui was founded. Mercurial, gifted, quick to learn, a brilliant polemicist in print and even better on a soapbox, Wang was the *enfant terrible* of the T'ung-meng-hui. Other men of his age were prominent — Chu Chih-hsin, for example, a very bright young man himself — but Wang was deferred to by leaders like Hu Han-min and sometimes even by Sun Yat-sen. Wang was from a gentry family that had come upon bad times. He went to Japan in 1904 and did not meet Sun until the summer of 1905, but they immediately became very close and remained so. Sun was often content merely to outline some general ideas and, impatient with detail, allow others to fill in what he had sketched. Wang and Hu became his major spokesmen, and while the more plodding Hu kept closer to Sun's blueprints than Wang, the latter was doubtless Sun's favorite. It was Wang, for example, who became the featured speaker when Sun was inaugurated as provisional president of the Chinese republic in 1912,[62] and it was Wang who composed the dying Sun's last testament in 1925. Reflective but also impetuous, Wang led the T'ung-meng-hui in its most demanding intellectual activity, the debate with Liang Ch'i-ch'ao, and he also made the revolutionaries' most daring and sensational stab at violence, an attempt to murder the regent in 1910.

These three prominent revolutionaries all differed substantially from Liang, whose vacillation between revolution and reform earned him the revolutionaries' contempt. Brooding and sensitive, Liang could not resist grappling with issues that lay far beyond his or any one man's ability to solve. How to renew a Chinese vigor he refused to believe had died? How to reconcile what was good in the old with what was good in the new? How even to decide what was good in both old and new? How best to get others to see what he saw? None

---

[61] See Shen Yen-kuo, *Chi Chang T'ai-yen hsien-sheng*, pp. 22–23. Maybon, in *La Politique Chinoise*, pp. 164–66, has some interesting comments on how the foreigners frustrated rather than abetted the Manchus; cf. Y. C. Wang, *Chinese Intellectuals*, p. 239.

[62] Chang Chiang-ts'ai, *Wang Ching-wei hsien-sheng hsing-shih hsü-lu*, p. 106.

of the revolutionaries wrestled so agonizingly with such questions; and the doubts that obsessed Liang did not seem to plague the revolutionaries quite so much.

More directly than the others, perhaps, Sun confronted the questions that troubled Liang, but he reveals to us none of Liang's uncertainty. Sun was too self-confident a man; it is likely that, given the five minutes with J. P. Morgan that found Liang speechless, Sun would have eloquently outlined a plan for Chinese banks and railroads. Wang Ching-wei dealt with some of the same questions as Liang, particularly those concerning the introduction of new ideas and institutions to China, but Wang was a man of brisk decisiveness and could resolve his intellectual doubts in action. It is ironic that Wang and Liang, bitter foes at a crucial stage in the Chinese revolution, shared many goals and some doubts about how to reach those goals; and thus they have both gone into history as political and intellectual chameleons, Wang as an opportunist [63] and Liang as a somewhat pitiable lost traveler, wandering and groping through a maze of impenetrable intellectual and emotional problems.[64]

It is thus possible to find points of similarity between Liang Ch'i-ch'ao and some of the revolutionaries that are not found among the revolutionaries themselves, testimony to the latter's diversity. They included dedicated traditionalists, violent anti-traditionalists, and many to whom tradition was a peripheral concern; the T'ung-meng-hui also included secret-society members among its leaders as well as men who were trained abroad; older men and young, bibliophiles and assassins, women on horseback like Ch'iu Chin and women like Ho Chen (Mrs. Liu Shih-p'ei) who shared and perhaps even shaped their husbands' revolutionary careers, overseas Chinese who had never seen their homeland and others who never left their ancestral homes, sons of Confucian scholars and sons of peasants, wealthy businessmen and struggling students — all these diverse elements in

[63] Howard L. Boorman, "Wang Ching-wei: China's Romantic Radical," *Political Science Quarterly*, LXXIX, 525.

[64] See Levenson, *Liang, passim,* and *Confucian China and Its Modern Fate,* Vol. I, "The Problem of Intellectual Continuity," pp. xviii–xix. However, cf. Philip C. Huang, "A Confucian Liberal: Liang Ch'i-ch'ao in Action and Thought" (unpublished Ph.D. dissertation, University of Washington, 1966), pp. 5–7, 111–14, 215–24.

the Chinese revolutionary movement reveal the swirling currents of the time.

The structure of the T'ung-meng-hui also reflected this diversity. Although it was a larger and more unified group than any revolutionary organization that preceded it, the T'ung-meng-hui nevertheless contained powerful centrifugal forces. The most important one was that the provincial branch offices in Tokyo were so strong relative to the head office; this can be seen in the latter's lack of funds, manpower, and authority on the one hand, and the members' close attachments to their fellow provincials on the other. Furthermore, T'ung-meng-hui headquarters moved from place to place; sometimes it was in Tokyo, sometimes Hong Kong, sometimes wherever Sun Yat-sen was. There were also branches scattered all over Southeast Asia as well as some in Europe and North America.[65]

Finally, the T'ung-meng-hui leadership at least as early as 1907 was riven by factionalism, which then continued throughout the life of the organization. The issues sometimes seem trivial; for example, Huang Hsing and Sung Chiao-jen are said to have been so angered by a disagreement with Sun Yat-sen about the flag the republic would have that they very nearly left the T'ung-meng-hui. But as Sung noted in his diary, these minor issues reflected deeper antagonisms; there were also other issues involving Chang Ping-lin, Sun, Wu Chih-hui, and a good number of the revolutionaries.[66]

These divisive tendencies were real and important, but the unifying forces were equally so. The top leaders, and particularly Sun Yat-sen, continued to be generally recognized by the membership throughout the T'ung-meng-hui's existence, although some groups and individuals did split off and some shifts in doctrine took place. There was a good deal of personal contact among the most important centers and between the head office and the provincial branches, since the leaders traveled from place to place and wrote to each other frequently. The numerous revolutionary organs also advertised for

[65] Shelley Cheng, "The T'ung-meng-hui . . . ," pp. 106–29, has details on the organization.

[66] For these disputes see Hsüeh, *Huang Hsing*, p. 51, and Wu Hsiang-hsiang, *Sung Chiao-jen, Chung-kuo min-chu hsien-cheng ti hsien-ch'ü*, pp. 49–51, 98, 158–60.

each other and republished each other's articles. The United States military attaché in Peking observed that the Chinese officers who had returned from studies in Japan possessed a feeling of community — "clannishness" he called it — that cut across the usual provincial loyalties.[67] Last and most important, although the various branches financed most of their own activities, funds for the major T'ung-meng-hui activities seem to have been either channeled through Sun and his chief lieutenants or given directly to local leaders for purposes scarcely distinguishable from Sun's own. Chang Ping-lin's outrage at Sun's inability (or unwillingness) to finance the *Min-pao* indicates how dependent the T'ung-meng-hui agencies were on Sun for financial support.

Thus although the T'ung-meng-hui was loosely organized, there were bonds that held it together. The picture is a composite one of a scattered and sprawling organization with a varied membership possessing certain divided loyalties, but with an important common purpose and a recognized though not unquestioned leadership. There was much confusion and inefficiency and a general lack of coordinated and integrated effort, but still the T'ung-meng-hui held together for seven years under extremely trying conditions and made a significant contribution to the development of a new China. Indeed, the very nature of its contributions may have been shaped by its mixed character. Its diversity allowed a variety of ideas and interests to come together, if only for a brief time, creating an atmosphere of vigor and excitement that added to the movement's drive and momentum. But the T'ung-meng-hui also found itself unable to forge bonds that would carry the movement beyond the achievement of its immediate objective. Conditions in the China of 1911 and afterward demanded a unity of purpose and concerted effort that may have been beyond the reach of any single organization; certainly the T'ung-meng-hui proved unequal to the task.

The revolutionary movement was aimed primarily at wrenching political power from the Manchus. Military activities were therefore of the highest importance, and though much energy was given to the articulation and dissemination of ideas, revolutionary writings were

[67] James H. Reeves, *Notes on the Chinese Revolution of 1911–1912*, p. 8.

attempts to convince and persuade, to plead a cause; they were items of propaganda as well as statements of principle or belief. Sometimes they were both, and sometimes only one of these; the line between them is not always easily drawn.

Of the military activities themselves little need be said here. The difficulties that dogged the revolutionaries were due to the weakness of their organizations as well as the immensity of their task. Short of funds and manpower, forced to rely upon unpredictable allies such as the secret societies and "roving braves" or bandits, plagued by inadequate planning, uncoordinated efforts, spies, and security leaks, T'ung-meng-hui plots were a series of fiascoes.

Financial troubles never eased.[68] By far the greatest part of the revolutionaries' income was used for military activities, and most of the contributions came from Southeast Asia. The principal obstacle to their fund-raising was competition from the reformists led by K'ang Yu-wei and Liang Ch'i-ch'ao. T'ung-meng-hui writers had to keep in mind the need to persuade overseas Chinese that the revolutionary cause deserved their support. This need and the fact that there was an important audience in Southeast Asia as well as in China and Japan affected the newspaper debates between the revolutionaries and reformers.

It is not surprising that at its very first meeting the T'ung-meng-hui decided to have an official journal. At Huang Hsing's suggestion it was first decided to employ Sung Chiao-jen's *Twentieth Century China* (*Erh-shih shih-chi chih Chih-na*) for this purpose. Shortly thereafter, however, Sung's journal was suppressed by the Japanese authorities, and the *Min-pao* was founded in its stead.[69] Twenty-four issues were published before it was proscribed on October 10, 1908. In 1910, Wang Ching-wei managed to publish two more issues. Chang Ping-lin was its editor and most prolific contributor during most of its existence, but Wang, Hu Han-min, Chu Chih-hsin, and many other T'ung-meng-hui leaders wrote frequently for the journal. Even Chou Tso-jen presented some translations from Kropotkin and the terrorist-novelist S. Stepnyak (Sergei M. Kravchinsky). Sun Yat-

---

[68] See Shelley Cheng, "The T'ung-meng-hui . . . ," pp. 201–5, 220–310, *passim*.

[69] *Min-pao*'s founding is described most interestingly by Sung Chiao-jen in his diary, *Wo chih li-shih*, pp. 75–88. *Min-pao* (No. 4, p. 145) claimed in mid-1906 that its circulation reached 10,000.

sen, however, contributed not one article to the official publication of the organization he headed, although his ideas were set forth by some of his followers, particularly Wang Ching-wei and Hu Han-min. Hu tells us that the preface to the first issue of *Min-pao*, which was printed over Sun's name, was dictated by Sun but written by Hu himself; presumably this may after all be considered Sun's article. Hu also pointed out that the first three principles of the *Min-pao* were to be identified with Sun's *San Min Chu I*.[70] *Min-pao* also published Sun's speech on the occasion of its first anniversary, and Sun published a few articles in other newspapers such as the *Restoration Daily* (*Chung-hsing jih-pao*) in Singapore.

In the third issue of *Min-pao*, its editor set forth its purposes.[71] The revolutionaries must understand the significance of the revolution, must know what they were fighting for. This meant, he emphasized, not merely grasping the concrete meaning of revolution, which was to overthrow the Manchus, but engaging in what he termed "abstract study." The revolutionaries must ask what the aims of the revolution should be. What methods should be employed and which avoided? What other matters should be promoted besides the overthrow of the Manchu regime? What kind of plans are there for post-revolutionary reconstruction? What effect would the revolution have upon China and the world at large? There were many such questions, Hu asserted, more than any one or two men could hope to solve, but if the T'ung-meng-hui failed to answer them, the revolution would bring only harm to the Chinese people.[72] It was with these problems in mind, Hu continued, that the T'ung-meng-hui had founded the *Min-pao*:

> The function of a revolutionary newspaper is to enable people to understand the revolution. A revolution has secret activities, but there should be nothing secret about its principles. Not only should they not be secret, but they should be spread to society, in order

---

[70] Hu Han-min, "Tzu-chuan," *Ke-ming wen-hsien*, III, 388.

[71] Hu Han-min, "Min-pao chih liu ta chu-i," *Min-pao*, No. 3 (Apr. 5, 1906), pp. 1–22. For translated excerpts from this article see W. T. deBary *et al.* (eds.), *Sources of Chinese Tradition*, pp. 763–67. Hu was *Min-pao*'s first editor, although Chang Chi, who spoke Japanese well, was named publicly in order to facilitate dealing with the Japanese authorities. Hu, "Tzu-chuan," *Ke-ming wen-hsien*, III, 388.

[72] Hu, "Min-pao chih liu ta chu-i," *Min-pao*, No. 3, pp. 2–3.

that they may pour into people's minds and create a public opinion. . . .[73]

Hu hastened to add that such a journal must be careful to do more than arouse emotions. If it failed to educate, it would not meet its responsibilities. Public opinion, he declared, has its greatest value when it relies upon reason to make judgments, while things done in the passion of the moment are of no benefit in the long run.

> A revolutionary newspaper must deal in abstract study, and if it cannot it is inadequate as a journal of revolution. If it can do this but fails to guide society's intellectual development and nurture people's abilities, it is also useless.[74]

Similar expressions of concern by other T'ung-meng-hui writers are not lacking, although most tended to emphasize that the first order of business was to smash the Manchu regime.[75] Hu Han-min had nevertheless sketched the framework within which the revolutionaries would attempt to explain their views of what China's main problems were and how they should be solved.

THE 1905 TURNING POINT

History is rarely generous enough to periodize itself neatly, but 1905 can be considered a major turning point. That summer, long years of change culminated in four key events that took place within just a few weeks of each other. One was the abolition of the traditional examination system, an event that symbolizes the fall of imperial China. The consequences for China's social order, educational system, and administrative structure were so direct and concrete that they meant imminent doom for traditional institutions. At almost the same time, the empress dowager decided to investigate foreign constitutional monarchies, apparently with a view to adopting a constitution for China. When China turned to the outside world for instruction in the art of government, it reversed centuries-old attitudes, and those who were imbued with tradition might understandably feel that the world had turned inside out.

[73] *Ibid.*, p. 4.
[74] *Ibid.*, p. 5.
[75] For example, see Wang Ching-wei, "Min-tsu ti kuo-min," Part II, *Min-pao*, No. 2 (Jan. 22, 1906), p. 17.

The Manchus' reforms were stimulated by the third important event of 1905, Japan's triumph over Russia. The effect upon Chinese observers was electric. Japan, the victor over China in 1895, an ally of Britain since 1902, had now defeated a major Western imperialist power. An Asian nation had become a world power, and her success was widely interpreted as one of constitutional monarchy over autocracy. Japan became a model for all thoughtful Chinese to study, whether they were government leaders, reformers, or revolutionaries. The fact that there was a lesson to be learned seemed to be further demonstrated by the October (1905) Manifesto in Russia, which promised a constitution for Japan's erstwhile foe; defeated Russia seemed to have concluded that in constitutionalism there was strength.

A few years earlier, many people might have followed the Manchus' lead. Had it been 1898 when the imperial commissioners boarded a train at Peking to leave for their ship and foreign lands, a Wu Yüeh might have been among those cheering their departure and wishing them well. In 1905 he was at the railway station, but he was there to throw a bomb. For the fourth event of that summer was the establishment of the T'ung-meng-hui, signaling a new and higher stage in the development of the revolutionary movement. For too many it was now too late for compromise.

Thus some forty-five years of halting, uneven, grudging, but nevertheless intensifying change began to accelerate and snowball. On the government side, the change from cautious "self-strengthening" in the 1860's to the risks of limited constitutional government in 1905 may not have been much ground to have covered in four and a half decades, but to Liang Ch'i-ch'ao and his followers it seemed to offer some promise for progress without revolution. Having changed his mind about revolution during his 1903 visit to the United States, Liang met K'ang Yu-wei and other leaders of the Society to Save the Emperor (*Pao-huang-hui*) at a crucial policy conference in Hong Kong early in 1904. The reformers mobilized their resources, mapped a reorganization of their society and its publications, and discussed strategy.[76] By 1905, Liang's arguments for peaceful reform were becoming a challenge the revolutionaries had to confront.

[76] Jung-pang Lo, *K'ang Yu-wei*, pp. 195–96.

Even if the Manchus' reforms accomplished little else, they opened new possibilities for those who insisted on a more rapid pace. With the old educational system gone and a new political framework in the making, Chinese students poured into Japan, where even greater changes had been in progress for decades; a few others went to France or elsewhere in the West. Abroad they were infused with a new spirit, and few could have returned to China with their minds unmoved, even if not all became revolutionaries. The United States military attaché in Peking observed in 1912:

> . . . the revolution has been largely effected through the work of Chinese who have gone to school in Japan during the last ten to fifteen years. . . . During the past few years the remark has been heard on all sides that the returned Japanese students [i.e. those Chinese who had returned from Japan] were revolutionary in spirit. . . . [They] returned to China republicans rather than monarchical reformers.[77]

That republican spirit did not originate in the early 1900's, but its scattered beginnings in the nineteenth century were so inchoate that they were easily obscured by reformers' greater interest in Western technology. In the wake of 1898's Hundred Days, Chinese interest in Western social and political thought blossomed.[78] Of the many factors contributing to this flowering, the most invigorating may have been the work of Yen Fu.[79] Yen's translations appeared opportunely, and they spoke to the issues of wealth, power, progress, and national salvation that were most on the minds of the new Chinese intelligentsia. Only a few shared Yen's admiration for Great Britain; most found something else in his work, perhaps the link between science and society that social Darwinism seemed to promise. The

[77] Reeves, *Notes*, pp. 7–8.

[78] An interesting indication of the changing attitudes of the time is the shift from the translation of foreign scientific and technological works that characterized the period from 1850–99 to the translation of works in the social sciences, history, and geography in 1902–4. See Tsuen-hsuin Tsien, "Western Impact on China through Translation," *Far Eastern Quarterly*, XIII, 305–27. Note the tables on pp. 315 and 319.

[79] See Benjamin Schwartz, *In Search of Wealth and Power: Yen Fu and the West*. Also, Y. C. Wang, *Chinese Intellectuals*, pp. 193–212. It is entirely possible, perhaps even likely, that Yen Fu's contribution as described here was far less than the contribution to revolutionary thought made by Japanese transmitters of Darwinism.

translations provided Chinese intellectuals with an entirely new vocabulary and a wide range of new ways of looking at the world that can only have been exhilarating and intellectually liberating, especially to young men newly arrived in the dynamic Japan of the early 1900's. Most of all, Darwinism and its associated ideas of inexorable evolution and progress hit them like an irresistible force.

It is difficult to determine the precise effect that such ideas may have had upon the students who streamed into Japan after the turn of the century. We know that their writings were full of such expressions as "the struggle for existence," which they applied chiefly to the world political situation. At the very least it can be said that these ideas contributed to the new questioning spirit, and that this spirit was gradually funneled into a torrent of political unrest. The main source of the students' discontent was China's weakness and her inability to withstand foreign aggression; the object of their dissatisfaction became the Manchu government. Tsou Jung and others then pointed to what they regarded as other hateful features of the Manchu regime and indeed of the entire Chinese political tradition. A growing anti-Manchuism fed the demand for a new form of government that was openly expressed in the T'ung-meng-hui Manifesto.

Before 1905 these sentiments were felt by no more than a few hundred Chinese, and except for Sun Yat-sen and a handful of others, they were young and inexperienced in the world outside China. By 1905 their numbers had grown, and older men had joined them. Some students, such as Chang Chi, had been in Japan for as long as six years. To them it appeared that each Manchu reform was a confession of weakness and therefore a signal for the revolutionaries to advance. When the Manchus sent the constitutional missions abroad, the revolutionaries accused them of merely hammering out a new shield. The students responded by welding their forces into a new spearhead. The battle had been joined anew.

PART TWO

# The T'ung-meng-hui's
# Political Program

# 3

# *A National Revolution: Drive Out the Manchus*

### NATIONALISM, OLD AND NEW

To drive the Manchus from China was the first point in the T'ung-meng-hui program,[1] but anti-Manchuism was of course not new. It can be traced to the very first years of Ch'ing times and the famous "Ming loyalists." Two of these men, Wang Fu-chih (1619–92) and Lü Liu-liang (1629–83), were frequently acknowledged by T'ung-meng-hui writers as their forerunners.[2] Wang formulated a concept of race according to which races had first been differentiated by the circumstances of geography; each race had then produced a distinctive culture which could not be borrowed by another race. Thus while foreigners might adopt certain Chinese customs, they could not really be assimilated and were therefore not fit to rule China. Lü contended that Confucius himself had said that only Chinese could rule China.[3]

[1] For convenient outlines of the T'ung-meng-hui's program compare its "Manifesto" in Ssu-yü Teng and John K. Fairbank, *China's Response to the West,* pp. 227–29, with the *Min-pao's* six principles in W. T. deBary *et al.* (eds.), *Sources of Chinese Tradition,* pp. 762–67.

[2] On Wang see Hsiao Kung-ch'üan, *Chung-kuo cheng-chih ssu-hsiang shih,* V, 629–40, and deBary, *Sources,* pp. 597–606. On Lü see Hsiao, *op. cit.,* V, 640–46. Their biographies may be found in Arthur W. Hummel (ed.), *Eminent Chinese of the Ch'ing Period,* II, 817–19, and I, 551–52.

[3] It is with these men that there seems to have arisen for the first time the question of the right of non-Chinese to rule China. Professor Vincent Y. C. Shih has noted ethnic issues arising in Sung and Yüan times, but in the first case, and

The virulent anti-Manchuism of the Ming loyalists gradually disappeared as scholars were drawn into the Ch'ing bureaucracy. But a new and violent anti-Manchuism appeared with the Taipings. "The most deadly weapon they used was the ethnic issue. They harped on the theme of the distinction between the Chinese and barbarian non-Chinese, and the conception of the superiority of the former over the latter." [4] The Taipings shared this part of their ideology with secret societies: "It gradually became the dominant feature of secret society ideology." [5]

The revolutionaries were heirs to a tradition of anti-Manchuism which probably was reinforced by their own association with secret societies. Moreover they were fully aware of their ancestry and looked even deeper into the past than we have.

We recall that, since the beginning of our nation the Chinese have always ruled China; although at times alien peoples have usurped the rule, yet our ancestors were able to drive them out and restore Chinese sovereignty so that they could hand down the nation to posterity. Now the men of Han [i.e., the Chinese] have raised a righteous [or patriotic] army to exterminate the northern barbarians. This is a continuation of heroic deeds bequeathed to us by our predecessors. . . .[6]

---

perhaps in the second as well, the issue was more economic than racial. "Some Chinese Rebel Ideologies," *T'oung Pao*, XLIV, 183–85, 190–91.

Yuji Muramatsu says that racial themes "found explicit popular expression in rebel ideologies" in the Southern Sung and were exploited by rebels against the Chin and Yüan. But even under conquest dynasties these appeals were never sufficient motive for rebellion. "Some Themes in Chinese Rebel Ideologies," Arthur F. Wright (ed.), *The Confucian Persuasion*, pp. 264–67.

[4] Vincent Y. C. Shih, "The Ideology of the Taiping T'ien Kuo," *Sinologica*, III, 7.

[5] *Ibid.*, p. 9.

[6] "The Manifesto of the T'ung-meng-hui, 1905," translated in Teng and Fairbank, *China's Response*, p. 227. For the Chinese text of this document see *HHKM*, II, 13–16.

Although I have accepted the Teng and Fairbank translation, several glosses should be added in view of the importance of the terms "nation" and "sovereignty." The phrase "beginning of our nation" is a translation of *wo Chung-kuo k'ai-kuo*; although "nation" is acceptable, the revolutionaries did use other expressions for it (see below, note 41). In the phrase "hand down the nation to posterity" there is no Chinese equivalent for "nation," and the only possible antecedent is *Chung-kuo*. The translation "restore Chinese sovereignty" is an expansion of the Chinese *kuang-fu* ("restore") without an object; again the only possible antecedent is *Chung-kuo*, and of course *kuang-fu Chung-kuo* was a com-

T'ung-meng-hui members considered themselves to be heirs to a noble tradition, but at the same time they were determined to be the trail blazers of a new era. Revolution, after all, is a break with the past, and if they were to be true revolutionaries they had to be not only inheritors but pioneers.

> . . . revolutions in former generations, such as the Ming Dynasty and the Taiping Heavenly Kingdom, were concerned only with the driving out of barbarians and the restoration of Chinese rule. Aside from these they sought no other change. We today are different from people of former times. Besides the driving out of the barbarian dynasty and the restoration of China, it is necessary also to change the national polity and the people's livelihood.[7]

The revolutionaries thus quite deliberately and self-consciously declared that anti-Manchuism was but one feature of a broader program — that the liberation of China from Manchu control was to be only the first step in a totally new direction. This higher objective to some extent shaped the character of the anti-Manchu campaign, as did also the fact that the revolutionaries' target was a foreign people. The desires to rid China of foreign control and to establish a republic led the revolutionaries to speak out for cultural distinctiveness, unity, the right of citizens to participate in government affairs, and many other principles that added up to a plea for national self-determination. Furthermore, in distinguishing between "heroes' revolutions" and its own "national revolution," the T'ung-meng-hui Manifesto called for a movement in which all people in the country would "bear the responsibility of revolution."[8] The revolutionaries were beginning to move toward new goals with new techniques, toward a new "national polity" (*kuo-t'i*) by means of mass action. In short, the Manifesto contains some of the earliest statements of modern Chinese nationalism.

---

mon revolutionary slogan. While it probably can be taken to mean "restore Chinese rule," the importance of the concept of sovereignty and Wang Ching-wei's recognition of its complexity make it advisable that I use the term carefully.

[7] "Manifesto of the T'ung-meng-hui," Teng and Fairbank, *China's Response*, p. 227. The revolutionaries used the same term (*ke-ming*) for their own and previous revolutions; however, the latter were characterized as "heroes' revolutions" (*ying-hsiung ke-ming*), whereas their own was a "national [or 'citizens'] revolution" (*kuo-min ke-ming*).

[8] *Ibid.*

How new was all this? That depends partly upon what one means by traditional Chinese "culturalism," Chinese rebel ideologies, and modern Chinese nationalism — not only upon what T'ung-meng-hui writers said and meant. Of these, I will refer here only briefly to culturalism and nationalism.[9] Traditional Chinese attitudes, it has been suggested, included "no sign of a feeling of cultural inferiority" but rather reflected "a complete confidence in cultural superiority that is notably lacking in nationalism." On the other hand, "modern nationalism has depended for its strength on the identification of the individual with the national political unit."[10] One may question whether the possession of an attitude of cultural superiority is an adequate criterion for distinguishing culturalism from nationalism. But identification of the individual with the national political unit is unmistakably associated with modern nationalism and not with pre-twentieth-century China. In this respect the T'ung-meng-hui constituted the first organized and historically really significant group of modern Chinese nationalists.[11]

THE T'UNG-MENG-HUI BRIEF AGAINST THE MANCHUS

Except for Tsou Jung and a few others in 1903 and 1904, the revolutionaries' attack on the Ch'ing before 1905 tended to focus upon its weakness vis-à-vis the foreign powers. After the establishment of the T'ung-meng-hui this kind of argument was rarely heard. The reasons seem clear. Compared with the decade 1895–1905, the threat to China's independence after 1905 probably seemed less immediate. It was in 1904 that the *entente cordiale* was formed, and almost immediately thereafter a series of crises began in Morocco and the Balkans that compelled Europe to concentrate on affairs closer to home and finally plunged her into war in 1914. In addition, it probably would have embarrassed the revolutionaries to remind their readers that the countries presented in *Min-pao* as models

[9] Reference was made earlier to rebel ideologies. Nationalism will be discussed at more length below. For the concept of "culturalism" see Edwin O. Reischauer and John K. Fairbank, *East Asia: The Great Tradition*, pp. 290–93.

[10] *Ibid.*, p. 292.

[11] See Joseph R. Levenson, *Confucian China and Its Modern Fate*, Vol. III: *The Problem of Historical Significance*, for the important distinction between what is "only historically significant" and "historically really significant" in modern China.

for Chinese nationalism and democracy were not only the same powers that had forced the unequal treaties upon China but were the ones still threatening her. It may be true that the danger from Japan made China's situation after 1905 hardly less precarious, but the revolutionaries, with their headquarters in Japan and anxious for Japanese help, were in no position to make an issue of Japanese imperialism. Finally, it was the reformers who tended to emphasize the international situation after 1905, arguing that revolution would create an opportunity for the powers to move into China on the pretext of restoring order and protecting foreigners' interests. Understandably, therefore, the revolutionists tended to minimize the current danger from foreign powers. They did not altogether cease to berate the Manchus for the defeats and humiliations China had suffered in the sixty-odd years that had gone before, but for the most part they turned to other issues.

The T'ung-meng-hui indictment of the Manchus can be discussed under three general headings. First, they had conquered China by military force, plundering widely and slaughtering wantonly, and once in power they had carried out discriminatory policies that relegated the Chinese people to an inferior position in society and had visited upon them a host of other oppressive measures. Second, they were foreign barbarians, an inferior race. Third, they were now attempting to perpetrate a gigantic hoax by posing as reformers who wanted to save China, chiefly by introducing constitutionalism.

The first two charges may not seem to require much discussion. It would indeed be tedious to recount in full the crimes with which the revolutionists charged the Manchus. Nor do they represent the kind of thought with which we are chiefly concerned here. But production of the anti-Manchu vitriol that was splashed across the pages of *Min-pao* and other revolutionary publications was a major T'ung-meng-hui industry. It commands some of our attention because it spilled over into the more temperate of the revolutionists' ideas and therefore tainted them, and because it consumed much energy that might have been devoted to more constructive purposes such as the "abstract study" Hu Han-min had demanded. Anti-Manchuism was itself an important aspect of the revolutionary mentality, and it both colored and stunted the development of other aspects. It contributed to an atmosphere in which differing minds found it hard to meet.

However creditable their effort to discuss more positive and far-reaching goals, the revolutionists were primarily concerned with the immediate and pressing problems of acquiring the power to achieve those goals. They were therefore activists and agitators first, and theorists only second. But even their anti-Manchu agitation led them to develop some important ideas, among which concepts of nationhood were the most significant. This fact alone makes even their most emotional diatribes of more than routine interest.

Finally, racist anti-Manchu attacks were inseparable from the republicans' struggle against constitutional monarchy. Even merely to acquire power they had to do more than arouse anti-Manchu sentiment; they also had to discredit constitutional monarchy. This meant opposing constitutional monarchy in principle, but it also meant proving that the Manchus were incapable of instituting a genuine constitutional government. In the background of revolutionary tirades against the Manchus, there always loomed the Manchus' proposal to grant a constitution. Time and again the three points noted above were hammered home to *Min-pao* readers in an effort to persuade them that a constitution granted by cruel and tyrannical barbarians would be mere sham. The revolutionaries obviously feared that the Chinese people would be misled into believing that the projected Manchu constitution showed a sincere willingness to permit popular participation in government and to effect a wide range of needed reforms. The fear took on a note of urgency because of the threat posed by Liang Ch'i-ch'ao, whose vivid writing, lively intellect, and growing reputation made him a formidable adversary. Arguing vigorously in behalf of constitutional monarchy and against revolution, Liang gave the revolutionaries no choice but to expend much of their ammunition on the proposed constitutional regime. Their anti-Manchuism cannot be understood without constant reference to their duel with the reformers.

### The Manchus as Oppressors

Of what, then, were the Manchus guilty? Of having "conquered China and enslaved our Chinese people," cried the T'ung-meng-hui Manifesto; they were guilty of slaughtering those who resisted "by the hundreds of thousands" and of "extreme cruelties and tyrannies." [12] As the months passed and revolutionary journalism flourished, other writers filled in the details. In this case as in others, Sun Yat-sen's views provide a convenient summary of most of the revolutionaries' later arguments, as well as interesting differences in emphasis.

In an article published in the United States a year before the establishment of the T'ung-meng-hui, Sun briefly recited the story of the seventeenth-century conquest; he then accused the Manchus of physically mistreating even the old and weak, burning homes, stealing property, forcing the Chinese to shave their heads, and slaughtering countless numbers of persons, "after which they employed their barbarian genius in so many ways that, caught in a tragic blood bath, the Chinese had no choice but to accept their fate." Determined to stifle the people's minds so as to make them permanently obedient, they destroyed all Chinese writings "relating to the facts of the Manchus' aggression and cruelty." They prohibited Chinese from forming private organizations and participating in national affairs. In time, the Chinese people lost their "spirit of patriotism" and even forgot they had become boarders under a roof no longer their own.[13]

Sun also listed what he called the "the ten most important cruelties we have suffered in the more than two hundred and sixty years of tyranny under the Tartar government." His charges were here stated in broad terms, such as "the Tartar government has sought to benefit itself rather than the people," but they show Sun's inclination to condemn the Manchus for not being a Western-style democracy. The Manchus had "blocked the people's material and intellectual development," deprived the Chinese of "all rights of equality and civil rights," infringed upon their "rights to life, liberty, and property," restricted

[12] Teng and Fairbank, *China's Response*, p. 228.

[13] Sun Yat-sen, "Chung-kuo wen-t'i chih chen chieh-chüeh," *Kuo-fu ch'üan-chi*, VI, 221. Sun's oversimplification of the Manchus' censorship policies is worth noting. See L. Carrington Goodrich, *The Literary Inquisition of Ch'ien-lung*; the aims of censorship are summarized on pp. 44–53.

Whatever the factual basis for Sun's charges, our questioning must not obscure the persistence and intensity with which the revolutionaries made them. It is not worth citing more than a few examples in our text, but the reader should keep in mind that the vast bulk of revolutionary writing was devoted to such matters. A convenient sampling of this material may be found in *50th Anniversary Documents*, Vol. XVI, especially pp. 143–313 and 466–97. See also note 83, below.

their "freedom of speech," and could deprive them of their "rights without recourse to law." [14]

It is of course highly significant that this article was originally published in the United States. If nothing else, it demonstrates Sun's capacity for adapting his presentation to the nature of his audience. Upon no other occasion in the period before the revolution did Sun state his opposition to the Manchus in similar terms. In his first formulation of the principle of nationalism (*min-tsu chu-i*), for example, Sun spoke only of the Manchus' being a foreign race that had usurped Chinese sovereignty (*cheng-ch'üan*). Sun's emphasis upon this political concept also contained a rebuke to those revolutionaries who advocated a more extreme anti-Manchuism, one that went beyond the issue of political domination. [15]

Other revolutionary writers discussed all these points at one time or another between 1905 and 1911, but it was the imperial censorship and the rule that Chinese must shave their heads for which the Manchus were most frequently and heavily attacked. [16] Other writers also stressed matters that were ignored by Sun. Aired most frequently was the charge that the Manchus had excluded the Chinese from the highest echelons of government, and that even Chinese who held key positions had their authority curtailed in many ways. The revolutionaries' chief target was the Ch'ing practice of appointing a Manchu and a Chinese to joint occupancy of important posts. T'ung-meng-hui writers argued that this system was grossly inefficient and had paralyzed the Ch'ing administration. They charged also that it reflected the Manchus' basic distrust of the Chinese and was only one of many ways in which the Chinese were controlled and discriminated against.

[14] Sun Yat-sen, "Chung-kuo wen-t'i chih chen chieh-chüeh," *Kuo-fu ch'üan-chi*, VI, 223.

[15] See Sun's speech on the occasion of the first anniversary of *Min-pao*, October 17, 1906. "San Min Chu I yü Chung-kuo min-tsu chih ch'ien-t'u," *Kuo-fu ch'üan-chi*, III, 8–10. Chün-tu Hsüeh, *Huang Hsing and the Chinese Revolution*, p. 42, notes Sun's objection to including the term "anti-Manchu" in the T'ung-meng-hui's name.

[16] See, for example, Wang Ching-wei's argument concerning hair style. It was an indignity to be forced to shave one's head, Wang said; appearance is an important part of a people's spirit. Wang considered this requirement part of an attack upon Chinese customs. "Min-tsu ti kuo-min," Part I, *Min-pao*, No. 1, p. 17.

Wang Ching-wei analyzed the system in some detail, comparing the Ch'ing administration to that of other conquest dynasties.[17] No fact, he declared, more clearly demonstrated the political inequality of the Chinese vis-à-vis the Manchus than that the latter were only one-eightieth as numerous as the Chinese but held two-thirds of the important official positions.[18] Wang did not claim that Chinese were not widely employed, but he insisted that they were more carefully controlled in the Ch'ing than they had been under any other conquest regime. Under the Chia-ch'ing emperor (r. 1796–1820), there had been some change, and power had begun to shift increasingly into Chinese hands. But, Wang continued, the Manchus had still monopolized key positions, especially those concerned with military affairs and foreign relations. Wang observed that one way for a ruler to keep his subjects docile was to cut them off from contact with foreigners. Thus, while Chinese had been permitted to serve in the Court of Colonial Affairs (*Li-fan-yüan*) in the early years of the Ch'ing dynasty, this practice had ceased during the reign of the K'ang-hsi emperor (r. 1662–1723).[19]

Wang emphasized that the Manchus were particularly anxious to reserve military power to themselves. The Manchus' talents, he told his readers, were confined to their ability to ride and shoot.[20] They had to rely upon military force to retain power, and had devised a number of methods to keep military affairs under their own control. Wang discussed these at some length, noting particularly how Manchu banner garrisons were strategically located to check the more

---

Subsequently he wrote that the Manchus had "completely destroyed" Chinese clothing styles. "Tsa po Hsin-min ts'ung-pao," Part II, *Min-pao*, No. 11, p. 31.

[17] "Min-tsu ti kuo-min," Part II, *Min-pao*, No. 2, pp. 6–13.

[18] Citing the *Ta-Ch'ing hui-tien* as his source, Wang noted the number of Manchus and Chinese holding positions ranging from Grand Secretaries (*ta hsüeh-shih*) to Secretaries to Ministry (*pu*) Presidents (*chu-shih*). Here, he asserted, was the evidence, and the *Ta-Ch'ing hui-tien* revealed that the same situation prevailed in other major branches of government including the Censorate (*Tu-ch'a-yüan*), Transmission Office (*T'ung-cheng-ssu*), Court of Judicature and Revision (*Ta-li-ssu*), Court of Sacrificial Worship (*T'ai-ch'ang-ssu*), Court of the Imperial Stud (*T'ai-p'u-ssu*), Court of Banqueting (*Kuang-lu-ssu*), Court of State Ceremonial (*Hung-lu-ssu*), and the Imperial Academy of Learning (*Kuo-tzu chien*). *Ibid.*, p. 9.

[19] *Ibid.*, pp. 9–10. See also Wang's "Lun ke-ming chih ch'ü-shih," Part II, *Min-pao*, No. 26, pp. 1–2.

[20] "Min-tsu ti kuo-min," Part I, p. 14.

numerous Chinese forces (*lü-ying*).[21] The general weakness and des-
uetude of the *lü-ying* he attributed to the Manchus' deliberate efforts
to deny the Chinese any significant military role.[22] Even when Chinese units were allowed to fight, he charged, it was generally against
other Chinese (as in the suppression of the *San-fan* Rebellion, 1673–
81) and under the leadership of Manchu generals.[23] The Manchus'
efforts to monopolize military power met with decreasing success, particularly after the middle of the nineteenth century, owing to the need
to raise forces to save the dynasty from the Taipings and other rebels.[24] The Manchus, Wang stressed, had permitted military decentralization and allotted military power to Chinese generals only
because of their selfish desire to survive and to retain power. After
the Taipings had been defeated, the Manchus had done everything
in their power to regain control.

No reader would miss the point that the Manchu concessions were
meant to be withdrawn after they had served the Manchus' purposes. Wang admitted that the Manchus had found it impossible fully
to regain the power they had relinquished and that regional power
posed a serious problem for them. Still the Manchus had maintained
their rule by using Chinese to fight Chinese, and therefore the victory of the armies of Tseng Kuo-fan and Li Hung-chang did not
mean, as some believed, a revival of Chinese military power.[25]

It was in the exercise of political and military authority that Wang
Ching-wei believed the Manchus had been most assiduous in sup-
pressing the Chinese. In his opinion military power had been even
less accessible to the Chinese than political power, because the Man-

---

[21] See "Man-chou li-hsien yü kuo-min ke-ming," *Min-pao*, No. 8, pp. 38–40.
For his description of the banner system see "Min-tsu ti kuo-min," Part II, p. 3.

[22] "Min-tsu ti kuo-min," Part I, pp. 15–16. Wang quoted as evidence the
authoritative military history of the Ch'ing (to 1821) by Wei Yüan (1794–1856),
*Sheng-wu chi.*

[23] "Min-tsu ti kuo-min," Part I, pp. 16–17, and Part II, p. 12.

[24] For a Western scholar's analysis of this problem see Franz Michael, "The
Military Organization and Power Structure of China during the Taiping Rebellion,"
*Pacific Historical Review*, XVIII, 469–83.

[25] "Man-chou li-hsien . . . ," pp. 38, 40–41, and "Min-tsu ti kuo-min," Part II,
pp. 12–13. See Franz Michael, *op. cit.*, pp. 478–83, where some further complexities are discussed. Also, Ralph L. Powell points out that "since the Taiping Rebellion the balance of military power had lain in the hands of Chinese provincial
officials." *The Rise of Chinese Military Power, 1895–1912*, p. 72.

chus were chiefly warriors and could rely on their own military skills but had no choice but to cooperate with the culturally more advanced Chinese in administering the state.[26]

Wang also discussed the Manchus' efforts to control financial affairs — their discrimination against the Chinese in the tax system and in the general enforcement of laws and application of punishments. The policies of unequal treatment of the Chinese in military, political, and financial affairs comprised one area of the Manchus' anti-Chinese policies, the one concerned with what Wang termed "rights in public affairs" (*kung-ch'üan*).

A second major field concerned personal rights (*ssu-ch'üan*), from which Wang singled out the right to own land as the one most blatantly violated by the Manchus. He described how, after the conquest, the new rulers had arbitrarily decided what land had no recognized owner, appropriated it by force, and distributed it to members of the imperial family and to various high officials.[27] When some of this land drifted back into Chinese hands, the government manipulated prices so as to purchase it cheaply and then turned it over to Manchu bannermen. Practices of this kind, along with others such as prohibiting bannermen from participating in trade, only contributed to the Manchus' decay by encouraging them to rely on privilege rather than productive labor.[28]

In sum, whereas China had had an "absolute monarchy" for six thousand years, the government of the last 260 years could be termed "an aristocracy." [29] What was an aristocracy? It was "a government of inequality." How did it differ from absolutism? Chiefly, it seemed, in being less respectable, for "there have been scholars who have justified absolutist government, but there have been no defenders of aristocracy." Wang continued: "All mankind should be equal," and

[26] "Min-tsu ti kuo-min," Part II, pp. 11–12.

[27] It is interesting to note that Wang quoted the regulations as stated in the *Huang-ch'ao t'ung-tien*, another example of his frequent attempts to document his charges. See "Min-tsu ti kuo-min," Part II, pp. 15–16. However, in Hummel, *Eminent Chinese*, I, 217, it is noted that such confiscation was more widely practiced in Ming than under the Manchus.

[28] "Min-tsu ti kuo-min," Part II, pp. 16–17. On these and related problems see Ma Feng-ch'en, "Manchu-Chinese Social and Economic Conflicts in Early Ch'ing," in *Chinese Social History*, ed. E-tu Zen Sun and John de Francis, pp. 333–51.

[29] "Min-tsu ti kuo-min," Part II, p. 1.

to distinguish people's rights and duties in terms of classes (*chieh-chi*) violates the principles of nature (*t'ien-li*) and is contrary to the proper nature of man (*jen-tao*). All countries, unfortunately, had to pass through a stage of aristocratic government. In Europe it had persisted for one thousand years down to at least the seventeenth and eighteenth centuries. China had been subjected to it long ago, before the Warring States period, and again in a somewhat different and more humiliating form under the Mongols; it had been eradicated by the Ming but had returned with the Manchus.[30]

Most writers did not make this earnest an attempt to conceptualize "inequality" and to fit it into an institutional and historical context. The general practice was merely to describe various examples of oppression to prove that the Manchus were incorrigible barbarians who hated the Chinese and were glad to trade Chinese lives and territory to the foreign powers to maintain their rule or who were so inept and corrupt that they were leading the Chinese and themselves to destruction.[31]

At its worst, revolutionary propaganda descended to the level of Wang Ching-wei's own cry (shortly before he himself attempted to assassinate the regent Tsai-feng) that the Manchus occupied China "because they enjoy killing."[32] The keynote of this argument was the difference between the races, and it suggests how Wang's rational arguments of 1905 and 1906, which were buttressed with a wealth of historical evidence and scholarly apparatus, became increasingly infected with racism by 1910.

### The Manchus as Manchus

"The Manchu government is evil because it is the evil race which usurped our government, and their evils are not confined to a few political measures but are rooted in the nature of the race and can neither be eliminated nor reformed."[33] "The present government is not a Chinese government but is that of a foreign tribe (*i-tsu*). Since

---

[30] *Ibid.*, pp. 1–2.

[31] For a typical example see Wang Tung, "Ke-ming chin-shih lun," *Min-pao*, No. 17, pp. 33–60.

[32] "Lun ke-ming chih ch'ü-shih," Part I, *Min-pao*, No. 25, p. 8.

[33] Hu Han-min, "The Six Principles of the People's Report (*Min-pao*)," deBary *et al.*, *Sources of Chinese Tradition*, pp. 763–64. See *Min-pao*, No. 3, p. 8, for the Chinese text, "Min-pao chih liu ta chu-i."

our interests are thus mutually opposed, our aims cannot but be different." [34]

For not a few revolutionary writers, statements such as these summed up the case against the Manchus. Their publications are filled with variations upon these basic themes: as barbarians the Manchus were innately evil, and as foreigners they could not act in the interests of the Chinese. Usually the writers confined themselves to citing instances of Manchu mistreatment of the Chinese and concessions to the foreign powers as evidence for both of these allegations. But some of the racial arguments have points that deserve our attention.

Ch'en T'ien-hua, for example, bolstered his position with two quotations from the *Tso-chuan*: "If he be not of our kin, he is sure to have a different mind." "The Teih [*sic*] and Jung are wolves, to whom no indulgence should be given." [35] For him, the authority of the classics was sufficient proof of the validity of the racial thesis. Race, however, provided only one count against the Manchus. For the other, Ch'en turned to history. No dynasty, he argued, had ever been able to sweep away its own accumulated evils. It had always been necessary for a new regime to arise before the misery of the people could be alleviated. This proved that the implementation of reforms without a revolution was no more likely than that "a raven's head may be white or a horse may sprout horns." [36]

Wang Ching-wei and Chu Chih-hsin discussed the racial issue in terms quite different from Ch'en's, but they were no less concerned to discredit the Manchus and deny them the right to rule China. Their aim was to demonstrate the principle that states should be organized by people who possessed a common history and culture. In Wang's case this was done by frequent reference to what he considered to be the basic principles of ethnology, sociology, and political science, along with remarks on Chinese and, occasionally, Western history. Chu relied mainly upon examples from European history.[37]

Chu began by distinguishing between the state (*kuo-chia*) as a

[34] Ch'en T'ien-hua, "Lun Chung-kuo i kai-ch'uang min-chu cheng-t'i," *Min-pao*, No. 1, p. 49.

[35] *Ibid.* The translations given here are those of James Legge. See Vol. V of *The Chinese Classics*, pp. 355 and 123. "Teih" should be "Ti."

[36] Ch'en, "Lun Chung-kuo i kai-ch'uang min-chu cheng-t'i," pp. 48–49.

[37] Chu Chih-hsin, "Hsin-li ti kuo-chia chu-i," *Min-pao*, No. 21, pp. 13–35. Wang's discussion is chiefly in Part I of his "Min-tsu ti kuo-min."

legal entity and the state as reflected in its people's psyche. The former he called "the state as viewed objectively," meaning that one recognized the existence of effective governing authority without reference to the right of those in power to hold that authority. However, the state also could be viewed "subjectively," from the standpoint of whether its subjects considered its existence justified by racial principles that were rooted in history.[38] The subjects of a state did not owe allegiance to it simply because it was the *de facto* governing authority. If one thought of nationalism (*kuo-chia chu-i*) in such purely "legalistic" terms, he said, then countries and areas that had been annexed by or ceded to another country should be expected to transfer their loyalty to it. The people of Alsace-Lorraine should be devoted to Germany rather than to France; Finland and Poland should not be seeking their independence from Russia, nor the Irish, Indians, and "Africans" from England, nor the "Indo-Chinese" from France; and the Jews should not be seeking to establish a homeland. In legal terms, what is in fact "genuine nationalism" would be considered "anti-nationalism" (*fei kuo-chia chu-i*).[39] To argue that the Chinese should regard the Manchu regime as a proper state worthy of their loyalty was to define nationalism as obedience. And it was also to deny that nationalism derives from the spirit of a people, from their feeling of identity built over a long period of time and manifested in shared customs. Concluding his long discussion of European nationalism, of which he found the German unification movement most representative, he summed up by saying that nationalism consisted "entirely in the aim of establishing an independent state"[40] and that that state could be based only upon a common racial and historical heritage.

Wang Ching-wei began his discussion by defining a nation (*min-tsu*)[41] as a "continuing human group [possessing] common charac-

[38] Chu Chih-hsin, "Hsin-li ti kuo-chia chu-i," pp. 14–15.

[39] *Ibid.*, p. 18, *passim.* Chu discussed many other examples of "genuine nationalism" in Europe, including the movements that established the Dutch Republic, the German Empire, and Norway.

[40] *Ibid.*, p. 30.

[41] Both Wang and Chu generally used the term *min-tsu*, whereas Ch'en T'ien-hua had employed *chung-tsu*. Wang, however, said *min-tsu* was a racial (*chung-tsu* or *tsu-lei*) concept. Chu, on occasion, also used *chung-tsu*. None made an effort to distinguish these terms. Since the revolutionaries also used the terms *min-tsu chu-i, kuo-min chu-i,* and *kuo-chia chu-i* for nationalism, it often is difficult to know

teristics." These he grouped under six headings: consanguinity, a common spoken and written language, the same territorial abode, common customs, common religion, and "common spiritual and physical [characteristics]." Wang emphasized that the ties binding such a group had to have existed continuously over a long period of time, so that in its history there had developed common relationships that made the nation "indestructible." [42]

Wang then contrasted the nation with a citizenry (*kuo-min*), which he defined as "the elements comprising a state (*kuo-chia*)." *Min-tsu* was an ethnological term, "citizen" a legal one; *min-tsu* was to be discussed in racial (*tsu-lei*) terms, whereas "citizen" was a political concept. All this led up to the fundamental questions: "Is a single nation necessarily a single citizenry? Is a single citizenry necessarily a single nation?" [43]

When a single *min-tsu* organized a state, that state was bound to be based upon equality and freedom, Wang wrote.[44] Equality existed because people of the same *min-tsu* had innate feelings of brotherhood toward one another; this was "natural equality" (*t'ien-jan chih p'ing-teng*). And freedom? Wang began with one of the phrases from the *Tso-chuan* that Ch'en T'ien-hua had also used: "If he be not of our kin, he is sure to have a different mind." [45] Wang then proceeded to argue the obverse of this dictum, that people of the same race *are* of one mind and work together harmoniously to overcome their problems. "Therefore, freedom is bound to be evenly distributed." Equality and freedom prevail. "Therefore, nationalism (*min-tsu chu-i*)

---

whether to render *min-tsu* as "race" or "nation." The point seems to be that the T'ung-meng-hui writers used these terms interchangeably; it was their aim to portray the Chinese as a distinct racial group, to identify race with nation and nation with state, and to argue that a state composed of one race was best.

There is much literature on problems of this sort, reflecting their complexity and contemporaneity. Helpful introductions to this literature are: Lin Yao-hua, "Kuan-yü min-tsu i-tz'u ti shih-yung ho i-ming ti wen-t'i," *Li-shih yen-chiu*, II, 171–90, and *Han-min-tsu hsing-ch'eng wen-t'i t'ao-lun chi*.

[42] "Min-tsu ti kuo-min," Part I, pp. 1–2.

[43] *Ibid.*, p. 3.

[44] However, he did subsequently mention that nationalism had developed into "imperialism" (*min-tsu ti-kuo chu-i*) in Europe. *Ibid.*, p. 4. In his time, of course, the term did not have all of its present connotations; to Wang it seemed to mean something like "national empires" rather than a modern "ism."

[45] See note 35. Wang, however, did not indicate any source.

is an original part of human nature." History showed that it could be temporarily submerged, but never eliminated.[46]

Wang then described what took place when a state was created out of different *min-tsu*. Two principal forms were possible. First, dissimilar *min-tsu* might organize a state without changing their individual characteristics, in which case (*a*) several *min-tsu* might retain their own language and customs, and as in Switzerland, might seek political unification, or (*b*) a conquering *min-tsu* might compel a vanquished one to submit to its authority, as Russia had compelled Finland and Poland.[47]

The second general category comprised instances of assimilation. Wang discerned four possible patterns: *min-tsu* of equal strength could fuse and become one new *min-tsu*; numerically superior conquerors could absorb their erstwhile foes; a defeated majority could be assimilated by conquerors who were exceptionally powerful despite their lack of great numbers; numerically inferior conquerors could be absorbed by a vanquished majority.[48]

Wang then sketched historical instances of foreign tribes having been assimilated by the Chinese. Only the Mongols had escaped assimilation, but at least it had not taken the Chinese long to overthrow them and regain their former position, "that of conquerors." [49] Wang took special note of the period from Chin (A.D. 265–420) to the founding of Sui (A.D. 589), when the Chinese, despite their extreme weakness, had assimilated the powerful barbarian conquerors.[50] With the exception of the Yüan (1260–1368) and the 265–589 periods, China's history exhibited the second pattern of assimilation, that of the conquering many (the Chinese) absorbing the defeated few.[51]

Since the fall of Ming, however, China had slipped out of the second pattern and was in danger of dropping into the third, i.e.,

---

[46] "Min-tsu ti kuo-min," Part I, pp. 2–3. Wang noted several examples of persistent nationalism in Western Europe; e.g., the Italian *min-tsu* had been divided since the fall of Rome, but in the nineteenth century had been able to carry out "nationalism" and establish the Kingdom of Italy.

[47] *Ibid.*, p. 3.          [49] *Ibid.*, p. 9.

[48] *Ibid.*, pp. 4–5.          [50] *Ibid.*, p. 8.

[51] *Ibid.*, p. 9. Wang made no mention of the Liao (907–1125) and Chin (1115–1234) dynasties in this context, although he did in others (above, note 17), but he appeared to associate the Khitan (Liao) and Juchen (Chin) with the (Yüan) Mongols, as people that the Chinese had ultimately been able to defeat but not assimilate.

of being assimilated by a small but powerful conqueror. To support this contention, Wang first sought to establish that according to the six criteria he had set down, the Manchus and the Chinese were distinctly different *min-tsu*. However, he chiefly emphasized the Manchus' origins as described in their own legends, besides noting their relation to the Juchen. Comparing the Manchus to the Chinese ("we descendants of the gods"), he contented himself with a few scornful remarks about the small area of the Manchus' homeland and their general backwardness, concluding: "We are as far apart as heaven and earth." [52]

In his definition of *min-tsu* and his discussion of assimilation patterns, Wang had established a basis for studying the relationship between the Chinese and the Manchus, and had also devised a framework for a concept of the nation-state.[53] But after his comparison of the Manchus and Chinese, his account became a routine discussion of the steps the Manchus had taken to preserve their identity and prevent their assimilation (e.g., prohibiting intermarriage with the Chinese and preserving the Manchu language and traditions). Wang claimed that the Manchus' anxiety to preserve their customs arose from their desire to keep themselves distinct from the Chinese and to confine their people to old ideas. After all, he said, the Manchus' customs are so inferior that they cannot be maintaining them because they consider them admirable.[54]

Wang accused the Manchus of attempting to assimilate the Chinese, citing as evidence such "material" devices as requiring the Chinese to adopt the Manchu hair style and "spiritual" ones aimed at eradicating the Chinese feeling that they were superior to other races. He pointed to the harsh treatment given to many well-known scholars who had remained bitterly opposed to the Manchus on racial grounds. He also quoted the Yung-cheng emperor's (r. 1723–1735) famous proclamation in which it was said that the virtue of the Manchus should not be measured by their place of origin any more than was the case with Shun and Wen Wang. Reasonable though this statement might appear, Wang warned, it was really an attempt

[52] *Ibid.*, p. 10.

[53] Compare the conception of race and the nation formulated by Chang Ping-lin in Chapter 6.

[54] *Ibid.*, p. 12. The entire discussion covers pp. 11–17.

to deceive the Chinese by substituting the Confucian ruler-subject relationship for racial principles. The Chinese must realize, said Wang, that the Manchus "are destroying our country and our race." [55]

Liang Ch'i-ch'ao had asked several simple but effective questions that pointed up some of the difficulties in Wang's anti-Manchu thinking. Could Wang deny that there were hateful Chinese as well as admirable Manchus? Could one then argue on purely racial grounds? Wang's derisive retort was that such questions only served to reveal the (presumably worthless) character of Liang's thinking.[56] Do the revolutionaries want to overthrow the Manchus because they are Manchus or because their government is bad? Both, Wang insisted.[57] Must the Chinese separate from the Manchus before they can establish their state, or could they absorb the Manchus, Moslems, Tibetans, Mongols, and other such groups in China? Here Liang invited Wang to choose Scylla or Charybdis. If Wang really meant that a state had to include only one national group, other groups either were free to split off from China or had to be absorbed. Wang stood firmly for assimilation by the Chinese.[58] Several years later he made it explicit that the Manchus too were welcome to be citizens of a greater China,[59] presumably on the same terms. Under persistent attack by Liang, Wang later elaborated upon his arguments, but could do little more than describe in more detail the differences between the Manchus and the Chinese in their history and culture.[60]

[55] *Ibid.*, pp. 17–21. A partial translation of the Yung-cheng emperor's proclamation may be found in Dun J. Li, *The Essence of Chinese Civilization*, pp. 129–31. The reference to Shun and King Wen appears on p. 130.

[56] Wang, "Min-tsu ti kuo-min," Part I, pp. 28–29.

[57] *Ibid.*, p. 29.

[58] *Ibid.*, p. 30. See also Wang's "Po Hsin-min ts'ung-pao tsui-chin chih fei ke-ming lun," *Min-pao*, No. 4, pp. 12–13.

[59] "Lun ke-ming chih ch'ü-shih," Part II, p. 20.

[60] See, for example, "Tsa-po Hsin-min ts'ung-pao," Part I, *Min-pao*, No. 10, pp. 43–56. It was actually K'ang Yu-wei who, more than Liang, emphasized what Manchus and Chinese shared rather than what divided the two. See, for example, K'ang's comment that if China's government was bad it was also the government of other dynasties, not only the Ch'ing. Quoted by Kao Liang-tso, "K'ai-kuo ch'ien ke-ming yü chün-hsien chih lun-chan," *Chien-kuo yüeh-k'an*, Vol. VII, No. 3, p. 4. Interestingly, Wang and others concentrated their fire on Liang. It was almost as if the modernizing wings of the two sides confronted each other, leaving the more traditional-minded to debate in their own way. Wang by no means ignored K'ang, but he also referred his readers specifically to Chang Ping-lin's answers

Racial arguments are inherently weak,[61] as Liang Ch'i-ch'ao had indicated to Wang, and could create hopeless contradictions for a movement that prided itself upon being the torchbearer of liberty, equality, and fraternity. Even without these two considerations, any serious attempt to prove that the Manchus deserved to be overthrown because they were barbarian conquerors who were destroying Chinese civilization and had enslaved the Chinese people would become enmeshed in a vast web of historical and sociological complexities.[62]

Analysis of the revolutionaries' anti-Manchuism, however, should take into account not only the content of the ideas but also the uses to which they were put. It can hardly be doubted that of all the ideas advocated by the T'ung-meng-hui, anti-Manchuism was the supreme propaganda weapon. Indeed, so great was the sheer propaganda value of anti-Manchuism that one sometimes hesitates to interpret it as anything more. In particular it must have served to smooth relations between the T'ung-meng-hui and the many fanatically anti-Manchu secret societies that joined the revolutionary movement. It also offered a simple explanation for economic problems, for the inability to cope with the Western onslaught, and for every other ill

---

to K'ang. See, for example, "Min-tsu ti kuo-min," Part I, pp. 26–28. Some of the differences between Chang and K'ang are touched on in Chapter 6.

[61] A good introduction to this question is Ashley Montagu, *Man's Most Dangerous Myth: the Fallacy of Race*. Other discussions I find to be helpful include David Fellman, "Racism," in Joseph S. Roucek (ed.), *Twentieth Century Political Thought* (New York: Philosophical Library, 1946), pp. 105–31, and Frank H. Hankins, "Race as a Factor in Political Theory," in Charles Edward Merriam and Harry Elmer Barnes (eds.), *A History of Political Theories: Recent Times* (New York: Macmillan, 1924), pp. 508–48.

[62] I do not wish to become similarly entangled, but a reading of Franz Michael, *The Origin of Manchu Rule in China*, will convey the magnitude of the problem. Professor Michael shows, among other things, that the Manchu victory was not a mere military conquest but a far more subtle process including a partial Sinification of the Manchus. When they entered China, most of the Manchus "were racially of Chinese stock" (p. 9), and in fact it is "difficult to say just how many Manchus were left outside the imperial clan itself" (p. 76). Furthermore the banner system and even the term "banner" were taken from the *wei-so* system of the Ming, a Chinese dynasty. Finally, the Manchu victory can be explained chiefly by the fact that their policies were "more Chinese" than those of their leading rival, who was himself a Chinese (p. 11). "It was the Chinese system, Chinese officials and Chinese ideas that enabled the Manchus to conquer China" (p. 79). But even if one granted that the Manchus were only barbarian conquerors, the classics may also be cited *against* the revolutionaries: "When the barbarian enters China (i.e., Chinese civilization) he becomes Chinese" (p. 9).

with which China was afflicted, and it provided convenient scape-goats as well. It wore the cloak of science, and so had added authority in a time when Western ideas were growing in prestige. Anti-Man-chuism also served a more specific purpose. It enabled the revolu-tionaries to attack the Manchus' proposed constitutional government in an effective way, if only because it was easily understandable. The revolutionaries would in any case attack the "pseudo-constitution" that did not fundamentally alter the autocratic nature of the govern-ment. But they would also argue that as barbarian conquerors, the Manchus found it impossible to carry out political reforms. And this, especially in the period before the constitution was proclaimed, was an extremely important argument.

### The Manchus as Constitutionalists

It will be recalled that at about the time of the founding of the T'ung-meng-hui the Manchus sent a mission abroad to study foreign constitutions. Subsequently, in September, 1906, shortly after the re-turn of the constitutional mission, the Manchus announced that a constitution and a series of administrative reforms were being pre-pared. The new system was soon proclaimed, and within a year there had been a flurry of reforms which, even if more nominal than real, caused the revolutionists much anxiety.[63]

Convinced that the Manchus were only disguising and not re-linquishing their control, the T'ung-meng-hui writers could not be sure that the Chinese at home and abroad shared this view. It also appeared likely that the foreign powers, and especially Japan, would now consider the revolutionaries even less deserving of support than they had previously.[64] Subsequent measures only heightened the

[63] For these reforms and those mentioned in the next paragraph see Meribeth E. Cameron, *The Reform Movement in China, 1898–1912*, pp. 100–135. E-tu Zen Sun, in "The Chinese Constitutional Missions of 1905–1906," *Journal of Modern History*, XXIV, 251–68, maintains that from September, 1906, on, it was increas-ingly apparent that these were empty reforms. Note the intent of the edict of September 1, 1906, discussed by Professor Sun on pp. 267–68. Professor Cameron, however, holds that the Manchus were willing to carry out serious reforms but unable to, chiefly because local officials had robbed the government of its power.

[64] Japanese attitudes toward the Manchu government and the Chinese revolu-tionaries are discussed in Marius B. Jansen, *The Japanese and Sun Yat-sen*, pp. 105–30. Japan preferred a weak but friendly constitutional monarchy in China

revolutionaries' concern. These measures included the establishment of a Bureau for the Compilation of a Constitution, the dispatch of another constitutional mission abroad, the announcement of regulations for the establishment of provincial and district assemblies and the election of their members, and finally, in August, 1908, the publication of the outline of the constitution, the parliament, and the election law. These were to be brought into final form within nine years.

As each measure appeared, the revolutionaries could attack it on its own merits. But until the constitution was actually produced, they would inevitably find it an elusive target. They were able to find much to criticize in the government's declared intention to imitate the Japanese system. However, residing in Japan, frequently in trouble with the Japanese authorities, and anxious to obtain Japanese support for their movement, the revolutionaries were unable to make free use of this weapon. They must have known how the Japanese constitution served the purposes of the oligarchy and how during a like period of preparation for it in Japan, political opposition and discussion were stifled.[65] But this knowledge could only heighten their anxiety; it could not be used to attack the Manchus' proposals.

Even if the Manchus themselves did not make extravagant claims for their constitution, there was always Liang Ch'i-ch'ao to contend with. Thus when Hu Han-min charged that the Manchus' "evils . . . are rooted in the nature of the race . . . ," he added that "even if there are a few ostensible reforms, the evils will remain just the same. The adoption of Western constitutional institutions and law will not change the situation . . . [contrary to the view of Liang Ch'i-ch'ao]."[66] Racial arguments were repeatedly linked to attacks on

and even helped the Manchus to plan their constitution. See also E-tu Zen Sun, "The Chinese Constitutional Missions of 1905–1906," *Journal of Modern History*, XXIV, 252–53, 255, 257, 267, where it is shown that the Manchus were hoping by means of these reforms to undercut the revolutionary movement, impress the foreign powers, and improve administrative efficiency.

[65] See Nobutaka Ike, *The Beginnings of Political Democracy in Japan*, pp. 171–88; G. B. Sansom, *The Western World and Japan*, pp. 358–59; and Hugh Borton, *Japan's Modern Century*, pp. 137–48.

[66] Hu Han-min, "The Six Principles . . . ," deBary, *et al.* (eds.), *Sources*, p. 764. Liang wrote a good deal on the virtues of constitutional monarchy as opposed to republican government. His debate with T'ung-meng-hui writers on this subject is discussed below in Chapter 4.

the Manchu constitution, and those attacks in turn were linked to arguments against Liang.

The revolutionaries therefore mounted an offensive against "the pseudo-constitution" that began with the first issue of *Min-pao* and was maintained to the last. When Ch'en T'ien-hua argued that the Chinese could not work in harmony with the Manchus and that the latter were incapable of reform, he was referring specifically to the proposed constitution and warning his readers that it was intended to trick them into abandoning the revolution. Chu Chih-hsin argued that the Manchus would not voluntarily surrender or even curtail the privileges they had held for so long and that therefore they had no real intention of establishing a constitution. The emperor would not allow a constitution that provided for equality between Manchus and Chinese, and the Chinese would accept nothing less. A Manchu monarchy and a constitution were therefore incompatible, Chu insisted, and the fundamental reason was the difference between the two races.[67] In brief, "the line dividing the races is the basis for the Manchus' inability to establish a constitution." [68] Until the line was erased, China would see no constitutional government; and the line could only be obliterated by revolution. Indeed, "in the present revolution it is revenge that comes first, and destroying the government next. . . . Even if they establish a constitution we Chinese cannot live together in peace with the Manchus." [69]

Again it was Wang Ching-wei who carried most of the journalistic burden. A constitution, he argued, represented the Manchus' last desperate hope for retaining political power; every other prop supporting their government had been either destroyed or seriously weakened.[70] Wang then analyzed the recommendations made by the first constitutional mission and approved by the court. He stressed that they were aimed at limiting regional power and returning authority to the central government. This, he contended, was not really a question of political relationships but a racial matter. "Therefore the problem can be assessed in one brief statement: *the reason the*

[67] Chu Chih-hsin, "Lun Man-chou sui yü li-hsien erh pu-neng," *Min-pao*, No. 1, pp. 36, 38, *passim*.

[68] *Ibid.*, p. 39.

[69] *Ibid.*, p. 34.

[70] "Min-tsu ti kuo-min," Part I, p. 24.

*Manchu government is planning centralization is that it is the inevitable result of a minority race controlling a majority race.*" [71]

Wang's reasoning illustrates the revolutionaries' approach to one of the most important and perhaps even the crucial problem they had to solve in order to discredit the government reforms and refute Liang Ch'i-ch'ao. The problem was essentially to persuade their readers that although the Manchus seemed to be doing much of what the revolutionaries thought should be done, all these Manchu moves were only a façade.

It would seem that strengthening the central government would have been an essential step toward preparing China to resist foreign aggression, restore domestic peace and stability, and carry out a program of modernization. The revolutionaries' proposals, however, paid surprisingly little attention to the desirability of centralization, and indeed their intentions are ambiguous. The T'ung-meng-hui Manifesto, for example, clearly suggested that at least some degree of "local self-government" would exist under the Chinese Republic; but the same document's land program, and perhaps even the social reforms it called for, implied a need for a degree of state power that might have been incompatible with very much local self-government.[72] The land program spelled out by Hu Han-min (and labeled "land nationalization" rather than the manifesto's "equalization of land rights" [73]) called for "collectivism," a great deal of action by "the state," and a "great variety of public programs," [74] all of which

[71] "Man-chou li-hsien . . . ," *Min-pao*, No. 8, p. 35; emphasis in original. Wang developed his argument at considerable length in "Hsi-wang Man-chou li-hsien che ho t'ing chu," *Min-pao*, No. 3, pp. 23–39 (numbered 1–17, since pagination of each article begins with no. 1), and No. 5, pp. 1–41. See especially the latter, in which Wang explained the need for a racial (*chung-tsu*) revolution in an attempt to refute Liang Ch'i-ch'ao's argument that racial and political revolutions were incompatible. See also Wang's "Yen-chiu min-tsu yü cheng-chih kuan-hsi chih tzu-liao," *Min-pao*, No. 13, pp. 17–37.

[72] See the translation in Teng and Fairbank, *China's Response*, pp. 228–29.

[73] See Harold Schiffrin, "Sun Yat-sen's Early Land Policy: The Origin and Meaning of 'Equalization of Land Rights,'" *Journal of Asian Studies*, XVI, 549–64, especially pp. 549–51, where Dr. Schiffrin explains his translation of *p'ing-chün ti-ch'üan* and distinguishes it from Teng and Fairbank's "equalization of land ownership" and some of the other possible interpretations of this concept. Hu's proposal for nationalization (*t'u-ti kuo-yu*) was more elaborate, explicit, and extreme. See "Six Principles," deBary, *et al.* (eds.), *Sources*, pp. 766–67.

[74] Hu Han-min, "Six Principles," quoted in deBary, pp. 766–67. The last phrase

would require a considerable degree of centralization. Wang Ching-wei also suggested that he envisioned a strong central government in, for example, his explanation of how a separation of powers did not damage "the unity of the state." [75]

All these were little more than general suggestions, and there were not very many of them. The revolutionaries did not take a consistently firm stand in favor of a strongly centralized republican government, and we are left to ask whether they really did not want one or whether they found the issue too uncomfortable to discuss. My own view inclines toward the latter position as the less unsatisfactory, since the alternative is more difficult to reconcile with their desire to be free of foreign domination and domestic strife, and since the only indication of their opposition to a highly centralized government is their objection to the Manchus' effort to produce one.

Wang Ching-wei's analysis offers support for this view. Centralization and decentralization, he explained, referred to the *exercise* of power and not to the actual *holding* of it; the power held by the state was indivisible, but responsibility for implementing or administering power could be parceled out. Whether a state followed a policy of centralized or decentralized administration depended on its own particular circumstances. In China at that time, circumstances were such that political considerations alone were not decisive; it was also, and chiefly, a matter of race. [76]

Wang explained that since the Manchus were conquerors (and therefore presumably insecure) and since they were too few in number to monopolize political power all over the country, they had to concentrate authority in such a way that a small group could hold all the reins. In addition, local self-government required the participation of each locality's inhabitants; since the Manchus were foreigners, and particularly because they were unfamiliar with agriculture, they were incapable of local self-government. In fact, if they were genuinely to attempt it, they could be successful only at the cost of losing their Manchu identity. [77] It was in this fashion, accord-

was not included in the deBary translation; see *Min-pao*, No. 3, p. 13, for the Chinese text.

[75] Wang Ch'ing-wei, "Po Hsin-min ts'ung-pao tsui-chin chih fei ke-ming lun," *Min-pao*, No. 4, pp. 21–22.

[76] "Man-chou li-hsien . . . ," *Min-pao*, No. 8, p. 35.

[77] *Ibid.*, pp. 35–38.

ing to Wang, that the racial barrier between Chinese and Manchus dictated the centralization policy.

Wang then developed his idea in two interesting ways. First, he pointed out how centralization had developed under the early Ch'ing emperors but had broken down in the nineteenth century, beginning with the Hsien-feng period (1851–62). The decisive turning point, he held, was the Taiping rebellion, when the central government was compelled to yield to provincial officials military and financial powers that until then had been deemed essential to the maintenance of central control. The continuing decline had been accelerated after 1900 (i.e., in the aftermath of the Boxer incident and the international expedition against China). Thus the Manchus had surrendered their monopoly of power only unwillingly, owing to the pressure of events, and they were not only prepared to restore it at the earliest opportunity but in fact had to restore central control in order to survive. When, during the Boxer incident, they found that their authority was so weak that governors and viceroys could ignore imperial orders to make war on foreigners, the Manchus were driven to desperate measures. They decided to carry out reforms in order to keep their own power. The constitution was therefore part of a scheme to reform the political system in such a way as to curtail the power of provincial officials.[78] In short, "it is establishing a constitution as seen from the outside, but beneath the surface it is centralization; the constitution is bait, centralization is the hook; [the constitution] buys Chinese [good will] with false hopes, while it fattens the Manchus on real power."[79]

One interesting point about Wang's analysis, then, is the detail in which he discussed the Manchus' efforts to maximize central control and how those efforts met with increasing failure after the rise of the Taipings. Although he knew how complicated a political and administrative problem this was, Wang insisted that race was the essence of the problem in the Ch'ing period. Second, Wang took it into account that the problem of centralization versus regionalism was not peculiar to the Manchus. When the problem existed in Han, T'ang, Sung, and Ming times, however, he held that it arose from the nature of absolute monarchy. The Manchus' centralization pol-

[78] *Ibid.*, pp. 38–43.
[79] *Ibid.*, pp. 43–44.

icy emerged partly because of the same causes but also for a "special reason" — race — and it was this special reason that Wang stressed.[80] From any point of view, then, whether the specific conditions of Ch'ing or the historic problems of Chinese government, Wang insisted that race was the decisive factor in Manchu centralization policy. The implication was that abolishing absolute monarchy would eliminate those problems faced by Chinese dynasties such as Han, T'ang, Sung, and Ming, and that overthrowing the Manchus would dissolve the "special reason" for the Ch'ing's administrative problems. In any case, the constitution was in Wang's opinion merely a screen behind which the Manchus would work to solidify their own power. He compared it to the *po-hsüeh hung-ju* examinations of 1679, at the same time implying that those who supported constitutional monarchy, like Liang Ch'i-ch'ao, were as much self-seekers and traitors to China as the scholars who had taken part in the examinations.[81]

Interestingly, Wang's treatment of Tseng Kuo-fan and Hu Lin-i was quite different. Although he scolded them for serving the Manchus, suggesting that they should have absorbed the teachings of Ming loyalists Wang Fu-chih and Huang Tsung-hsi, he excused them on the grounds that the "principle of race" (*min-tsu chu-i*) was stunted in their time; even if it had been flourishing, however, without "nationalism" (*kuo-min chu-i*), they could have been expected to understand only loyalty to the ruler and not love of country. "If Tseng and Hu were alive today," he added, "I am certain that they would be members of the revolutionary army." [82]

This is another example of Wang's tendency, at least in 1905–6, to be less extreme than many of his comrades. In *Min-pao*'s first anniversary supplement, *T'ien-t'ao* (*Heaven's Punishment*), for ex-

[80] *Ibid.*, pp. 41–42.

[81] "Lun ke-ming chih ch'ü-shih," Part II, pp. 10–11. These examinations were instituted by the K'ang-hsi emperor in an attempt to attract into government service those scholars who had refused to cooperate with the Manchus. All who passed were assigned to the compilation of the Ming dynastic history. Of the 188 scholars invited to participate, 152 did so. Many who refused, including Ku Yen-wu, later participated indirectly in the compilation of the history. This special examination thus played an important role in drawing the Confucian scholars into the Ch'ing bureaucracy. See Hellmut Wilhelm, "The Po-hsüeh hung-ju Examination of 1679," *Journal of the American Oriental Society*, LXXI, 60–66.

[82] "Po Hsin-min ts'ung-pao tsui-chin chih fei ke-ming lun," p. 17.

ample, Tseng Kuo-fan and others who had defended the Ch'ing against the Taipings were condemned as "traitors" and grotesquely caricatured.[83]

Wang's criticism of Manchu constitutionalism was not based solely on race. It included sentiments that linked him to other democratic revolutionaries, but those sentiments were usually linked also to the Manchus' alien character: "A constitution embodies the will of the people. It is not something that the government can determine for them. Its basic purpose is to extend the power of the people to observe and direct the actions of the government. Would that [Manchu] government establish laws to restrict itself?" He concluded it would not, because it had a government of foreign conquerors which treated the host people as a vanquished people. Favors would not freely be conferred on Chinese slaves by their Manchu masters, he told his countrymen, and it was not proper that the Chinese beg for them.[84]

Liang Ch'i-ch'ao had argued that the Manchus should be given the opportunity to produce their constitution. While waiting for it, the revolutionaries could continue their military preparations. Then, if it was indeed an unacceptable constitution, the justification for revolution would be plain to all, and the revolutionaries would be in a far better position militarily and better able to gain popular support. Wang dismissed this proposal on two counts. First, the Manchus' faults were irremediable. One could no more hope that the Manchus would satisfy the revolutionaries than one could expect "that the horse will sprout horns or the ram give milk." [85] Second, there was no time to lose. If the revolutionists were to wait the necessary years, the government might have made itself too strong. Time and again he emphasized that a constitution would cloak the Manchus' power with a false legitimacy that would discourage opposition. Not gradualism (*chien-chin chu-i*) but urgency (*chi-chin chu-i*) was the watchword,

[83] *T'ien-t'ao* appeared in April, 1907. Its contents tended toward the crude anti-Manchuism that permeated the revolutionary press. The Manchus' crimes were repeatedly and vividly portrayed, and the supplement concluded with a selection of writings by the ill-fated assassin Wu Yüeh. Among other things, Wu explained why, of the two ways he recognized in which the Manchus could be eliminated (revolution and assassination), this era was the one of assassination. In brief, *T'ien-t'ao* amounted to a strident call for violent retribution against the Manchus.

[84] "Min-tsu ti kuo-min," Part I, p. 25.

[85] "Tsa-po Hsin-min ts'ung-pao," Part III, *Min-pao*, No. 12, p. 27.

he cried, not only now but after the revolution as well, lest China be unable to protect her independence from the ambition of the powers. "This is a time of struggle to the death between the government and the people." Since the Manchus were carrying out an "anti-Chinese policy" (*p'ai-Han cheng-ts'e*) to "save themselves," the Chinese had no alternative but "anti-Manchuism" (*p'ai-Man chu-i*). Wang ridiculed the policy of peaceful and patient petitioning that Liang asked for: "Can anyone, after all this time, still think peaceful means will move that unfeeling alien government? Don't they know yet they have been made fools of?" [86]

The revolutionaries were deeply convinced, it is clear, that the Manchus were insincere in proposing and incapable of administering a constitutional regime. There is no doubt that the revolutionaries' attack on the proposal stemmed from a basic hostility to the Manchus as well as from a conviction that China should be a republic, both of which attitudes antedated the Manchus' reform proposals. The revolutionaries' anti-Manchu writings as well as those on republican government were influenced by the plans for a constitutional monarchy. Anti-Manchuism now became a far more complex matter than it had been before 1905, even in its fullest formulation as expressed by Tsou Jung.

It continued to serve as a bellows with which to whip up the fires of revolution. But it was now the chief weapon in the struggle against the idea of constitutional monarchy as well. Unable to attack a nonexistent constitution, T'ung-meng-hui writers inveighed against its sponsors. Here it was used not only against the Manchus, but also against Liang Ch'i-ch'ao and the Society to Protect the Emperor. Would the Manchus now, after two hundred and sixty years, voluntarily share with the Chinese the political and military power they had taken such pains to monopolize? Would they suddenly accept on the basis of equality a people they had discriminated against in so many ways? The old arguments concerning oppression and racial differences had a new focus and direction, for the revolutionaries

---

[86] *Ibid.*, pp. 34–35. This entire article is a clear example of how an occasional reference to possible danger from the foreign powers was scarcely noticeable in the mountain of other abuse the revolutionaries heaped upon the Manchus. In addition, the revolutionaries wrote many articles in which the main theme was to minimize the danger of foreign intervention.

were now led into a discussion of constitutional monarchy as a form of government. Thus Liang could be attacked as both a traitor to China and a misguided constitutional monarchist. As part of this debate the revolutionaries would be led to elucidate further the nationalism they were in the process of defining.

THE CONTINUING STRUGGLE:
REVOLUTIONARIES VERSUS REFORMERS AFTER 1907

The great degree to which the revolutionaries' invective against the Manchus was related to the Ch'ing's proposed constitution and Liang's support for it suggests that the reformers remained a more formidable opposition, and for a longer period, than we have been accustomed to think; or at least it may be said that historians have not done justice to the reformers' political role in the post-1898 period. We have noted that the revolutionaries found it difficult to criticize a constitution that had not yet appeared, but it was not long before there were at least some indications of what the Manchu government had in view. Toward the end of 1906 many of its proposals had been publicized. By 1907 at the latest there was enough basis for discussion of their proposals, for in that year two of the commission members published a book that revealed their thinking quite clearly.[87] And yet these proposals attracted far less of the revolutionaries' attention than Liang's writing.

One reason for the revolutionaries' limited discussion of specific Manchu reforms was that their energies were diverted to activities other than writing. Wang Ching-wei and Hu Han-min, for example, wrote very little for some time after the spring of 1907. Sun Yat-sen was expelled from Japan in March of that year, and other T'ung-meng-hui leaders such as Wang and Hu soon followed him. For about a year they were traveling, raising money, and promoting uprisings. Between May, 1907, and May, 1908, there were at least six revolts involving the T'ung-meng-hui. Wang, during this period and the following eight months, traveled all over Southeast Asia.[88]

Hu Han-min was similarly occupied, except that after the failure

[87] This was *Ou-Mei cheng-chih yao-i* by Tuan-fang and Tai Hung-tz'u. See E-tu Zen Sun, *op. cit.*, pp. 256–64.

[88] Chün-tu Hsüeh, *Huang Hsing*, pp. 65–72, has a brief account of the uprisings and Wang's travels.

of the May, 1908, uprising he was assigned to Singapore. For more than a year thereafter he continued to travel widely, trying to rally support for the revolution, but Singapore remained his base of operations from about June, 1908, to September, 1909. During those fifteen months one of his responsibilities was to manage a newspaper, the *Restoration Daily* (*Chung-hsing jih-pao*).[89] From that vantage point Hu led the revolutionaries in a debate with the *Tsung-hui pao*, a publication of the Society to Protect the Emperor.

Hu's writing in 1908–9 was shaped by several factors. First of all, the movement had been going badly. The revolts were dismal failures, and internal squabbling was becoming more frequent and intense; in particular, Chang Ping-lin's attack on Sun Yat-sen was threatening to tear the movement apart. In addition to factional rivalries, the T'ung-meng-hui found itself faced with disagreement on substantive issues. As a result of their defeats and the clashing ambitions and divergent backgrounds of their leaders, the revolutionaries were forced to re-examine their strategy and tactics. Among the issues Hu stressed, for example, was whether the T'ung-meng-hui should continue to rely militarily on secret societies. The ease and rapidity with which so many uprisings were put down led Hu to conclude that instead of depending upon secret-society forces the revolutionaries should build a regular army. Sun Yat-sen rejected this idea for two reasons. One was that regular army troops were always difficult to control, the other that even the many failures had already had an impact that was "not negligible"; still almost unfailingly optimistic, Sun held that "every defeat is a seed of success."[90]

The numerous issues dividing the revolutionaries around the middle of 1908 were no doubt accentuated by events in Peking, where the Manchus had a busy summer. One momentous step they took was to suppress Liang Ch'i-ch'ao's Political Information Club (*Cheng-wen-she*), an act which capped months of stiffening Ch'ing resistance to reformist demands and curtailment of reformist activity. Another step by the court was to announce specific plans for its constitution and a parliament. Coming so soon after a series of successes in crushing attempts at revolution, these energetic moves

[89] Yao Yü-hsiang, *Hu Han-min hsien-sheng chuan*, pp. 3–4.
[90] Hu, "Tzu-chuan," in *Ke-ming wen-hsien*, III, 401. Other and sharper disagreements are referred to below in Chapters 5 and 6.

provided a sharp contrast to those of the disorganized revolutionaries. It would be surprising if the T'ung-meng-hui leadership had not felt itself under intensifying pressure to revive its movement. Hu's writing in 1908–9 suggests that he was under pressure of this sort.

A third factor that influenced Hu Han-min's thinking in this period was his new location. His shift to Southeast Asia was significant in two ways. First, it was symptomatic of a change in the revolutionary movement. By the middle of 1908, the T'ung-meng-hui organization, which had always been far from tight, was loosening rapidly. As the Japanese became less hospitable and the T'ung-meng-hui ended its third year in Japan with little visible accomplishment to show for its efforts, more and more revolutionaries returned to China. Their purpose, according to Hu, was to promote the revolution more actively or directly (lit.: "for the actual promotion of the revolution"); as the revolutionaries spread into the Chinese interior, the Tokyo headquarters became less important. The movement's center shifted to Hong Kong and then to Southeast Asia, within the vast expanses of which the nominal leaders, Sun Yat-sen, Wang Ching-wei, and Hu, traveled around.[91] The T'ung-meng-hui had become that geometrical impossibility and political improbability, a multi-centered revolutionary conspiracy.

The Southeast Asian environment also gave T'ung-meng-hui writers a different immediate audience. The overseas Chinese had always been important to the propagandists, but now they became the primary target. Not only were the T'ung-meng-hui leaders living in their midst, but Hong Kong and Southeast Asia had become the main arena for the struggle between the revolutionaries and the Society to Protect the Emperor. Hu's perception of the overseas Chinese therefore affected the slant of his writings. He perceived that the overseas Chinese had lost so much of their cultural heritage that they had to be totally re-educated. "Their thought, language, and customs must all be Sinified (*Chung-kuo hua-lo*)," he wrote. (Hu even professed satisfaction that most overseas Chinese had not cut off their queues, since it was the only way he could distinguish them from the host people.) The audience to which the republicans were

[91] "Tzu-chuan," pp. 399–400. Chang Ping-lin was meanwhile exerting more influence in the Tokyo remnant of the T'ung-meng-hui, or at least so it appears from his domination of *Min-pao* after the spring of 1907.

now addressing themselves they viewed almost as a primitive society, riddled with superstition and anachronistic customs.

Distasteful as this was, Hu observed, the revolutionaries could not disparage the overseas Chinese for their "tribalism" (*pu-lo chu-i*).[92] Hu believed that the unique circumstances of the overseas Chinese had made them easy prey for the Society to Protect the Emperor. For example, they were easily impressed by the imperial institution and anyone who served it. Thus Hu charged that K'ang Yu-wei had been able to deceive "the extremely simple-minded overseas Chinese" by identifying himself as the Kuang-hsü emperor's teacher and offering them the dual prospect of saving China and becoming officials, all the while serving the emperor together with Han-lin scholars. "The overseas Chinese were ignorant concerning the racial question and political ideas," Hu wrote, and they would accept whatever K'ang or the court told them. In this manner the reformers had gained a considerable following among the overseas Chinese in Southeast Asia. Only after Hu and his comrades came to the area had K'ang's victims been awakened from their dreams and made aware they had been tricked. Sun Yat-sen had enlightened them little by little when he spoke in Southeast Asia during his travels before 1905, and subsequently T'ung-meng-hui branches had made further inroads. The founding of the *Restoration Daily* then initiated a debate with the reformers somewhat like the one that had taken place in Tokyo; the difference was that the opposition was now weaker. Wang Ching-wei and Hu Han-min divided the labor, Wang concentrating on international problems and Hu on the constitution, but both were guided by Sun Yat-sen's ideas. They wrote very simply and clearly, Hu tells us, so that the overseas Chinese might understand.[93]

Finally, the revolutionaries worked less to develop their ideas after

---

[92] *50th Anniversary Documents*, XV, 30–31.

[93] *Ibid.*, pp. 32–33; "Tzu-chuan," pp. 401–2. In the latter Hu mentions two little books he and Wang wrote, but I have seen no other reference to these items.

The reform-revolution debate in Southeast Asia is analyzed in Ch'i Ping-feng, *Ch'ing-mo ke-ming yü chün-hsien ti lun-cheng*, pp. 122–32. Mr. Ch'i, who has had access to more of the sources for this 1908–9 period than I, concludes that the Southeast Asia debate very much resembled the earlier debate in Japan. The only significant new features were that Sun Yat-sen took a more active part and that the appearance of the "Outline of the Constitution" in August, 1908, affected the terms of the debate; present indications are that these new features did not change the debate significantly, but the subject remains to be studied in depth.

mid-1908 because their major intellectual competitor, Liang Ch'i-ch'ao, had been removed from the arena. The Political Information Club had been suppressed, and Liang's *New People's Miscellany* had ceased publication toward the end of 1907; its successor, *Cheng-lun*, suffered the same fate less than a year later.[94] The reformers were also overwhelmed with financial problems in 1907–8, and when in the midst of political and economic travails the Kuang-hsü emperor died, the reform movement went into a tailspin from which it never recovered.[95] With no emperor to protect, the last hope of the Society to Protect the Emperor seemed lost. Liang did not give up — he continued to write, organize, and attempt to persuade one Manchu leader or another to accelerate reforms [96] — but his problems only intensified; he finally confessed in 1910 that constitutional reform was hopeless, although he would continue to "pray for the improvement of the government." [97]

Beginning about the end of 1907, the propaganda struggle against republicanism was carried on under the leadership of Yang Tu in his newspaper *China News* (*Chung-kuo hsin-pao*). Yang was a disciple of the Englishman Edward Jenks (1861–1939), whose book *A History of Politics* had been translated by Yen Fu in 1904.[98]

[94] Chang P'eng-yüan, *Liang Ch'i-ch'ao yü Ch'ing-chi ke-ming*, p. 339.

[95] Jung-pang Lo, *K'ang Yu-wei*, pp. 208–14; Ting Wen-chiang (ed.), *Liang Jen-kung hsien-sheng nien-p'u*, II, 284–308.

[96] Ernest P. Young, "The Reformer as a Conspirator: Liang Ch'i-ch'ao and the 1911 Revolution," *Approaches to Modern Chinese History*, ed. Albert Feuerwerker, Rhoads Murphey, Mary C. Wright, pp. 239–45.

[97] Ting Wen-chiang, *Liang Jen-kung hsien-sheng nien-p'u*, II, 312.

[98] See Benjamin Schwartz, *In Search of Wealth and Power: Yen Fu and the West*, pp. 174–85.

Yang Tu (1875–1932) was a *chü-jen* of 1897 who went to Japan in 1902, became involved in revolutionary activity but, although anti-Manchu, refused to join the T'ung-meng-hui; instead, he eventually cooperated with the Manchu constitutional reform program. In general, he tried to stake out a position between Liang Ch'i-ch'ao and the revolutionaries. After 1911 he became an active supporter of Yüan Shih-k'ai. By the end of his life he had switched radically again; in 1930, for example, he was associated with Lu Hsün and others in several organizations which are said to have been leftist, and he developed a very close relationship with Chou En-lai. See Wu Hsiang-hsiang, "K'uang-tai i-ts'ai Yang Tu," in *Min-kuo cheng-chih jen-wu, Wen-hsing ts'ung-k'an*, XIII, No. 1, pp. 69–85.

The Jenks book provides a good example of how minor Western works became foci of controversy among Chinese intellectuals. *A History of Politics* was one

Among Jenks' ideas, some seem particularly relevant to the issue of anti-Manchuism. He argued, for example, that since all states originated as military organizations and since all modern political communities owed their existence to successful warfare, states inevitably have to be organized along military lines. Also, the state is not "merely the nation organized for governmental purposes"; indeed, state and nation "never are identical." [99]

Yang Tu's efforts to wed such ideas to K'ang Yu-wei's and incorporate them into a rebuttal of T'ung-meng-hui nationalism were taken lightly by Hu Han-min, who apparently did not deem it necessary to reply. Hu tells us merely that an article written by Wang Ching-wei at the end of 1905 was the answer to Yang Tu. [100] It is a revealing commentary on the bitter rivalry within the T'ung-meng-hui that Hu made no reference to a lengthy article by Chang Ping-lin which was devoted entirely to explaining why Jenks' book was inapplicable to China. [101] Only a short time before, and indeed in the very article of Wang's to which Hu refers, the republicans were referring to Chang Ping-lin as the man who had the answers to K'ang Yu-wei. In any case, it is clear that Hu Han-min did not feel Yang Tu required the point-by-point ripostes he and Wang had felt compelled to deliver to Liang Ch'i-ch'ao. On the contrary, Hu and Wang felt their opposition in the Southeast Asia newspaper debate was so inconsequential that responding became merely a peripheral activity. [102] In brief, when revolutionaries such as Hu Han-min did return to the propaganda and ideological side of their struggle in mid-1908, a number of factors combined to give ideas a different and lesser place in the movement than they had occupied before 1908.

One change in the later writing of the revolutionaries was that they attacked specific features of the Manchu reform program, but the purely racial onslaught also continued. Hu Han-min, for example, wrote a careful and thoughtful point-by-point critique of the Au-

title in a series called "The Temple Primers," which were intended to be "small volumes of condensed information introductory to great subjects" to meet "the needs of the general public" and to serve as introductions to more specialized studies. See the publisher's note at the beginning of the 1900 edition.

[99] Jenks, *A History of Politics*, pp. 73, 140, 147, *passim*.
[100] Hu Han-min, "Tzu-chuan," in *Ke-ming wen-hsien*, III, 400.
[101] Chang Ping-lin, "She-hui t'ung-ch'üan shang-tui," *Min-pao*, No. 12, pp. 1–24.
[102] Hu, "Tzu-chuan," p. 402.

gust 27, 1908, imperial edict in which the government outlined its proposed constitution and election procedures.[103]

In his critique Hu stressed many of the same points he and others had been making for years. The Manchus' constitution was really a stratagem by which they hoped to keep the Chinese majority down, monopolize all power, and maintain the position of conquerors; they had been able to monopolize military and financial control for some two hundred years but had been losing their monopoly since the Taiping rebellion, which explained why they had to take steps to regain it; the constitution was therefore a euphemism for centralization; the Manchus held to an "anti-Chinese" (*p'ai-Han*) policy; the Manchus were now gaining power at the expense of the Chinese as a result of their new policies; the Manchus talked reconciliation but practiced suppression of the Chinese; the Manchus were lying despots with whom one could not deal in a peaceful manner, and indeed had been deceitful ever since the beginning of the dynasty, when they had pretended to respect Confucian principles of ruler-subject relationships; in this way the Manchus had been able to fool traitors such as Tseng Kuo-fan, and now that Western ideas of freedom and equality had enabled people to see through the old ideas, the Manchus were trying to use the idea of constitutionalism instead. "Thus the Manchus wildly hope to make use of a constitution to manacle the Chinese and make us slaves for eternity, never to revive." [104]

Even amid their most careful and thoughtful political analyses the revolutionaries spewed racial invective. China's political atmosphere became increasingly inflamed, and rational discussion became increasingly difficult. At the same time, even in their bitterest

[103] The edict is translated in Pao Chao Hsieh, *The Government of China (1644–1911)*, pp. 371–74. See also Cameron, *The Reform Movement in China, 1898–1912*, pp. 113–15, and Li Chien-nung, *The Political History of China, 1840–1928*, ed. and trans. Ssu-yü Teng and Jeremy Ingalls, pp. 218–20, where the date is wrongly given as Sept. 22. The translators apparently thought Li was rendering the date according to the lunar calendar. See the Chinese edition, *Chung-kuo chin pai-nien cheng-chih shih*, I, 265. Hu's critique was published in *Chung-hsing jih-pao* (*Restoration Daily*) in a number of installments between September 24 and October 9, 1908. Its title was "Wu-hu, Man-chou so-wei Hsien-fa Ta-kang" (Alas, the Manchus' So-called Outlines of the Constitution). A substantial portion of it has been reprinted in *50th Anniversary Documents*, XV, 229–59.

[104] *50th Anniversary Documents*, XV, 236. See pp. 229–36 for the other references cited in this paragraph.

denunciations of the Manchus, Chinese continued to grope toward
new ways of identifying themselves. In particular, Chinese intellectuals were beginning to identify themselves as members of a Chinese
nation-state.

NATIONALISM, NEW AND OLD

A recurring problem faced by the Chinese revolutionaries, besides
understanding the new ideas they dealt with, was the difficulty of
placing those ideas concurrently in Chinese and Western historical
settings. Napoleon was a hero to Tsou Jung, Yang Tu, and most other
Chinese nationalists, but modern European nationalism was an ille-
gitimate offspring of Napoleonic internationalism; it was a movement
born of Napoleon's forcible violation of his dependent and allied
states.[105] The reaction to the Napoleonic idea of a European continent
tied together by common legal, administrative, and economic systems, with one army and one foreign policy, was of course a highly
complex one. Conditions differed from country to country, and so
did French methods; thus the character and extent of French influence varied, and so did the nationalism of each country. Western
college students still fail examinations asking them to analyze nineteenth-century European nationalism, and Western scholars still find
areas of disagreement concerning its character and significance. If
young Chinese had some trouble understanding it sixty years ago, we
should not be surprised.

In the West, modern nationalism developed partly out of a long
process of social and political change, partly as a reaction to foreign
control, and partly because of the example of the strength and pros-
perity enjoyed by unified nations such as Britain and France. Con-

[105] The development of the feeling of common history and destiny that is so
central to modern nationalism can be traced back to the twelfth century. And
popular nationalism, the feeling of the people (chiefly property owners) that they
had an interest in, and deserved to have a voice in, affairs of state, certainly made
its voice heard in the seventeenth and eighteenth centuries. See Robert R. Palmer,
"The National Idea in France before the Revolution," *Journal of the History of
Ideas*, I, 95–111. But the feeling of all inhabitants of a nation that they were
citizens, and the embodiment of Europeans' hopes and loyalties in the nation,
only began to come to fruition during the French Revolution and Napoleonic
Wars. An essential part of this process was the reaction to the Enlightenment view
of the unity of mankind, for while this view flourished, nationalism could not
achieve full expression.

cepts such as Herder's "Volksgeist" were employed by intellectuals to convince a people that its character was unique owing to its common history, traditions, customs, language, and religion. To preserve these features of a distinctive community, to guarantee each individual his place in it, and to affirm and express the common destiny, it was necessary to erect a state upon the cultural foundation. The nation-state became, in Renan's memorable phrase, "a plebiscite of every day," the object of men's supreme loyalty. Ironically, the nation came to be regarded as the source of cultural life, instead of the other way round. Thus a world of sovereign nation-states emerged. An important aspect of this process was its revolutionary character; since Europe was marked by multi-national empires, such as Austria, and divided peoples, such as the Italian, nationalist movements stood in opposition to the existing political order. There sprang up secret societies with initiation rituals, secret passwords, spy networks, and pseudonyms, plotting revolts and circulating revolutionary literature.

The ways in which the development of the Chinese nationalist movement paralleled this process are clear, but some of the differences must be noted. One obvious and fundamental difference is that China began from a vastly different base. Furthermore, she was not afforded the luxury of some seven hundred years of gradual (although often jarring) social, economic, intellectual, and political transformation within which European nationalism evolved. The vast complex of beliefs, attitudes, customs, and institutions that characterized imperial China cannot even be adumbrated here, but it is obvious that the role of the family in Chinese society, the nature of personal and group loyalties in China, and the Chinese view of other peoples represent a context in which modern nationalism would find it difficult first to take root and then to grow as it did in the West. Thus while the Chinese nationalists, like their European counterparts, emphasized their common cultural characteristics, related them to the need for a new political order, and used similar methods to those employed by groups such as the Carbonari, concepts such as the rights of sovereign states did not come easily to them.

In addition, the Chinese nationalists could not avoid using old terms and frames of reference that gave their ideas a curiously mixed character. Ch'en T'ien-hua quoted from the *Tso-chuan* but he also drew upon Rousseau. Chu Chih-hsin buttressed his arguments with references to Western history. Wang Ching-wei attempted to make use of Western scholarship, but he relied a great deal on Chinese history. In his last call to his comrades, for example, in the final issue of the *Min-pao*, it was in Mencius' language that Wang summarized the revolutionaries' determination to revolt. If a child fell into a well, one rushed forward to save him with no thought of personal risk or any possible gain. This was the "feeling of commiseration" (*ts'e-yin chih hsin*) natural to all men; this was courage, and, at its purest, this was *jen*.[106] Now the Chinese people had fallen into the Manchu well; how could one bear to see them suffering and unable to free themselves?

> Who would say that our determination to revolt does not derive from this feeling of commiseration? Men cannot bear the destruction and humiliation of their own kind (*t'ung-lei*) and of what history has recorded and their forefathers bequeathed. The pathetic sight of the destruction of their country leads men to reflect upon its past and produces this feeling of commiseration.[107]

With much quoting from Mencius and Wang Yang-ming, Wang Ching-wei then described it as a matter of being true to one's nature as a man to rush to the rescue of the stricken Chinese; only by overthrowing the Manchus could the Chinese fully realize their feeling of commiseration and their "good conscience" (*liang-chih*).[108]

Thus for Wang Ching-wei, what had begun as an attempt at scientific analysis of race and the nation, using the latest concepts formulated by Western scholars, turned out to be something quite different. And for the T'ung-meng-hui, what was one kind of revolution when Sun Yat-sen described it for American readers, was quite another when Wang Ching-wei and others were addressing a Chinese audience. Furthermore, the Chinese audience itself ranged from businessmen abroad and in the treaty ports to students (themselves with diverse interests and leanings) in Japan and elsewhere overseas, and

---

[106] "Ke-ming chih chüeh-hsin," *Min-pao*, No. 26, p. 1. (In this issue of *Min-pao*, the pagination of each article began with number one. There was no consecutive pagination for the issue as a whole. The pages of this article are thus numbered 1 to 8 but were actually pp. 21–28 of the magazine.)

[107] *Ibid.*, p. 2.

[108] *Ibid.*, *passim*. For the specific references to the famous concepts of Mencius and Wang Yang-ming, see pp. 5 and 7 respectively.

to the population at home, even including, it was doubtless hoped, the illiterate masses. But whatever part deliberate calculation may have played, the more significant point is that the past, of necessity, lived on. And much of it was not fertile soil for modern nationalism.

Compared with what had gone before, however, the T'ung-meng-hui attack on the Manchus marked an unmistakable development of Chinese nationalism. Particularly noteworthy are Sun Yat-sen's comments on China's "spirit of patriotism," Chu Chih-hsin's concept of national self-determination as the feeling of identity based on a common history and expressed in an independent state, and Wang Ching-wei's ideas of the characteristics of a nation and its relation to the state, perhaps most notably his idea of loyalty to the state rather than personal loyalty to a ruler. If their sentiments bore some similarity to rebel ideologies,[109] and if the revolutionaries themselves acknowledged their debt to the past by their language and otherwise, we should not be misled into underestimating the dissimilarities and the new elements that were present. Modern nationalists in countries that have proud traditions are sometimes even less able to escape their tradition than others of their countrymen, despite their greater desire to do so. Particularly is this the case in lands that are or have been under foreign domination or whose people feel that they are "behind" in some way. These men desire change, and so they must criticize the old; but they must fan whatever embers of national pride they can find, and if it is at all possible they must justify their claim to self-rule by pointing to a history of independence and achievement. Sometimes they must even prove they have the characteristics of a nation. Thus the Indian poet-nationalist Henry Derozio (1809–31) wrote a sonnet to India's youth calling upon them to

> . . . dissipate the gloom
> That long has made your country but a
>     tomb,
> Or worse than tomb, the priest's, the
>     tyrant's den.

[109] Both Shih and Muramatsu have noted that demands for "equality" were common among rebels. Muramatsu adds that "alien beliefs" were important, but by "alien" he means non-Confucian. Shih also notes that religious beliefs were significant elements of rebel ideologies. See note 3 above.

But he also wrote an encomium to the same pre-British India:

> My country! in the day of glory past
> A beauteous halo circled round thy brow,
> And worshiped as a deity thou wast.
> Where is that glory, where that reverence now?[110]

This is the common dilemma of modern nationalists. The men of *Min-pao* may have been thinking in similar terms when they chose four pictures for display in their first issue. First there was Huang Ti, "the world's first great nationalist" (*min-tsu chu-i ta wei-jen*) and "the founding father of the Chinese nation"; then side by side were Rousseau, "the world's first great democrat," and Washington, "the world's first founder of a republic"; finally there came Mo Ti, "the world's first great advocate of equality and fraternity."

Even in the most turbulent times it is no easy matter for men to cut themselves off from their heritage even if they desire to. In this early stage of China's intellectual revolution, nowhere was the clash between East and West more violent than in men's minds. Few people, especially intellectuals, escaped being a battleground for sharply conflicting loyalties. But were these conflicts hopelessly irreconcilable? Ho Ch'i and Hu Li-yuan wrote their proposals for westernization in pure *wen-yen*; K'ang Yu-wei studied Western astronomy even as he concentrated upon adjusting Confucianism to the modern world; even a radical westernizer such as T'an Ssu-t'ung praised Confucius. When Wang Ching-wei used the language and imagery of Mencius he can hardly have prevented the content of Mencius' ideas from infiltrating his own, much less those of his readers.

Language doubtless influences the concepts it expresses and writers' and readers' understanding of those concepts. But one should not overlook the possibility that Wang's use of Mencius, or any modern Chinese intellectual's use of traditional terms, reflects no more attachment to the ideas those terms represent than an educated Westerner's use of terms from Plato, Aquinas, or Shakespeare. Writers in *Min-pao* used traditional language and concepts rather casually. One derives no clear impression of intellectuals grappling with an agonizing problem of building pride in a nation while being

---

[110] See *Sources of Indian Tradition*, compiled by William Theodore deBary, Stephen Hay, Royal Weiler, and Andrew Yarrow, pp. 569–71.

ashamed of its culture. Perhaps the Manchus were an unseen blessing. China's problems could be explained as *their* doing; get rid of the barbarian conquerors and the rest would be relatively easy. In any case, the presence of the Manchus allowed the Chinese revolutionaries to escape the dilemma of other modern nationalists. They avoided the possible embarrassment of answering questions about the inadequacies of the traditional order; at the same time they neglected the grim but necessary task of deciding exactly what was wrong with the traditional order and not only with those who had lately presided over it. Their attempt to explain what they wanted to build would suffer from their limited explanation of why they wanted to destroy.

Anti-Manchuism, whatever its drawbacks, united many otherwise irreconcilable interests. It provided a stimulus and focus for a new feeling of commonality, a feeling that all who suffered under Manchu rule had something in common that transcended all differences. As a sentiment around which so many rallied in an organized movement to unseat the Ch'ing dynasty, anti-Manchuism became the core of a new nationalism.[111]

It may be said that before 1905, Chinese "nationalism" was a compound of the old "culturalism," rebel and secret-society ideologies, and beginning in the nineteenth century, some Western ideas. The proportions changed rapidly around the turn of the century, and with Tsou Jung the solution began to take on Western coloring. With the T'ung-meng-hui, a new nationalism marked by some traces of traditional overtones was overtaking the old "nationalism" with its modern shadings.

[111] Cf. Josef Fass, "A Few Notes on the Birth of Nationalism in China," *Archiv Orientalni*, XXXII, 376–82.

# 4

# *A Political Revolution: Establish a Republic*

It may be true that all revolutionaries know more surely what they oppose than what they favor. It seems obvious that revolutionaries live in the present like other men and that men are better able to know the present and past than the future. But revolutionaries are not altogether like other men. One of the ways they differ is in their perceptions of past, present, and future. Alienated from existing values, beliefs, and institutions, they are also alienated from the past that produced those values, beliefs, and institutions. The very alienation that begins to form men into revolutionaries blurs their vision: as men turn their eyes from a present and past they increasingly reject to a future they increasingly desire, their ability dispassionately to perceive present and past is dulled. A vision of future possibilities changes their perception of existing and past conditions. The present and past may become so clouded by the future that they are less visible. Revolutionaries identify themselves with the future so much more than with the past and present that it sometimes becomes more real for them; in this sense, they may know what they favor more surely than what they oppose.

The Chinese revolutionaries, therefore, may not fairly be criticized for being predominantly negative, or for attacking the existing system without proposing an alternative, for offering dissent and destruction with no blueprint for the future. Sun Yat-sen once summed up the T'ung-meng-hui program as follows:

In brief, the aim of our revolution is to plan for the welfare of the masses. Because we do not approve of the monopoly held by a Manchu minority, we desire a national revolution (*min-tsu ke-ming*). Because we do not approve of the monopoly held by the monarch, we desire a political revolution. Because we do not approve of the monopoly held by a wealthy minority, we desire a social revolution.[1]

In this passage Sun indicated what the T'ung-meng-hui proposed to leave behind, and in so doing he implied what the new direction should be. Elsewhere, he and his comrades tried to specify the nature of the political and social revolutions.

The fundamental and most obvious political aim of the T'ung-meng-hui revolutionaries was to establish a republic. Few writers neglected to point out that while former "revolutions" had failed to change the political system, this one would. Certainly the key documents of the movement made this intention abundantly clear from the time the T'ung-meng-hui was founded. Individual writers, however, had different ideas about republicanism. Sun Yat-sen called for a republic in his Tokyo speech of 1905 and in another commemorating the first anniversary of the *Min-pao* fifteen months later.[2] Wang Ching-wei objected to the term "constitutional republic" (*kung-ho li-hsien*) and preferred to say that China would establish a "constitutional democracy" (*min-ch'üan li-hsien*).

The reason I do not call it a constitutional republic is that the term republic has both a broad and a narrow meaning. Its broad

[1] Sun Yat-sen, "San Min Chu I yü Chung-kuo min-tsu chih ch'ien-t'u," *Kuo-fu ch'üan-chi*, III, 14. *Min-tsu ke-ming* can also be translated "racial revolution." See above, Chapter 3, note 41.

[2] See Ssu-yü Teng and John K. Fairbank, *China's Response to the West*, p. 227, for the T'ung-meng-hui Manifesto's reference to former revolutions, and p. 228 for point three of the four-point program, establishment of the republic. Also Hu Han-min, "Min-pao chih liu ta chu-i," *Min-pao*, No. 3, pp. 9–11, for the second principle of the T'ung-meng-hui journal; W. T. deBary *et al.* (eds.), *Sources of Chinese Tradition*, pp. 764–65, has an abridged translation.

For Sun's 1905 speech, entitled "Chung-kuo ying chien-she kung-ho-kuo," see Sun's *Kuo-fu ch'üan-chi*, III, 1–6. Another version of the speech is given on pp. 6–8. The 1906 speech is in *ibid.*, pp. 8–16. Because the major questions involved in studying the "social revolution" have been discussed at some length by other scholars and because of my own interests, this study is concerned mainly with the "political revolution."

meaning also includes patrician government (*kuei-tsu cheng-chih*) and therefore I do not use it.[3]

The revolutionaries did, in fact, use different terms. Hu Han-min employed *kung-ho*, precisely the term to which Wang objected. So did Sun, in his 1905 speech, but in 1906 he spoke of a "democratic constitutional form of government" (*min-chu li-hsien cheng-t'i*). In the T'ung-meng-hui Manifesto the favored usage was simply "people-state" (*min-kuo*), a term commonly translated today as "republic."

All this may mean only that there was still no generally accepted Chinese term for "republic," although Wang Ching-wei's remark suggests that something more than translation was involved. Or it may suggest different emphases by different writers, or even a widespread unfamiliarity with ideas of republicanism and democracy. Some revolutionaries, of course, wanted neither. In any case, what did republican government mean to the Chinese revolutionaries? What did they mean by "democracy" and other terms they used such as "liberty, equality, and fraternity," "a national revolution" (*kuo-min ke-ming*), "a people's revolution" (*p'ing-min ke-ming*), and the like? Why did they want China to be a republic, and how did they think their political ideals could be realized?

REPUBLICAN GOVERNMENT IN THEORY

The revolutionaries spelled out their ideas not only because they understood that they had to look beyond the overthrow of the Manchus, but also because they had to answer Liang Ch'i-ch'ao and the reformers. This necessity largely determined what issues were discussed and what form the revolutionaries' arguments took. Furthermore, finding themselves in a public debate, both sides often attempted to score debaters' points at the sacrifice of more constructive thought. And always in the background was the proposed Manchu constitution, an obvious target for the revolutionists but also, at least in their eyes, a possible source of support for their opponents.

Liang posed the fundamental issue between them. The Chinese people, he wrote, were not yet qualified to carry out the responsibilities of republican citizens. Indeed, in 1905–6 he believed that even

[3] Wang Ching-wei, "Po Hsin-min ts'ung-pao tsui-chin chih fei ke-ming lun," *Min-pao*, No. 4, p. 28. Presumably, Wang had in mind the Roman republic.

constitutional monarchy was beyond China's reach, although it is true that he wavered in this belief and for most of the T'ung-meng-hui period supported constitutional monarchy. But he was convinced that China was not ready for a republic. His central argument was that the establishment of a republic required a revolution, and since those who would carry out the revolution were unaccustomed to democracy, a "strong man" would soon gain control and institute a new absolutism. Liang envisioned a period of "enlightened absolutism" during which the Chinese people would prepare for democratic government, but the nature of this government and the manner of transition to it remained unclear.[4]

This general view provided the basis for Liang's debate with Wang Ching-wei. For his ideas on monarchy, constitutionalism, and republicanism, Liang had drawn upon many Western writers. Most prominent among them were the German jurists Johann Kaspar Bluntschli (1808–81), Max von Seydel (1846–1901), and Conrad Bornhak (1861–1944).[5] Liang enjoined the revolutionaries to consider Bornhak's views on the evils of republican revolution, which provided the chief basis for Liang's position, and on constitutional monarchy. Wang took up the challenge with gusto, for both he and Liang seem to have read similar Japanese translations of German works.[6]

[4] Liang's most complete statement of these views is in his "K'ai-ming chuan-chih lun," *Hsin-min ts'ung-pao*, No. 73, pp. 1–24; No. 74, pp. 1–15; No. 75, pp. 1–50; No. 77, pp. 1–10. The best brief survey of his ideas is in Hsiao Kung-ch'üan, *Chung-kuo cheng-chih ssu-hsiang shih*, Vol. VI. See especially pp. 743–53, on which I have drawn heavily. The article just noted is summarized on pp. 750–52.

See also Joseph R. Levenson, *Liang Ch'i-ch'ao and the Mind of Modern China*, pp. 157–58, for Liang's arguments against revolution and republicanism. A recent writer has commented that "Liang's opposition to Sun Yat-sen's party probably had more influence on his thinking than is suggested [by Levenson]." J. Gray, "Historical Writing in Twentieth Century China," *Historians of China and Japan*, ed. W. G. Beasley and E. G. Pulleyblank, p. 201. The most detailed study of these questions is Chang P'eng-yüan, *Liang Ch'i-ch'ao yü Ch'ing-chi ke-ming*.

In general, it can be said that Liang hoped for China to develop a system closely resembling England's, although owing to a number of circumstances (perhaps including his attitude toward Yen Fu, who was closely associated through his translations of Mill and Spencer with English thought) Liang relied more on German theorists.

[5] The Japanese had been intensely interested in German constitutionalism, and their own constitution of 1889 was modeled on that of Prussia. See Nobutaka Ike, *The Beginnings of Political Democracy in Japan*, pp. 174–78. The writings of German thinkers must have been most plentiful and readily available in Japan.

[6] Wang on several occasions criticized Liang's understanding of Japanese, citing

Bornhak had argued that a republic was inherently unable to fulfill the main function of the state, which was to resolve conflicts of interest among different segments of the population. The reason was that in a republic there existed no authority outside the people themselves, and they could not always be counted upon to resolve their own conflicts peacefully. When such a stalemate occurred, as it was bound to, a republic could only sink into strife out of which some form of absolutism would arise. A monarchy, on the other hand, possessed the very attribute that a republic lacked, for in Bornhak's view the state and the monarch were one, and political authority resided in his person: "The whole power of the state is the power of the prince, and all constitutional law is the law of the prince." [7] Such a monarch, who of course also stood outside the conflicts he was to resolve, could best fulfill the functions of the state.[8]

Wang began his reply by identifying Bornhak's conception of the state with that of Seydel, whose follower Bornhak was. Seydel, he pointed out, had held that the monarch's relationship to the state was the same as a person's relationship to his possessions. The monarch was thus the possessor (lit.: "subject," *chu-t'i*) of authority and the people were its "object" (*k'e-t'i*).[9] Or as Rupert Emerson puts it, Seydel believed that a land and a people became a state by being

passages he had mistranslated, and he once stooped to imputing to Liang deliberate falsification of the Japanese. See Wang's "Tsa-po Hsin-min ts'ung-pao," Part I, *Min-pao,* No. 10, pp. 52–53; also "Hsi-wang Man-chou li-hsien che ho t'ing chu," *Min-pao,* No. 5, pp. 1–2, for Wang's personal comments on Liang Ch'i-ch'ao's intelligence and learning.

[7] Quoted by George H. Sabine and Walter J. Shepard in their "Translators' Introduction" to H. Krabbe, *The Modern Idea of the State,* p. xxv. See also Rupert Emerson, *State and Sovereignty in Modern Germany,* p. 76, note 53. Since Liang and Wang did not always spell out the ideas of the Western thinkers they referred to and since the thinkers are not very well known, I have added some information where it seemed necessary.

[8] Quoted by Liang Ch'i-ch'ao, "K'ai-ming chuan-chih lun," *Hsin-min ts'ung-pao,* No. 75, pp. 11–13. See also Wang Ching-wei, "Po Hsin-min ts'ung-pao tsui-chin chih fei ke-ming lun," *Min-pao,* No. 4, pp. 4–6. Liang himself did not similarly attack republican government. He condemned his opponents because they were revolutionaries and because, he said, they only masked their ambitions with pretty names (*mei-ming*), constitution and republic. It was clearly revolution to which he was objecting. See "K'ai-ming chuan-chih lun," *Hsin-min ts'ung-pao,* No. 75, p. 14.

[9] "Po Hsin-min ts'ung-pao tsui-chin chih fei ke-ming lun," *Min-pao,* No. 4, p. 7. For the corresponding debate in Japan, see Frank O. Miller, *Minobe Tatsukichi,* p. 27, and *passim,* especially pp. 43–72.

ruled, much as things became property by being owned. As things are the objects of ownership, land and people are the objects of ruler-ship.[10] Wang conceded that this was somewhat different from Born-hak's conception, but he maintained that the two were basically the same, since both regarded the monarch as the subject of governing power.[11]

Wang took exception to the views that the state was indistinguish-able from its ruler and that it was the object of governing authority. He set against the Seydel-Bornhak-Liang conception his own ver-sion of the juristic personality of the state, which turned out to be remarkably similar to that of Georg Jellinek (1851–1911).[12] The state was an independent personality and itself the subject of gov-erning authority. For the state, Wang asserted, is created by human efforts; individual men possess a desire for order, out of which there is formed a collective will:

> This collective will (*ho-ch'eng i-li*) has as its elements each in-
> dividual will, and exists independently of them. Each particular will
> possesses [its own] personality, and the general will (*tsung-i*) also
> has a personality [of its own]. The former is called the single per-
> sonality, the latter the collective personality (*ho-ch'eng jen-ke*). The
> state is the collective personality. It therefore has its own will and is
> not dependent upon another power for its existence. The parliament
> in a democracy and the monarch in a monarchy are the highest
> organs for carrying out the will of the state. They are not the state.[13]

Wang later contended that since according to this theory of state sovereignty, the monarch is a mere organ of the state, the theory stood opposed to absolute monarchy. Indeed, an understanding of it

---

[10] Rupert Emerson, *State and Sovereignty in Modern Germany*, p. 74. Emerson adds that since in Seydel's view the ruler creates law, his title to rule must precede law. Thus, quoting Seydel, the king "derives his power from no legal source, especially from no delegation on the part of the people or of the State. He rules with his own power and for that very reason this power knows no sphere which is legally withdrawn from its operation." He is not part of a larger and higher organization.

[11] Bornhak and Seydel have, in fact, been linked as believing that political authority is personified in the monarch. See Sabine and Shepard, "Translators' Introduction" to H. Krabbe, *The Modern Idea of the State*, p. xxv.

[12] See *ibid.*, pp. xxx–xxxi.

[13] Wang Ching-wei, "Po Hsin-min ts'ung-pao tsui-chin chih fei ke-ming lun," p. 8.

was essential for any discussion of democracy.[14] If the monarch were regarded as the embodiment of the state, as he was by Bornhak, it should follow that upon his death the state would cease to exist, Wang added. Finally, Wang could not agree that the people were objects of government; they were rather to be regarded as the subjects of rights and duties.[15] Thus in a state in which sovereignty[16] resides with a parliament, the people can elect and be elected as representatives. Such a parliament is a national body, an organ of the state that represents the people as a whole and not particular interests of certain groups. Bornhak's conception of a parliament was the "old-fashioned" one (*ku-tai chih i-hui kuan-nien*) according to which each member represented the interests of those who elected him rather than the interests of the people as a whole. The modern concept, as exemplified by Paul Laband (1838–1918) and Jellinek, was just the reverse. Therefore, Bornhak's contention that only a monarch could be above conflicts of interests among the people was unfounded, and his central criticism of republican government was without substance.[17]

Liang had further argued that in a republic one of two things would inevitably occur. Either sovereignty would inhere in the parliament, in which case that institution would come to dominate the executive and establish a "parliamentary absolutism," as he believed was about to happen in the United States; or a system providing for separation of powers would be instituted, thus violating the principle of the indivisibility of sovereignty. "Sovereignty tends to concentrate in one [organ of government] as naturally as water flows

[14] Wang, "Tsai po Hsin-min ts'ung-pao chih cheng-chih ke-ming lun," Part I, *Min-pao*, No. 6, p. 84.

[15] "Po Hsin-min ts'ung-pao tsui-chin chih fei ke-ming lun," p. 9.

[16] It was not until some months later that Wang specifically discussed and attempted to define sovereignty. See "Man-chou li-hsien yü kuo-min ke-ming," *Min-pao*, No. 8, p. 51. Here he noted that sovereignty was an extremely complex concept that he interpreted to mean "the highest independent power in the state, or in other words, that power which is not subject to limitation by other people." This last, he said, was part of its negative aspect, and was in fact an insufficient explanation. In foreign constitutional or legal usage its content was more definite. For reasons of convenience and consistency he would use a simple definition: "Sovereignty is the highest power in the state, the source of all other power, and the power that controls all state affairs."

[17] "Po Hsin-min ts'ung-pao tsui-chin chih fei ke-ming lun," pp. 9–11. See also Wang's "Tsai-po Hsin-min ts'ung-pao chih cheng-chih ke-ming lun," Part I, pp. 88–90, for the continuing discussion of this issue in similar terms.

downhill . . . and [government] inevitably becomes an enlightened absolutism." [18]

Wang Ching-wei, noting scornfully what he called Liang's attempt to support his position with legal props ("he employs law to embellish his writings the way women use jewelry"), apologized for attempting to correct him despite his own "lack of training and experience." [19] Wang rejected the view that power inevitably tended to be concentrated in one organ of the government, calling on Jellinek for support. The latter had demonstrated, and others had agreed, that a well-conceived separation of powers negated this possibility. In such a system, Wang continued, no organ of government was under the orders of any other organ; so far as its own functions were concerned it was "completely independent." Thus any two or more organs of the state stood in "interrelated positions"; it was not the case that one compelled and another submitted. Outside any one organ there were others upon whose powers it could not encroach. Liang was thus wrong in asserting that under constitutional democracy (Wang's preferred term, it will be recalled) all sovereignty lay with the parliament and that such a form of government would inevitably become a parliamentary or popular absolutism.[20]

[18] Liang Ch'i-ch'ao, "K'ai-ming chuan-chih lun," *Hsin-min ts'ung-pao*, No. 75, p. 9. Liang was actually presenting some views of a Japanese legal scholar, Hozumi Yatsuka (1860–1912), which he himself did not fully accept. See *ibid.*, pp. 9–10. Liang went on to argue his main point, which was that at her present stage of development China was most suited for "enlightened absolutism as preparation for a constitutional system." *Ibid.*, p. 11. Cf. note 9 above for the reference to Japan; Professor Miller's discussion, when compared with Chinese thought before 1911, clearly shows the startling degree to which the debate between Wang and Liang revolved around the issues raised by Minobe.

[19] Wang had, according to his most faithful follower and biographer, received an LL.D. in Japan in 1906 after three years of study. See T'ang Leang-li, *Wang Ching-wei: A Political Biography*, p. 19. This of course does not mean that he obtained sound training, since many schools attended by Chinese in Japan gave their students little more than a "degree." Wang himself tells us that he studied law and politics in Japan, concentrating on constitutional systems in the West. It was in these three years, it seems, that he first came in contact with Western ideas. He writes that the new concepts of the state and popular sovereignty swept away his old ideas (he had received a classical education and earned the *sheng-yüan* degree). See his "Tzu-shu," in *Ming-chia chuan-chi*, pp. 46–47. Cf. Howard L. Boorman, "Wang Ching-wei: China's Romantic Radical," *Political Science Quarterly*, LXXIX, 507.

[20] "Po Hsin-min ts'ung-pao tsui-chin chih fei ke-ming lun," p. 20. Wang later tried to clarify this by departing from Jellinek's view that in every state there is a

Wang conceded more merit to Liang's statement that the United States system violated the principle that sovereignty is indivisible, but he insisted that a separation of powers did not necessarily mean divided sovereignty. Jellinek had held that although the state was a single entity it did not need to rely upon one organ to act. Other writers had also pointed out that Montesquieu had not wished to reduce the unity of the state but to promote that unity while preventing absolutism. Thus, Wang concluded, "If China can imitate the three-power division of the American constitution, while also making her parliament the supreme organ, she too will be able to bring forth the reality of democratic government." [21]

Liang countered with the charge that the system proposed by Wang was unworkable. A parliament could not represent the "general will" of which Wang had spoken, because a representative's views would inevitably deviate from those of his constituents. The only way to ascertain the general will, therefore, was to submit all legislative and administrative affairs to a direct vote. Invoking the authority of the man *Min-pao* had called "the world's first great democrat," Liang observed that even Rousseau had recognized the impracticability of such a system for large states. [22]

Wang agreed that Rousseau had not considered a representative

---

legally unlimited authority that establishes law and is above it (i.e., that holds *sovereign* power rather than merely the power to govern). This, although with some important refinements, was the view of all political thinkers who held to the legal sovereignty of the state. See Francis W. Coker, *Recent Political Thought*, pp. 501–3. Wang tried to distinguish between a "supreme organ" (*tsung-lang chi-kuan*) and a "highest organ" (*tsui-kao chi-kuan*). The former implied that a single organ held all power, and he therefore preferred the latter, which in a republic (here, he said, using the term in its "narrow sense" to mean democracy) should be applied to the parliament. However, he then said that the "meaning" of the two was the same, but their "usage" was different. "Tsai-po Hsin-min ts'ung-pao chih cheng-chih ke-ming lun," Part I, pp. 88–89.

[21] "Po Hsin-min ts'ung-pao tsui-chin chih fei ke-ming lun," pp. 22–23. It was this use of "supreme organ" that Wang later attempted to amend.

It is worth noting that Wang called for a three-power system. Five and one-half months later Sun Yat-sen was to present the first formulation of his five-power constitution. Wang, whose relationship with Sun was extremely close in this period, appears to have known nothing of his views on this question. It seems possible that the idea of the five-power constitution only took shape in the few months before Sun announced it.

[22] Liang Ch'i-ch'ao, "Lu-sou hsüeh-an," *Yin-ping-shih wen-chi, chüan* 9, pp. 11b–12a. See also *Hsin-min ts'ung-pao*, No. 76, pp. 7–9. I am grateful to Mr. Chang P'eng-yüan for directing me to the source of these remarks by Liang.

system to be truly democratic. He himself supplied Rousseau's famous statement to the effect that the liberty of Englishmen ended when they elected their members of parliament, after which they became slaves. This, however, only proved that

> . . . in purely theoretical terms real democratic government means the direct exercise of sovereignty by the whole body of the people, but speaking realistically, true democratic government often only exists as an ideal. In practice, a representative system is its basic principle, while direct exercise of sovereignty by the people is the exception. This is set forth in *The Social Contract*. One cannot proceed from this to speak of the people's general will as difficult to realize. Why? Because a representative system does not wrest the people's rights from them and give those rights to their representatives. The latter represent the people in the exercise of their rights. Therefore a parliament is a reflection of the people's thoughts.[23]

Wang condemned as crude and superficial Liang's view that a parliament could not mirror the general will and his criticisms of the intimidation and deceptions that often characterized elections. He admonished Liang to distinguish between flaws that were inherent in the system and defects that could be eliminated by seeing to it that laws were carefully drawn.

Liang, however, had put his finger on a basic weakness in Rousseau's conception, one that Rousseau himself had seen and been helpless to correct. The "general will" could never be more than a majority opinion. Wang also complicated matters for himself by quoting Rousseau's statements that once the state had been established all within its borders would be required to obey the general will, and if a decision of parliament (one that is in accord with the wishes of the majority) should run counter to the view of an individual, that would be "sufficient to prove the incorrectness of that view." Rousseau, Wang declared, meant that the general will is formed out of the freely expressed opinions of individuals. "Thus the individual's obedience to the general will means but obedience to himself. This by no means involves the destruction of freedom." Wang concluded by noting that later scholars had praised Rousseau for converting

[23] Wang Ching-wei, "Tsai-po Hsin-min ts'ung-pao chih cheng-chih ke-ming lun," Part I, p. 95.

"individualism" (*ke-jen chu-i*) to "collectivism" (*t'uan-t'i chu-i*).[24]

The ominous tone of this last remark echoed one by Ch'en T'ien-hua in the first issue of *Min-pao*. "What we seek is the freedom of the group; we do not seek the freedom of the individual. . . . In a republic the majority decides, and it cannot but restrict the freedom of the minority."[25] Ch'en went on to say that (presumably in the early stages of a republic) the masses are not equipped to make important decisions, and they therefore "elect their betters to represent them" and to decide wisely.[26] He condemned the Manchus for interfering with individual rights on the grounds that they did it for the benefit of the few who held power rather than on behalf of all; he drew no further lines against such interference other than that it should be done in the general interest.

Ch'en committed suicide only a few weeks after he wrote this article, and we cannot know how he might have refined his thinking. Wang's ideas were developed at much greater length, but he attempted little more than to prove that the principles of political science neither made a monarchical state unavoidable nor popular self-government impossible. A republic was theoretically a viable system chiefly because the popular will could adequately be expressed

[24] *Ibid.*, pp. 97–98. At least one recent scholar has not praised him for this dubious achievement. Characterizing Rousseau as the founder of the "romantic cult of the group," George H. Sabine observes: "The more authority its spokesmen have, whether they are called representatives or not." *A History of Political Theory*, pp. 592–93. Cf. J. L. Talmon's view that "Rousseau's 'general will' . . . became the driving force of totalitarian democracy," which Professor Talmon contrasts with "liberal democracy" and which he thinks led to later totalitarianism; *The Origins of Totalitarian Democracy*, pp. 6, 38–49, *passim*.

For a fascinating discussion, from a different angle, of Rousseau's concept of representation as applied in the course of the French Revolution, see Gordon H. McNeil, "Robespierre, Rousseau, and Representation," *Ideas in History*, ed. Richard Herr and Harold T. Parker, pp. 135–56.

[25] Ch'en T'ien-hua, "Lun Chung-kuo i kai-ch'uang min-chu cheng-t'i," *Min-pao*, No. 1, p. 48. Note the striking similarity between the first sentence and Sun Yat-sen's remark in his 1924 lectures: "On no account must we give more liberty to the individual; let us secure liberty instead for the nation." *San Min Chu I*, trans. Frank W. Price, p. 213. The two men were of course speaking in different contexts, but there was enough similarity between the situations in which they were involved and the attitudes of the men to warrant our attention.

[26] Ch'en, "Lun Chung-kuo i kai-ch'uang min-chu cheng-t'i," p. 48. The term freely translated here as "their betters" literally means "those whose level is higher than that of most people."

through a parliament which, together with the executive and judicial branches of government but occupying a higher position than either, comprised a collective body in which sovereignty resided.

Despite Wang's limited purposes, his debate with Liang helped to crystallize a number of important issues: how to guarantee the responsibility of elected officials to the electorate, how to ensure that the popular will would be adequately expressed and implemented, how to avoid majority tyranny — in short, some of the basic issues of democratic government. If Wang seems inconsistent, or perhaps even cavalier, in his treatment of the last problem, it is nevertheless to his (and Liang's) credit that these issues were formulated and discussed; indeed, it is remarkable that both these men identified these problems so clearly and discussed them so openly in view of their limited experience with Western ideas and the gravity of the clash between their respective movements.

A modern political scientist might easily expose any number of soft spots in the thinking of Wang and Liang. Perhaps Liang shared too much of Hozumi Yatsuka's pessimism about the dangers of absolutism, and perhaps he contradicted himself on this and other points. Perhaps Wang was unable to reconcile the principle of separation of powers with his notion of sovereignty. But such weaknesses seem minor in comparison with the level and focus of the discussion. The weaknesses may reveal which features of democratic thought were most difficult for Chinese intellectuals to grasp, or how frequently each man yielded to the temptation to score a debater's point against the other. But what is most remarkable is that the leading Chinese intellectuals of the time were debating about modern representative government, and were not debating whether or not to have it but what kind to have. The debate not only identified for Chinese readers the theoretical issues that had been crucial in the West for centuries, but it showed that China's political and intellectual climate, or at least weather, had changed dramatically since 1898. The debate reveals a set of assumptions and values that Wang and Liang, revolutionary and reformer, shared. In essence, those assumptions and values can be lumped together under the rubrics of government by consent and a division of power. And it is the latter, according to at least one acknowledged authority, that is the "basis of civilized government" and "what is meant by constitutionalism." [27]

It was with the concepts of popular sovereignty and shared power that Wang attempted to resolve some of the dilemmas of democratic government that had emerged in his debate with Liang. He did so in a most interesting way. Wang had placed great emphasis upon a system of popularly elected representatives, but he stressed even more the importance of government by law. It was here that he found a basic difference between constitutional democracy and absolutism:

> What are citizens? They are the elements of which the state is composed. They are united on the basis of liberty, equality, and fraternity, and in this spirit the laws of the state are established. Laws represent the general will of the people. The government is commissioned (*wei-jen*) by the laws of the state. Therefore it is called a state that is governed by law, or a constitutional form of government. Hence the government is fundamentally and radically different from absolutism.[28]

Thus the general will was expressed not only in a representative body but in law as well. And the law was considered superior to the state:

> The fact is that under absolutism those who govern may freely do evil, but under constitutional [government] they cannot. The difference between [government by] morality and [government by] law resides in whether or not there exists the power to compel [the ruler]. Now if one urges a dictator, "You may not do evil," this is a moral admonition. If he insists on doing evil, what recourse is there? But under a constitution the conduct of government organs complies with laws. If they violate the law, they achieve nothing. Thus even if they desire to do evil they cannot. When those who govern cannot do evil if they desire to, peace and order can long be preserved in the state. Thus constitutional [government] is in its essential principle immeasurably superior to absolutism.[29]

Wang was here referring specifically to the principle that the authority of each branch of government was to be carefully defined by law. If any one branch attempted to exceed that authority and

---

[27] Carl J. Friedrich, *Constitutional Government and Democracy*, p. 5.

[28] Wang Ching-wei, "Min-tsu ti kuo-min," Part II, *Min-pao*, No. 2, p. 18.

[29] "Po Hsin-min ts'ung-pao tsui-chin chih fei ke-ming lun," p. 25.

encroach on the sphere of another branch, it would be checked by the laws that defined the area of each branch's authority. Wang saw clearly that there was a relation between the concepts of separation of powers, checks and balances, and government by law.

Throughout his discussions of constitutional government, Wang stressed two points. Above all, a constitution had to define and limit the powers of the government. Second, it had to make explicit the rights and duties of the people. The first purpose was to be accomplished chiefly by basing the constitution on the principle of the separation of powers. Wang made no point more frequently or more emphatically than this: power could not be concentrated in one organ of government. We have already noted that Wang advocated a separation of powers, as in the government of the United States. In his subsequent writings on this subject he did little more than reassert the principle of divided authority in a system of interrelationships in which each organ had its sphere of authority clearly demarcated by law.[30]

To Wang it was also a fundamental characteristic of constitutional democracy that the rights as well as the duties of the people were defined by law. Again he stressed that this was a way of distinguishing constitutional democracy from absolutism.

> To look at [the difference between constitutional democracy and absolutism] from the point of view of individual rights, absolutism in no way recognizes the liberty of the people. Therefore the state has only rights with respect to the individual, but no obligations, while the individual has only duties to the state, but no rights. Under constitutional [democracy] both the state and the individual have their rights and their duties. The two are thus vastly different.[31]

Citizens of a constitutional democracy, he added, were free to express their opinions and would tend to engage in many kinds of cooperative enterprises. Those forced to live under absolutism were obedient, passive, and indifferent, and the more they were imposed upon by the government, the more their abilities were stifled.[32]

---

[30] For other affirmations of this principle see Wang's "Tsa-po Hsin-min ts'ung-pao," Part II, p. 28; "Min-tsu ti kuo-min," Part II, p. 18; "Po Hsin-min ts'ung-pao tsui-chin chih fei ke-ming lun," p. 30. See also notes 20 and 21.

[31] "Min-tsu ti kuo-min," Part II, pp. 18–19. See also "Po Hsin-min ts'ung-pao . . . ," p. 30.

[32] *Ibid.*, p. 27.

These yardsticks of what Wang regarded as true constitutional government were almost invariably held up against the projected constitutional reforms of the Manchus, and without exception the reforms were found to fall short. In this connection Wang made one statement that had important implications if he meant it to be a general principle and not merely an *ad hoc* argument against a Manchu constitution. Monarchy, he wrote, meant that the highest organ of government was controlled by one man, whereas in a democracy it was controlled by a majority of the people.

> Governments are thus distinguished according to the nature and function of the highest organ of the state. If all the powers of government are held by one organ, it is called absolutist government. If this organ either is limited by others or must cooperate with others in order to exercise the powers of government, it is called constitutional government. Hence the difference between absolute monarchy and constitutional monarchy is that while both have a monarch as the highest organ, in the former he alone holds supreme governing power, and in the latter there are other organs which limit his power. If one asks whether the power of the highest organ can really be limited, [the answer] cannot be sought in a legal document. It should be sought in the actual power of the people (*kuo-min shih-shih-shang chih ch'üan-li*). The actual power of the people is the cause that brings the constitution into existence; it is not a result that occurs after the constitution is produced. If the actual power of the people can limit the power of the ruler, the constitution is effective. Otherwise, it is mere words.[33]

This paragraph, a useful summary of Wang's conception of the outstanding features of constitutional government, suggests that Wang was acquainted with Locke's idea that the people possess natural rights which precede the codification of such rights. It also shows Wang's explicit recognition that even the most ingeniously devised constitution has meaning only if it institutionalizes popular sovereignty; Wang understood the realities of political power and was more than a blind believer in the magic of constitutional government. Another example of this understanding is his plea for "no taxation without representation." This, he said, was more than a slogan. It was proper that since taxes come from the people, they ought to be

[33] "Man-chou li hsien . . . ," p. 53.

determined by the people through their representatives. But more than this, if the government ever desired to reassert absolute control, it would be denied the funds it needed. Control of the purse was a power as well as a right.[34]

Wang's next problem was to elaborate upon these ideas, to draw out their implications and apply them to the Chinese context. In particular, it remained for Wang to show why the principles of democratic government could best be expressed in China by a republican system. This task proved to be greater than the task of understanding democratic principles.

Nowhere is this more striking than in Wang's attempt to defend republicanism with the ideas of Laband and Jellinek. Although these men were the leaders of the new movement in German administrative law that denied the identification of the state with the ruler, this fact by no means made them spokesmen for republicanism. On the contrary, they were devout monarchists who sought to justify the authority of imperial government by making it a *Rechtsstaat*, a state whose activities are under legal limits. Laband summarized it in this way: "The state can require no performance and impose no restraint, can command its subjects in nothing and forbid them in nothing, except on the basis of a legal prescription." [35] As Rupert Emerson points out, despite the differences between Laband, Jellinek, and their followers on the one hand, and Seydel on the other, all agreed that "in the German conception of the State, the power of all organs in an absolute or in a constitutional monarchy must be regarded as deriving from the monarch." And even if Laband and Jellinek regarded the state rather than the monarch as the possessor of sovereignty, the difference between them and Seydel was still slight, because "the view of State and sovereignty of all these writers was after all merely an outgrowth of the long and honored tradition of monarchical rule." Emerson then goes on to stress their respect for monarchy and the weakness of the idea of popular sovereignty in Germany at that time.[36]

Although it may be an effective tactic to refute one monarchist view

[34] "Lun ke-ming chih ch'ü-shih," Part I, pp. 13–14.
[35] Quoted in Sabine and Shepard, *op. cit.*, p. xxxvi.
[36] Emerson, *State and Sovereignty*, pp. 74–76.

with another, it can be very difficult to develop from monarchism a theoretical basis for "constitutional democracy" or republicanism. The problem can be seen clearly in Jellinek, whose chief contribution to political theory has generally been considered to be his concept of the autolimitation of the state. He held that the state's submission to law was voluntary — that since the state was sovereign but limited, the limits must be self-imposed.[37] This was precisely the principle to which Wang had so directly and eloquently taken exception.

The German theories Wang attempted to build upon had grown out of the concern with problems of the state that had dominated nineteenth-century German political thought. The German thinkers of that period concentrated on the state because they considered it "the instrument of German national liberation and unification."[38] This fact alone would go far toward explaining why Chinese revolutionaries found German political thought absorbing. In addition, of course, the Japanese had made the ideas available to the Chinese and had also seemed to make the ideas work in Japan. Much of this body of thought was neutral with respect to the precise form of government it might lead to, as Minobe Tatsukichi argued forcefully when accused by Hozumi Yatsuka and others of using the ideas to undermine the authority of the emperor; Minobe claimed to be analyzing the nature of the state without raising the issue of monarchism versus republicanism.[39] Minobe's biographer, however, has pointed out that although the concept of *Rechtsstaat* has a long history and several facets, "it has existed as a vital proposition only in the presence of monarchy. Instrumental in the transition from absolute to constitutional monarchy, it also raised up in the state personality an obstacle to the assertion of popular sovereignty."[40]

We are left with several possible conclusions. One is that Wang understood all or most of this rather clearly, and accepted the concept of *Rechtsstaat* on the grounds that the obstacles it might pose to popular sovereignty were more than compensated for by the strong theoretical underpinning it gave to a powerful state. Another is that his degree of understanding either is unclear to us or matters less

[37] *Ibid.*, pp. 60–61. See also *Encyclopedia of the Social Sciences*, VIII, 379b.
[38] Frank O. Miller, *Minobe Tatsukichi*, p. 9.
[39] *Ibid.*, pp. 26–31. Minobe's debt to Jellinek was so great that one of his students was to call him "the Jellinek of Japan." *Ibid.*, p. 12.
[40] *Ibid.*, p. 10.

than his desire to find respectable ideas with which to counter Liang Ch'i-ch'ao. A third possible conclusion is that Wang's appreciation of the concept was so limited that he simply could not see its wider implications. There is no sure way to ascertain when a man's understanding is limited and when his seeming lack of understanding is rather to be explained either by his attempt to modify other men's ideas and adapt them to different conditions and purposes or by an arbitrary but deliberate eclecticism that simply ignores the problem of faithfulness to the inner consistency and meaning of the original ideas. But I think that what mattered to Wang Ching-wei was less that he be true to Jellinek than that Jellinek's ideas could be used to refute Liang Ch'i-ch'ao and discredit the Manchu reforms; if the ideas would serve these purposes but not lead ultimately to a theoretical foundation for constitutional democracy, Wang would probably have accepted the half loaf gratefully.

A thinker can of course select from various theories the points that suit his own purposes, and then proceed to weave a new fabric out of these threads. But Wang had only chosen what would serve his needs in the debate with Liang Ch'i-ch'ao; his ideas were not then converted into the ingredients of a new theory. He knew too little of the intellectual and political matrix in which the ideas he borrowed had been formed. Had he understood, for example, that the differences between Seydel and his opponents were interwoven with the question of states' rights under the Bismarckian constitution, he might have discussed this key issue in relation to China. Young intellectuals like Wang Ching-wei were compelled by the goals they had set for themselves to deal with ideas they had not yet had time to digest, taken from societies whose differences from China they had not yet adequately analyzed. One of their most noticeable omissions, and the one hardest to explain is their failure to analyze specific Chinese problems and relate their proposals to the solution of those problems.

In Wang's case, at least, it does not seem unreasonable to ascribe this failure partly to the lack of time. Most of his writings for *Min-pao* appeared between November, 1905, and May, 1907; a few others were published in the two numbers of *Min-pao* that he managed to issue in January and February, 1910. In the summer of 1907 he was called upon to leave Tokyo and assume other responsibilities in

Southeast Asia. There Wang was instrumental in the revolutionaries' successful competition with the reformers for the support of the overseas Chinese. After the defeat at Hokow in the spring of 1908, Wang turned his attention to plotting a sensational assassination, an effort that culminated in his attempt to take the regent Tsai-feng's life in March, 1910. Thus after the spring of 1907 Wang's energies were channeled into the more commonly traveled avenues of revolution. Considering the amount and quality of his writings in the first thirteen issues of *Min-pao*, there is reason to think that Wang, who was only twenty-four years old in 1907, might have had a good deal more to say on the subject of democratic government had he continued to write.

In addition to the propaganda campaign in Southeast Asia and the revolts within China in 1907–8, another problem that claimed the attention of Wang and other followers of Sun was the split within the T'ung-meng-hui (discussed below in Chapter 6). A by-product of the schism was that *Min-pao* from this time until its suppression in October, 1908, was, in effect, the organ of Sun's opponent, Chang Pinglin. Under these circumstances it was not likely that anyone writing in *Min-pao* would give much expression to the theory of republican government. Sun Yat-sen's followers carried on in journals such as the *Restoration Daily* in Singapore, but the issues of this journal I have seen do not permit me to say that republicanism claimed a significant portion of their attention.

### THE PROBLEM OF FOUNDING A REPUBLIC

One barrier Wang faced was that the ideas he attempted to employ were better suited to a constitutional monarchy such as Liang Ch'ich'ao preferred; indeed, it is even possible that Jellinek's ideas could better have been adapted to the Manchus' needs than to the revolutionaries'. But a second, closely related, and more impenetrable barrier was one all democratic revolutionaries have faced. The needs of carrying on a revolutionary movement conflict with the goals of democratic revolution; and the further a society is from democracy before the revolution, the harsher this truth is. Revolutionary change great enough to bring a society to democracy necessitates a degree of upheaval that is difficult to channel into peaceful democratic processes. The more drastic and extensive the change men try to bring about, the more they are forced to devote themselves to means rather than ends. The more rapid and far-reaching the transformation men want to effect, the more they find themselves having to resort to violence. The more they resort to violence, the more they alienate those who share the revolutionaries' original ideals but are so opposed to the use of force that they break away from the revolution; conversely, when revolution reaches a violent phase it attracts men who are driven by thirst for adventure and other motives that have little to do with democratic revolution. The Chinese saw this problem and addressed themselves to it. But it may be an insoluble one.

In China before 1911, men like Wang Ching-wei fought men like Liang Ch'i-ch'ao so bitterly that one could hardly guess that they shared as many purposes as they did.[41] The differences between them, such as those discussed earlier in this chapter, were not insignificant, but at least on the surface it appears that Wang and Liang had more in common with each other than Wang had with Chang Ping-lin and his secret-society cohort T'ao Ch'eng-chang or than Liang had with the Empress Dowager Tz'u-hsi and I-k'uang. What made these men line up the way they did? What logic is there in the political alignments of 1903–8? Some answers may be sought in the nature of the dispute about whether and how a republic might be established.

*Planning the Transition*

Liang Ch'i-ch'ao, although his position was not altogether consistent, had argued less that republicanism was unworkable than that a revolution could not result in the establishment of a viable republic. It seems clear that as a strong advocate of popular sovereignty and individual freedom he had far more sympathy for the revolutionaries' declared goals than his antipathy toward revolution permitted him to have for their methods.[42] Replying to Liang's arguments, therefore, the revolutionaries found themselves defending not only the

[41] See my article, "Reform and Revolution in China's Political Modernization," in Mary C. Wright (ed.), *China in Revolution: The First Phase, 1900–1913*.

[42] Even in his plea for "enlightened absolutism" it is clear that Liang regarded it as a transitional stage leading to constitutional government and that he objected to revolution rather than to democracy. See *Hsin-min ts'ung-pao*, No. 75, pp. 10–11, 14 ff.; No. 77, pp. 1–10. Note also Professor Hsiao Kung-ch'üan's comment that as seen from his thought as a whole, Liang was "a moderate democrat." *Chung-kuo cheng-chih ssu-hsiang shih*, VI, 753.

principle that liberty and equality could best be secured under a republic but also the premise that a republican system could be established successfully in China after a revolution. This, in turn, involved the T'ung-meng-hui writers in the counterargument that meaningful constitutional government could not be put into effect under the Manchus. It is of course true that the revolutionists would have devoted much attention to these questions even if there had been no Liang Ch'i-ch'ao. But Liang, by concentrating his fire on revolution as a means, forced the revolutionaries to defend their methods when they might otherwise have been more at liberty to discuss their ends.

The reformers argued that revolution would expose China to both internal and external danger. Revolution would bring civil war, destruction, and chaos, and would also create two other dangers. One was that a military strong man might seize power and even attempt to found a new dynasty. The other was that the foreign powers might intervene and that such action might lead to the partition of China.

The revolutionaries flatly denied both possibilities. Sun Yat-sen, in his 1906 speech, recognized the existence of these problems but said that the revolutionaries need only avoid a struggle among themselves. If some nourished the ambition to establish a new dynasty, there would be a civil war that would give the foreign powers their opportunity; but as long as his comrades aimed at the establishment of a "people's government" (*kuo-min cheng-fu*) by a "common people's revolution" (*p'ing-min ke-ming*) there was no danger.[43]

This thesis was the subject of a lengthy explanation by Wang Ching-wei. Wang maintained that a revolution created the hazard of internal chaos only if its aims were not suited to the particular society in which it took place. If its aims were suitable, the destruction that must inevitably accompany a revolution could bring only good results. The only point to consider was whether the destruction really furthered the chosen ends. If it did, it was not destruction but improvement. The goals of the revolutionary movement were to establish a nation-state, a constitutional democracy, and state socialism. The destruction was to be directed at the barbarian conquerors and their evil despotism. The aims were good and suited to China, the means furthered the ends, and there was therefore no danger.[44]

[43] Sun Yat-sen, "San Min Chu I yü Chung-kuo min-tsu chih ch'ien-t'u," pp. 10–11.

[44] Wang Ching-wei, "Po ke-ming k'e-i sheng nei-luan shuo," *Min-pao*, No. 9,

Wang turned to Chinese history for evidence to support these propositions. In an argument that is not easy to follow he claimed there had been four "people's revolutions" (*kuo-min ke-ming*) in Chinese history.[45] These he distinguished from other dynastic changes in that the four were not aimed merely at establishing a new dynasty. He then drew the moral that no revolutionary should harbor any longing to be emperor, or more fundamentally, that the revolutionaries should be dedicated to higher and more constructive goals. Then they would not fight among themselves, and the revolution would not be destructive.[46]

The revolutionaries did not deal directly with the question of the disorder that might be caused by revolution. The point they sought to make was that if the overthrow of a dynasty was in accord with the objective historical situation, the merest push would topple it with scarcely any effort on the rebels' part.[47] The only danger then would be that the victors would fight among themselves for the spoils. But, as Wang put it, the collapse would be a "natural" development,[48] not a violent revolution. In other words, if the Manchus were weak enough, their regime would fall virtually without a struggle.

Despite the frequent references to Liang's arguments, this effort was not only an answer to the reformers but also a warning to some of the less "progressive" elements in the revolutionary movement. Wang was far more concerned to point out the dangers implicit in any attempt to establish a new dynasty than he was to refute the charge that revolution meant internal disorder. At the stage of their movement when they were debating with Liang, the revolutionaries tended to minimize the disorder that would accompany the overthrow of the Manchus rather than acknowledge that it was necessary and healthy. There was no exaltation of "struggle" as a moral or political purga-

---

pp. 27–30. Hu Han-min later summarized the same argument, referring his readers to Wang's fuller discussion. See "Yü *Kokumin shimbun* lun Chih-na ke-ming-tang shu," *Min-pao*, No. 11, pp. 131–32.

[45] Wang, "Po ke-ming k'e-i sheng nei-luan shuo," p. 31. The four were those that overthrew Ch'in, Wang Mang, Sui, and Yüan. Wang thus departed from the T'ung-meng-hui Manifesto, which had claimed that former revolutions were "heroes' revolutions (*ying-hsiung ke-ming*) but today we have a national revolution." Teng and Fairbank, *China's Response*, p. 227. Teng and Fairbank translate *Kuo-min ke-ming* as "national revolution."

[46] Wang Ching-wei, "Po ke-ming k'e-i sheng nei-luan shuo," p. 34.

[47] *Ibid.*, pp. 34–35.

[48] *Ibid.*, p. 35.

tive, such as one finds among later Chinese revolutionaries. But the
T'ung-meng-hui made no secret of its fear that a would-be emperor
would spring from its midst.

The second part of the reformers' argument was answered more
directly. Sun Yat-sen sounded the keynote for the revolutionaries.
The only way to avoid the partition of China by the foreign powers,
he wrote in 1904, was to have an energetic government that would
earn their respect. It was the feeble Manchu government that invited aggression; a vigorous new government would not.[49]

Other writings elaborated on this theme. Sun himself added that
the corruption and backwardness of the Manchus were a threat to
world peace and the balance of power, and argued that the Russo-
Japanese War would not have occurred if China had been able to
play a more positive role in world affairs.[50] Moreover, he told his
American audience, the Manchus were anti-foreign but the Chinese
were not. China had accepted Buddhism, a Chinese dynasty had
welcomed the Jesuits, and China had a long history of overseas trade;
it was the Manchus who had "prohibited the entire country from having intercourse with foreigners. . . ."[51] Thus if China would establish "a civilized government," benefits would accrue not only to the
Chinese but to the whole world. The new government would open all
of China to foreign trade, railroads would traverse the length and
breadth of the country, the production of raw materials would increase steadily, foreign goods would be sold in China in ever-increas-
ing amounts, and China's international trade would be far greater
than ever before. It was therefore in the interests of the Western
powers to aid in the establishment of a new government in China.
"America is the leader of Western civilization, a Christian people,
the teacher of our future new government. Are there Lafayettes
among you?"[52]

[49] Sun Yat-sen, "Po Pao-huang pao," *Kuo-fu ch'üan-chi*, VI, 227.
[50] "Chung-kuo wen-t'i chih chen chieh-chüeh," p. 221.
[51] *Ibid.*, p. 222.
[52] *Ibid.*, p. 226. This is another example of Sun's ability to make a simple and artful
appeal to a particular audience. He had begun this article by noting that the
United States had a special interest in China's problems because of American
interest in trade and in China's possibilities as a market (p. 220). It is also typical
of the revolutionaries' shift around 1903–4 from an emphasis on opposition to
Western imperialism to attacks on the Manchus combined with appeals for Western
support.

The arguments were then that revolution would produce a new, vigorous, and stable government and so would prevent rather than cause partition, and that it was in the interest of the foreign powers to have such a government in China. Both points were discussed at length by Wang Ching-wei and Hu Han-min and frequently referred to in T'ung-meng-hui proclamations and other writings.[53] Little of substance was added, but several points are worth noting. There were repeated affirmations that the new government would honor all existing treaties between China and other countries, and that every effort would be made to ensure that no harm came to the foreigners' persons or possessions during the revolution.[54] Sun Yat-sen accompanied such assurances with appeals for foreign assistance, and Hu Han-min asked that the foreign powers observe neutrality.[55] This concern for the attitude of other countries helps to explain why the revolutionaries' anti-Manchu writings contained relatively few references to China's treatment by the foreign powers. For the time being, at least, the revolutionaries did not feel strong enough to assert any intention of abrogating the privileges that the Manchus had been forced to grant to the powers; moreover, they were anxious to obtain foreign aid.

In answering the reformers' charges that revolution would lead to disorder and partition, the T'ung-meng-hui writers offered chiefly the hopes that the Manchus would collapse without great resistance, that the revolutionary ranks would not be split by a struggle for power, and that the foreign powers would see that they stood to profit from the revolution. The only attempt to formulate a planned transition to republican government was Sun Yat-sen's three-stage program.

[53] See the following: (a) Wang Ching-wei, "Po ke-ming k'e-i chao kua-fen shuo," *Min-pao*, No. 6, pp. 17–39; (b) Hu Han-min, "Min-pao chih liu ta chu-i," *Min-pao*, No. 3, pp. 14–21; (c) Hu Han-min, "Yü *Kokumin shimbun* lun Chih-na ke-ming-tang shu," pp. 131–34.

[54] For the reference to honoring treaties see *HHKM*, II, 33, and Hu Han-min's "Min-pao chih liu ta chu-i," p. 21. For the care to be taken with regard to foreign interests during and after the revolution see *ibid.*, p. 17, and Wang's "Po ke-ming k'e-i chao kua-fen shuo," pp. 18–20. Note the attempt, as in Wang's article (p. 18), to distinguish between the Boxers (whose "aim was to support the Ch'ing and wipe out the foreigners") and the T'ung-meng-hui (which "is anti-Manchu and not anti-foreign"). Foreign readers were undoubtedly expected to recall that the Manchus had also supported the Boxers.

[55] "Min-pao chih liu ta chu-i," *Min-pao*, No. 3, pp. 20–21.

Sun's plan was first adumbrated in the T'ung-meng-hui Manifesto. There it was stipulated that the establishment of constitutional government would take place within nine years after the outbreak of revolution. The first step would be to eliminate "the accumulated evils" of the Manchu regime along with the government itself. Among the evils to be abolished were shaving the head and wearing the queue, foot-binding, and opium-smoking, as well as official malpractices. The changes would require a maximum of three years, the first stage of Sun's program, termed the period of "government by military law." The manifesto stipulated, however, that "where real results are achieved before the end of three years, the military law shall be lifted and a provisional constitution shall be enacted."[56]

The second stage was to be "government by a provisional constitution." In this period, scheduled to last six years, the people were to elect local officials, and "all rights and duties of the Military Government toward the people and those of the people toward the government shall be regulated by the provisional constitution, which shall be observed by the Military Government, the local councils, and the people. . . . Six years after the securing of peace in the nation the provisional constitution shall be annulled and the constitution shall be promulgated."[57] Finally, there would be "government under the constitution. . . . The military and administrative powers of the Military Government shall be annulled; the people shall elect the president, and elect the members of parliament to organize the parliament. The administrative matters of the nation shall proceed according to the provisions of the constitution."[58]

Perhaps the revolutionaries could have used this outline as a basis for approaching the many questions it left unsolved. The idea of introducing constitutional government by stages, the idea that later became Sun's well-known concept of tutelage, offered at least one possible starting point, but it also had its dangers. The dangers inherent in a concept of tutelage are familiar enough that no discussion of them is necessary here. All that needs to be mentioned is that the

[56] "The Manifesto of the T'ung-meng-hui." Teng and Fairbank, *China's Response*, pp. 228–29. No distinction was drawn between the objectionable practices that had been introduced by the Manchus and those that antedated the Ch'ing.

[57] *Ibid.*, p. 229.

[58] *Ibid.*

principle of tutelage, like many other ideas of the revolutionaries, did not distinguish them clearly from Liang Ch'i-ch'ao and his supporters Liang's idea of "enlightened absolutism" was a very similar concept The difference lay in who would do the tutoring and how long it would take.[59]

It cannot yet be said with certainty that the revolutionaries did not address themselves to the complexities of sweeping away "accumulated evils," devising, promulgating, and enforcing provisional and permanent constitutions, effecting transitions from stage to stage, holding elections, in short the key problems of actually implementing a new form of government. Indications are that the revolutionaries did not deal with these questions in any significant detail, but the subject awaits further research.[60] One remains curious to know how their solutions to these problems would compare with those of the Manchus and Liang Ch'i-ch'ao.

One problem the revolutionaries did face was the relation between military and civil authority in the time of transition. It was Sun Yat-sen who attempted a solution, although his idea comes to us through the writings of Wang Ching-wei. Wang described Sun's plan in an effort to refute Liang's charge that a revolution would lead only to dictatorship under a military strong man.

Sun recognized that the aim of establishing democracy would conflict with the need to rely on military force, and that military men could not be expected to relinquish voluntarily the power they would acquire as leaders of a successful revolution. The important thing was to determine beforehand the relationship between civil and military authority.[61] At a time when troops were being used, he said, "absolute power" (*chuan-ch'üan*) should reside with the military, since the power of the people was still undeveloped. However, he added:

[59] For a fuller discussion of the tutelage concept as employed by Liang and the revolutionaries, see Chang P'eng-yüan, *Liang Ch'i-ch'ao* . . . ," pp. 235–41.

[60] My tentative conclusions are based on the incomplete materials available to me. These are substantial enough to give me some confidence that after the spring of 1907, in view of the conditions at that time, the revolutionaries did not deal with such matters to any significant degree. But the available materials were not sufficiently complete, especially for the period after mid-1908, to permit firm conclusions about what the revolutionaries did not discuss. References below to their omissions should be understood in this light.

[61] Wang Ching-wei, "Min-tsu ti kuo-min," Part II, pp. 20–21.

. . . the two should not encroach upon each other but must support each other. As military power advances one degree, civil power also advances one degree. When peace is established, military power is transferred to the civil authority. All is then peaceful and perfect. To determine these relations there should be a provisional constitution. At the beginning of the revolution there must be a military government established. This military government has absolute power in regard to military affairs and political power as well. For example, when a *hsien* is pacified, the military government and the people draw up an agreement providing for their rights and duties toward each other. The military government issues orders for the organization of local administrative offices and appoints officials to manage them, while the people organize a local assembly. This assembly is not immediately like the assemblies of modern republics. Its chief duty is to see whether the work of the military government is in accord with the provisional constitution. When *hsien* B is pacified, then *hsien* A joins with it and they jointly observe the constitution; they are then joined by *hsien* C and so on throughout every province and prefecture. If the people violate the provisional constitution, the military government can compel them to comply with it. If the military government violates it, the territories under its jurisdiction can join together and refuse to carry out their duties, and withdraw recognition of the military government. At the beginning of the revolution, with no firm base yet established and outlaw elements very strong, even the most stupid of men will not take to killing each other. Then, after the military success, with the assemblies of eighteen provinces on guard at its rear, the military government would find the way to absolute power blocked even if it sought such power.[62]

Sun concluded with the observation that this experience in local government would provide a basis for participation in full constitutional government under the republic.

Sun had pointed out a basic problem, but the solution he proposed was only a beginning. There remained the question of how civil authority was to be asserted. The role to be played by the military also remained undefined. Relationships between the military government and the people, the method by which local assemblies would be formed, the nature of the provisional constitution, and other fundamentals of government were not yet specified. Finally, as Liang Ch'i-ch'ao pointed out, if the military government violated the provisional constitution, the only recourse Sun left to the people was rebellion; and unless the revolutionary leaders were men of superior character such as the world had never seen, Sun's provisional constitution would remain but a scrap of paper.[63]

Wang Ching-wei then attempted to answer Liang's criticisms of the provisional constitution as an instrument of transition. Law, he declared, was meaningless if it was merely a collection of written clauses that did not express the beliefs and needs of society. But law that was a manifestation of those beliefs and needs would be effective. From this Wang drew the conclusion that "if the principles of nation and citizenship (*min-tsu chu-i* and *kuo-min chu-i*) are widely accepted by the people, the provisional constitution will be produced in response to their needs." [64] The unanswered questions were how such principles were to become widely accepted and, more specifically, whether the overthrow of the Manchus and the founding of a republic were essential preliminaries.

The dangers implicit in the tutelage concept emerged clearly. There is evidence that at least one prominent revolutionary writer regarded the period of military government as one in which drastic action could be taken without fear of opposition. Feng Tzu-yu argued that a "social revolution" should be initiated as soon as the revolutionary army went into action, because the revolutionaries would then have the power to act arbitrarily.[65]

The three-stage formula, so far as I can now ascertain, was all that the revolutionaries presented as a program for establishing their new government. The only other proposal that even remotely resembled such a program was put forth by Wang Ching-wei only a few

---

[63] For Liang's criticisms of Sun's scheme see *Hsin-min ts'ung-pao*, No. 75, pp. 15–17.

[64] "Po Hsin-min ts'ung-pao tsui-chin chih fei ke-ming lun," p. 16.

[65] "Min-sheng chu-i yü Chung-kuo cheng-chih ke-ming chih ch'ien-t'u," *Min-pao*, No. 4, pp. 108–9. Feng called the military government a "completely arbitrary (*wu-tuan*) government." *Ibid.*, p. 115. Feng's concept of "social revolution" meant first the establishment of what he called "state socialism" and later a transition to "complete socialism."

months after his attempt to elaborate on Sun's. In the intervening period the Manchus had formally announced for the first time that they would promulgate a constitution and reorganize their administration. Although Wang had persistently denounced the Manchus' proposals as fraudulent, he welcomed them when they were enacted as an opportunity for the Chinese to become more active in local government. If the reforms were meant seriously, the Manchus would be obliged to undertake a wide variety of tasks they had long neglected, including census-taking, repair and construction of public works, communications facilities, opening mines and schools, and instituting relief programs. Obviously, he said, the Manchus would have to depend upon localities to do much of this work themselves. This was the opportunity, said Wang: "In my estimation, *affairs that have not yet been attended to are potential powers. Whoever is first to deal with them is the one to seize the power.*"[66] Wang urged the revolutionaries to participate in such work as a means of building local power groups into self-governing units, stressing police and educational work as two particularly fruitful routes to power and influence. But Wang never went beyond this germ of the idea of using the Manchus' reforms to effect a gradual liberation of local areas from central control. Certainly he never even hinted at any way to move from this into republicanism.

The idea is of interest in two ways. One is that it represents a qualification of Wang's otherwise uncompromising belief that the Manchus' reforms could benefit only themselves. Another is that the revolutionaries left unexplored this moderate course of political action. Wang's insight into the possibilities offered by this course was acute. But the fact that the ideas he sowed failed to bear fruit suggests the planting season for such fragile hopes had passed. It was October of 1906 when Wang's article appeared, and by that darkening autumn the chill climate of Chinese politics was already suitable only for hardier seedlings. Anti-Manchuism sank into Chinese soil hungry roots that left little nourishment for theories of republicanism or carefully planned transitions to a new polity.

After a full year of the T'ung-meng-hui's and *Min-pao's* existence the struggle between government and anti-government forces had

---

[66] Wang Ching-wei, "Man-chou li-hsien . . . ," p. 48. Emphasis in original.

sharpened and deepened. The air had been filled with such deafening recrimination and invective that quiet gradualist proposals were not likely to be heard. The revolutionaries' plan for making the transition to republican government remained Sun Yat-sen's three-stage formula, in which the first step was to eliminate the Manchu regime by force. The revolutionaries hoped they might then establish a military government that within three years would succeed "in eradicating all traditional evils and abuses." [67] No less immediate a prospect of a new world, no less radical a plan, no less utopian a dream would satisfy the new Chinese intelligentsia.

TRANSITION TO WHAT?

The revolutionaries devoted little attention to the specific form of their future government. There was much theorizing about parliaments and sovereignty and thinking in general terms about elections, equality, freedom, and democracy, but only one effort was made to sketch the actual institutional framework within which these ideals would be translated into action. This was Sun Yat-sen's proposal concerning the constitution of the future Republic of China, which he set forth in a speech in 1906.

Sun began by citing the United States constitution as the best of all such written documents but said that it was now outdated. Although it had been amended many times, it had undergone no basic change. In the meantime the country had advanced rapidly, and its constitution was no longer suitable. For this reason — Sun at first gave no other — China need not copy the system of the United States.

It seems odd that of all the reasons Sun might have given for not imitating the constitution of another country (including the danger of applying to Chinese society the practices of a very different society), he should have chosen the reason that the American system was no longer suited to the United States itself. Sun did not stop to explain in what ways history had overtaken the United States constitution. He was more concerned to show that the system was inadequate, and indeed it soon appeared that it was not changes over time but a basic weakness of the system itself to which Sun was objecting. His aim was to see to it that China would not follow but would lead. "My

[67] "The Manifesto of the T'ung-meng-hui," Teng and Fairbank, *China's Response*, p. 229.

idea is that the constitution of the future Republic of China should create a new principle, to be called 'the five-power division.'" [68]

This was Sun's first pronouncement of the now familiar scheme for which he was to campaign so energetically during the next two decades.[69] To the legislative, executive, and judicial functions Sun proposed to add examination and control. The examination branch, a fourth independent organ of government, would have the function of circumventing the election and appointment of unqualified government officials. All public servants would be required to submit to examinations, supervised by the examination branch. For examples of what he hoped to avoid, Sun pointed to the United States, where men whose only talent was oratory were often elected to office and numerous patronage appointments were given to unqualified party workers.

The control branch would be concerned with "supervision and impeachment," and would prevent the legislative branch from dominating the executive. In the United States, Sun maintained, the Congress used these powers with such telling effect that it often established a "Congressional absolutism." Only a president of the caliber of Lincoln, McKinley, or Theodore Roosevelt could maintain executive independence. Sun again emphasized that executive power must be vested in an independent branch of the government.[70]

This was virtually all Sun had to say about China's future constitution. And the T'ung-meng-hui writers had nothing to add. In the eighteen issues of the *Min-pao* published after Sun made this speech, and in the few other T'ung-meng-hui writings available, there are no further discussions of the political system that would be es-

[68] "San Min Chu I yü Chung-kuo min-tsu chih ch'ien-t'u," p. 15.

[69] Sun's later formulation is available in many editions and translations as "The Five-Power Constitution." This earliest expression of it has never been translated.

[70] *Ibid.*, p. 16. Sun took note of China's traditional examination and censorial institutions. He called the former "bad" and the latter "the slave of the emperor." In 1924 he said that these two branches of government came "from old China" where "they were very effective." To link them with the three branches common in the West was "to combine the best from China and the best from other countries. . . ." See *San Min Chu I*, trans. Frank W. Price, pp. 356–57.

McKinley's place in the trio of American presidents is unexplained. Perhaps his Far Eastern policy made him seem to be a strong president. Note above Liang Ch'i-ch'ao's similar statement concerning the power of a parliament. Like the revolutionary-modernizers, Liang was also interested in having a strong central government. See pp. 87–90, 112–13.

tablished after the revolution. It should be noted, however, that only four numbers of *Min-pao* went to press between Sun's speech and his departure from Tokyo; a fifth appeared before Wang Ching-wei left for Southeast Asia. Subsequently *Min-pao* was dominated by Chang Ping-lin, who was critical of republicanism.

What then could the revolutionaries say when Liang Ch'i-ch'ao maintained that China was not ready for a republic? How indeed does one justify the adoption of a form of government that one has not described? Now deeply pessimistic about how rapidly China could move toward democracy,[71] Liang had stressed that for republican government to be successful, the people had to have reached a certain level of education and had to possess the habit of participating in political affairs. Parliament, after all, was the most important organ of a republican government; were the Chinese people ready to manage complex affairs ranging from impeachment and law-making to evaluating budgets? Would politically immature people fulfill their duty to vote? Would they not be subject to bribes, pressures, and selfish interests? [72] Moreover, there were a host of practical problems to deal with: defining what constituted a Chinese citizen for voting purposes, delimiting voting districts, taking a census, appointing officials and police to supervise elections, devising civil and criminal codes, and many other things as well. In sum, constitutional government could not be established overnight or without careful planning and preparatory work.[73]

The revolutionaries' answers were that speed was of the essence, that Liang's was the gloomy pessimism of the timid, and that he underestimated the Chinese people and failed to see the many embryonic elements in China's past that fitted her for democracy. Past rulers, especially the Ch'ing, had aborted the embryos, and the Manchus,

[71] Philip C. Huang, "A Confucian Liberal: Liang Ch'i-ch'ao in Action and Thought," p. 127, points out that Liang's reversal on this issue was so drastic that he had even become elitist.

[72] Liang Ch'i-ch'ao, "K'ai-ming chuan-chih lun," *Hsin-min ts'ung-pao*, No. 77, pp. 1–6. This was before the Manchus had announced their intention to initiate constitutional government. Liang was arguing here against any kind of constitutional government for China, not only a republican form.

[73] *Ibid.*, pp. 6–9. See above, Chapter 1, for the discussion of Liang's change of mood and thinking after his visit to the United States in 1903. Further analysis of his concept of "enlightened absolutism" may be found in Philip C. Huang, "A Confucian Liberal . . . ," pp. 129–33.

as barbarians, could not conceive anew such civilized forms. Finally, China could learn from the examples of the West and Japan.

The possibility of building upon Chinese precedents and learning from the West and Japan became the revolutionaries' chief arguments against Liang and on behalf of their program. First, the T'ung-meng-hui insisted that China should have a republic immediately because a republic was the most advanced form of government. They rejected the views that republican government should develop slowly and gradually and that China should first have a constitutional monarchy. As Sun Yat-sen put it, "the future of China is like building a railroad. Thus if we were now building a railroad, would we use the first locomotive ever invented or today's improved and most efficient one?" [74] Besides, Sun had also written, first to establish constitutional monarchy and then a republic would require two revolutions instead of one. To destroy once was serious enough. Why do it twice? [75] Sun, it appeared, had ruled out any possibility of peaceful and gradual change.

Second, it was possible for China to have a republic immediately because her people had both the native talents and the necessary experience. Sun asked: are the Chinese inferior to the Hawaiians, who were uncivilized and even cannibalistic a century before but after contact with foreigners "in one leap became a republic"? Or to the American Negroes, who had been slaves but were now free citizens of a republic? The answer was obvious. In fact, the level of the Chinese people was "somewhat higher" than that of other peoples.[76] As for experience, Sun pointed to China's "village and clan self-government," which, he said, included conducting trials and managing defense, education, and road repair. China might not be up to Western standards, but she was not entirely lacking in experience, and the matter was after all one of degree rather than of the presence or absence of experience.[77]

Ch'en T'ien-hua likewise claimed that the Chinese people had developed institutions much like the organs of local self-government that were so esteemed in the West, and had done so without govern-

---

[74] Sun Yat-sen, "Chung-kuo ying chien-she kung-ho-kuo," p. 4. For Liang Ch'i-ch'ao's reply to this remark see *Hsin-min ts'ung-pao*, No. 75, pp. 25–27.

[75] "Po Pao-huang pao," p. 230.

[76] Sun Yat-sen, "Chung-kuo ying chien-she kung-ho-kuo," p. 4.

[77] "Po Pao-huang pao," p. 229.

ment leadership or formal training in government and law. The only problem was to release their natural talents from the bonds that held them under the Manchu regime.[78]

Hu Han-min added that "the greatest difficulty in establishing a constitutional government, as experienced by other countries, is the struggle of the common people against both the monarch and the nobility." Since China had no nobility, and in fact no class differences at all, the establishment of constitutional government would be easier in China than in other countries.[79] Hu confidently predicted that China would have a successful revolution and republic "because Chinese nationalism and democratic thought" were "well developed." [80]

Wang Ching-wei made a more systematic examination of China's past. Contrary to what Liang alleged, the Chinese people had possessed the spirit of liberty, equality, and fraternity, although it had been lost in *Chan-kuo* times (B.C. 403–221). Therefore, since "constitutional democracy is a system that is based upon this spirit, the spirit of the system must be suited to our people." [81] Wang never explained in what form this spirit had manifested itself. But he also found that China had traces of other essentials of modern constitutional government in her past, such as the concept of reciprocal rights and duties between the state and the people. "Since the time of Yao and Shun, China has known that the people are the basis of the state." In the Three Dynasties, Wang continued, it was accepted that the ruler was obliged to obey the will of Heaven, which was that the people be cared for. If he did not, Heaven "would cast

---

[78] Ch'en T'ien-hua, "Lun Chung-kuo i kai-ch'uang min-chu cheng-t'i," pp. 42–44. Ch'en, unfortunately for the revolutionaries, concluded this article with the assertion that between revolution and constitutional democracy there should be a stage of "enlightened absolutism." Liang Ch'i-ch'ao, of course, pounced upon this remark to attack the *Min-pao* writers for contradicting each other, as well as to ridicule Ch'en's views (see *Hsin-min ts'ung-pao*, No. 75, pp. 39–45, for his discussion of Ch'en's article; pp. 43–45 deal with the "enlightened absolutism" issue). Wang Ching-wei then replied that a difference of opinion between two men could not be termed a contradiction, adding that this was a time for discussion and the free exchange of ideas rather than complete identity of views. (See *Min-pao*, No. 4, p. 3.)

[79] "The Six Principles of the People's Report," deBary *et al.*, *Sources of Chinese Tradition*, p. 764.

[80] *Ibid.*, p. 765.

[81] "Po Hsin-min ts'ung-pao tsui-chin chih fei ke-ming lun," p. 29.

severe punishment down upon him." In that period, therefore, the power of the Chinese people to control the ruler was greater than in the times that followed. "This was the spirit of China's moral law." [82] This spirit had to be renewed, adjusted to the modern world, and combined with Western ideas and practices, but its mere existence simplified China's task.

Wang believed that the problem was further eased by the opportunity China had to learn from the experience of other countries. Like every other T'ung-meng-hui writer known to me, Wang held that in this way China could avoid the mistakes other countries had made and accomplish in decades what had taken the others centuries to do. He did, however, stress more than any of the other revolutionary writers that because each country had its own peculiar characteristics and problems, the form of constitutional democracy varied from one country to another. [83] But while he noted that China would also have its own unique version and could not simply copy from the United States, England, or France, he made no attempt to describe that system or the particular problems China would have to deal with.

Similarly, Ch'en T'ien-hua said that Japan had in forty years leaped from China's level to the status of a "first-class world power." Could not China, with her vastly greater size and population, learn from Japan and the West and become a leading power still faster? Ch'en noted the rapid progress that had taken place in teaching methods and called it to the attention of those who said that because China would find it difficult to educate all her people democracy would not work. [84] He added that one of the Chinese people's most serious faults was their lack of respect for the military and general absence of military spirit. If China's education became equal to Japan's, and her military officers as able, then her armed forces would be on a par with her neighbor's. Ch'en then discussed at some length the need for the government to foster a martial spirit as Japan had done. [85] Sun Yat-sen lauded Japan in similar terms. Now that the students had seen with their own eyes what Japan had accomplished, he added, a new tide of reform was taking shape. [86]

[82] *Ibid.*, p. 30.          [83] *Ibid.*
[84] Ch'en T'ien-hua, "Lun Chung-kuo i kai-ch'uang min-chu cheng-t'i," pp. 44–45.
[85] *Ibid.*, pp. 46–47.
[86] "Chung-kuo ying chien-she kung-ho-kuo," pp. 2–3.

It is a striking feature of the revolutionaries' interest in the experience of other countries that they spoke less of copying or imitating than they did of learning from other countries' mistakes and avoiding the problems that had plagued other states. Even in the case of Japan, it seemed to be less important to them to propose a model than to show that the goal they wanted to reach could be reached. The interesting point concerns what they wanted. When Wang Ching-wei spoke of compressing centuries into decades he was referring to the development of democratic ideas and institutions, and his objects of study were the English, American, and French systems. His dependence on German political theorists can be traced to the training he received in Japan and the limited writings with which he was acquainted. He seems to have genuinely believed that those whose views he accepted, Laband and Jellinek, were representatives of a republican or at least anti-monarchical current of thought. And it was the United States constitution that he proposed as a model for China's. Ch'en T'ien-hua and Sun Yat-sen, on the other hand, were more concerned with China's becoming a world power. Indeed, their reference to Japan was precisely in these terms; they certainly were not pointing to her as an example of republicanism or even of constitutional democracy.[87]

It is also noteworthy that those revolutionaries who discussed democracy at all spent fully as much time searching their own past for democratic traces as they did examining the theory and practice of democracy in the modern world. Before attempting to explain this phenomenon it may be helpful to examine some of the revolutionaries' other writings that also exhibit these and some other features of revolutionary thought.

It will be recalled that the T'ung-meng-hui writers considered their revolution to have three aspects. In addition to a racial revolution that would expel the Manchus and restore Chinese sovereignty and a political revolution that would replace the imperial system with a republican form of government, there was to be a social revolution aimed at a dimly visualized social and economic equality.[88] The revo-

---

[87] In a far more thorough study of Ch'en T'ien-hua than can be attempted here, his central concern with making China strong emerges clearly. See Ernest P. Young, "Ch'en T'ien-hua (1875–1905): A Chinese Nationalist," *Papers on China*, XIII, 113–62.

[88] See pp. 106–7 for Sun Yat-sen's summary of the aims of the revolution; note

lutionaries were less clear about the third part of their program than any other. Indeed Sun Yat-sen in one speech advocated promoting a social revolution but also seemed to plead for preventing one. Just a few moments before he described the threefold revolution, Sun observed that Europe and the United States were faced with problems that made social revolution there "absolutely unavoidable." [89] In China these problems were still minor, but if she waited too long to solve them, they could not be dealt with except by revolution. And revolution "is to be used only when absolutely necessary." He concluded: "When we carry out the national and political revolutions (*min-tsu ke-ming, cheng-chih ke-ming*), we must at the same time try to improve (*kai-liang*) the social and economic order and prevent a social revolution. This is truly [our] greatest responsibility." [90] Here Sun seemed to imply that China did not yet require a social revolution but only "improvement," and he said clearly that the principle of people's livelihood was the guide to such improvement.[91]

Was social change to be gradual and moderate? Chu Chih-hsin, the T'ung-meng-hui's chief writer on social revolution, disagreed. Indeed, one of his chief contributions to revolutionary literature was his widely hailed article entitled "The Social Revolution Should Proceed Simultaneously with the Political Revolution." [92] Indeed, no other T'ung-meng-hui writer suggested that social revolution was unnecessary, although Hu Han-min at times implied it. Since Sun

also the T'ung-meng-hui Manifesto in Teng and Fairbank, *China's Response*, pp. 227–28, and the first three of the *Min-pao*'s Six Principles in deBary, *et al.*, *Sources*, pp. 762–67. This aspect of revolutionary thinking has been studied by Western scholars more than any other. See Harold Schiffrin, "Sun Yat-sen's Early Land Policy: The Origin and Meaning of 'Equalization of Land Rights,'" *Journal of Asian Studies*, XVI, 549–64; Robert A. Scalapino and Harold Schiffrin, "Early Socialist Currents in the Chinese Revolutionary Movement," *ibid.*, XVIII, 321–42; and Schiffrin and Pow-key Sohn, "Henry George on Two Continents: A Comparative Study in the Diffusion of Ideas," *Comparative Studies in Society and History*, II, 85–109.

[89] "San Min Chu I yü Chung-kuo min-tsu chih ch'ien-t'u," p. 12.

[90] *Ibid.*, p. 11. Years later Sun was to insist that he opposed revolution as an answer to "social questions" and preferred "peaceful methods." See *San Min Chu I* (Price translation), *op. cit.*, pp. 409–11.

[91] "San Min Chu I yü Chung-kuo . . . ," p. 12.

[92] "Lun she-hui ke-ming tang yü cheng-chih ke-ming ping-hsing," *Min-pao*, No. 5, pp. 43–66. But see below, p. 143 for the similarity between Sun and Chu.

himself was inconsistent rather than deviant, it is best to accept social revolution as a T'ung-meng-hui principle. There was less discussion of it and perhaps therefore less agreement; or perhaps because it was not agreed upon it was not fully discussed.

What did social revolution mean to its advocates? And how was it to be carried out? As far as the revolutionists' attempts to answer these questions are concerned, I have nothing to add to what other scholars (cited in note 88) have told us. But it is worth re-emphasizing that the T'ung-meng-hui writers without exception called for the establishment of some kind of "socialism." Also without exception, they undertook to explain its meaning and its development in the West only in the most general terms and, what is most puzzling, without explaining why it was necessary for China. "There are many socialist theories, but they all aim at levelling economic classes," wrote Hu Han-min, who had said China had no classes.[93] Chu Chih-hsin called for the establishment of "state socialism" and the elimination of private property and the division that it caused between the rich and the poor; except in the case of Russia, he pointed out, it was precisely for the purpose of wiping out laissez-faire that socialism had arisen. Chu defined laissez-faire as "the system of absolute recognition of private property."[94] The inequalities inherent in this system were not so serious in China as in the West, but they would be before long if China did not carry out a social revolution.[95] The reasons for the existence of these inequalities and why they were bound to worsen were not examined.

Thus, like Sun Yat-sen, Chu seemed to be calling for a social revolution in order to avoid a more violent social revolution. Their observation of the West told them that social revolution was imminent there, and it almost seemed as if their demand for Chinese equality in the world made it mandatory that China move in the same pattern as other nations. Sun, however, did not share Chu's position on the abolition of private property.

As we have noted in discussing the revolutionaries' political ideas,

[93] Hu Han-min, "The Six Principles of the People's Report," deBary, *et al.*, *Sources*, p. 766.

[94] Chu Chih-hsin, "Lun she-hui ke-ming tang yü cheng-chih ke-ming ping-hsing," p. 47. For a summary of this article see Scalapino and Schiffrin, "Early Socialist Currents . . . ," pp. 329–31.

[95] Chu Chih-hsin, "Lun she-hui . . . ," pp. 49–50.

they spoke more of studying the West to learn how to avoid its mistakes than of imitating it. In fact this emphasis was even more pronounced in the economic sphere than in the political, since there were those who wanted to imitate the American or British political systems in full or in part but none who spoke of copying Western or even Japanese social or economic institutions. Of course the revolutionaries wanted to "modernize," but it is remarkable that despite their frequent reference to the Japanese example, none undertook to analyze her economic transformation. For the Chinese revolutionaries "social revolution" meant building "socialism," which was justified not in terms of its superiority as a method of organizing society for industrialization in particular or "modernization" in general but chiefly as a way to secure social and economic justice.

Each T'ung-meng-hui writer stressed that socialism aimed at erasing the line between rich and poor, or at making the nation's wealth the property of all the people, or at guaranteeing each person employment and a fair share of the wealth produced. Feng Tzu-yu did mention that the single-tax system would also increase China's productive power and provide the government with a steady and substantial income, but he stressed repeatedly that socialism's chief accomplishment would be to eliminate economic inequality; indeed, it would even "advance mankind's spirit of morality and honor." [96] Sun Yat-sen also stressed that his *min-sheng* principle would eliminate poverty, although he placed perhaps equal emphasis on his belief that the single tax would make China "the richest country on earth." [97] In general, when the revolutionaries discussed their social and economic goals they emphasized the benefits to individuals that would result from greater social justice for all; they put less stress on "the nation" or "society" or similar abstractions than when they discussed their political goals. It would seem to be of some importance that socialism came to China with so strong and clear an emphasis on its humanitarian principles, but this is a subject that cannot be explored here.[98]

[96] Feng Tzu-yu, "Min-sheng chu-i yü Chung-kuo cheng-chih ke-ming chih ch'ien-t'u," p. 104.

[97] *Kuo-fu ch'üan-chi*, III, 14.

[98] For further discussion of this and related questions see Martin Bernal, "The Triumph of Anarchism over Marxism, 1906–1907," *China in Revolution: The First Phase, 1900–1913*, pp. 97–142.

The revolutionists usually noted that they could take only the idea of socialism from abroad, since it had nowhere been put into practice. Feng Tzu-yu, who found "state socialism" thriving in Germany and Japan (and believed it was a necessary step toward "complete socialism"), praised these countries' nationalization of various industries but declared that the "first principle" of state socialism was "equalization of land rights" (*p'ing-chün ti-ch'üan*), the doctrine of Henry George.[99] Thus Feng came around to full agreement with his comrades. And it is in their identification of socialism's first principle with such vague land programs and with the ideas of Henry George that the revolutionaries' predicament becomes clearest to us. For while it is clear that they had some understanding of the broad aims of socialism, they had not had the time to analyze the difficulties of applying it to China. In their pressing circumstances there could be no deliberate and systematic comparison of the Chinese problems that socialism was intended to solve and the particular evils that concerned Western socialists. Moreover, knowledge of the differences among different socialist schools was almost nonexistent at this early stage of China's intellectual revolution; the very selection of George as their master suggests some of the limitations imposed by circumstances upon the revolutionaries in their study of George, socialism, and China's economic and social problems.[100]

[99] Feng Tzu-yu, "Min-sheng chu-i . . . ," p. 110. "P'ing-chün ti-ch'üan" has been commonly translated as "equalization of landownership" (see, for example, Teng and Fairbank, *China's Response*, p. 228). Feng, however, also called it (p. 114) "land nationalization" and said that it meant the abolition of private ownership of land.

[100] Schiffrin and Sohn have found, for example, that although George contributed significantly to the revival of socialism in England in the 1880's, his ultimate influence was on middle-class businessmen rather than on socialists ("Henry George on Two Continents," pp. 85–95). As Robert L. Heilbroner has pointed out, George, while going beyond Ricardo in his concern for the working class, shared Ricardo's view that it was capitalists who were being robbed (by landholders) of "honest profit." (*The Worldly Philosophers*, p. 179.) In this connection it is of some interest that Marx, in his unfinished last chapter ("Classes") of *Capital*, identified landowners as a third class in capitalist society; see Shlomo Avineri, "Marx and the Intellectuals," *Journal of the History of Ideas*, XXVIII, 270. But Marx never developed this idea enough to catch the attention of Asian revolutionaries, whereas George's major emphasis fell increasingly on the responsibility of landowners for society's ills. For Henry George as a "Christian Socialist" see Charles Gide and Charles Rist, *A History of Economic Doctrines*, trans. R. Richards, pp. 534–40, *passim*.

CHINA'S NEW INTELLIGENTSIA
AND SOME PROBLEMS OF INTELLECTUAL REVOLUTION

There are important similarities between Wang Ching-wei's political discussions and other revolutionaries' writings on socialism. Jellinek, a respected theorist, was Western and contemporary, and insofar as he challenged conventional ideas and institutions and was an apostle of German national power, he appeared to deal with a problem very much like the one that faced the Chinese revolutionaries. Similarly, George was a Western thinker, had a considerable following, and seemed even to many in the West at the end of the nineteenth century to be blazing new trails in economic thought. To ardent young Chinese nationalists, aroused at China's backwardness and inertia in a dynamic world, the very title *Progress and Poverty* was magnetic. A plan to banish want by concentrating on the problem of land rents could hardly fail to interest a member of a poverty-stricken agricultural nation. Considering George's popularity in the West, particularly his influence upon the Fabians (which might possibly have led Sun, who studied socialism in England when the Fabian Society was flourishing, to regard George as the father of modern socialism), it is not difficult to understand why he had so much appeal for the Chinese revolutionaries.

When young Chinese intellectuals encountered ideas like those of Jellinek and George, their reactions to those ideas, like the reactions of any individual to new ideas, were shaped by their own needs, desires, and backgrounds. Their reactions are our best clues to their thoughts and feelings. The ideas they chose and the way they interpreted those ideas reveal their hunger for doctrines that could guide them to the best way of strengthening the state without sacrificing popular sovereignty; similarly they hoped to ensure social equality, eliminate poverty, and promote general economic and social harmony and well-being. It is difficult to be more precise about these goals than they were.

Kato Hiroyuki, who introduced to Japan the idea of the *Rechtsstaat*, was dismayed to find people interpreting its idea of natural rights to mean popular sovereignty; [101] Jellinek doubtless would have

[101] See David Abosch, "Katō Hiroyuki and the Introduction of German Political Thought in Modern Japan: 1868–1883" (unpublished Ph.D. dissertation, University of California, Berkeley, 1964).

been similarly dismayed at being thus interpreted by the Chinese. Henry George might not have been dismayed by his popularity among Chinese revolutionaries, but as a man who "may be best characterized as petty-bourgeois" [102] and who was concerned chiefly with problems created by the industrial revolution, especially in large American cities, he would have been surprised that his ideas should have become the major doctrinal points of reference for early Chinese socialism. Jellinek and Henry George were not writing for men like Wang Ching-wei and Sun Yat-sen, but the Chinese revolutionaries viewed Western ideas from their own angle of vision, and from where they stood Jellinek and George came closer than any other Western thinkers they knew to advocating the kind of political and social revolution they wanted.

The process by which a man absorbs a new idea is complex. His preconceptions, immediate needs, and distant goals guide his choices in many ways, coloring the alternatives, highlighting some and dimming others; but perhaps some ideas dart so quickly and sharply to his innermost core that they slice cleanly past the subjective influences. A man's choices are affected by the sequence in which he encounters new ideas — it might make a great difference if he read Darwin before Marx rather than the other way round. Where and when he encounters certain ideas will also matter, and so will who presents them — Wang Ching-wei at twenty-two reading Jellinek in Japan after the Russo-Japanese War is different from Wang at seventeen in Kwangtung reading Yen Fu's translation of Mill; both Wangs are very different from Sun Yat-sen reading Henry George in English while riding the Union Pacific across the Great Plains to Chicago. The variables could be enumerated almost indefinitely.

[102] Eric Roll, *A History of Economic Thought*, p. 464, is the source of this quotation. Whether or not the following anecdote supports Roll's assessment, it may be of some interest to those concerned with interaction between cultures. It might have startled George's Chinese admirers to know that he was a staunch opponent of Chinese immigration, a harsh critic of the Chinese as people, and doubtful that they could understand Western ideas. In an article published in the *New York Tribune* on May 1, 1869, one which is said by his son to reflect views he held until his death in 1897, George condemned Chinese as "utter heathens, treacherous, sensual, cowardly and cruel. . . . Their moral standard is as low as their standard of comfort. . . . No plan for making them tell the truth seems to be effective. . . . The Chinese seem to be incapable of understanding our religion; but still less are they capable of understanding our political institutions." Quoted by Henry George, Jr., *The Life of Henry George*, pp. 194–95.

Wang had available to him many ideas besides Jellinek's; Sun knew more than George. Chinese with similar backgrounds made different choices or interpreted Jellinek and George differently from Wang and Sun. We have stressed the rather obvious appeal of national power combined with both the rule of law and at least popular expression, if not popular sovereignty, in the case of Jellinek, and the similarly obvious appeal of George's interest in land problems. It is worth adding that Germany, her disciple Japan, and the United States might well have seemed to Chinese to be the most vigorous nations in the world at this time; they might well have seemed in 1905 to represent the wave of the future, which would have predisposed the Chinese to be interested in Jellinek, Minobe, and George.

Finally, Henry George's attraction for the Chinese suggests other possible lines of interpretation. The immense importance of Sun Yat-sen's position among the Chinese revolutionaries is evidenced partly by their acceptance of George. None of the revolutionaries' ideas were more exclusively traceable to Sun than those of George, which he relayed to them. Sun was interested in George partly because he seemed to offer a means of accumulating national wealth, but even more, it has been suggested, because he advanced ideas aimed at preventing social revolution. Indeed it was as a means of dealing with social problems created by industrialization rather than economic problems themselves, according to this interpretation, that Sun valued George's thinking.[103] This interpretation has much merit, but there is another side to the problem.

It was Sun Yat-sen more than any other person who linked the many parts of the revolutionary movement. When members of a small revolutionary affiliate called the *Kung-chin-hui* objected to his land program, Sun retreated to a position that would appease them without alienating his more radical followers. Still, radicals like Feng Tzu-yu and Chu Chih-hsin did not retreat. For them the land program remained revolutionary. Why then were they also Georgists? Chu, for example, had read Marx and Engels. Other Chinese were adopting other socialist or anarchist ideas. Those who knew other doctrines but held to George may have done so out of loyalty to Sun or for other reasons. But one other possibility is suggested by the position

[103] For a fuller explanation see Schiffrin and Sohn, "Henry George on Two Continents . . . ," especially pp. 103–5 and 108–9.

George had in the intellectual currents of the time, particularly as seen by other socialists.

Writing in 1887 to hail a "revolution" in the United States, Engels also discussed George.[104] It would have taken ten years to carry out such a revolution anywhere else, Engels said, but in only ten months American workers had become a self-conscious proletariat and organized themselves into a revolutionary political party. Since this was all so new, however, the United States labor movement still expressed itself in a variety of ways. Of the three major forms it took, the one under the leadership of Henry George in New York City, Engels deemed the least promising. It seemed to him "that the Henry George platform, in its present shape, is too narrow to form the basis for anything but a local movement, or at best for a short-lived phase of the general movement." Engels could have been forgiven had he made a much more optimistic assessment of George's potential, since less than three months earlier George had made a remarkably strong showing in the New York mayoralty election; furthermore *Progress and Poverty*, published in 1879, had been a popular seller. But Engels found two main weaknesses in George's platform: First, his insistence that land monopolization was the sole cause of poverty and misery did not take into account other means of production besides land. Second, his solution even to the land problem was too moderate — it was too far from "a total revolution of the whole system of social production." George's proposals went no further than "the extreme section of Ricardian bourgeois economists who, too, demanded the confiscation of the rent of land by the State."

For Engels, therefore, Henry George's ideas were not aimed at preventing social revolution; at this stage of history George was revolutionary but not revolutionary enough. I suggest that what Engels regarded as George's weaknesses may have been regarded as strengths by the Chinese. To put it another way, the differences between Marxism and Henry George's ideas that are underlined by Engels' comments also go far toward explaining why Chinese who had read both preferred George.

[104] My source for this paragraph is Engels' preface to the American edition of *The Condition of the Working Class in England*. The preface is reprinted as one of the appendices to a recent edition, trans. and ed. W. O. Henderson and W. H. Chaloner, pp. 352–59.

When the Chinese viewed the future, they saw a radically different China — a constitutional democracy expressing the popular will but dedicated at least as much to strong executive government and national power as to social and economic equalitarianism, and probably more to all of these aims than to individual liberty. The revolutionaries did not spell all this out very clearly; they gave relatively little of their energies and attention to problems beyond those directly related to gaining power. But it must also be said that the Chinese revolutionaries do not compare unfavorably with other revolutionaries in these respects. Failure to describe the future in detail is not the same as lack of attention to it. For revolutionaries every criticism of the present derives ultimately from a sense of the future.

If this is so, how does one explain the revolutionaries' numerous references to the past? Just as Wang Ching-wei found the spirit of democracy in China's past and others found that the Chinese had experience that would facilitate popular government, Hu Han-min and Feng Tzu-yu found Chinese precedents for socialism in the ancient "well-field" system,[105] and Feng found them even more developed in Wang Mang, Wang An-shih, and the Taipings.[106] Chu Chih-hsin also found that the social revolution could build on much that already existed in Chinese tradition.[107] One could multiply such examples manyfold. Do they indicate a lingering attachment to the past, perhaps an emotional tie devoid of intellectual conviction, or an unquenchable traditionalism, or a cynical effort to impress some traditionalistic people whose support the revolutionaries were seeking?

These and similar explanations are unconvincing. In fact, one marvels that the Chinese revolutionaries did not refer to traditional precedents and the like far more than they did. Many of them had strong classical educations. Traditional terminology was still the language of educated men, and traditional concepts were not so depleted or stigmatized that the revolutionaries avoided them when they seemed apt or likely to be effective. If the revolutionaries had really been traditional men they would have sought, like K'ang Yu-wei, some means to identify themselves systematically with some

---

[105] Hu called it "a model" for land nationalization. See deBary, *Sources*, p. 766. Feng, "Min-sheng chu-i . . . ," pp. 105, 110–11, equated it with the doctrine of equalization of land rights.

[106] *Ibid.*, pp. 105–6.

[107] Scalapino and Schiffrin, "Early Socialist Currents . . . ," p. 331.

progressive slice of China's rich and varied tradition. Most of all, they could not avoid the nationalist's need to foster a sense of cultural unity and pride, particularly since their movement was anti-Manchu and anti-imperialist.

In view of the many factors that might have inclined the revolutionaries toward relying heavily upon traditional formulas, therefore, one cannot help being impressed by how much they avoided the practice. And when they did not avoid it, they were matter of fact about it. Classical allusions seem as natural in their writing as phrases from the Bible do in ours. If "well-field" may have meant more to them than "forbidden fruit" does to Westerners, its use by the Chinese nevertheless seems less impressive than their references to the general will, representative government, constitutionalism, and the like. Their hearts and minds were torn, but the larger parts of both were being claimed by the West.

Still, the traditional component in the revolutionaries' thinking ought not to be ignored. Illustrative of the breakneck speed with which intellectual revolution was snowballing in China, the practice of proving new systems suitable for China on the basis of past precedents quite clearly distinguishes most T'ung-meng-hui men from those who were to dominate the Chinese intellectual scene after about 1915. The New Youth of the New Thought Movement were not to sully their ideas with what they regarded as the refuse of China's past. In fact, the ideas of this group were already taking shape in the decade before 1911, and within the T'ung-meng-hui itself, although far off in Paris.

# PART THREE

# Discordant Elements
# in the Revolutionary Movement

# 5

# *The Anarchists*

When *Su-pao* was forced to close in 1903, Wu Chih-hui fled to Hong Kong and from there continued on to Europe. After two years in England Wu moved to Paris, where he renewed his acquaintance with Chang Ching-chiang and Li Shih-tseng.[2] At the same time Sun Yat-sen was traveling in the United

[1] A useful account of the revolutionary movement in Europe may be found in Feng Tzu-yu, *Ke-ming i-shih*, II, 132–41. Chu Ho-chung has written a valuable firsthand report that must, however, be used with caution, particularly with regard to Chu's own role. See "Ou-chou T'ung-meng-hui chi-shih," *Ke-ming wen-hsien*, II, 251–70. Chang Chi has a diary of his stay in Europe from November, 1910, to November, 1911, which, though it adds little to our knowledge of anarchist ideas, reveals a good deal about the pursuits of those who were caught up in the anarchist movement. See *Chang P'u-ch'üan hsien-sheng ch'üan-chi* (Complete Works of Mr. Chang P'u-ch'üan), pp. 253–82. These and other materials have been conveniently brought together in *50th Anniversary Documents*, XI, 379–443.

[2] Li Shu-hua, "Wu Chih-hui hsien-sheng sheng-p'ing lüeh-shu," *Wu Chih-hui hsien-sheng ti sheng-p'ing*, pp. 55–56.

Li, a son of Li Hung-tsao (see Arthur W. Hummel [ed.], *Eminent Chinese of the Ch'ing Period*, pp. 471–72), had gone to Paris in 1902 to serve as an attaché in the Chinese legation. Li met Wu in Shanghai before leaving for Europe. Thus began a friendship that was to last until Wu's death more than half a century later. In Paris, Li was quickly drawn into scholarly and political pursuits, taking a keen interest in biology, the theory of evolution, and Kropotkin's application of Darwinism to social problems.

Chang Ching-chiang (1877–1950, perhaps less well known by his *ming,*

States and Europe, where he eventually met with revolutionary elements among Chinese students in Belgium, France, Germany, and England. Wu did not align himself with Sun at first but joined the T'ung-meng-hui before the end of 1905. Li and Chang did not enlist until two years later.[3]

Meanwhile, Wu, Li, and Chang proceeded to form their own group, the World Association (*Shih-chieh-she*). Chang returned to China in 1906, stopping in Singapore to purchase a printing press and engage a printer. Before the end of the year Wu and Li had begun to publish a pictorial magazine, but it failed to attract readers and ceased publication after two issues. On June 22, 1907, they produced the first issue of *The New Century* (*Hsin shih-chi*),[4] a magazine dedicated to promoting revolution, but a revolution that was very different from what the T'ung-meng-hui advocated. It was to be world-wide in scope and aimed at the destruction of all states and all private property. To put it briefly, the program of these Chinese revolutionaries was the anarchism of Michael Bakunin (1814–76) and Peter Kropotkin (1842–1921), although the Chinese recognized that there were differences between these two anarchist thinkers.[5]

---

Jen-chieh), the son of a wealthy merchant, was also an attaché in the Chinese legation in Paris. Excited by anarchist ideas, he soon became an ardent revolutionary and was a major financial contributor both to Sun Yat-sen and to the Paris group. See Feng Tzu-yu, *Ke-ming i-shih*, II, 227–30. Chang met Wu in London in early 1905, when both met Sun Yat-sen for the first time. See Li Shu-hua, "Wu Chih-hui . . . ," p. 56. Chang's biography is in Boorman and Howard (eds.), *Biographical Dictionary of Republican China*, I, 73–77.

[3] Feng Tzu-yu, *Ke-ming i-shih*, II, 135. Some sources say Wu was not sworn into the T'ung-meng-hui until 1906.

[4] In all, 121 issues of *Hsin shih-chi* (hereafter cited as *HSC*) were published, the last one appearing on May 21, 1910. During its three-year existence, the journal came out weekly with almost unbroken regularity until September, 1909. The last eight issues were spread over seven months. Together with several other publications of the World Association, which were appended under the title *Hsin shih-chi ts'ung-shu* (hereafter cited as *HSCTS*), *Hsin shih-chi* was reprinted by photolithograph in Shanghai in 1947. Citations of these materials refer to the 1947 edition.

[5] The *Hsin shih-chi* writers were quite clear about the distinctions to be drawn among various anarchist thinkers. In 1907 Li Shih-tseng translated an article that distinguished seven schools of anarchist doctrine. The leaders, in addition to Bakunin and Kropotkin, were William Godwin (1756–1836), Pierre Joseph Proudhon (1809–65), "Max Stirner" (pseudonym of Johann Kasper Schmidt, 1806–56), Leo Tolstoy (1823–1910), and Benjamin R. Tucker (1854–1939). See "L'Anarchisme," subtitled "Shih-chieh ch'i-ke wu-cheng-fu chu-i chia" (Seven of the

Since anarchism was at the height of its popularity in France around the turn of the century, it is hardly surprising that the Chinese who lived there, themselves resentful of the authority wielded by the Manchu government, would take an interest in them.[6]

## The Setting in France: Ideas and Politics

It has been suggested that when Ch'en Tu-hsiu studied the West he was already strongly biased against Chinese tradition and was therefore disposed to condemn tradition in general.[7] The vehemence with which the *New Century* writers attacked Chinese tradition and the passion with which they embraced anarchism indicate that the same may be said of them. One finds no hint in their writings of even the slightest willingness to accept any but the most radical ideas. The only merit of the past was that it provided the tools for a rapid and thoroughgoing destruction of existing institutions and customs. Indeed, from anarchism itself they chose the most extreme and activist doctrines.

Anarchist ideas have been traced at least as far back as Zeno of Citium (342–270 B.C.).[8] Modern anarchists took their inspiration from such varied sources as the fifteenth century Anabaptists (one of whom influenced Tolstoy), the onetime Benedictine monk and

World's Anarchists), in *HSCTS*, pp. 33–50. Li then appended a cleverly devised chart that classified the seven according to their positions on certain issues, such as the form of organization, if any, that would replace government, and whether they advocated the abolition or retention of private property. *Ibid.*, pp. 39–40.

I am grateful to Dr. Martin Bernal for pointing out to me that Li's translation was of a digest of *Der Anarchismus* by Paul Eltsbacher (see the English translation by Steven T. Byington under the title *Anarchism*, New York, 1960) and that the chart was based on chap. 10 of that book.

[6] Wu Chih-hui, it will be recalled, had already been engaged in anti-Manchu activities in Tokyo and Shanghai. Li Shih-tseng was not yet a revolutionary, but he had been impressed by the courageous spirit Wu had displayed in Tokyo and was sympathetic to the student movement. (Statement by Li Shih-tseng, personal interview, Taipei, October 25, 1958.) Mr. Li familiarized himself with the writings of Lamarck and Kropotkin soon after he reached Paris. He abandoned his position in the Chinese legation in order to free himself for study, experiments, and writing.

[7] Benjamin Schwartz, "Ch'en Tu-hsiu and the Acceptance of the Modern West," *Journal of the History of Ideas*, XII, 64.

[8] Francis W. Coker, *Recent Political Thought*, p. 192. See also *Encyclopedia of the Social Sciences*, II, 47a. Two valuable detailed studies of the history of anarchism are James Joll, *The Anarchists*, and George Woodcock, *Anarchism: A History of Libertarian Ideas and Movements*.

later renowned writer Rabelais (1495–1553), Garrard Winstanley and the Diggers (seventeenth century), the seventeenth- and eighteenth-century advocates of natural rights, the Physiocrats, the classical economists, and the socialists.

As this list suggests, anarchism has encompassed widely differing ideas, and even where its adherents have been in basic agreement there have often been marked divergencies in emphasis and important shadings of detail. The fundamental tenet that has united all anarchists is opposition to coercive authority. This position is based upon the view that man is by nature good and, if not interfered with, will build the best possible society. From this general conception, however, has flowed a wide variety of notions about the nature of that good society, ranging from fully collectivist to extremely individualistic formulations. The seven anarchists discussed by the members of the World Association reflect these divergencies. But the Chinese anarchists were in agreement with their Western contemporaries, who also tended to subscribe more to the doctrines of Bakunin and Kropotkin than to any others. It was at the hands of these two men that anarchism was given its fullest formulation, although there were important differences between them.[9]

Among the seven anarchists we have named, Bakunin and Kropotkin were the staunchest collectivists, and of the two Kropotkin was the more extreme. Tucker and Stirner were ardent individualists, the latter going so far as to condemn all social organization and advocating its violent destruction and the prevention of any subsequent association.[10] Tucker favored voluntary societies, but he reserved to each individual the privilege of refusing to participate, and he denied any association the right to monopolize any social service. Both Bakunin and Kropotkin, however, believed that men would inevitably organize themselves into social units. For them the important point was that men should not be forced into associations against their will.

Bakunin [11] believed that those who owned the means of produc-

[9] Coker, *Recent Political Thought*, pp. 200–202.

[10] Coker suggests that Stirner's ideas hardly fit the modern definition of anarchism; *Recent Political Thought*, p. 201.

[11] See *ibid.*, pp. 202–7, and G. D. H. Cole, *A History of Socialist Thought*, II, 213–36, for brief introductory surveys. Also, Joll, *The Anarchists*, pp. 84–114, *passim*; E. H. Carr's *Michael Bakunin* (London, 1937) is the best biography. G. P. Maximoff (ed.), *The Political Philosophy of Bakunin: Scientific Anarchism*,

tion were able to control the state and the mass of the people. Therefore, a central point in his doctrine was common ownership of the means of production, although he specified that this did not mean the abolition of all private property. Still more basic was his view that the state is inherently immoral because it functions by coercion. All states, he declared,

> . . . have been condemned to perpetual struggle — a struggle against their own populations, whom they oppress and ruin, a struggle against all foreign States, every one of which can be strong only if the others are weak — and since the States cannot hold their own in this struggle unless they constantly keep on augmenting their power against their own subjects as well as against the neighbor States — it follows that the supreme law of the State is the augmentation of its power to the detriment of internal liberty and external justice.[12]

In sum: "the morality of the State then is the reversal of human justice and human morality."[13] "Liberty, morality, and the humane dignity of man consist precisely in that man does good not because he is ordered to do so, but because he conceives it, wants it, and loves it."[14]

The state was to be smashed by violent revolution, but in addition, the "*immediate* and *direct* aim" of revolution was "economic equality."[15] The new system would be organized on the principle of "free federation and organization from below upward," culminating in "the unity of all of the peoples of the earth."[16] Bakunin also spoke of the need for "a United States of Europe" in order to prevent "any civil war among people comprising the European family."[17]

Bakunin had great respect for science and at times came very close to describing it as the sole source of truth and knowledge. But he also expressed some reservations on this score, and despite his

---

is a valuable source book. Since much of the Chinese anarchists' energy was devoted to translating Bakunin and, to a far greater extent, Kropotkin, a brief summary of their main ideas seems appropriate.

[12] Quoted in Maximoff, *op. cit.*, p. 139.
[13] *Ibid.*
[14] *Ibid.*, p. 145.
[15] *Ibid.*, p. 372. Emphasis in original.
[16] *Ibid.*, p. 273. See also pp. 297–98.
[17] *Ibid.*, p. 274.

inconsistency on the question we may agree that Bakunin did not believe that science could solve all the problems of men.[18]

Kropotkin's [19] claim that his doctrines were rooted in science was less reserved and somewhat more justified than Bakunin's. Trained in geology, geography, and ethnology, Kropotkin had published several important papers based upon his own field research in the Russian Far East. He had also read widely in biology. In 1902 he published his *Mutual Aid*, an attempt to apply the theory of evolution to social questions. Kropotkin firmly believed that the study of human affairs could bear fruit only if it followed the methods of the natural sciences, and his own studies were based upon prodigious research and supported by masses of data.

Kropotkin's ideas were founded on the belief that struggle is but one principle of animal (including human) existence, and that the vital factor in evolution was cooperation or mutual aid.

> Sociability is as much a law of nature as mutual struggle. Of course it would be extremely difficult to estimate, however roughly, the relative numerical importance of both these series of facts [warfare and killing on the one hand, and mutual support, mutual aid, and mutual defense on the other]. But if we resort to an indirect test, and ask Nature: "Who are the fittest: those who are continually at war with each other, or those who support one another?" we at once see that those animals which acquire habits of mutual aid are undoubtedly the fittest.[20]

[18] See *ibid.*, p. 24, Rudolf Rocker's "Introduction" to Maximoff's source book. For some of Bakunin's statements on science see *ibid.*, pp. 68–81. Note p. 80: Science "must not interfere with the real or practical organization of society." This view did not, however, prevent him from speaking of "the immutable law of Socialism" (*ibid.*) or believing that his own ideas were based upon science (Coker, *Recent Political Thought*, p. 203).

[19] Useful short essays on Kropotkin may be found in Coker, *Recent Political Thought*, pp. 207–17, and Cole, *A History of Socialist Thought*, II, 342–52. The best detailed treatment is George Woodcock and Ivan Avakumovic, *The Anarchist Prince* (London, 1950). For the book that impressed the Chinese anarchists most see Kropotkin's *Mutual Aid, A Factor of Evolution* (originally published 1902, now in many editions), parts of which Li Shih-tseng translated into Chinese in *Hsin shih-chi*. Kropotkin was an extremely prolific writer, and many of his other publications were known to his Chinese followers and partly translated. A useful compendium is *Kropotkin's Revolutionary Pamphlets*, edited with Introduction, Biographical Sketch, and Notes by Roger N. Baldwin.

[20] Peter Kropotkin, *Mutual Aid, A Factor of Evolution*, pp. 5–6. Kropotkin supported this view with a vast array of his own observations and the researches of other scientists.

In human society, Kropotkin maintained, the natural disposition toward mutual aid and the establishment of interrelationships based upon equality were thwarted by coercive institutions. The very existence of the state, religious organizations, and private property was a denial of man's natural ability to cooperate spontaneously. These institutions divided men into nations, religious denominations, and economic and social classes, whereas if left to themselves men would gradually evolve a world community unmarred by such distinctions. Like Bakunin, Kropotkin held that the state was evil because it relied on force.[21] Religion was an inadequate explanation of nature and tended to make people accept injustice. Property-holders exploited the propertyless. Kropotkin contended that if such obstacles to the development of human nature were removed, small groups of voluntarily cooperating producers and consumers would be formed.[22] Out of these there would grow ever widening free federations until finally the very idea of ownership would be discarded and there would exist a communist society based upon the principle of "from each according to his ability, to each according to his needs." For "the ethical progress of our race, viewed in its broad lines, appears as a gradual extension of the mutual-aid principles from the tribe to always larger and larger agglomerations, so as to finally embrace one day the whole of mankind, without respect to its diverse creeds, languages and races."[23]

Although Kropotkin thought the economic order could be changed gradually, he believed that the state had to be smashed immediately and completely. There could be no slow transition to a stateless society. "When cooperation is not forced by government, natural wants will bring about a voluntary cooperation. Overthrow the state and a free society will rise up at once on its ruins."[24] The abolition of the state could only take place by means of violent revolution. Because of the apathy and backwardness of the masses, political action by constitutional means was futile. It was also wrong in principle. Government itself was immoral, and therefore so was par-

---

[21] Kropotkin supported without qualification Bakunin's views on the state. See his "Bakunin and the State," in *Kropotkin's Revolutionary Pamphlets*, pp. 165–69.

[22] See *Mutual Aid*, pp. 223–92, for Kropotkin's evidence drawn from his studies of human society.

[23] *Ibid.*, p. 224.

[24] Quoted in Coker, *Recent Political Thought*, p. 215.

ticipation in government; more specifically, he condemned the practice of representation on the theory that no man could represent another except when he was placed under instructions in regard to one specific issue and was subject to immediate recall.[25] It was clearly impractical for representative government to operate in this fashion.

Finally, let us note Kropotkin's conviction that the future would be as he described it. "It is no longer a matter of faith; it is a matter for scientific discussion."[26]

Li Shih-tseng arrived in France in the year that Kropotkin published his *Mutual Aid*; Wu Chih-hui reached England less than a year later.

Anarchist ideas had about reached the peak of their popularity and influence, although anarchism was beginning to merge with syndicalism and to become somewhat diluted by trade unionism.[27] Since the establishment of the Second International in 1889, the anarchists had been involved in a new kind of struggle. The central issue among socialists had become whether to seek power by participating in the rapidly developing parliamentary movements, as was urged by Social Democratic parties in France and Germany especially, or to rely on "direct action" (i.e., the general strike), as the anarchists demanded. In France it was chiefly because of this issue, although there were others of importance, that the socialists remained divided up to 1905, the rival groups holding separate congresses and formulating their own programs. Nominal unification was achieved in 1905, but the trade unions, in which anarchist influence was of key importance, remained independent. From 1902 to 1909, what has been called the "heroic period" of French syndicalism, the central issue remained whether to cooperate with the state or destroy it. The anarchists led the fight for the latter position, arguing that the state (and

[25] Cole, *A History of Socialist Thought*, II, p. 359.

[26] Quoted in Coker, *Recent Political Thought*, p. 124. Kropotkin believed that anarchism was firmly rooted in science (see "The Place of Anarchism in Modern Science," *Kropotkin's Revolutionary Pamphlets*, pp. 150–54), but he established rigorous criteria for scientific investigation and was cautious in appraising the precision attainable by the "social sciences" as well as their ability to support prediction. See *ibid.*, pp. 146 ff.

[27] This discussion is based chiefly on Cole, *A History of Socialist Thought*, Vol. III, Part I (see especially the Introduction and pp. 323–91), and Woodcock, *Anarchism*, pp. 257–69, 293–324.

employers) were enemies to be smashed, not partners in reform. For about a decade the anarchists were able to dominate the largest workers' movement in pre–1914 France.[28]

In the France of this period the anarchist program faced serious obstacles. Many of its adherents were thought to have compromised themselves by giving support to the Third Republic when opponents of Dreyfus used the famous case to attack republican government. Moreover, the government's action in abolishing the privileged position occupied by the Roman Catholic Church was regarded by some as evidence that the state could effect reform and that it was not an unqualified protector of religion. Nevertheless, French workers lagged far behind their counterparts in England and Germany in economic and social welfare measures; and although it tended to be socialist, the working class in France was small and relatively inert. Syndicalist leaders such as Victor Griffuelhes made it their chief task to whip up sentiment for the attack on the state.

The chief obstacle facing the anarchists was their own inherent tendency toward disunity and the premium they placed upon acting as individuals. At no other time were anarchists more disorganized than in the late nineteenth and early twentieth centuries. Their spirit is exemplified by the unanimous approval given an Italian delegate to an 1882 anarchist congress when he said, "We are united because we are divided." [29] In disunity there was strength, they felt, and by this standard they were powerful indeed; it must have delighted their Chinese followers to add to the strength of the T'ung-meng-hui in a similar fashion.

It was in this intellectual and political climate that the World Association and the *New Century* magazine were born. Furthermore, to an already turbulent atmosphere the Chinese came as restless men, dissatisfied with their own society. Some of them were already committed to revolution and had tasted failure; it would not be surprising if they arrived in Europe feeling bitter and frustrated.

## The Ideas of the Chinese Anarchists [30]

The ideas of Bakunin and Kropotkin were the basis of the Chinese anarchists' beliefs.[31] Where the two disagreed, as on the question of

---

[28] Woodcock, *Anarchism*, pp. 296–97.
[29] *Ibid.*, p. 260.
[30] The Chinese anarchists' ideas have been described by Robert A. Scalapino

private property, the Chinese tended to support Kropotkin. A useful introduction to these ideas, which helps to clarify their relationship to other ideas of the time, is a small pamphlet published by the World Association.[32] Here it was pointed out that although "liberty" and "equality" were regarded as two key points by revolutionaries, the revolutionary parties had failed to go beyond these ideas. Moreover, they were terms that were subject to misuse by opportunists. "Therefore, in order to determine their exact value and cleanse them of impurities, we add two lines to these terms: liberty is the absence of government (*wu-cheng-fu*); equality is the common ownership of property (*kung-ch'an*)."[33]

The first aim required the destruction of authority (*ch'iang-ch'üan*) in the present society, the prevention of its re-establishment in the future, "and the protection of the liberty of the individual." Each person's development would be according to his own needs and desires. All groupings of individuals would build up gradually from below, finally culminating in the Great Community (*Ta-t'ung*). The second concept, which was now called "communism" (*kung-ch'an chu-i*), aimed at "transferring to the public the sources of the wealth of the entire world," and at implementing the principle of "from each according to his ability, to each according to his needs."[34]

The similarity between these statements and those of Bakunin and

---

and George T. Yu, *The Chinese Anarchist Movement*. The pre-1912 period is discussed in pp. 1–25. In subsequent pages the authors explore the relationship between anarchism and Marxism-Leninism in China. For earlier Chinese anarchism see Hsiao Kung-ch'üan, "Anarchism in Chinese Political Thought," *T'ien Hsia Monthly*, Vol. III, No. 3, pp. 249–63.

[31] Li Shih-tseng's translation of fragments of Bakunin's writings may be found in *HSC*, Nos. 8 and 9. His translations of Kropotkin are in *HSC*, Nos. 12, 15, 16, 17 ("Kropotkin's Theory"); Nos. 31, 32, 34–38, 44–52 (*Mutual Aid*); Nos. 41, 47, 49 (*Law and Authority*); Nos. 58–62, 66–83 (*The State, Its Historic Role*); Nos. 102–8 (Kropotkin's diary while imprisoned in Russia for revolutionary activities). Numerous other writers were translated, but none received more than a fraction of the attention given to Kropotkin.

[32] "Anarchie and Communism," titled in Chinese "Wu-cheng-fu chu-i yü kung-ch'an chu-i" (Anarchism and Communism). This was a 1907 translation by Li Shih-tseng of an article by the prominent Italian anarchist, Carlo Cafiero (d. 1892). Cafiero was a follower of Bakunin who finally abandoned anarchism in the 1880's, went mad, and died in a mental hospital, tortured by the fear that he was receiving more than his deserved share of sunshine. See Joll, *The Anarchists*, pp. 117–24, and Woodcock, *Anarchism*, p. 344, and *passim*. Li's translation may be found in *HSCTS*, pp. 41–48.

[33] *Ibid.*, p. 42a.        [34] *Ibid.*

Kropotkin is obvious. It is also clear that the anarchists' opposition to authority brought them into direct conflict with their "comrades" on the *Min-pao*. "All governments are the enemies of equality and liberty," wrote Li Shih-tseng. How could one hope to realize these ideals through an institution that was inherently inimical to them? But "if there is no government, the goals of liberty and equality have been reached." [35] Deriding his countrymen's concern that China might be destroyed, another writer stated it with passion:

> Of all the grand things in the world, what could be better than the dissolution of states? I should like to see the destruction of every state on earth in the 20th century. What is more, I should like China to be the first. [36]

The *New Century* writers did not shrink from aiming their shafts directly at "the revolutionary party." In general, their argument was that the T'ung-meng-hui advocated only a partial revolution and therefore a meaningless one. [37] It was not enough that some writers such as Chu Chih-hsin and Feng Tzu-yu had called for an immediate social revolution and the abolition of private property. If any form of political authority was established, the main business of the revolution would be unfinished. Li Shih-tseng demonstrated this point in an interesting manner. To show that "the evolution of thought is the same as other kinds of evolution," he ranked what he called ten Chinese schools of thought in order of their development and degree of perfection. At the very bottom was the most outmoded traditional thought as typified by the "three bonds and five constants" school (*san-kang wu-ch'ang p'ai*); in the middle were various reform groups such as the "self-strengtheners," or those who stood for an amalgamation of Chinese foundation and Western application (*Chung-Hsi t'i-yung p'ai*); next to the top was the T'ung-meng-hui, the "equality and liberty school" (*p'ing-teng tzu-yu p'ai*), and finally there were the anarchists, the "truth and evolution school" (*chen-li chin-hua p'ai*). [38] The *Min-pao* writers were simply one step behind.

[35] "Lai-shu fu-ta," *HSC*, No. 6, p. 1b.

[36] Anonymous, "Wang-kuo?" (Destroying the country?), *HSC*, No. 48, p. 1b.

[37] For a typical discussion in these terms see Li Shih-tseng (translator; author unknown), "Wu-cheng-fu chu-i k'e-i chien-chüeh ke-ming-tang chih tse-jen hsin," *HSC*, No. 58, pp. 10–13.

[38] "Chin-hua yü ke-ming," *HSC*, No. 20, p. 2.

Similar arguments were advanced in other *New Century* articles, often in terms of the doctrine of evolution, the argument being that the principles of nationalism and democracy were stages in a progression that led to socialism and finally to anarchism.[39] The anarchists also objected to anti-Manchuism on the grounds that it was irrational and contrary to the principle of universal harmony among all men.[40] This charge was echoed by a small and short-lived anarchist society that was established in Tokyo by Liu Shih-p'ei[41] and Chang Chi, and which maintained close relations with the Paris group.

Liu and Chang founded the Society for the Study of Socialism in June, 1907. Liu opened its first meeting, however, by declaring that its program was "not merely to carry out socialism but to make anarchism our objective."[42] Liu and Chang founded the society "because the Chinese people only understand the principle of race (*min-tsu chu-i*); they do not consider the misery of the people's lives and do not seek a fundamental (*ken-pen*) revolution."[43] Liu went on to say that opposition to the Manchus meant a fight against government and privilege; it was not aimed at extending the privi-

[39] See Scalapino and Yu, *The Chinese Anarchist Movement*, p. 14.

[40] *Ibid.*, p. 20. See also Li Shih-tseng's argument against nationalism (*kuo-chia chu-i*) and his demand that national boundaries be abolished. "Ke-ming," *HSCTS*, pp. 5–8, and especially p. 6.

[41] Liu Shih-p'ei (1884–1919) was a noted classical scholar who had become a *chü-jen* in 1902. The next year he failed in the metropolitan examinations and then went to Shanghai, where he became involved in the revolutionary movement and adopted the name Kuang-han ("Restore the Han"). Later he joined the Restoration Society (Kuang-fu-hui) and wrote for the *Russia Alarm* (*O-shih Ching-wen*) and *Warning Bell Daily* (*Ching-chung jih-pao*). In 1907 he went to Japan, where he joined the T'ung-meng-hui, wrote for the *Min-pao*, and then turned to anarchism. Two years later he broke with the revolutionary movement and entered the service of the Manchus. See Boorman, *Men and Politics in Modern China, Preliminary Fifty Biographies*, Part I, pp. 98–100; Feng Tzu-yu, *Ke-ming i-shih*, II, 231–33; and Hidemi Onogawa, "Liu Shih-p'ei and Anarchism," *Acta Asiatica*, No. 12, pp. 70–99.

[42] The meeting was reported in *HSC*, Nos. 22, 25, and 26 under the title "She-hui chu-i chiang-hsi hui ti-i-tz'u k'ai-hui chi-shih." It was reprinted from Liu's journal, *T'ien-i pao*. The author was Liu's brother-in-law, Wang Kung-ch'üan. Liu's comment may be found in *HSC*, No. 22, p. 4b. This item is also included in a selection of articles from *T'ien-i pao* published in Chang Nan and Wang Jen-chih (eds.), *Hsin-hai ke-ming ch'ien shih-nien-chien shih-lun hsüan-chi*, Vol. II, Part 2, pp. 944–47; Liu's comment is on p. 944.

[43] *HSC*, No. 22, p. 4a. Liu's views on race had not always been so lofty; see Onogawa, "Liu Shih-p'ei and Anarchism," pp. 75–77, and below, note 70.

leges of the Chinese. Those now advocating an anti-Manchu revolution, he charged, were only some students and various small organizations. If they were successful, the benefit would accrue to a minority. Liu called for an effort to gain the support of workers and peasants in order to create a "revolution by the majority," from which the masses would derive the benefit.[44]

Another writer in *New Century* attacked the Chinese overseas students even more bitterly, but on different grounds. Ch'u Min-i [45] complained that in "the era of the glory of science," Chinese students should concentrate on seeking knowledge (presumably by concentrating on scientific or technical subjects) that would equip them to be leaders in the improvement of society. As it was, they were only seeking their own pleasure and comfort.[46] Li Shih-tseng had earlier advanced this idea more pointedly. Chinese students, he charged, chose to study law and political science partly because they were the means to gaining official positions. "Therefore we call [the studies of] law and political science euphemisms for studying to be an official." [47]

The disagreements between these branches of the revolutionary movement could thus descend to accusations of this kind. The Tokyo republican members, in turn, were fond of chiding the Europe-based anarchists for remaining far from the scene of battle. But the differences between the two groups concerned weightier matters. The Chinese anarchists subscribed to beliefs that were fundamentally at variance with those of other participants in the Chinese revolutionary movement. Anti-Manchuism, nationalism, and democracy, cardinal tenets of the T'ung-meng-hui, were sharply attacked in the *New Century*. It is true that on certain issues the anarchists advanced arguments that are almost identical to those found in the *Min-pao*.[48]

---

[44] *HSC*, No. 22, p. 4c. The Tokyo anarchists are treated in more detail below.

[45] Ch'u Min-i (1884–1946) had an American tutor as a child and then was a student of political science and economics in Japan from 1903 to 1908. There Wang Ching-wei and Chang Ching-chiang became two of his closest friends. He went to Paris with Chang in 1908 and joined the anarchist movement. Subsequently he affiliated himself with Wang Ching-wei, and later was executed as a "national traitor." See Boorman and Howard (eds.), *Biographical Dictionary*, I, 467–69.

[46] Ch'u Min-i, "Hsü wu-cheng-fu shuo," *HSC*, No. 60, p. 7a–b.

[47] "T'an hsüeh," *HSC*, No. 7, p. 2a.

[48] See, for example, Li Shih-tseng's explanation of why a revolution would not

But the two groups not only were opposed on most major questions; they differed in regard to the very questions that they deemed crucial, not to mention the sources from which they took their inspiration and the conceptual bases of their beliefs.

The *Min-pao* writers were probably the first to attempt to formulate a concept of Chinese nationalism in its modern Western sense. Outraged at China's weakness, resentful toward the foreign powers and yet jealous of them, and stirred by Japan's modernization and the dynamism they felt all around them, the republican revolutionaries were determined to secure for China a new position in the world. She was to be strong and wealthy, and respected as an independent member of the world community of nations. To this end, the Chinese people had to be awakened to the unique characteristics that made them a nation — distinct from, equal to, and perhaps even somewhat better than other nations. They also had to learn that the power to make China a modern nation was in their own hands and minds. Much of the revolutionaries' anti-Manchu propaganda as well as their discovery of Chinese precedents for new political and economic systems was used for these purposes.

The Chinese anarchists had only contempt for these ideas, partly because they believed in universal brotherhood and opposed what they regarded as narrow nationalism, but also in part because they desired a total break with tradition. To them, the view that China had had ideas and institutions comparable to those of the modern West betrayed a lingering attachment to antiquity that had to be severed.

Ch'u Min-i made precisely this point in *New Century*. Characterizing the Chinese as "slaves of the ancients," he insisted that the "reason China has not been able to progress with the world is that she reveres antiquity and is contemptuous of modernity." The West, in contrast, "reveres the modern and has contempt for the ancient . . . and therefore is about to make the present triumph over the past and make unlimited progress." The Chinese "speak of the ancients as sages who knew everything, whose every word was truth." Ch'u then

---

result in the partition of China by foreign powers, "Ke-ming," pp. 5b–6a. Even in this case, however, Li made it clear that the loss of China was secondary to other issues: "Why fear partition? Let us only fear the loss of our freedom and equality." *Ibid.*, p. 5b.

attacked those who traced every new idea to a supposed Chinese origin, noting that Lao-tzu had been called the creator of anarchism, communism had been identified with the well-field system, and similar treatment had been accorded to nationalism, democracy, and many other concepts. "In sum, all of the Westerners' new learning was already familiar to our men of antiquity," he scoffed. Ch'u maintained that new ideas were produced only when time and circumstances were suitable; they could not be dredged up from the past.[49]

## LIU SHIH-P'EI AND THE CHINESE ANARCHISTS IN JAPAN

There is some irony in the fact that Liu Shih-p'ei, during his anarchist phase, had spoken in precisely the terms to which Ch'u Min-i objected. China's government, he said, had been rooted in Confucianism and Taoism for thousands of years. "Both of these theories advocated non-interference (*fang-jen*) rather than interference (*kan-she*). . . . In name there was a government; in fact, it was as if there was no government. . . . Therefore in all the world anarchism will be easiest [to achieve] in China, and China should be the first [to reach it]."[50]

It is thus entirely possible that Ch'u Min-i's ire was directed more at Liu Shih-p'ei and the other Chinese anarchists in Japan than it was at anyone else. For *T'ien-i pao*, the organ of Chinese anarchism in Japan, was permeated with reverence for China's past, comparisons between traditional China and the contemporary West that treated China more favorably, and the argument that China's past uniquely fitted her for anarchism. One even detects on occasion a certain longing for the simple, rustic, and primitive life, close to nature, that figured so prominently in traditional Chinese as well as Western anarchism but was relatively lacking in the modern Chinese variety.

In an attack on militarism and property, for example, Liu Shih-p'ei argued that measures such as equal division of land, which were necessary in order to eliminate the profit motive and distinctions between rich and poor, could well take place first in China. So could

---

[49] "Hao ku," *HSC*, No. 24, p. 2b.

[50] Quoted in [Wang] Kung-ch'üan, "She-hui chu-i chiang-hsi hui ti-i-tz'u k'ai-hui chi-shih," *T'ien-i pao*, No. 6 (Sept. 1, 1907), in Chang Nan and Wang Jen-chih (eds.), *Hsin-hai ke-ming ch'ien shih-nien-chien shih-lun hsüan-chi*, Vol. II, Part 2, p. 945.

an end to war. The reason was that ever since ancient times Chinese thought had regarded soldiers and merchants with contempt.[51] Together with his wife, Ho Chen, Liu subsequently developed the logical corollary of this view, the idea that China's special qualities militated against her studying and copying from the West. Liu's respect for Chinese thought, and particularly for the traditional Chinese view of merchants and soldiers, was now woven into a more far-reaching criticism of industrialization and military modernization. This led him in turn to attack other features of modern civilization such as law. Chinese law, he held, was both different and better.[52] Indeed, the rule of law in modern governments favored the rich and was a plague on the people; China's old system, which relied on local custom, was not as bad.[53] Liu thus came to the conclusion that "worshipping Western methods" offered no hope for China; Western civilization, infected with materialism and utilitarianism, should not be a model for China.[54] In brief, "Europe, America and Japan only have pseudo-civilizations (*wei wen-ming*)."[55]

Liu's explanation was that China had the great advantage of being much farther removed from her feudal era than Europe and Japan were from theirs. Thus the Europeans and Japanese were more accustomed than the Chinese to being controlled. China, having left feudalism behind thousands of years before, enjoyed much looser government; moreover, government in China relied on virtue rather than divine authority. Liu argued in this fashion that Chinese tradition was similar to anarchism and that anarchism could therefore be put into practice more easily in China than in the West.[56]

These views clearly separated Liu and his followers in Japan from the vast majority of Chinese anarchists and other revolutionaries. Such attitudes toward tradition and, more significantly, criticisms of

[51] Liu Shih-p'ei, "Fei-ping fei-ts'ai lun," *T'ien-i-pao*, No. 2 (June 25, 1907), in Chang Nan and Wang Jen-chih, *Hsüan-chi*, II, 904.

[52] Ho Chen and Liu Shih-p'ei, "Lun chung-tsu ke-ming yü wu-cheng-fu ke-ming chih te-shih," *T'ien-i pao*, Nos. 6 and 7 (Sept. 1 and Sept. 15, 1907), Chang and Wang, *Hsüan-chi*, II, 953–56.

[53] Liu Shih-p'ei, "Lun hsin-cheng wei ping-min chih ken," *T'ien-i pao*, Nos. 8–10 (combined issue, Oct. 30, 1907), in Chang and Wang, *Hsüan-chi*, II, 972–73.

[54] *Ibid.*, pp. 968–70.

[55] Ho Chen and Liu Shih-p'ei, "Lun chung-tsu ke-ming . . . ," p. 956.

[56] *Ibid.*, pp. 957–58. See also Liu Shih-p'ei, "Lun hsin-cheng wei ping-min chih ken," p. 974.

the West, were rarely expressed in revolutionary literature. Even when he directed his attention to the modern world and his hopes for man's future, Liu could hardly avoid a wistful look backward. Things were simpler in the past, he complained, when merchants did not have to be educated and scholars did not have to learn about military affairs. Nowadays merchants and even farmers had to study, and life had become much more complex.[57]

These ideas are not at all surprising in view of Liu's stature as a classical scholar and in the light of his later career. He turned against the revolution in 1908, served the Manchus in some shady spy operations, and subsequently supported monarchical restoration in general and Yüan Shih-k'ai's effort in particular. With Chang Ping-lin he devoted a good part of his energies even during the revolutionary movement to writing treatises on traditional scholarly subjects for the *Kuo-ts'ui hsüeh-pao* (National Essence Journal). Liu's connection with the revolution may therefore be dismissed by some as merely a brief aberration in his career, but it lasted for five of his first twenty-five years and involved him in two revolutionary organizations and at least three revolutionary publications. If, in the perspective of his entire life, his revolutionary period was only a brief aberration, that makes it more significant, not less. For it suggests there was something in the air that affected men of widely varying dispositions. Liu may not have been a committed revolutionary, but his reasons for abandoning the revolution are obscure; highly personal factors, having to do with intraparty squabbles and pressures from his strong-willed wife and brother-in-law, were probably decisive.[58] But for a brief period he shared much with all Chinese revolutionaries, and with the other Chinese anarchists he agreed more than he disagreed.

Liu differed most from the *New Century* group in his attitude toward the West, but important though this difference was, Liu was

[57] Liu Shih-p'ei, "Jen-lei chün-li shuo," *T'ien-i pao*, No. 3 (July 10, 1907), in Chang and Wang, *Hsüan-chi*, II, 911.

[58] See Feng Tzu-yu, *Ke-ming i-shih*, II, 232, and Hu Han-min, "Tzu-chuan," p. 400. Liu's wife, Ho Chen, seems to have been a formidable woman. She was the moving spirit behind the founding of *T'ien-i pao*, which she undertook after coming into contact with some of the more extreme elements among Japanese socialists. The journal was considered the organ of her Association for the Recovery of Women's Rights (*Nü-tzu fu-ch'uan hui*). See Chang and Wang, *Hsüan-chi*, II, 1074–75. I have been unable to identify any writers in *T'ien-i pao* other than Liu, Ho Chen, and Wang Kung-ch'üan.

still more like than unlike the Paris anarchists. His attitude toward Chinese tradition was not entirely different from theirs. Liu was occasionally very critical of it. He attacked the examination system, the class divisions, the spirit of self-seeking, and much more.[59] Ho Chen and Liu specifically criticized those who "only advocate nationalism (*min-tsu chu-i*)" partly for clinging to outdated ideas of China's uniqueness and superiority. Arguing that such ideas can lead to "nationalistic imperialism (*min-tsu ti-kuo chu-i*)," Ho and Liu condemned all ideas of superiority. "Why hold on to old ideas about China and foreign barbarians?" [60]

Inevitably, Liu found it impossible to be absolutely evenhanded in his discussions of China and the West, but his criticism of the latter was not due simply to a lingering traditionalism. On the contrary, Liu's praise of Chinese tradition must be understood as a reflection of his hostility to Western civilization. If there had to be government, he preferred to keep the old system rather than adopt Western forms.[61] But what he wanted most was to have no government at all. This was the dominant sentiment expressed in *T'ien-i pao*. Everything else Liu and his associates wrote was related to this central theme.

Liu saw very close links between the existence of governments, national boundaries, social classes, wealth and property, and armies. Citing numerous examples from the West and China, he outlined nothing less than the course of human history. In their desire to amass wealth, he wrote, men had employed soldiers and fought each other. As a result, fissures developed between rich and poor, noble and low, educated and uneducated, rulers and ruled. Empires were created and armies established to protect them. Rulers used soldiers and wealth to control their subjects. Accordingly, in order to put an end to fighting and destroy classes, armies and fortunes had to be abolished, governments overthrown, national boundaries erased, and all land and property divided equally among the people. Ultimately the desires for profit and ownership of things would be eliminated, whereupon greed and fighting would also disappear. Then there would be no more distinctions between strong and weak, rich and poor, governing and governed, served and serving.[62]

---

[59] For an example see "Lun hsin-cheng wei ping-min chih ken," p. 969.

[60] Ho Chen and Liu Shih-p'ei, "Lun chung-tsu ke-ming . . . ," pp. 951–52.

[61] *Ibid.*

[62] Liu Shih-p'ei, "Fei-ping fei-ts'ai lun," pp. 900–904. It is worth noting that Liu

As this rather Utopian image evolved into a concentrated attack on government in particular, it acquired some interesting features. One was an attitude toward classes that anticipated some Chinese Communist views. An anonymous author in *T'ien-i pao* wrote optimistically about the burgeoning social revolutions that were beginning to sweep the world in the wake of racial and political revolutions, but he argued that the root of the matter — the very existence of classes — had not yet been touched. To dig that deeply it was necessary to create a huge organization of the workers of the world and to divest capitalists of everything they owned.[63]

Liu Shih-p'ei's views were not quite the same, but they were no less reminiscent of modern communism. In one curious passage, for example, he praised Hsü Hsing, a contemporary of Mencius, for his "everyone a farmer" concept. Hsü, Liu said, had his shortcomings, but in advocating the shattering of class distinctions he had demonstrated the proper spirit.[64] More significantly, Liu wrote frequently of how industrialization resulted in the division of society into two classes, capitalists and workers. Capitalists had rights but no responsibilities; workers had duties but no rights. Even in China the process of social division was under way, and commoners were being controlled by the wealthy as a new class of arrogant aristocrats such as Chang Chien arose.[65]

Rifts such as those between classes represented, to Liu Shih-p'ei, a long process of degeneration. From a common origin and natural equality humanity had descended to a condition of man-made

---

was expressing similar but not quite identical views at the same time in *Min-pao*. See his article "Pei-tien p'ien" (Lament for the Tillers), *Min-pao*, No. 15 (July 5, 1907), pp. 19–34, in which Liu analyzed the history of agricultural problems and solutions that had been attempted since ancient times. He concluded that the major contemporary problem was due to class division and advocated that the land should be "held in common by the people" (*t'u-ti wei kuo-min so kung-yu*) in order to destroy the division. Interestingly enough, in his *Min-pao* article he added a note on how this kind of economic and social change was related to democratic government. Cf. note 70, below.

[63] "She-hui ke-ming ta feng-ch'ao" (The Great Tide of Social Revolution), *T'ien-i pao*, No. 2 (June 25, 1907), in Chang Nan and Wang Jen-chih, *Hsüan-chi*, II, 905–7.

[64] Liu Shih-p'ei, "Jen-lei chün-li shuo," p. 913.

[65] Liu Shih-p'ei, "Lun hsin-cheng wei ping-min chih ken," pp. 971–72, and "Wu-cheng-fu chu-i chih p'ing-teng kuan," *T'ien-i pao*, Nos. 4, 5, 7 (July 25, Aug. 10, Sept. 15, 1907), in Chang and Wang, *Hsüan-chi*, II, 926–28.

inequality.[66] This inequality Liu analyzed in terms of three sets of relationships: between government and people, capitalists and workers, strong nations and weak.[67] "In sum," he concluded, "the evil of government is that those above oppress those below. The evil of private capital is that the wealthy control the poor. The evil of states is that the strong oppress the weak." As long as these three evils continued to exist, only governments, individual men, and individual states would benefit, rather than the masses of humanity all over the world.[68]

The concern for human equality and for mankind as a whole was a major point of agreement between the Japanese and European branches of Chinese anarchism. The Tokyo group also took issue with anti-Manchuism from this standpoint. Liu and his wife rejected the notion that different races should not live together. They also denounced the idea that if more than one race inhabited a state one should rule the other; here they referred specifically to the Chinese case and explicitly rejected this major T'ung-meng-hui principle, even going so far as to suggest that if it were acceptable for one race to rule another a case might be made for Manchu rule in China. But their idea of nationalism was to get rid of all inequalities, not only those that existed between Chinese and Manchus but also those between India and England, Annam and France, the Philippines and the United States, and Central Asia and Russia. The Lius sharply criticized the T'ung-meng-hui ("the so-called revolutionary party") because so few of its members went beyond anti-Manchuism. Ho and Liu advocated not only a world-wide anti-colonial movement but also a "majority revolution" in China itself. Interestingly, they compared the Chinese to the French revolutionaries, who, they believed, had not extended their movement beyond Paris, and to the Americans, who had not extended theirs beyond the bourgeoisie. In contrast to such geographically and socially limited revolutions, both of which left the masses of poor still in their misery, Liu Shih-p'ei and Ho Chen found that the Russians were carrying their ideas to all classes throughout the country. When the Russians would succeed in their revolution, the Lius predicted, they would be sure to carry its benefits much farther than the French or Americans had. To avoid

[66] *Ibid.*, pp. 919–23.    [67] *Ibid.*, pp. 923–29.    [68] *Ibid.*, p. 930.

having a small minority reap the benefits, therefore, revolution had to "emerge from the people as a whole." [69]

This position created obvious disagreements between the anarchists and the T'ung-meng-hui. Two kinds of attempts were made to resolve them. First, the anarchists made it clear that they were only opposed to racism and not to criticisms the T'ung-meng-hui directed at specific Manchu wrongdoing. Second, they pointed out that overthrowing the Manchus had to precede an anarchist revolution and thus could be considered a necessary stage in the historical process. [70] These attempts had at best only uneven success. One reason was that all writers for *T'ien-i pao* cared far more about universal harmony on earth (a sort of "*Ta-t'ung* now!" sentiment) than they did about getting along with the T'ung-meng-hui. The second and closely related reason was that Liu and Ho were already campaigning vigorously for introducing anarchism as soon as the Manchus fell; in the very same article that purported to show anarchism was not in conflict with the anti-Manchu revolution, they also insisted that no government should be set up after the Manchu collapse. [71] In addition, they and others went into considerable detail about the evils of republican government. Constitutional monarchy was of course worse still, since half the parliament always consisted of nobles, but republicanism (or constitutional democracy, as it was more commonly termed) was not a great deal better. In such systems half the parliament was made up of capitalists, corruption was rife, and property qualifications limited the electorate; more important still, as long as the upper class controlled industry and the masses depended on industry for their livelihood, the rich would always be in control. [72] Furthermore, a representative system left minorities unrepresented. In the end, the anarchists' basic point was that any government required a bureaucracy and therefore was a system in which some persons con-

[69] Ho Chen and Liu Shih-p'ei, "Lun chung-tsu ke-ming . . . ," pp. 951–52.

[70] For example, *ibid.*, pp. 947–51. Typically, Liu Shih-p'ei also tried a third solution, writing articles for *Min-pao* in which he supported T'ung-meng-hui anti-Manchuism, even going so far as to compare the Manchus to the British in India and the French in Annam. See his three-part article "Pien Man-jen [in the last two parts, Man-chou] fei Chung-kuo chih ch'en-min," *Min-pao*, No. 14, pp. 39–111; No. 15, pp. 35–62; No. 18, pp. 1–25. The comment on Britain and France is in Part 3, p. 22.

[71] Ho Chen and Liu Shih-p'ei, "Lun chung-tsu ke-ming . . . ," pp. 952–53, 957.

[72] Liu, "Lun hsin-cheng wei ping-min chih ken," pp. 970–71.

trolled others; at best, majority rule meant the few would be ravaged by the many.[73]

Another writer took more direct aim both at reformers, such as Liang Ch'i-ch'ao, and at the T'ung-meng-hui, bluntly declaring both to be misguided and self-seeking.[74] Still another frothed more passionately. Government and justice, he declared, are incompatible and mutually exclusive. Even in the United States, "the world's number one republic," elections were won by those who spent the most. The form of government was of no consequence. Monarchy or democracy, constitutional monarchy or republic, "as long as there is government it is a murder weapon, an instrument of greed. . . ." The title of this article aptly summed up its anonymous author's creed.[75]

Views of this sort, vehemently and frequently repeated, linked the Tokyo and Paris anarchists. The Japan group, with its more critical attitude toward the West and its lack of interest in science, its stronger attachment to Chinese tradition, and of course its early abandonment of revolution, differed in very important ways. Liu also made one brief attempt to distinguish anarchists from socialists, whereas the Paris group considered itself socialist. The attempt is interesting because of the special place Liu assigned to socialists and anarchists: they were the only two groups that "want to reconstruct the world." It is also interesting that Liu criticized the socialists' methods because they would solve only those problems connected with property and capital; socialists not only would not destroy the state but would strengthen it.[76] In none of this, however, did the Tokyo and Paris anarchists differ from each other quite as much as all the anarchists did from the T'ung-meng-hui. The latter did consider themselves socialists who wanted a powerful state, and they did not hesitate to rebuke the anarchists on occasion although the task was left to minor *Min-pao* writers.[77]

---

[73] Liu, "Wu-cheng-fu chu-i chih p'ing-teng kuan," pp. 925–26.

[74] Chih-ta [identity unknown], "Pao-Man yü p'ai-Man," *T'ien-i pao*, No. 3, in Chang and Wang, *Hsüan-chi*, II, 915–16.

[75] "Cheng-fu che wan-o chih yüan yeh" (Government Is the Source of All Evil), in *T'ien-i pao, ibid.*, pp. 914–15.

[76] Liu, "Wu-cheng-fu chu-i chih p'ing-teng kuan," pp. 930–31. See also p. 918, where Liu identifies individualist, communist, and socialist forms of anarchism. It seems clear that Liu was criticizing T'ung-meng-hui "socialism."

[77] For example, Lei Chao-hsing, "Cheng-fu shuo," *Min-pao*, No. 17, pp. 87–97.

The anarchists, however, wrote confidently of the day when all government would be eliminated. "Therefore," said Liu, "we stand for realizing the natural equality of man, destroying artificial inequality, overthrowing every organ of rule, abolishing every association based on class or occupation, and uniting all the people of the world into one great mass to plan the complete happiness of mankind." Liu then drew up a sequence of stages beginning with the abolition of the state and proceeding through eliminating national and racial boundaries, equalizing power, pleasure, and pain, and finally reaching absolute sexual equality. The method to be followed he diagrammed as beginning with publishing books and magazines and engaging in speeches and other agitation to enlighten people with anarchist teachings. This stage would be followed by organizing workers, calling strikes, refusing to pay taxes, punishing "robbers of the people" (and killing them if necessary), until at last government would be gone, and equality and anarchism would be ushered in. Then, Liu proclaimed, "universal happiness will be at hand!" [78]

### WU CHIH-HUI AND CHINESE ANARCHISM

Liu's was a dream that all anarchists shared. But China produced in this era yet another variant of the anarchist dreamer. Wu Chih-hui, although in general agreement with most of the anarchist ideas described above, was by no means reluctant to attack the Manchus and even to argue for the restoration of Chinese rule.[79] He also warned his comrades against misunderstanding the concept of the Great Community (*Ta-t'ung*). It was not to be thought of as a specific condition of society, a final point at which to stop, for this would be contrary to the eternal progress implicit in the theory of evolution. The concept indicated a direction along which to proceed, not a final objective.[80]

One important feature of Wu's writings was his attack upon religion. If the Paris anarchists' unlimited faith in science qualifies

---

Lei argued that the *Ta-t'ung* sought by anarchists could come only by a long process of evolution and only when the entire world was ready for it. For now, it was still a "yu-cheng-fu" (lit., "having government") era.

[78] Liu, "Wu-cheng-fu chu-i chih p'ing-teng kuan," pp. 931–32.

[79] See "Yü-lun," *Wu Chih-hui hsüeh-shu lun-chu ti-san-pien*, pp. 140–41.

[80] "Shu tzu-yu ying-yeh kuan-chien hou," *Wu Chih-hui hsüeh-shu lun-chu ti-san-pien*, p. 19.

them in one respect as precursors of the radical Chinese intellectual movement of the next two decades, Wu's hostility to religion, which was shared but not expressed as often or as vehemently by his colleagues, qualifies them in another. Indeed, Wu himself was to be in the forefront of the pro-science, anti-religion group in the famous 1923 debate.[81]

Wu began his discussion with the statement that socialism was anti-religion and religion was anti-socialist; the two were "absolutely different." [82] The difference lay in the moral content of religion and socialism, Wu contended. Religion possessed a modicum of morality, but because its "degree of evolution" was low, it also contained a far greater measure of superstition. Socialism, on the other hand, stood much higher on the evolutionary ladder and therefore surpassed religion in moral content and was devoid of superstition.[83] The morality of socialism [84] included all that was good in religion and more besides, while it excluded all the evils of religion. Hence there was no further place in the world for religion, and it had to be opposed.[85]

*New Century* readers took issue with Wu on several counts. One, for example, argued that morality was inherent in religion and the latter need only be reformed, not abolished.[86] Wu's reply now denied to religion even the faint praise he had extended earlier. Religion was designed for those unenlightened souls who were unable to seek truth with their minds, he charged. Moreover, the basic problem was to reform society; here religion had nothing to offer, and in fact it had

[81] The debate and its broader context are treated in D. W. Y. Kwok, *Scientism in Chinese Thought, 1900–1950.*

[82] "Tsung-chiao tao-te yü she-hui chu-i," *Wu Chih-hui hsien-sheng ch'üan-chi,* VI, 2. (This article appeared in *HSC,* No. 42.)

[83] *Ibid.,* pp. 2–3. To illustrate this conception Wu provided a diagram in which he added that the "pseudo-morality" (*wei tao-te*) of religion included a "class concept," whereas socialist morality was dedicated to the destruction of classes. *Ibid.,* pp. 3–4.

[84] Wu did not explain in detail what he meant by the "morality of socialism." He noted only that its characteristics were "selflessness (*wu-wo*), altruism (*po-ai*), etc.," and that it meant "the destruction of classes, the abolition of the spirits, etc." *Ibid.,* p. 4. *Po-ai* was commonly used in revolutionary writings for "fraternity" in the liberty-equality-fraternity triad. However, the anarchists also translated "altruism" with these two characters. See "L'Anarchisme," in *HSCTS,* p. 39a.

[85] "Tsung-chiao tao-te yü she-hui chu-i," p. 5.

[86] "Tsung-chiao wen-t'i" in *Wu Chih-hui hsien-sheng ch'üan-chi,* VI, 7. This article may also be found in *HSC,* Nos. 54 and 55; see p. 3b in each.

no good features at all and should be eradicated.[87] There was no need to accept myths concerning the Creation in order to explain nature; "the universal principle of evolution enables men to understand. There is no point in talking about [anything being] unfathomable." [88] This same principle, evolution, made it clear that religion must be eliminated and socialism must come to the fore; and not only socialism but "today's newest socialism, which is specifically termed anarchism." Wu concluded: "Because we hope to hasten the progress of mankind, we can only promote science; we should not advocate superstition." [89]

Wu's identification of the new with the good was never clearer than when he compared "all the religions of olden days" with "the socialism we now hope for," and found that the "degree of evolution" determined that the morality of the latter was purer and "more complete." [90] His faith in science generally, and in evolution specifically, linked him to his *New Century* colleagues in the first decade of the twentieth century, to the *New Youth* magazine writers (of which he was one, although an infrequent contributor) of the next decade, and to the worshipers of "Mr. Science" of the 1920's. The development of these ideas in the *New Century* between 1907 and 1910 reveals the speed at which the Chinese intellectual revolution was progressing. Although the political struggle had hardly begun, the intellectual battle was already being carried on along a broad front that extended far beyond China. The Manchus had yet to be overthrown and a new government established; revolutionaries were attempting to instill in the Chinese people new concepts of nationalism and popular government. For others, however, these principles were already outmoded. Some believed that by Western standards China had yet to enter the nineteenth century, while others sought to rush her into the twentieth. Still others looked even further into the future and, interestingly enough, among them were the two enemies, Wu Chih-hui and Chang Ping-lin, whose conceptions had something in common with those of their mutual opponent, K'ang Yu-wei, as well as with those of Liu Shih-p'ei.

Wu Chih-hui's vision of a future world community was barely adumbrated in the one brief article he devoted to it, and it would

[87] *Ibid.*, pp. 9–11.        [88] *Ibid.*, p. 18.        [89] *Ibid.*, p. 19.
[90] "Tsung-chiao tao-te yü she-hui chu-i," pp. 2–4.

therefore be unfair to compare it with K'ang's *Ta-t'ung-shu* or even with Chang's singular conception. But a brief description of Wu's plan will help us to understand more fully the character of Chinese anarchist thought and its place in China's revolutionary movement and modern intellectual history.

Wu proposed the elimination of all national boundaries and the adoption of a single common language.[91] Scientific training would occupy 70 to 80 per cent of the educational curriculum, and the remainder would be devoted to "anarchist morality." The result would be that a universal moral code would replace government by law. In such a society, for each to produce according to his ability would not be considered a duty, nor would it be considered a right for each to receive according to his needs; presumably, both would be accepted as natural principles of existence, and the very concepts of rights and duties would have been banished.

There would be no private property, no governing and no governed. But Wu did not propose a return to the original state of nature. He conceived of an organized society, and although he was not clear about how it would come about, he had many ideas about what it would look like. He sketched plans for homes, communities, and transportation facilities, the latter to include flying balloon routes and a system of conveyer belts for pedestrians making short trips. Wu specified the distance to be maintained among different communities (three to five *li*) and stipulated that each would provide room, board, and recreation facilities for those who desired to travel; no one would be required to have a fixed place of residence. Each house would have flowers in front, trees in back, and a terrace looking out upon the trees. To build the many houses that would be needed, all palaces, temples, monuments, pagodas, and the like would be torn down and the materials used for new construction.

Wu stressed the importance of the educational system. Engineering

---

[91] This discussion is based upon Wu's "T'an wu-cheng-fu chih hsien-t'ien," in *Wu Chih-hui hsüeh-shu lun-chu*, pp. 254–57. (This article may also be found in *HSC*, No. 49.) On this same subject, Professor D. W. Y. Kwok has very kindly allowed me to see his manuscript "The *Ta-t'ung* Thought of Wu Chih-hui," which he presented at the International Conference on Asian History, August, 1964, Hong Kong. See also Hidemi Onogawa, "Liu Shih-p'ei and Anarchism," pp. 80, 90 ff., for Liu's similar concept and its relation to K'ang Yu-wei's idea of "Ta-t'ung" and to other currents in older Chinese thought.

studies would have top priority so that immediate transportation and construction needs could be met. Special attention would be given to research in hygiene and medicine in order to lengthen life expectancy. He even hoped for the elimination of the "cannibalistic" custom of meat-eating.[92] The sciences and every other specialized subject would be familiar to all, and there would be no further need for "snobbish" academic titles such as the Ph.D. Wu also spoke of the need for a diversified economy which would make the most of each person's capabilities and in which each would be free to follow his chosen profession.

It would be unwise to regard this brief and Utopian statement as a serious plan for a future society. But it illustrates graphically the ideals to which Wu and his comrades were dedicated and sheds some interesting light on the mood of these men. It might be speculated that schemes such as Wu's and perhaps even movements such as the anarchists' are born of a marriage between frustration and desperate hope, and are akin to what Schumpeter has characterized as "the kind of radicalism whose intensity is in inverse proportion to its practical possibilities, the radicalism of impotence."[93]

The spirit of these men and the circumstances in which they found themselves may offer a parallel with the Chinese intelligentsia of the next decade. The failure of the Chinese republic and the disillusionment with the Western democracies after World War One, combined with the victory of the Bolsheviks in Russia and the resulting heightened interest in "scientific socialism," have frequently been cited as decisive influences upon the Chinese radical movement. The Chinese anarchists, similarly disillusioned and also inclined to draw upon the scientific and materialistic side of Western civilization, were attracted by a theory that seemed to make change and "progress" laws of history. This theory, Darwinian evolution, became in Kropotkin's hands a new view of human society and one that neatly suited men who were already favorably disposed toward effecting change by

[92] Some of the anarchists took an oath to refrain from eating meat, smoking, drinking, and various other habits that they regarded as harmful. Li Shih-tseng was still a vegetarian in 1959, when I last saw him.

[93] Joseph A. Schumpeter, *Capitalism, Socialism, and Democracy*, p. 328. For an interesting contrasting view see Wilbert E. Moore's 1966 Presidential Address to the American Sociological Association, "The Utility of Utopias," *American Sociological Review*, XXXI (1966), 765–72.

means of "struggle" and accepting "westernization" and science. It is important too that anarchist doctrine was intensely activist; both Bakunin and Kropotkin endorsed violence and even assassination. The Chinese anarchists' position is demonstrated by the praises heaped upon Wang Ching-wei in the last issue of *New Century* for his attempt to assassinate the Prince Regent. The anarchism of Kropotkin and Bakunin thus provides a "scientific" explanation of history and a plan of action to eradicate the obstacles that barred the "natural" course of events. The similarity to the impression made upon other Chinese radicals by Marxism-Leninism is unmistakable.[94]

THE CHINESE ANARCHISTS AND THE REVOLUTIONARY MOVEMENT

It is amply clear that the Chinese anarchists differed from other T'ung-meng-hui writers in spirit and in their basic principles. Why, then, did they support the revolutionary movement? The obvious answer seems to be also the chief explanation: it "was a marriage of convenience and friendship, not of logic." [95] For one thing, the anarchists considered the overthrow of the Manchus to be an essential first step toward China's attainment of anarchism. As Li Shih-tseng put it, expelling the Manchus was one stage in the revolution; the revolution began with the elimination of all authority, and this in turn started with the overthrow of the Manchu emperor.[96]

Sun and Wu Chih-hui also had a common enemy in Chang Ping-lin,[97] who began to attack Sun in 1907. In 1909 Chang and several other members of the T'ung-meng-hui, including T'ao Ch'eng-chang, issued a manifesto criticizing Sun.[98] The major allegations were that

[94] For a further discussion of this phenomenon and the post-1911 relationship between the anarchist and communist movements in China see Scalapino and Yu, *The Chinese Anarchist Movement*, pp. 39–44, 54–61.

[95] *Ibid.*, p. 26. See pp. 21–26 for a discussion of this question.

[96] Li Shih-tseng, "Ke-ming," p. 5a. Li subsequently argued that China need not pass through stages of constitutional monarchy and republican government, contrary to what some claimed. His reasoning was identical to Sun Yat-sen's analogy with railroad building mentioned earlier: a civilization in which candles were still relied upon for lighting need not go through stages of using kerosene and gas before it introduced electricity. He took care, however, to explain how the theory of evolution provided for such leaps. *Ibid.*, pp. 6b–7a.

[97] Scalapino and Yu, *The Chinese Anarchist Movement*, pp. 24–25; Onogawa, "Liu Shih-p'ei and Anarchism," p. 97.

[98] Scalapino and Yu (p. 25) date this manifesto in October, 1907; Tsou Lu says it was issued after the Anking uprising (which took place on November 19, 1908).

Sun had inflated his own importance in the movement by taking the title *tsung-li*, and that he had used party funds to amass a personal fortune. Wu, who had been on bad terms with Chang for years, was a logical choice to lead the counterattack in Sun's behalf, particularly in view of the fact that Chang was by now the dominant figure on *Min-pao*.[99] However, one may question the degree to which "Sun and the Paris group were brought even closer together"[100] because of this. Although it is true that Sun was "defended" in the pages of *New Century*, the character of that defense deserves our attention.

In the late summer or early fall of 1909, Sun wrote to Wu in his own defense, and appealed to Wu to publish his explanation. Sun made no mention of Chang Ping-lin and suggested that T'ao be regarded as the author of the manifesto.[101]

On November 13, 1909, *New Century* published its attack upon the writers of the anti-Sun manifesto. It was not written by Wu, but was contained in a letter written to Paris by someone who called himself "a member of the revolutionary party."[102] This defense of Sun began with a brief quotation from the anti-Sun manifesto, in which it was asserted that when the T'ung-meng-hui was founded,

---

See *Chung-kuo Kuo-min-tang shih-kao*, p. 74. We know that Chang and T'ao sought funds from Sun to re-establish the *Min-pao* after the Japanese authorities forced it to close in October, 1908; they entertained the idea of moving it to the United States. See Lo Chia-lun, *Kuo-fu nien-p'u ch'u-kao*, I, 206. This indicates that Tsou Lu may be correct, since Chang and T'ao probably would not have asked Sun for money after issuing such a manifesto. Sun himself made no mention of the manifesto until the fall of 1909, when he appealed to Wu for help. Wu wrote three articles attacking Chang in 1908 but made no reference to the manifesto; the chief issues concerned the *Su-pao* incident and Wu's proposals for the adoption of an international language. See *HSC*, Nos. 28, 44, 63. The feud between Sun and Chang seems to have broken out in 1907, moderated during 1908, and resumed with new intensity late in 1908 or early in 1909.

[99] It is possible that Wu and Chang were enemies even prior to the *Su-pao* incident. See Scalapino and Yu, *The Chinese Anarchist Movement*, p. 68, note 68. These authors hold that because of the relationship between Wu and Chang "it was easy for the Paris group led by Wu to defend Sun against an old enemy." *Ibid.*, p. 25.

[100] *Ibid.*, p. 24.

[101] "Tsai Ou chiang ch'ü Mei-kuo shih chih Lun-tun Wu Ching-heng han" (Letter to Wu Ching-heng [Chih-hui] in London, written in Europe as I was about to go to America), in Sun Yat-sen, *Kuo-fu ch'üan-chi*, V, 85.

[102] "Ch'üan, ch'üan, ch'üan" (Take Heed, Hear Me, Take Heed), *HSC*, No. 115, pp. 4–11. It was continued in the next issue five weeks later. See *HSC*, No. 116, pp. 9–13.

Sun's rhetoric and his supposed ability to gather funds among his many followers in Southeast Asia enabled him to be named *tsung-li* even though he possessed no other particular merit.[103] The writer took issue with this statement, but noted that Sun "is only one man in the affairs of the revolution" and "the T'ung-meng-hui is only a small group among the organs of the revolutionary party"; besides, having a *tsung-li* "and other such titles" was only for administrative purposes. "This year 'A' will do it, and next year it will be 'B.' Any group, even in academic circles, has such a title. None of them regard him [a *tsung-li*] as an individual with special qualifications." [104] "A *tsung-li* is only the public servant of one society and he is chosen in rotation according to ability. . . . The *tsung-li* of the T'ung-meng-hui is only the *tsung-li* of the Tokyo student society. Why contrive a title such as head (*t'ung-ling*)?" [105]

The writer then went on to criticize the authors of the manifesto for giving the title "supreme head" (*ta t'ung-ling*) to the *tsung-li* of the T'ung-meng-hui; they seemed to think, he said, that the T'ung-meng-hui was China and that its *tsung-li* would be the head of the Chinese Republic. That would be decided by the Chinese people once the revolution was successful. The T'ung-meng-hui could not arrogate this responsibility to itself, he concluded, and Sun did not necessarily possess the qualifications for the position, although he conceded that even if Sun were not elected head he would surely be given another high post.[106]

The writer had thus defended Sun partly by denying the importance of his organization and the post he held in it. Sun, interestingly enough, after reading this article, promptly wrote to Wu to thank him for printing it, expressing satisfaction with the criticism of T'ao Ch'eng-chang.[107] It seems clear that Sun did not complain about

[103] *HSC*, No. 115, p. 8b.

[104] *Ibid.*, p. 9a. Compare these statements with those of Lin Chüeh-min that Sun's position depended upon whether or not "he does his duties well," that it was controlled by the party members, and that the members were not followers of any one individual. Quoted by Shelley Cheng, "The T'ung-meng-hui: Its Organization, Leadership and Finances, 1905–1912," p. 146.

[105] "Ch'üan, ch'üan, ch'üan," p. 9b.

[106] *Ibid.* The article continued with an unqualified refutation of the charge that Sun had mishandled party funds.

[107] "Chih Wu Ching-heng ch'ing yü Hsin shih-chi p'ing-lun Jih-Hua hsin-pao p'o-huai tang-shih miu-lun ko-han," in Sun Yat-sen, *Kuo-fu ch'üan-chi*, V, 89. This included a total of five letters. The first one, cited here, was written on

having been relegated to a lesser role in the revolutionary movement as long as he was exonerated of the charges of being overambitious, self-seeking, and dishonest.

Sun then added that in a recent letter from Tokyo he had been informed that Chang had unleashed another attack "that is even more vile than T'ao's" and which he could not even bring himself to discuss. He appealed to Wu to retaliate.[108] Nine days later Sun wrote again, advising Wu that Chang's (still unspecified) charges had been published in a letter to a Singapore newspaper. Sun stressed that Chang had great prestige owing to his martyrdom in jail and because of his writings; unless his accusations were refuted he could do great harm to the party. He called upon Wu to do this in the very next issue of *New Century*.[109]

Only three days later, Sun, now obviously very upset, wrote once again, asking Wu to expose Chang's own misconduct.[110] He asked that Wu send him the evidence of Chang's implication in Liu Shih-p'ei's spying activities in behalf of the Manchus. Sun re-emphasized that Chang was "a towering figure" in the party with great influence among the overseas students and that it was important to have solid evidence of his wrongdoing.[111] Forgetting, perhaps in his haste and anxiety, to tell Wu his forwarding address, Sun had to write Wu again that same day.[112] In his last letter Sun said that he found these developments "unbearable"; he requested that Wu send him extra copies of the articles refuting T'ao and Chang, so that he could circulate them among his followers as he traveled.[113]

Wu published his attack on Chang in the next issue of *New Century*, as Sun had requested.[114] He noted that the anti-Sun manifesto

---

December 4, 1909. In it Sun makes it clear that he considered T'ao to be the author of the manifesto. Wu later confirmed this, but no one denied that Chang was also one of the sponsors.

[108] *Ibid.*, p. 90.

[109] *Ibid.*, Letter of December 13, 1909. Wu's journal was now appearing only once a month, probably owing to financial difficulties.

[110] Wu claimed to have proof that Chang was still associated with his old friend Liu Shih-p'ei, who had by now betrayed the revolutionary cause.

[111] *Ibid.*, Letter of December 16.

[112] *Ibid.*, pp. 90–91. Sun was then in New York and was soon to leave for San Francisco.

[113] *Ibid.*, p. 91. Letter of January 3, 1910.

[114] "Tang-jen," *HSC*, No. 117, pp. 1–10. This issue was published on January 22, 1910.

had been written by T'ao Ch'eng-chang and had already been discussed in an earlier issue of *New Century*; he would therefore concentrate on Chang Ping-lin's subsequent article.[115] The latter was
actually aimed chiefly at Wang Ching-wei, who, after *Min-pao* had
been forced to cease publication in October, 1908, managed to
bring out two more issues early in 1910. Chang was particularly
outraged because Wang, in order to evade the wrath of the Japanese
authorities who had shut down *Min-pao*, issued the two numbers
under the imprimatur of the World Association in Paris. Chang's
charges against Sun seem to have been similar to those contained
in the 1907 manifesto; the attack that Sun considered unmention-
able was not revealed. Wu defended Sun against the accusation that
he had personally profited from party funds and then proceeded to
revile Chang for "selling out the revolution."[116] He concluded by
mentioning that he had not yet seen Chang's latest attack on *him*
because of the ban that had been placed upon circulating *Min-pao*,
and he asked that someone send him a copy.[117]

The role played by the Chinese anarchists in the revolutionary
movement is difficult to assess. Although they found some immediate common interests with other elements in the movement, such as
the desire to overthrow the Manchus and the wish to discredit Chang
Ping-lin, these were not interests that were central to them. Anti-
Manchuism embarrassed them; and while Wu's feud with Chang was
intense and, as we shall see, far from casual intellectually, it was
carried on largely without reference to the revolutionary movement.
It was only when Sun personally appealed to Wu for help that he
entered the political arena with vigor. Apart from this one incident,
Wu and the other *New Century* writers concerned themselves almost
exclusively with promoting the doctrines of science and anarchism.
In terms of geography and politics they remained on the fringes of
the revolutionary movement. The Tokyo anarchists were hardly
closer to the political center of the T'ung-meng-hui.

[115] *Ibid.*, p. 4b. Wu offered no further comment on the first *Hsin shih-chi* article
"defending" Sun, the implication being that he approved of the views expressed.
Indeed, the fact that it was published in *Hsin shih-chi* indicates that this was the case.

[116] *Ibid.*, p. 6b. The letters purporting to link Chang with Liu Shih-p'ei may be
found on pp. 6b–9b.

[117] *Ibid.*, p. 10b. Wu was referring to Chang's "Kuei Hsin shih-chi."

With reference to intellectual development, however, the anarchists were in some ways closer to the T'ung-meng-hui and to the mainstream of modern Chinese thinking. I hasten to add that doubtless there are numerous reasons why anarchism should not be taken this seriously. Clemenceau is supposed to have said he felt sorry for anyone who had not been an anarchist at twenty, and many would similarly dismiss anarchism as little more than an expression of youthful exuberance and rebellion. It is also easy to exaggerate some of the obvious relationships between anarchism and modern communism; the men we have discussed, after all, did not become Communists. Furthermore, anarchism's principles differ sharply from all other varieties of socialism in several important respects. In reply to his own question, "What is property?" Proudhon issued the defiant answer that has probably done more to link these doctrines than anything else: "Property is theft." But he also said, "Whoever puts his hand on me to govern me is an usurper and a tyrant; I declare him my enemy!" And his anarchist followers have usually interpreted that "whoever" rigorously enough to include even cadres of political parties that claimed to represent the propertyless classes. To the anarchists, democratic political movements, even if less abhorrent because they were less organized, were not much better. Few anarchists in East or West have dissociated themselves from Proudhon's cry, "Universal suffrage is the counterrevolution!" Organized movements to effect political reforms, though they included some anarchists from time to time, have invariably and rigidly proved to be incompatible with anarchism. What, then, are the connections between the Chinese anarchists, the T'ung-meng-hui republican movement, and the intellectual revolution?

The first connection is that many Chinese saw no way to separate anarchism, socialism, communism, and republicanism. As prominent a fighter for the republic as Sung Chiao-jen, who like so many other T'ung-meng-hui leaders considered himself a socialist, wrote that "true socialism will not succeed unless you support anarchism and communism." [118] Liao Chung-k'ai published translations of articles dealing with anarchism and socialism in similarly respectful terms, although he distinguished the two and noted that his socialist author

[118] Quoted in Martin Bernal, "The Triumph of Anarchism over Marxism, 1906–1907," p. 136.

represented a moderate Christian socialism.[119] Despite Liu Shih-p'ei's one brief attempt to distinguish between socialism and anarchism, the Chinese anarchist organization in Japan was called the Society for the Study of Socialism; it declared its objective to be the achievement of both anarchism and socialism.[120] Its journal carried several translations of Engels including one of his prefaces to "The Communist Manifesto" and chapter one of the Manifesto itself.[121] Finally, the anarchist movement in Paris identified itself fully with socialism.[122]

In general, socialism was at least as important as republicanism in giving the T'ung-meng-hui a common core of belief. Voices were raised among the revolutionaries against republicanism, but I have yet to see a criticism of socialism in the revolutionary literature of this period. The T'ung-meng-hui, in its genuine concern to promote social as well as political change, found allies among the anarchists, whose overwhelming stress was upon the social and economic rather than the political.

This kind of support, however, does not seem to have contributed very much to the revolutionary movement, except in terms of intangible and indirect effects in shaping the general intellectual climate of the time. The anarchists, like their T'ung-meng-hui allies, fostered the belief that socialism was a moral doctrine of social justice and equality. In addition, they promoted some unique ideas that differed from those of other revolutionaries but which nevertheless shared some common ground with them. The anarchists tried to promote a new world view in much the same spirit as Tsou Jung agitated "to sweep away thousands of years of despotism" and Sun Yat-sen insisted China could do as well as Hawaii which "in one leap became a republic." [123] The spirit resembled what has been called the "uto-

---

[119] See "She-hui chu-i shih ta-kang" (An Outline of the History of Socialism), *Min-pao*, No. 7, pp. 101–11; "Wu-cheng-fu chu-i chih erh-p'ai" (Two Branches of Anarchism), *Min-pao*, No. 8, pp. 131–38; "Wu-cheng-fu chu-i yü she-hui chu-i" (Anarchism and Socialism), *Min-pao*, No. 9, pp. 1–7 (last section; consecutive pagination in this issue stopped at p. 120; this article is actually on pp. 145–51 of the magazine). Dr. Martin Bernal has identified the translator as Liao Chung-k'ai.

[120] Cf. note 42 and related text above. T'an Pi-an holds that the Chinese at this time blended socialism and anarchism into their own version of populism. See his "O-kuo min-ts'ui chu-i tui T'ung-meng-hui ying-hsiang," *Li-shih yen-chiu*, 1959, No. 1, pp. 35–37.

[121] *Ibid.*, p. 36. See also Chang and Wang, *Selected Essays*, II, 1075.

[122] Note Wu Chih-hui's discussion of "socialist morality" above, pp. 178–79.

[123] See pp. 38 and 138 for the statements by Tsou and Sun.

pianism of the (1958) Great Leap Forward." [124] In the case of the anarchists, and perhaps of the leaders of the New Culture Movement as well, this utopianism derived from an uncritical and indeed highly emotional belief in the omnipotence of science. To Wu Chih-hui, even in 1924, science was capable of providing man with virtually unlimited understanding, and Western wealth and power were attributable solely to the development of modern science.[125] From a belief in the omnipotence of anything it is but a short step to utopianism.

The Chinese anarchists, like their Western counterparts, promised far more than they or even Evolution could deliver, thereby arousing hopes and expectations they could not satisfy. The world envisioned by Western anarchists "was indefinitely postponed until the millennial day of reckoning; it was a kind of revolutionary pie-in-the-sky, and one was expected to fast until mealtime." [126] The Chinese revolutionary movement as a whole generated desires that could not be fulfilled, thereby contributing to widespread discontent and the growth of still more radical movements. The anarchists took the process a step further. It is a phenomenon that is far from new. In other times and places, "in other situations of mass disorientation and anxiety," and against a background of disruption of old ideas and institutions, there have appeared movements aiming at limited and realistic reforms. Relying on mass insurrection, however, these movements have produced on their radical fringes a millenarian group that ultimately led to a fanaticism going far beyond the goals of the original movement.[127] The T'ung-meng-hui, already quite radical in comparison with all that preceded it, produced a branch that similarly went far beyond the republicans' original intentions. One wonders whether revolutions do not nourish within themselves seeds of the next revolution.

[124] Franz Schurmann, *Ideology and Organization in Communist China*, pp. 296 and *passim*.

[125] Kwok, *Scientism in Chinese Thought*, pp. 43–44.

[126] Woodcock, *Anarchism*, p. 472.

[127] Norman Cohn, *The Pursuit of the Millennium*, pp. v, 315–19.

# 6

## *Chang Ping-lin*

Students of the 1911 revolution are likely to find that Chang Ping-lin's role in it is one of their thorniest problems. In some respects he was the most conservative thinker in the movement; in others he was the most radical. His ideas can be traced to a variety of sources, ranging in time and space from ancient China to the modern West and differing in principle as widely as the Legalists and the anarchists. The influences that worked upon certain aspects of Chang's thought, such as his virulent anti-Manchuism, can be isolated with some accuracy, and the pattern of his thinking on such subjects can be grasped. But taken together, his ideas seem like a surrealist mural depicting man in conflict with himself and his world.

Professor Hsiao Kung-ch'üan has aptly called attention to the consistent note of protest in Chang's thought.[1] In this respect Chang resembles his comrades in the revolutionary movement. But if Chang was China's most pessimistic political thinker,[2] the trend of his thought was directly contrary to an important element in revolutionary thinking, its confidence in China's future. Chang was of a rare turn of mind, and he must be treated more as a unique individual than as a representative of a wing in the revolutionary movement. Of those who allied themselves with him politically, the most promi-

[1] Hsiao Kung-ch'üan, *Chung-kuo cheng-chih ssu-hsiang shih*, VI, 869.
[2] See *ibid.*, p. 870.

nent either were not intellectuals (e.g., T'ao Ch'eng-chang) or did not accept his ideas (e.g., Chang Chi). His staunch followers were few and of lesser importance in the movement (e.g., Huang K'an and Wang Tung). Nevertheless Chang Ping-lin was unquestionably the most outstanding scholar among the revolutionaries,[3] and there is no reason to doubt that his influence was considerable, even if its exact nature is difficult to ascertain. Furthermore, his life and thought have an importance apart from the revolutionary movement of which the T'ung-meng-hui was a part.

CHANG'S TWISTING PATH TO REVOLUTION

As a youth Chang Ping-lin was heavily exposed to anti-Manchu ideas and greatly influenced by them. His grandfather read to him of Ku Yen-wu (1613–82) and Wang Fu-chih (1619–92) and introduced him to the story of Tseng Ching (1679–1736) and Lü Liu-liang (1629–83).[4] Like many of his contemporaries, Chang was also inspired by tales of other Ming patriots, notably Cheng Ch'eng-kung, of whom he had read in Ch'üan Tsu-wang's writings.[5] Indeed, Hsü

---

[3] *Ibid.*, p. 843. See also Man-hua [T'ang Tseng-pi], "T'ung-meng-hui shih-tai Min-pao shih-mo chi," *Ke-ming wen-hsien*, II, 221. The literature of the 1911 revolution is replete with similar comments. Chang took his training under several noted scholars, among whom the most prominent was probably Yü Yüeh. Chang was already twenty-one when he entered the famous *Ku-ching ching-she* in Hangchow, where Yü was teaching. See Chang Ping-lin, *T'ai-yen hsien-sheng tzu-ting nien-p'u*, pp. 3–4.

[4] Hsü Shou-shang, *Chang Ping-lin*, pp. 27–28. Shen Yen-kuo, *Chi Chang T'ai-yen hsien-sheng*, pp. 1–9. Both of these works are extremely useful, offering detail on Chang's life, excerpts from his writings, and discussions of his ideas and influence. Both show Chang in a favorable light, but Shen's treatment, while less detailed in parts, is considerably more objective than Hsü's. See also Chang, *Nien-p'u*, p. 2.

Ku and Wang, noted scholars, were outstanding among the "Ming loyalists" of the seventeenth century. On Ku, see Hsiao Kung-ch'üan, *Chung-kuo cheng-chih ssu-hsiang shih*, V, 611–20, and Arthur W. Hummel (ed.), *Eminent Chinese of the Ch'ing Period*, I, 421–26. Some of Chang's basic concepts were taken from Ku Yen-wu; see Chang Ping-lin, "Ke-ming chih tao-te," *Min-pao*, No. 8, pp. 26–31. For Wang, consult Hsiao, *op. cit.*, V, 629–40, and Hummel, *Eminent Chinese*, II, 817–19. The Tseng Ching and Lü Liu-liang case is described in Hummel, *Eminent Chinese*, II, 747–49, and I, 551. See also Hsiao, *op. cit.*, pp. 640–46.

[5] Hsü Shou-shang, *Chang Ping-lin*, p. 28. Ch'üan's writings were a major repository of information concerning the Ming loyalists. See Hummel, *Eminent Chinese*, I, 203–5.

Shou-shang writes that after the failure of the reform movement in 1898 Chang chose to flee to Taiwan, where he hoped that he might find traces of Koxinga's spirit.[6]

Chang joined K'ang Yu-wei's Ch'iang-hsüeh-hui in 1895 because, according to Feng Tzu-yu, his reading of Western books (in Chinese translations) convinced him that it was necessary to implement reforms if China was to be saved.[7] The following year Chang joined the staff of the *Shih-wu pao*, which was then edited by Liang Ch'i-ch'ao and a close friend of Chang's, Hsia Tseng-yu.[8] Chang is said to have been a firm supporter of the reform movement at this time, except for his opposition to a Confucian religion.[9] But Chang tells us that he already objected to K'ang's interpretation of Confucianism and doubted that reform was possible as long as the Manchus held power.[10] These views had not yet prevented Chang's cooperation with the reformers, but as a staunch advocate of the Old Text school he was later to clash bitterly with K'ang on this issue alone.

With the collapse of the reform movement in 1898, Chang was in danger. A Japanese friend helped him to obtain a position as a writer for a Taipei newspaper,[11] and from that vantage point Chang urged his erstwhile comrades K'ang Yu-wei and Liang Ch'i-ch'ao to renounce the Manchus. He is reported to have written that Sun Yat-sen, with a smattering of Western education, was able to distinguish clearly between the races and thus to call for a revolution, while the two noted literati could not tell right from wrong and so continued to

---

[6] Hsü Shou-shang, *Chang Ping-lin*, p. 32. This may seem a bit farfetched, but Chang himself suggests something of the same sort in his "Chang hsü" (Preface) to Lien Heng, *Taiwan t'ung-shih*, I, 1. However, see note 11, below.

[7] Feng Tzu-yu, *Ke-ming i-shih*, I, 53. See also Chao Chin-yü, "Lun Chang Ping-lin ti cheng-chih ssu-hsiang" (On the Political Thought of Chang Ping-lin), *Li-shih yen-chiu*, 1964, No. 1, p. 32. Chang himself made only a vague and very brief reference to this association with K'ang, which he dates in 1896; see his *Nien-p'u*, p. 5.

[8] Chang, *Nien-p'u*, pp. 4–5.

[9] Feng Tzu-yu, *Chung-hua min-kuo k'ai-kuo ch'ien ke-ming shih*, I, 112.

[10] Chang Ping-lin, *Nien-p'u*, pp. 5–6. Chang was an adherent of the "Old Text" school of Confucianism. The similarities and differences between this and the "New Text" school are analyzed in a paper given at the 1968 meeting of the Association for Asian Studies by Professor Jack L. Dull of the University of Washington. The paper will be published shortly in an expanded version.

[11] The prospect of a job and safety appears to be a more likely reason than that given by Hsü Shou-shang for Chang's trip to Taiwan. See Lin Kuang-hao, "Chang T'ai-yen yü T'ai-wan hsin-wen chieh," *Chang-liu*, XXIV, No. 8 (Dec. 1, 1966), 9.

serve the barbarians.[12] The remark is interesting partly for what it reveals of Chang's early opinion of Sun: he was disdainful of Sun's education but nevertheless appreciative of his aim. Still more noteworthy is the suggestion that Chang, willing until that time to support reform, had now (late 1898 or early 1899) become a revolutionary and that racial considerations were important in his decision.

Chang's anti-Manchu sentiments seem not to have caused a break between him and Liang, for it was at Liang's invitation that Chang went to Japan in 1899. There he met Sun Yat-sen for the first time; ironically, it was Liang Ch'i-ch'ao who introduced them. According to one biographer Chang had no direct connection with T'ang Ts'ai-ch'ang's ill-fated plot in 1900, which the K'ang-Liang group financed, but he was nevertheless put on the Manchus' wanted list again. He had taken part in one meeting called by T'ang, at which Yen Fu, Jung Hung (Yung Wing), Wen T'ing-shih, and many others were also present. Even though Chang denounced T'ang's plan and warned him against allowing himself to be used by K'ang Yu-wei, Chang was condemned by the Manchus along with all the others who attended the preliminary meeting.[13]

Chang carelessly dallied for a time at his home and even stopped to visit his old teacher Yü Yüeh. He then availed himself briefly of the protection offered him as a teacher in a school managed by American missionaries. But the Manchus ferreted him out, and early in 1902 he managed a narrow escape to Japan. There he renewed and deepened his acquaintance with Sun Yat-sen.[14] Chang's career as a revolutionary was now launched.

This crucial phase of Chang's life remains mysterious in several important ways. It is not altogether clear what interests he shared with K'ang Yu-wei that were sufficient to override their differences and permit Chang to support K'ang from 1895 to 1898. Their sharply opposed conceptions of Confucianism and Chang's deep anti-Man-

---

[12] Feng, *Chung-hua min-kuo k'ai-kuo ch'ien ke-ming shih*, I, 113.

[13] Hsü Shou-shang, *Chang Ping-lin*, p. 32. On T'ang's plot see E. Joan Smythe, "The Tzu-li Hui," *Papers on China*, XII, 51–68. Hsü (p. 36) notes that Chang remonstrated with T'ang for acting in the name of assisting the Kuang-hsü emperor, reminding him that the proper aim was the overthrow of the Manchus and restoration of Chinese rule. Chang, *Nien-p'u*, pp. 7–8, confirms this. See also Feng, *Ke-ming i-shih*, I, 54. It was at this meeting that Chang cut off his queue to demonstrate his unqualified and irrevocable hostility toward the Manchus.

[14] Chang Ping-lin, *Nien-p'u*, p. 8.

chuism would seem to have precluded fruitful cooperation. Apparently, however, the beliefs they had in common, such as that it was necessary to learn from Japan and reform Chinese institutions in order to prevent foreign conquest, constituted a basis for agreement.[15]

A more intriguing puzzle is exactly when and why Chang abandoned reform in favor of revolution. Did it really occur as early as suggested above? If so, why did he and Liang Ch'i-ch'ao continue to work together? Was Chang's anti-Manchuism as deep as his remark concerning Sun Yat-sen suggests? If so, why did it not prevent his supporting K'ang Yu-wei? In the absence of further evidence, equal credence must be given to the view that Chang did not become openly and unequivocally revolutionary until 1900 or 1901. This view holds that it was the Manchus' inability to resist the foreign powers in the Boxer incident that finally persuaded Chang to become a revolutionary.[16]

Perhaps the most likely explanation is that the lines between revolutionaries and reformers were not yet clearly drawn, and most of those who would later join one or the other of these camps had not yet fully committed themselves. In the wreckage of the Hundred Days, the Boxer chaos, T'ang Ts'ai-ch'ang's and Sun Yat-sen's 1900 uprisings, and the furor over Russia's move into Manchuria, it probably took most intellectuals many months to find their bearings. The desire for change was wide and spreading, and there were few men with serious pretensions to influence who did not favor some degree of change in 1901–2. But the speed, the sequence, and the direction that change should take baffled all. As men groped and stretched for answers they assumed similarly awkward and shifting postures. Only between 1902 and 1905 did their positions stabilize. Chang Ping-lin himself suggests something of this sort when he classifies K'ang's group as having been revolutionary in 1897–1901.[17]

---

[15] See Chao Chin-yü, *loc. cit.*

[16] *Ibid.*, pp. 33–34; also Hu Shen-wu and Chin Tson-qi (Chung-chi), "Hsin-hai ke-ming shih-ch'i Chang Ping-lin ti cheng-chih ssu-hsiang" (The Political Ideas of Chang Ping-lin at the Time of the 1911 Revolution), *Li-shih yen-chiu*, 1961, No. 4, pp. 3–4.

[17] *Nien-p'u*, p. 6. Cf. my article "Reform and Revolution in China's Political Modernization," in Mary C. Wright (ed.), *China in Revolution: The First Phase, 1900–1913*, pp. 67–96. Some interesting perspectives on the relationship between Chang Ping-lin and Liang Ch'i-ch'ao may be found in Chiang Fu-sen, "Chang T'ai-yen yü Liang Jen-kung," *Ta-feng*, LXXIX, 2561–62. Chiang calls both Chang

Chang's new position is thus best seen in his attack on K'ang Yu-wei, published in 1903 and widely regarded as an extremely influential piece of revolutionary literature.[18] Chang took great pains to expose what he regarded as K'ang's two most grievous errors. The first was K'ang's view that since the Manchus had already been assimilated by the Chinese there was no reason for anti-Manchuism; the second was K'ang's idea that China could be saved by reform, whereas revolution would bring only chaos.[19] In his 1903 article, Chang rejected the assimilation theory in terms quite similar to those later used by the T'ung-meng-hui writers. K'ang, he said, preferred to ignore racial differences, but the principle of race (*min-tsu chu-i*) had been part of human nature from earliest times, and racial characteristics were ineradicable. In the modern world, Chang continued, racial groups were to be distinguished more by historical factors than by nature. If one looked far enough into the past, he would find that nature had developed all living things from a common source; it was history that made for differentiation.[20] Other races had, after all, mingled with the Chinese and adopted Chinese customs, but they had not acted as oppressors. The Manchus, on the other hand, had imposed their own customs (e.g., the queue) upon the Chinese and maintained their own language; far from becoming Sinified they had attempted to assimilate the Chinese. In addition, unlike other races to which K'ang had referred, the Manchus had not submitted to Chinese rule. The respect they showed to Confucius and their acceptance of Confucian principles were devices designed to protect their position as rulers and to trick people into regarding them as Chinese. Finally, Chang noted the ten-day massacre at Yangchow in 1645, observing

---

and Liang advocates of reform (*ke-hsin*). Even later Chang was less vituperative toward Liang Ch'i-ch'ao than were Wang Ching-wei and Hu Han-min, and he was more interested than persons such as Huang Hsing in pursuing efforts to effect a reconciliation with Liang; see Chang's *Nien-p'u*, p. 11.

[18] This was the article entitled "Po K'ang Yu-wei lun ke-ming shu." Like all of Chang's writings referred to below, this may be found in his collected works, *Chang-shih ts'ung-shu*, Vol. IV. I have used the version provided in *Chung-kuo chin-tai ssu-hsiang shih ts'an-k'ao tzu-liao chien-pien* (Source Materials on the History of Modern Chinese Thought), pp. 598–611. Note also his famous *Ch'iu-shu*, written in 1902 (according to his *Nien-p'u*, p. 9).

[19] Hsiao, *Chung-kuo cheng-chih ssu-hsiang shih*, VI, 849–50.

[20] "Po K'ang Yu-wei . . . ," pp. 598–99. Chang used the term *min-tsu chu-i* fully two years before Sun did.

that whereas in other incidents one leading figure had instigated a slaughter, in the Yangchow massacre all the Manchus had demonstrated a desire to wipe out the Chinese. Therefore "Chinese hatred of the Manchus should be hatred of them all." [21]

This last remark was sharply pointed. Just as the T'ung-meng-hui writers were later to condemn Liang Ch'i-ch'ao and other reformers as self-seekers who served the Manchus only in the hope of obtaining wealth and high position, Chang accused K'ang of seeking to regain the Manchus' favor in the hope that he might be forgiven for past sins. K'ang, he said, was hoping that the Kuang-hsü emperor might regain power and again reward him with a high position.[22] Chang warned that Kuang-hsü, like any other emperor, enjoyed the privileges that his position afforded and would not voluntarily surrender any of them to benefit the Chinese. Even if the present emperor were exceptional in this respect, he was only one man and, as the events of 1898 had shown, too weak in the face of the formidable opposition ranged against reform.[23]

Chang then turned to the question of revolution versus reform. He conceded that revolutions required bloodshed but maintained that constitutional government and freedom had to be fought for in China just as in the West, where these privileges had been won only by force of arms. Even the establishment of a constitutional monarchy would cause fighting.[24] Actually, he reasoned, it would be easier to accomplish a revolution than to establish a constitution under the Manchus, because the people supported the idea of revolution. The revolution lacked only a leader, whereas the constitutional movement lacked both leadership and popular support. Indeed, an unheralded hero might already be present among the revolutionaries; Washington and Napoleon also were unknown at one time. Some said that China could not produce such men, he added, but it could not be denied that Yao and Shun were Chinese. There was thus no need for the Chinese to think in terms of Western paragons; they could instead hope for another Yao or Shun to emerge to lead the revolution and save the Chinese race.[25]

[21] *Ibid.*, p. 600.    [22] *Ibid.*, p. 598; also, p. 610.
[23] *Ibid.*, pp. 602–3; also, pp. 604–5. It is striking to observe the extent to which Chang's argument was directed at the Kuang-hsü emperor and what Chang regarded as K'ang's blind faith in him.
[24] *Ibid.*, p. 604.    [25] *Ibid.*, pp. 605–6.

Chang saw that it was not enough to say that revolution would be easier to accomplish than constitutional reform. The question remained how the aims of revolution could be achieved. Chang offered no plan at this time, but he was confident that "human wisdom arises from struggle, and today it need rely only upon revolution to guide its development." Chang suggested Li Tzu-ch'eng (1605?–45) as an example of one who had begun as a common bandit but who, enlightened by struggle, had become a benefactor of the people. In Li's time, however, a movement such as his brought about the elevation of a hero, but today the result would necessarily be democracy. "The rise of democracy (*min-chu*) truly is dictated by current conditions. . . ."[26] At this stage of his development, Chang sounded much like the men who were soon to be his colleagues on the *Min-pao*.

Soon after he wrote this article, Chang was imprisoned for three years as a result of the *Su-pao* case. His courage and determination are shown by the fact that those slated for arrest had been warned of the danger and given ample time to flee. Only Chang chose to remain, and one biographer quotes him as having attempted to persuade Tsou Jung to join him: "For the revolution, we must shed blood. . . ."[27]

Chang's imprisonment made him something of a martyr. It enhanced his own reputation and stimulated revolutionary fervor among his compatriots. In addition, those three years were important for Chang's intellectual development. He was deeply impressed, first of all, by the fact that he had been tried by foreigners in a foreign court in China. The experience seems to have dramatized for him China's weakness and the degree to which she had been imposed upon by foreign powers.[28] Even more important, Chang became, in prison, a serious student of Buddhism. It was only at this time, he said, that he came to appreciate the truths of Mahayana doctrine; he proceeded to study the basic texts of the Fa-hsiang sect intensively.[29]

[26] *Ibid.*, p. 606.

[27] Shen Yen-kuo, *Chi Chang T'ai-yen*, p. 17. Tsou was swayed for the moment, but finally decided to flee. After a brief period during which he was sheltered in the home of a Christian missionary, Tsou gave himself up to the authorities.

[28] *Ibid.*, pp. 22–23. See also Chang Huang-chi, "Chang T'ai-yen hsien-sheng tsai yü i-wen lu," *HHKM*, I, 394.

[29] Shen Yen-kuo, *Chi Chang T'ai-yen*, p. 20. Prisoners were allowed to receive books, provided that Western works were not included. *Ibid.*, p. 19, and Chang Huang-chi, "Chang T'ai-yen . . . ," p. 395.

Chang noted that he had studied some Buddhist works before 1903, "although I never really mastered them thoroughly. When I was imprisoned in Shanghai, I devoted myself single-mindedly to the work of Maitreya and Vasubandhu, whose approach . . . resembled my life-long [pursuit] of sound learning and was therefore easy to accept. . . ."[30]

Despite the extremely harsh conditions in prison, owing to which about one hundred inmates are reported to have perished each year, when Chang emerged in July of 1906 he was in good health. As a noted scholar he was accorded special treatment. He was first given tailoring work and later made a cook, and so was able to supplement the meager fare to which other prisoners were restricted. He also was exempted from strenuous labor such as rock-crushing, at which merchants were employed.[31] Upon his release from prison Chang went directly to Tokyo, where he formally joined the T'ung-meng-hui and became the editor of *Min-pao*. For the next two years he was its most prolific writer.

### RELIGION AND NATIONALISM

When Chang Ping-lin arrived in Tokyo, a massive student rally was held in his honor. Chang himself was the principal speaker, and his talk was made the lead article in the next issue of *Min-pao*, which was also the first under his editorship. As Chang's first public statement after his release from prison, this speech marks his re-entry into the revolutionary movement and offers a useful introduction to the ideas Chang was to propound in the period we are considering.

Chang began his talk with a brief sketch of his own background, noting that his hatred for the Manchus had been aroused by the writings of Ming loyalists such as Wang Fu-chih. He came quickly to the question of what had to be done at this time. There was no need, he said, to discuss such matters as politics, law, and military science, for his listeners had all studied these subjects. Besides, "in my view, the most important thing of all is feeling (*kan-ch'ing*). Without it you may have countless Napoleons and Washingtons, but they will always be individual men, unable to band together. . . . To fulfill

[30] Quoted by Liang Ch'i-ch'ao, *Ch'ing-tai hsüeh-shu kai-lun*. Translated by Immanuel C. Y. Hsü, *Intellectual Trends in the Ch'ing Period*, p. 112.
[31] Shen Yen-kuo, *Chi Chang T'ai-yen*, pp. 23–27.

this feeling, there are two things that are most important. The first is to employ religion to promote faith (*hsin-hsin*) and the morality of the people. The second is to employ the 'national essence' (*kuo-ts'ui*) to stimulate racial spirit and patriotic fervor." [32]

Chang then proceeded to discuss religion and *kuo-ts'ui*. Citing Bentham and Spencer, he condemned those who "worship utility and consider religion to be of no consequence. For without religion, morality will not advance, and each will pursue his own interests in a struggle for existence." [33] The West had Christianity, he observed, and while it was a decidedly inferior religion, without it Europe and America could not have developed to the point they had. The question was: "What religion should China use?" Chang first considered the possibility of a Confucian religion. Confucianism, he conceded, had some extremely good features, notably its freedom from mysticism and abstruseness. However, it was inextricably linked with ideas of status and privilege, and since "today we desire to carry out a revolution and promote democracy (*min-ch'üan*)," these ideas would be like little germs that would infect the whole movement. "Therefore a Confucian religion absolutely may not be used." [34]

For Chang Ping-lin the answer lay with Buddhism. "Basically, China may be called a Buddhist country. Buddhist theory compels the intelligent to believe in it, and its rules (*chieh-lü*) make it irresistible to the uneducated. Reaching all levels, high and low, it is the most useful religion." [35] Critics might ask why in the past two thousand years Buddhism had failed to have the beneficial effects Chang expected it to have. His reply was that Buddhism had become corrupted by unenlightened practitioners who introduced much superstition and ritual. There was a pattern in history that had to be followed in politics

[32] Chang Ping-lin, "Yen-shuo lu," *Min-pao*, No. 6, p. 4.

[33] *Ibid.*

[34] *Ibid.*, p. 5. It is worth noting that Chang now used the term *min-ch'üan* for "democracy," whereas in 1903 he had used *min-chu*. In the intervening period Sun had named his Three People's Principles, in which *min-ch'üan* meant "democracy." An eminent philologist, Chang was not likely to use words carelessly.

[35] *Ibid.*, p. 6. Chang's emphasis on the practical value of religion, despite his condemnation of utilitarianism, is striking. It seems clear that Chang's argument is directed against K'ang Yu-wei's effort to change Confucianism into a religion. Note also Professor Hsiao's point that K'ang Yu-wei valued religions chiefly "for their effectiveness as social or moral forces." "K'ang Yu-wei and Confucianism," *Monumenta Serica*, XVIII, 186.

and religion. Political systems developed in three stages: government by a nobility, then monarchy, and finally republicanism. If a society proceeded directly to the third from the first, remnants of the first would survive. Similarly, religious systems began with polytheism and progressed through monotheism to a godless religion. Ancient Chinese Taoism, Chang asserted, was polytheistic, but it was followed directly by Buddhism, which is atheistic. The required second stage had failed to materialize. As a result, people came to regard Buddha as a spiritual being composed of all the Taoist spirits merged into one. Thus Buddhism had been debased. Now, however, Christianity had come to China, and the normal progression had been re-established. The time was therefore right for Buddhism.[36]

Chang anticipated that he would be asked to explain why India, the original home of Buddhism, had fallen under foreign rule. Without attempting carefully to correlate the decline of Buddhism with vulnerability to conquest, a difficult task at best, Chang merely argued that India's political demise took place for other reasons. Despite the efficacy of religion, it could not save a country that did not possess highly developed political and legal institutions. "China already has political and legal [institutions] and so cannot go the way of India."[37]

Chang then turned to the question of *kuo-ts'ui*, or "national essence." "To promote *kuo-ts'ui* does not mean that people should believe in a Confucian religion. It only means that people should cherish the history of the Chinese race."[38] In broad terms, there were three aspects of *kuo-ts'ui*. First there were China's unique language and literature. Next there were China's institutions, and here Chang observed that although her system of absolute monarchy should not be valued, it was neither wise nor sufficient to think only of demolishing the old system. Some features could be reformed, and others revived; for example, "one especially excellent thing that absolutely cannot be matched by the West is the *chün-t'ien* system, which corresponds to socialism."[39] China's legal system also contained elements of so-

[36] "Yen-shuo lu," pp. 7–8.

[37] *Ibid.*, p. 8.

[38] *Ibid.*, p. 9.

[39] *Ibid.*, p. 12. A convenient explanation of the *chün-t'ien* ("equal-field") system may be found in Edwin O. Reischauer and John K. Fairbank, *East Asia: The Great Tradition*, pp. 158–63. The system was in operation chiefly between

cialism, Chang maintained, because punishments were applied equally to all. So did the examination system, because it offered to the poor some hope of becoming officials. In sum, "all of China's institutions tended toward socialism," [40] and "today when we revere China's institutions we only revere socialism." [41]

The third aspect of *kuo-ts'ui* was the great men of China's past. Chang found that two were most admirable and deserving of emulation: Liu Yü and Yüeh Fei, "both of whom employed southern troops to defeat the barbarians. [Their example] can heighten our spirit." [42] China also had many men of learning who warranted esteem. Chang noted that although China had failed to develop science, her philosophy was not to be taken lightly. But he specifically excluded the Neo-Confucianists, contending that "the most learned men were the philosophers of Chou and Ch'in," especially Chuang-tzu and Hsün-tzu. More recently there was Tai Chen, who, "although he taught only Confucianism, did not follow the Sung school. . . . In his books he of course did not openly attack the Manchus, but we can see that his work contains no lack of deep hatred for them." [43]

Chang then concluded: "What I have said in the foregoing is that the method for accomplishing things today [rests] entirely upon two factors: religion and *kuo-ts'ui*." [44]

Chang's emphasis on these two points clearly distinguishes him from all other thinkers in the revolutionary movement. One cannot help wondering what thoughts passed through the minds of Chang's listeners when he expounded on the importance of religion. Most of them were doubtless new to the revolutionary movement and excited by their novel activities. They were learning to handle weapons, make bombs, send and receive coded messages, and do the other things involved in becoming part of an armed conspiracy. At the same time they were studying Western law and politics in order to

---

the fifth and eighth centuries. It was intended to prevent land ownership from becoming concentrated in the hands of large owners.

[40] "Yen-shuo lu," p. 12.

[41] *Ibid.*, p. 13.

[42] *Ibid.* Liu Yü (r. 420–423) was the founder of the short-lived Liu Sung dynasty (420–479). Yüeh Fei (1103–41) was the famous Sung general who championed an aggressive policy toward the Chin in north China.

[43] *Ibid.*, pp. 13–14. On Tai Chen (1724–77), see Hummel, *Eminent Chinese*, II, 695–700.

[44] "Yen-shuo lu," p. 14.

equip themselves to be builders of a new China. Chang's reputation was of course known to them. In *Min-pao* they had been reading their younger leaders — Wang Ching-wei, Hu Han-min, Chu Chih-hsin — as they attacked the Manchus and called for a republic. Now there came into their midst the scholar-revolutionary who had dared in print to mock the emperor and who at thirty-eight was one of the senior figures in the movement. Expectations must have run high,[45] but Chang's audience was not treated to its usual fare.

Despite his divergence from his compatriots, Chang remained very much in the forefront of the movement until 1912. His continuing status raises questions about his relationship with the rank and file and with the other leaders and about his influence in the movement. What made Chang a T'ung-meng-hui leader? How and to what extent did he make his influence felt? Some answers are suggested by Chang's brief reference to socialism. There were many facets to the thought of Chang Ping-lin. I have emphasized his stress on religion and *kuo-ts'ui*, because they seem to be among the most fundamental and abiding features of his thinking. To understand his role in the revolutionary movement, however, attention must also be given to some less basic aspects, for it was in these that his views coincided with those of his comrades. For example, in the brief reference to socialism noted above, Chang sounds much like Feng Tzu-yu and Chu Chih-hsin, despite his tendency to find in Chinese history a more widespread and highly developed socialism than they did. Another example is the occasional approval Chang bestowed upon republicanism, such as his reference to patterns and stages in political history. The little that Chang wrote in this vein must have been of great importance to the revolutionaries, for it put the weight of an acknowledged classical scholar behind their own arguments. In their competition with the erudite K'ang Yu-wei and Liang Ch'i-ch'ao, the revolutionaries were sorely in need of such support. Chang's immense learning, his stature as a scholar, and his impeccable anti-Manchu record (he had not even taken the examinations) were a rare combination. In his

---

[45] Hsü Shou-shang, whose first contact with Chang took place at this meeting, tells us that more than seven thousand people came to see "the great revolutionary, China's savior," *Chang Ping-lin*, p. 46. Feng Tzu-yu estimates the attendance at two thousand-plus, *Ke-ming i-shih*, I, 56. Chang himself says seven thousand, *Nien-p'u*, p. 11. In any case the crowd was large, and many waited outside in the rainy night for a glimpse of Chang.

scholarship he easily rivaled K'ang; and as an opponent of the Manchus he lay claim to principles of loyalty and integrity that formed a basis for his attack on K'ang, whom he reviled for currying the favor of the Manchus, especially the Kuang-hsü emperor. Paradoxically, Chang's scholarly talents may even have served the revolutionary cause better because they were rooted in the more traditionally acceptable Old Text doctrines.

Some of Chang's basic views dovetailed neatly with those of other T'ung-meng-hui writers. First, of course, Chang shared their opposition to the Manchus, and the common desire to bring about the downfall of the Ch'ing regime doubtless overrode his differences with them. The most important differences concerned long-range goals. For most of the revolutionaries the purpose of overthrowing the Manchus was to permit the building of a new China that would in many ways resemble Western nations, whereas for Chang the aim was quite different. But the immediate goal took priority, and the revolutionaries hoped that Chang's prodigious learning could bolster their anti-Manchu arguments.

Chang Ping-lin's attack upon the Manchus and his conception of the national revolution need not be described in detail,[46] but certain salient features require mention and elaboration. As his reply to K'ang Yu-wei's argument indicates, Chang's characterization of the Manchus' crimes closely resembled those of Wang Ching-wei and other T'ung-meng-hui writers. His concept of "nation" also was similar to Wang's in its emphasis on common cultural characteristics, but Chang also advanced a racial thesis almost identical to the one that Ch'en T'ien-hua derived from the *Tso-chuan*. His argument may not have been consistent, but it served the revolutionary cause nevertheless.

On the one hand Chang contended, true to the belief of his acknowledged master, Wang Fu-chih, that "cultural identity (*wen-hua hsiang-t'ung*) arises from consanguinity."[47] As Professor Hsiao

[46] Joseph R. Levenson has discussed these questions in some of his writings. A convenient summary may be found in his *Confucian China and Its Modern Fate*, I, 88–97. For Professor Hsiao Kung-ch'üan's treatment of the subject see his *Chung-kuo cheng-chih ssu-hsiang shih*, VI, 844–51.

[47] "Chung-hua min-kuo chieh," *Min-pao*, No. 15, p. 6. Cf. Ch'en T'ien-hua, above, p. 77. Note Wang Fu-chih's view that out of different physical environ-

Kung-ch'üan has noted, it was from this position that Chang was able to counter K'ang Yu-wei's view that foreign tribes were assimilable.[48] Chang, buttressing his argument with etymological analyses of various characters for "China" and an exegesis of the *Kung-yang* commentary, thus neatly complemented Wang Ching-wei in the latter's counterattack against Liang Ch'i-ch'ao.[49] For while Wang struck chiefly at Liang's understanding of Western ideas and institutions, Chang attempted to refute K'ang's interpretations of the classics, foremost among which was K'ang's adherence to the *Kung-yang* doctrine that the differences between the Chinese and barbarians were purely cultural.[50]

It is ironic that Chang found himself allied with Wang against K'ang, since Chang's world view was in many ways closer to K'ang's than it was to Wang's. Indeed, even K'ang's attack on the authenticity of the Old Text classics, which he published in 1891, had not deterred Chang from joining the Ch'iang-hsüeh-hui in 1895. And K'ang's concern for preventing the Chinese tradition from being engulfed by a tide of westernization was shared by Chang. It is unlikely, for example, that Chang would have disagreed with the basic aims of K'ang's Society to Protect the Emperor: "To preserve intact the country's territory, its people, and its tradition": and "to study matters relative to the preservation of the country, the race, and the tradition."[51] However, different conceptions of "race" and "tradition," which always kept some distance between the two men, finally drove them irretrievably apart once political differences were added. The

---

ments there emerge racial differences which in turn are the source of cultural differences. Hsiao, *op. cit.*, V, 637.

[48] *Ibid.*, VI, 847.

[49] "Chung-hua min-kuo chieh," pp. 1–5. This article seems to have been written in response to Yang Tu's "Chin-t'ieh chu-i shou" (Doctrine of Gold and Iron). See Hsü Shou-shang, *Chang Ping-lin*, pp. 28–29. Chang did not mention K'ang by name, but he pointedly criticized "drawing upon the Ch'un-ch'iu to falsify the true meaning of history. This can be traced to Liu Feng-lu and others like him who served the Manchus." "Chung-hua min-kuo chieh," p. 5. Liu (1775–1829) was an outstanding *Kung-yang* scholar whose critical analyses of the *Tso-chuan* made him anathema to an Old Texter like Chang Ping-lin. See Liu's biography in Hummel, *Eminent Chinese*, pp. 518–20. For K'ang Yu-wei's place in the *Kung-yang* tradition see Kung-ch'üan Hsiao, "K'ang Yu-wei and Confucianism," pp. 136–43.

[50] See *ibid.*, p. 174.

[51] Quoted in *ibid.*

elements of antagonism between K'ang and Chang were always present; politics provided the catalyst.

From our vantage point in time, Chang and Wang Ching-wei seem to be unlikely helpmates. But such marriages of convenience were not uncommon in the revolutionary movement; indeed, they help us to understand the divorces that followed and occasionally, as in this case, even preceded the Manchus' collapse. Revolution makes strange bedfellows. The entire phenomenon, in fact, points up the primacy of politics in this period. Intellectual disagreements, even of a fundamental nature, could be tolerated as long as immediate political aims were shared. But when the political consensus broke down it revealed latent schisms; rent by divisions, the Chinese intelligentsia split into factions which went off in all directions at once.

Chang's anti-Manchuism provided considerable common ground for cooperation with the T'ung-meng-hui, even though it stemmed from beliefs that demonstrate the vast difference in temperament and outlook between Chang and most other revolutionaries. For example, Chang's view of Manchu-Chinese relations was not as unequivocal as his remark on cultural identity would suggest. Although he believed that culture derived from race, he did not deny that other races had in the past merged with the Chinese. If so, why not the Manchus? Chang's answer was that assimilation of foreign tribes was possible if sovereignty lay with the Chinese. Chang indicated that despite racial differences assimilation was possible if the Chinese held political power.[52] It is true that he was capable of a more virulent racism, as attested to by some later remarks: the Manchus were brigands and "stealing is their nature (*t'ien-hsing*)"; "the Manchus' chaotic government is not the result of their laws and regulations but is due to their nature and customs."[53] But a more persistent note is exemplified by the following quotation: "What we mean by 'down with the Manchus' is by no means confined to saying: 'Your name is Aisin Gioro while we are of the *Chi* and *Chiang* families, and we fear that you will defile our posterity.' We also mean that you have destroyed our country and usurped our sovereignty."[54]

[52] "Chung-hua min-kuo chieh," p. 6. See also his "She-hui t'ung-ch'üan shang-tui," *Min-pao*, No. 12, p. 16. This is Chang's discussion of Yen Fu's translation of a book by Edward Jenks; see Chapter 3, note 98.

[53] "Man-chou tsung-tu ch'in-t'un chen-k'uan chuang," *Min-pao*, No. 22, p. 38.

[54] "She-hui t'ung-ch'üan shang-tui," p. 15. *Chi* and *Chiang* refer to Huang Ti

Chang's views on assimilation were firmly based upon a concept of the nation-state; for him, nationalism (*min-tsu chu-i*) was inseparable from politics.[55] Like Wang Ching-wei, Chang visualized a "mono-national state"[56] that closely approximated the Western idea of national self-determination, and he proposed that the Manchus be accepted as "naturalized citizens."[57] In one important respect he went beyond his comrades, for he explicitly recognized that the Moslems in China might have the same hatred for the Chinese that the Chinese had for the Manchus.[58] Chang was certainly not in favor of permitting minorities to split away from China and establish independent nations, partly because he believed that they were not ready for independence and partly because he hoped for the reestablishment of China's borders as they were under the Former Han dynasty. Nevertheless, he was willing to regard China's relationship with Sinkiang as an "alliance" in which the two would act as "complementary wings to cut off Russia's right arm." He hoped the Moslems would see that it was in their own interest to assimilate with the Chinese, but he clearly recognized that they might not.[59]

Chang's anti-Manchuism raises the question of his relationship to other traditionalists as well as to other revolutionaries. Joseph R. Levenson has suggested that Chang differed from other conservative scholars who became revolutionaries in that his revolutionary views were derived "from his concern to save the 'Chinese essence.'"[60] In addition, Chang's conception of the "Chinese essence" was different from that of other traditionalists, and he wanted to do more than preserve it. It is sometimes held that Chang was entirely traditional in attaching great importance to morality. But Chang did so for essentially pragmatic reasons, and despite certain similarities to Confucianism his conception of morality was quite different.

Chang regarded religion highly because it was useful in promoting morality. And why promote morality? "I believe that the decay

---

and Shen Nung, i.e., to the earliest Chinese; Aisin Gioro refers to the ancestral clan of the Manchus.

[55] Hsiao Kung-ch'üan, *Chung-kuo cheng-chih ssu-hsiang shih*, VI, 849.

[56] *Ibid*; see also note 78, p. 875.

[57] "She-hui t'ung-ch'üan shang-tui," p. 16.

[58] *Ibid.*, p. 18; "Chung-hua min-kuo chieh," p. 16.

[59] *Ibid.*

[60] Levenson, *Confucian China and Its Modern Fate*, I, 89.

of morality is the basic reason for the destruction of our country and our race." [61] The answer, clearly, was that a revival of morality was necessary to save the country and the race. But what did Chang mean by morality? He had already said that Confucianism was inappropriate to a democratic movement and that without morality men would pursue their own selfish interests. Now Chang went on to explain that morality was a matter of overcoming mutual suspicion and replacing it with trustworthiness, solidarity, and feelings of common purpose and mutual sacrifice. There is no doubt that in Chang's eyes morality was a means, not an end, since "those who do not have morality are unable to revolt." [62] Professor Hsiao has written that "the Confucianists considered morality to be the highest aim of government; Chang regarded morality as a tool that was necessary for government." And if under different circumstances immorality was called for, Chang would not hesitate to permit or even advocate it.[63] The same tools could be used for revolution as well. But Chang's conception of morality was also related to his nationalism. It is striking that his explication of morality sounds much like a recommendation for creating a nation-state. Consciously or not, Chang was working toward creating feelings of political identity and common destiny, vital elements of modern nationalism that are often said to have been lacking in the China of Chang's time.

Finally, there remains the question of how Buddhism fits into this conception. Its main appeal to Chang seems to have been its usefulness, since in contrast to Confucianism, Chang seemed to imply, Buddhism was incompatible with class distinctions and thus more consistent with democracy. Or at the very least, Buddhism was held to be attractive to the masses as well as to intellectuals.

It is of course true that Buddhist ideas had been features of many anti-dynastic movements in China's history.[64] But the character of those movements and of the intellectual, social, and political contexts in which they flourished was so at variance with the T'ung-meng-hui and its time that parallels are difficult to draw. Chang favored

[61] "Ke-ming chih tao-te," *Min-pao*, No. 8, p. 15.

[62] *Ibid.*, p. 18.

[63] Hsiao Kung-ch'üan, *op. cit.*, VI, 858.

[64] See Vincent Y. C. Shih, "Some Chinese Rebel Ideologies," pp. 185–90, *passim*; also Yuji Muramatsu, "Some Themes in Chinese Rebel Ideologies," pp. 245–48, *passim*.

different ideas than did the earlier Chinese rebels who were inspired by Buddhism, and he used them for different purposes and in a more sophisticated fashion. He did not, for example, foster the notion that a Maitreya would appear and save humanity. Nevertheless, his ideas contained certain mystical overtones which, combined with his anti-Manchuism, occasionally made him seem as close in spirit to the anti-Yüan rebel Han Shan-t'ung as to his T'ung-meng-hui comrades. At most these ideas may have contributed in a small way to the secret-society atmosphere in which the T'ung-meng-hui functioned. In any case, they underline once again what a curious variety of ideas found expression in the revolutionary movement.

Chang sometimes accented the utility of Buddhism, or at least those virtues that might foster the revolutionary spirit. A clue to his objectives can be discovered in the following passage:

> The present age is not the age of Chou, Ch'in, Han, and Wei. In those times things were far simpler, and even the commonplace sayings of Confucius and Lao-tzu were adequate for teaching the people and perfecting customs. Today, however, conditions are different. Even theories of transmigration are inadequate. If we do not explain immortality (*wu-sheng*), we shall be unable to eliminate the fear of death. If we do not eradicate the idea of personal possession (*wo-so*), we shall be unable to eliminate the worship of wealth. If we do not speak in terms of equality, we shall be unable to eliminate the slave mentality. If we do not make it clear that all living things are [potential] Buddhas, we shall be unable to eliminate the sense of inferiority that leads men to yield in the face of adversity. If we do not exalt the three Wheels [Buddha's deeds, words, and ideas] and the purity of [Buddha], we shall be unable to eliminate the belief that one deserves credit for good deeds.[65]

Chang had found in Buddhism a doctrine that would foster the virtues of courage, selflessness, equality, service, and duty. Perhaps most interesting of all is his suggestion that Buddhism can lead men to an awareness of their potentialities and thus inspire them with confidence in their ability to deal with the problems they face. The utilitarian spirit in which Chang promoted Buddhism is marked, but his deep commitment to Buddhist ideals is also impressive.

The mood of this article, which was published in November, 1906,

---

[65] "Chien-li tsung-chiao lun," *Min-pao*, No. 9, p. 25.

was strikingly different from the profound pessimism that was to envelop Chang less than a year later. In 1906 Chang was still optimistic about Buddhism and the future. His next step was to turn to history for proof of Buddhism's value. With the decline of Confucianism that accompanied the fall of Han, he wrote, the moral values of the Chinese people had been steadily and rapidly eroded.

> Buddhism then made its entrance and saved the situation. The people regained their purity, thus initiating the full flowering that culminated in T'ang. In Sung times Buddhism again became insignificant, and people's hearts became base. China soon fell to foreigners, and there was no escape.[66]

In Chang's opinion China's most glorious age owed much to Buddhism, and her greatest shame was connected with its decline. Chang then elaborated upon the importance of Buddhist ideas and related them to more recent times. At the end of Ming, he wrote, those who remained most persistently and implacably hostile to the Manchus were either Buddhist scholars or followers of Wang Yang-ming. The Meiji reformers in Japan had also been guided by principles derived from Wang Yang-ming. Wang's philosophy had little to recommend it except that it was based upon Buddhism. Of the various Buddhist schools Chang favored Ch'an because of its emphasis upon the individual human mind as opposed to reliance upon supernatural beings. Here, Chang contended, Ch'an flowed directly into the mainstream of Chinese thought. For despite the important issues that divided Mencius and Hsün-tzu or the Ch'eng-Chu and Lu-Wang schools, "they all have as their common point of origin the phrase 'depend upon oneself, and not upon others.'" It was because Ch'an harmonized best

[66] "Chi Yin-tu Hsi-p'o-ch'i Wang chi-nien-hui shih," *Min-pao*, No. 13, pp. 97–98. The meeting referred to in the title of this article honored the Maratha leader Sivaji (1627–80), whose campaigns against the Moguls Chang compared to those of Chu Yüan-chang against the Mongols. Like Chu, he declared, Sivaji "arose from among the people to overthrow a Mongol Empire and enable the Indian people to secure independence." *Ibid.*, p. 94. It is worth noting that Sivaji was a deeply religious man whose movement flourished amid a wider Hindu revival in western India. Chang, who preferred to regard India as the homeland of Buddhism rather than as a Hindu civilization, also liked to think of Chu Yüan-chang as having drawn his inspiration from Buddhism. It does not seem farfetched to suggest that Chang placed himself in the same tradition — a promoter of religion and a leader of his people's struggle for freedom from foreign control.

with this dictum that it became the most successful school of Buddhism in China.[67] But Confucianism, and particularly the Wang Yang-ming school because it was closest to Ch'an, was also to be valued, since it made men dependent upon their own efforts. Chang was less certain about Christianity, but he conceded that for men to "get along with each other in society" it was better to have some kind of faith than to have none at all. In any case, he concluded, his aim was more to heighten the Chinese people's "self-awareness" than to undertake a religious crusade, which would only set the Chinese against each other.[68]

It was in this way that Buddhism was made to serve the cause of nationalism. Chang's constant emphasis was on instilling in the Chinese people the courage and confidence to act, and to act with an awareness of their identity and destiny. The note of ambiguity one may detect in his admonition to "rely on oneself" becomes significant only in the light of his later views. At this time, in the spring of 1907, Chang meant that the Chinese people were masters of their common fate. His conception of religion and nationalism reinforced the T'ung-meng-hui program. The underlying incompatibility was not yet obtrusive or significant.

THE INDIVIDUAL, SOCIETY, AND THE STATE

*A Time of Trouble and Transition: The System of the Five Negations*

A striking shift in Chang's mood became evident in September. For the first time in print, Chang raised his sights to the distant future. If it was necessary to have a government, he said, then a republic was probably the least harmful form it could take.[69] But even the best of republics provided only a "preliminary and iniquitous method" of meeting the world's problems and could be nothing more than a temporary expedient. "If we aspire to the supreme good, we must soar to the Great Void (*t'ai-hsü*)." To do this it was necessary to have "the pseudo-government of a republic" as a base. "Only after

[67] "Ta T'ieh-cheng," *Min-pao*, No. 14, pp. 113–14. T'ieh-cheng was the pen-name used by Lei Chao-hsing, a contributor to *Min-pao* and a founding member of the T'ung-meng-hui. See Chapter 5, note 77.

[68] *Ibid.*, p. 122.

[69] "Wu-wu lun," *Min-pao*, No. 16, p. 2.

another one hundred years shall we see the system of the five negations." [70]

First among the five, Chang named *wu-cheng-fu*, by which he meant the abolition not only of government but of private property and the family as well. The existence of governments and nation-states led to international conflict, while property led to a struggle for wealth and thereby produced class distinctions and further conflict. The family system fostered love and therefore jealousy; it should not be regarded as a source of happiness. "Basically, there is no happiness, only less suffering." [71]

The second "negation" concerned "fixed abodes" (*wu-chü-lo*). Chang argued that the facts of geography placed some people at an advantage in relation to others and thus led to conflict. For example, those who lived in cold and dry lands found it more profitable to conquer warm and fertile areas than to improve their own territories. Thus it was not enough to eliminate governments or even national boundaries; it was also necessary to institute annual migrations of peoples in order that all might share equally in nature's beneficence.[72]

These two "negations" could be carried out simultaneously, Chang continued, but "the period of final perfection" [73] would not be reached until three more were gradually effected. Governments were made by men, and therefore as long as mankind existed there was always the danger that political institutions would be re-established. More fundamentally, however, men would always fight, injure, and kill each other; "to love supremacy is their nature." [74] The root of this problem was man's illusion that the self is real (*wo-chien*). Its solution was the third "negation," that of mankind (*wu-jen-lei*), by which Chang meant to propagate the Buddhist idea that the self has no individual independent reality (*wu-wo*) — an idea that would enable men to break the chain of existence. The process would be slow and arduous, but eventually there was "bound to be a day [when men will] tran-

[70] *Ibid.*, p. 4.    [72] *Ibid.*, pp. 5–7.
[71] *Ibid.*, p. 5.    [73] *Ibid.*, pp. 9–10.
[74] *Ibid.*, p. 11. Chang credited men of antiquity such as Hsün-tzu with having the insight to see the evil nature of man, but he pointed out their failure to recognize that concepts such as *li* and *fa* were the creations of men and therefore also evil. Thus the measures they advocated for meeting the problems caused by human nature were unworkable. *Ibid.*, p. 15.

scend the world." [75] This having been achieved, it would be necessary to guard against the danger suggested by the doctrine of evolution, which demonstrated that man developed from simple forms of life. Thus the fourth "negation" was that of all living creatures (*wu-chung-sheng*).[76] All living things having been negated, there could be no further illusion that the world was real, and thus the fifth "negation" (*wu-shih-chieh*) would follow as a matter of course. At this point, presumably, the "supreme good" as represented by the "Great Void" would have been achieved.

A possible explanation for the pessimism that suddenly overtook Chang at this time is that the events of the summer of 1907 had reduced him to despair. The revolutionary movement had been going badly. Uprisings in May and June had turned into fiascoes. Shortly thereafter, Chang learned that the revolutionaries' supplier of arms, Kayano Nagatomo, had bought old-fashioned guns for the revolutionary troops. Having already accused Sun of using party funds for his personal benefit earlier in the year, Chang now added the charge that both Sun and Huang Hsing were guilty of promoting uprisings without adequate preparation, thereby ensuring their failure and sacrificing many lives.[77] Together with Chang Chi, Sung Chiao-jen, T'an Jen-feng, Pai Yü-huan, and others who had also supported his earlier attack on Sun, Chang demanded that Sun be removed from the position of *tsung-li*. Liu K'uei-i, who was then acting vice-chairman of the party, refused to call a meeting to consider the demand, and the threat to Sun's position was repulsed.[78]

Chang remained unreconciled, and his criticisms of Sun continued. In 1909, supported by T'ao Ch'eng-chang, he renewed his demand that Sun be ousted, charging that Sun was using the revolution for personal ends. Chang met defeat once again, and in 1910 he withdrew from the T'ung-meng-hui. T'ao, who in 1907 had revived the Restoration Society (Kuang-fu-hui) in Southeast Asia, now moved its headquarters to Tokyo. Chang Ping-lin was chosen to head the society, with T'ao as his deputy.[79]

[75] *Ibid.*, p. 8.

[76] *Ibid.*

[77] Hu Han-min,"Tzu-chuan," p. 399.

[78] Liu K'uei-i, *Huang Hsing chuan-chi* (Biography of Huang Hsing), p. 16.

[79] Chang Huang-chi, "Kuang-fu-hui ling-hsiu T'ao Ch'eng-chang ke-ming shih," *HHKM*, I, 525–26.

It was therefore in the spring and summer of 1907 that the first rift appeared between Chang and Sun; serious from the beginning, it led within three years to a complete break. Combined with the decline in revolutionary fortunes, the dispute might well have been responsible for the pessimism that found expression in Chang's "five negations." In any case, Chang's outlook had changed in ways that further alienated him from most of his comrades.

## Chang Ping-lin on Government

The new direction of Chang's thinking is seen in his conception of government.[80] It will be recalled that in his opening speech to the T'ung-meng-hui in July, 1906, Chang had spoken of republicanism as the most advanced form of political organization. His writings in the next ten months contained no hint that he disapproved of government in general or republicanism in particular. In his nine articles and several shorter items published in *Min-pao* between July, 1906, and May, 1907, Chang concerned himself almost exclusively with attacks on the Manchus and discussions of religion and the Chinese tradition.[81] But after Wang Ching-wei left Tokyo, Chang became *Min-pao*'s chief political writer, and his writings overwhelmingly dominated the next eleven issues.

His political writings began to appear in June, 1907, with a study of Chinese political institutions written "to commemorate the achievements of former Kings." His hope was to have ancient practices understood and appreciated but not imitated; his readers could be assured that he would not idealize them.[82] The study itself was primarily philological and cannot be analyzed here, but in his introductory remarks Chang revealed something of his political philosophy. He began by noting that even some of the less admirable features of Chinese politics were no worse than what one found in the West. The employment of courtiers (*chin-ch'en*) by Chinese ministers was an evil, he declared, but "is it improved upon by the monarchical or republican governments of Europe and America?" His argument was that the manner in which candidates for elections spent money on their campaigns was essentially no different from pur-

---

[80] See Hsiao Kung-ch'üan, *Chung-kuo cheng-chih ssu-hsiang shih*, VI, 851–58.
[81] See *Min-pao*, Nos. 6–13.
[82] "Kuan-chih so-yin," *Min-pao*, No. 14, p. 1.

chasing an official position. Everyone seemed to admire France and the United States, but they were no less corrupt. "If governments are as despicable as this, it is not only despotism but constitutional democracy as well that should be done away with." Chang then compared the relationship between a government and the people to that of excrement and plants: without the first, the second could not grow, but that fact did not make the first any cleaner.[83]

> Our aim is simply to restore our ancestral land. Restoration is the duty we bear and what our own feelings demand. After the restoration there is no alternative but to proceed to the establishment of a republic. But that is not our duty, nor is it dictated by our own feelings. To look at it another way, there is no liking it or disliking it, bitter or sweet, black or white.[84]

These views complement those expressed in the "five negations." Government in all its forms was lowly, as were all man-made institutions, but it served to develop man's ability to dispense with government and was therefore necessary for a time. As Chang later explained, it was a republican form of government that could best pave the way for the abolition of government, and therefore there was no alternative to it. However, a republic was acceptable only if it undertook certain reforms: equal distribution of land, government-established factories in which the workers would divide the profits equally, a limitation upon inheritance to prevent wealth from being passed on to descendants, and investing the people with the power to remove their representatives from office. Without economic equality and direct popular control, Chang maintained, a republic would be less desirable than autocracy.[85]

A democratic and representative system he held to be inappropriate for a country of China's size and population. It was difficult enough to persuade people to pay for a new road or bridge that would benefit their own community; it would be still more difficult to obtain support for measures designed to aid the whole nation.[86] A parliament resembling those of Western countries was bound to be either too large to be manageable or too small to be representative, he as-

---

[83] *Ibid.*, p. 2.
[84] *Ibid.*, pp. 2–3.
[85] "Wu-wu lun," pp. 2–3.
[86] "Cheng-wen-she yüan ta-hui p'o-huai chuang," *Min-pao*, No. 17, 113–14.

serted. If one man represented 100,000 people there would be 4,000 delegates. If there were too few representatives, they would be unable to familiarize themselves with their constituents' problems and needs and therefore unable to represent them properly.[87] Chang's belief in a common national purpose and his confidence in the possibility of instilling a sense of nationhood in people by means of republicanism were showing signs of fading.

In July, 1908, the Manchu government announced its plan for the establishment of provincial assemblies and the election of their members. In August an imperial commission submitted its proposal for a constitution, electoral laws, and a parliament, recommending that a period of nine years be allowed for gradual implementation. The empress dowager approved the plan on the day she received it. It seems clear that it was these events which elicited from Chang his most detailed statement on representative government, for it appeared in the issue of *Min-pao* that followed the court's action and was directed specifically at the reforms proposed by the Manchus.

Chang's discussion amounted to a severe indictment of representative government, based chiefly on the theory that it was incompatible with equality. "Representative government," he said in the very first sentence, "is a remnant of feudalism." Western parliaments exhibited to him a common feature: an upper house composed of nobles or, in democratic countries, of "prominent elders." China, long removed from her feudal period and unblemished by the class divisions that were institutionalized in representative government, should not adopt such a system. Chang countered the arguments of those who pointed to the Japanese example by saying that Japan was much closer to her feudal era and still characterized by a division between nobility and commoners, whereas in China "all people are equal." [88]

Chang then suggested a variety of reasons why the system envisioned by the Manchus was unworkable. These included the problem of China's population, which he had pointed out in an earlier article, but more important was his conclusion that whether instituted by Manchus or Chinese, as part of a monarchy or democracy,

[87] *Ibid.*, p. 114.
[88] "Tai-i jan-fou lun," *Min-pao*, No. 24, p. 1.

representative government in China would bring only corruption and chaos. "In sum, representative government is of necessity inferior to absolutism." [89]

Chang expected that he and his comrades would now be accused of contradicting their doctrine that China should establish a republic. He explained that the revolutionaries had come to think that a hereditary monarch was intolerable and, partly owing to their favorable impressions of the United States, that a republic headed by a president was best. But they had failed to understand that with the benefits of a presidential system came the defects of elected representatives. The president would be a man with experience in both local and national government, whose record would be known to all and who would presumably be dedicated to the national interest. Representatives, however, were less likely to be chosen because of their qualifications than because they had local influence or power or simply a glib tongue. In the United States representatives, once they were in office, were protected by the law from prosecution for corruption as if they were emperors. Did China want to exchange one emperor for several thousand? [90]

In addition, there was the problem of population and the fact that a federal system was unsuited to current Chinese conditions. China's present task was to achieve peace and unity, to forge common bonds of language and customs, and to overcome sectional and provincial antagonisms and rivalries.[91] Chang's pre-eminent concern for a system geared to advancing China's interests as a nation and overcoming divisive tendencies was nowhere stated more clearly.

The problem of how to limit the power of the president still remained. Chang proposed that the president should manage only executive functions and national defense. In foreign affairs he would be merely the nation's "representative"; in other matters he was not to interfere. These limitations were intended to provide for a clear separation of powers.[92] In the event of war or other similarly critical situations, the people would make their wishes felt by sending to the capital one representative from each county (*hsien*).[93] Unlike a standing representative assembly, this group would meet to vote

[89] *Ibid.*, p. 8.   [91] *Ibid.*, p. 8.   [93] *Ibid.*, p. 12.
[90] *Ibid.*, pp. 8–10.   [92] *Ibid.*, p. 11.

only on one specific issue; each member would be charged with expressing the view decided upon by a majority of his constituents.[94] In effect Chang was proposing a national plebiscite on questions of first importance.

Chang also called for an independent judiciary, whose head would hold equal rank with the president. Similarly, education would comprise a separate branch of the government, with its chief official on a par with the heads of the executive and judiciary branches. Only elementary schools and military academies would be under government jurisdiction; all others would be "independent." [95] Chang placed great emphasis upon the rule of law, which would be equally applicable to all. Laws would be "determined by neither the government nor business interests" but by specialists in law and history. He made a particular point of the requirements that laws should be beyond the president's power to change and that all officials should be subject to them.[96] Punishments would be imposed in proportion to the harm that had been done: thus a thief might suffer a heavier penalty for pilfering a very small amount from a poor man than for stealing a much larger sum from a very wealthy person.[97] Severe restrictions would be placed upon the use of official position to further one's personal financial interests.[98] Requests for tax increases would be referred to local officials, who would in turn submit them to the people; without public approval there could be no increase. Only in those areas that approved such an increase would one be effected. The government budget would be made public annually. "All of this is designed to curb the wealthy and the strong and to relieve the poor and the weak." [99]

Chang then concluded with a lengthy exegesis of the Manchus' proposed constitution, noting at the outset that it was modeled on Japan's and inferring that "their aim is neither to assist the people nor to protect the state but only to uphold reverence for the court." [100] Quoting comparable passages from the Japanese constitution, Chang went on to attack the overpowering position the proposed Manchu

[94] *Ibid.*, p. 16.
[95] *Ibid.*, p. 11. See also pp. 14–15 for further comments on the importance of keeping education from becoming a government monopoly.
[96] *Ibid.*, p. 11.   [98] *Ibid.*, p. 13.   [100] *Ibid.*, p. 18.
[97] *Ibid.*, p. 12.   [99] *Ibid.*, p. 12.

constitution gave the emperor and the very limited role it assigned to the projected parliament. Sallies against the Manchus and their right to continue on the throne followed the pattern we have seen in his and other revolutionaries' writings.[101]

It is difficult to explain why Chang associated representative government with feudalism and class divisions. Perhaps he was thinking of parliaments as they first developed in the thirteenth century, when they represented estates of the realm rather than the interests of individual citizens. Or he may have had in mind the Prussian constitution, the best known to the Chinese revolutionaries of all Western constitutions. Whatever the case, he was unevenly informed about the functioning of representative government in the early-twentieth-century West. He was also unable to resolve some basic contradictions in his thinking. For example, he recognized the need for unity and centralization in China, but his preference for direct democracy, his highly impractical proposal on tax increases, and his suggestion that there be in effect three heads of government, all equal in status, would have interfered with unity and centralization. Nevertheless, he analyzed some of the important problems that the Chinese would face in their effort to introduce democratic political forms as the basis of a strong nation-state, including China's size, diversity, and the strength of local loyalties, the question of popular control of elected representatives, and the need for an impartially administered legal system. Although his concrete proposals may not have been uniformly well constructed, he addressed himself to specific Chinese political problems more than any of his comrades did. Despite his deep pessimism, his ultimate rejection of government and indeed of organized society and even of life itself, Chang gave a good deal of thought to the problems of China's post-revolutionary government. In view of the timing of these writings, which coincided with Chang's split with Sun, it may not be too much to suggest that Chang was making a bid for political leadership of the revolutionary movement. If this last must remain conjectural, it is nevertheless clear that Chang had

---

[101] *Ibid.*, pp. 18–27. Cf. Hu Han-min, "Wu-hu, Man-chou so-wei Hsien-fa Ta-kang," in which Hu pointed out the ways in which the Japanese constitution failed to limit the power of the emperor and how the Manchus' constitution would fail even more dismally.

parted company with his fellows on many questions of representative government.

## Chang's Individualism

Chang Ping-lin's profound distrust of authority and his hostility toward the state stemmed from a deep belief in individuality. The individual was central in Chang's political thought.[102] He believed not only that the state's activities were mean, but that the state had no nature of its own (*tzu-hsing*), that its functions were only those assigned to it by the particular needs of the time, and that there was no fundamental rational principle (*li*) that justified its existence.[103] It is only individual things that are real, he argued, and when they combine to form larger units, such units have no reality; "in sum, the individual is real, the group is illusory." [104] And again: "I maintain that of all the things men pool their energies to form there is not one that is to be valued." [105] Nevertheless, he conceded that sometimes it was necessary to have a state; since China was weak and in danger, and since other states would not disband overnight, China too needed a state merely in order to survive.[106] As for the reality of individual men, Chang was compelled to acknowledge that by his own theory they too were unreal, since they were made up of less complex particulars. But at least they were simpler elements than states and were therefore closer to reality.[107]

From this conception Chang drew important conclusions concerning human relations.

> Man is not born for the sake of the world, or for society, or for the state, or for other men. Therefore, man has no original obligation toward society, the state, or other men. Such obligations are matters that develop later. He must first have a debt to someone else; then he has something to repay to him. If he is unencumbered by debts, he has nothing to repay. In human relationships the limits are determined by the absence of harm. To go beyond this and require that men be virtuous cannot be allowed. . . . If I exert my energies for the benefit of others and seek no reward, this is based

---

[102] Hsiao Kung-ch'üan, *op. cit.*, VI, 859.

[103] "Kuo-chia lun," *Min-pao*, No. 17, p. 1.

[104] *Ibid.*, p. 12. See also p. 3, where Chang lists several collective bodies including the state, all of which he declared to be "unreal" (*hsü-wei*).

[105] *Ibid.*, pp. 8–9.        [106] *Ibid.*, p. 12.        [107] *Ibid.*, p. 4.

upon my own feelings of love; there is no outside law that deter-
mines it. . . . For harming oneself without harming others, one
may not be reproached. For doing what benefits oneself but does
not benefit others, one may not be reproached. Only for what harms
others may one be reproached.[108]

Another quotation will make Chang's position still clearer:

Men are not born to harm each other; therefore men need not do
evil, and it [evil] can be done away with. Men are not born to help
each other; therefore it is not their duty to do good and they may
not be so compelled. Between good and evil there must be a middle
"neutral" (*wu-chi*) line. To go beyond the line of what is neither
good nor evil and invoke what is called *kung-li*, is to restrain men
too strictly.[109]

[108] "Ssu-huo lun," *Min-pao*, No. 22, pp. 2–3. Chang's next line should be added
to complete his idea, but I have omitted it from the text because of translation
difficulties. It reads: "This may be termed the difference between *ch'i-wu* and
*kung-li*." The latter term is frequently translated as "universal principles," a
rendition which is meaningful when contrasted with Chang's nominalism but
which does not seem to provide an adequate antithesis to *ch'i-wu*. *Ch'i-wu* comes
from the *Chuang-tzu* in which the second chapter is called "*Ch'i-wu lun*," translated by Fung Yu-lan as "The Equality of Things and Opinions." Kuo Hsiang's
commentary reads as follows: "Everything is what it is. The opinions of the one
and the other are different; that they both have opinions is the same." (*Chuang
Tzu*, trans. Yu-lan Fung, Shanghai, 1933, p. 43.) Fung says that the "fundamental
idea" of this chapter is that "There is nothing that is not good, and no point of
view that is not right." (*A History of Chinese Philosophy*, I, 236.) He further
notes that this concept is intimately related to Chuang-tzu's belief in complete
liberty and that it also distinguishes his philosophy from Buddhism, which "maintains that there is nothing in the world which is good and no point of view which
is not false." *Ibid.* Thus Fung's translation of *ch'i-wu* as "the equality of things"
may be understood to include the conception of complete liberty, which seems to
be the sense in which Chang Ping-lin used it. *Kung-li* may then also be understood
in terms of Chuang Tzu's opposition to all political and social institutions on the
grounds that they impose uniformity upon individuals who ought to be allowed to
remain different. "Water, which is life to fish, is death to man." As Fung points
out, Chuang-tzu was entering a protest against the application of artificial fixed
standards to differently constituted beings. (*Ibid.*, p. 228.) Chang's contraposition
of *ch'i-wu* and *kung-li* thus seems to set liberty against constraint.

Scholars who wish to pursue the matter may turn to Chang's own lengthy
treatise, "Ch'i-wu lun-shih" (A Discussion of *ch'i-wu*), in *Chang-shih ts'ung-shu*,
Vol. (*han*) II, No. (*ts'e*) 13.

[109] "Ssu-huo lun," p. 5. For the term *wu-chi*, here translated as "neutral" and
"what is neither good nor evil," see William Edward Soothill and Lewis Hodous,
*A Dictionary of Chinese Buddhist Terms*, p. 382; also, p. 178 for the Buddhist
concept of four delusions (*ssu fan-nao*) from which the title of this article comes.

With the exception of his "Essay on the Five Negations," it is in Chang's conception of human relations that the note of protest in his thought is most clearly evident. Furthermore, it is Chang's aversion to authority and his suspicion of the reasons for which men band together to undertake collective action that make his thought intelligible and his relationship to his contemporaries at least partially discernible. A restless and nonconforming spirit, Chang seems to have been continually at odds with those whose company he shared, if not, indeed, with himself.[110] He was a Confucian scholar who rejected Confucian morality, a revolutionary who called for the preservation of China's "national essence," a nationalist who advocated the abolition of all distinctions among nations and denied that individuals have any obligations to each other, and a leader of the republican movement who condemned representative government.

Perhaps the only explanation for these contradictions is that Chang's life was a frustrated search for personal expression, direction, and identity. Growing to manhood in the last three decades of the nineteenth century, Chang was one of those tragically disoriented individuals who because they possess the intelligence and sensitivity that in other times would have enriched their lives, suffer most when they are placed by time and circumstance in life situations where they do not fit. Never fully reconciled to the old order (as is indicated by his unwillingness to enter the examinations under the Ch'ing), he could not fully accept its passing, perhaps because he feared that it would take all of Chinese tradition with it. What is the "Essay on the Five Negations" if not a cry of anguish? Characteristically, his response to the disappointments of 1907 was twofold: "the hopeless and suicidal nihilism"[111] of that essay was followed by his proposal

---

[110] It is worth noting some interesting similarities between Chang and Li Chih (1527–1602). Li was an extreme nonconformist whose ideas were a mixture of Confucianism, Taoism, and Buddhism. Like Chang he denied absolute truth and fixed standards, rejected government in practice, and believed that it was the nature of man to seek his own individual welfare. See Hsiao Kung-ch'üan, "Li Chih: An Iconoclast of the 16th Century," *T'ien Hsia Monthly*, VI, No. 4, pp. 317–41. Note Professor Hsiao's emphasis on Li's "love of liberty," pp. 322 ff. Li was a follower of Wang Shou-jen, and his thought owed much to Wang's stress on "good conscience" and the freedom of the individual mind; Chang Ping-lin's grudging approval of Wang can probably be traced to this same characteristic of the great Ming philosopher's theory of mind.

[111] Hsiao Kung-ch'üan, *Chung-kuo cheng-chih ssu-hsiang shih*, VI, 870. Chang's nihilism was almost surely closely related to his belief in Buddhism.

for direct democracy; withdrawal from the T'ung-meng-hui was followed by leadership of the Restoration Society. The only connecting link seems to be so desperate a plea for individual freedom that in his darkest moments he asked liberation from life itself. In his refutation of K'ang Yu-wei, Chang had said that bondage under the Manchus was unbearable: "If we are not free, it is better to be dead." [112] When a short time later the Manchus had him arrested, he seemed willing to prove with his life that this statement was more than a slogan to stir his readers. In 1907 another setback seemed to produce a similar reaction.

CHANG VERSUS WU CHIH-HUI: A SIDE CURRENT AND A PORTENT

Many of Chang's comrades in the T'ung-meng-hui may have been no less disturbed by the events of their time. But none of them viewed the decline of traditional China with such profound ambivalence as Chang, and all of them seemed better able to accept the view that the revolution would inaugurate a new and glorious age. Perhaps they were better able to identify themselves with the new course that China was to take. Chang remained out of sympathy with it, partly because of his attachment to the old China and partly because it was fundamental to his character, personality, and intellectual outlook to rebel against conformity and organized society. But Chang's ambivalence may also have had another source: it is possible that Chang glimpsed more of the future than any of his contemporaries did and that he recoiled from it. For an examination of this possibility we turn to his feud with Wu Chih-hui.

Chang's philosophical anarchism may appear to provide a link between his thinking and that of Wu Chih-hui. Chang was aware of the current of Western anarchist ideas that flowed among the Chinese students in Japan, and it is quite possible that he was influenced by them. But his anarchism is of a negative character that probably owes much more to Chinese anarchists such as Wu Neng-tzu.[113] In addition, his personal feud with Wu Chih-hui was violent enough to preclude any meeting of their minds. The fundamental point,

[112] "Po K'ang Yu-wei lun ke-ming shu," p. 608.

[113] See Hsiao Kung-ch'üan, "Anarchism in Chinese Political Thought," *T'ien Hsia Monthly*, III, 249–63.

however, is that there was a deep philosophical gulf between the two men.

One of the most interesting expressions of their differences emerged in their debate on language reform. Wu and his followers advocated the world-wide adoption of Esperanto. Chang demurred on practical grounds, discussing at length the manifold problems of replacing Chinese with an alphabetic writing system, but he also objected to the effects such a step would have on tradition. "Do those who today uphold anarchism also desire to destroy learning?" he asked.[114] They did not understand how language develops and changes over time, the problems of preserving the continuity between earlier writings and the present, and the difficulties that the adoption of a new language would create for those who wanted to read ancient books, however it might facilitate translation of foreign books.

> Is language useful primarily for translating foreign languages or for understanding our ancient books? They will say that our histories and biographies entomb the deeds of dead men, that our literature is empty verbiage, that is of no practical benefit to the people, and that even to abandon it in its entirety is permissible. They do not realize that the difference between man and the birds and beasts is precisely that he has the concept of what is past and what is yet to come. If we say that the sense of the past may be erased, then that of the future may also be excised, and man will know only this instant and nothing more.[115]

Chang and Wu held diametrically opposed views of tradition that reflected basic differences in their whole intellectual outlook. The clash was strikingly revealed in another series of exchanges between the two men. Chang had written that anarchism was not suitable for China and, indeed, that as formulated by Wu it hardly deserved to be called a philosophy.[116] Wu replied that it was only a philosophy such as anarchism, with its basis in modern science and particularly

[114] "Po Chung-kuo yung wan-kuo hsin-yü shuo," *Min-pao*, No. 21, p. 55.

[115] *Ibid.*, p. 70. Chang's deep concern for the preservation of Chinese tradition is evidenced by the fact that despite his voluminous writings for *Min-pao*, he also was a frequent contributor to *Kuo-ts'ui hsüeh-pao* (The Chinese Essence Journal). Some of his writings were published in both periodicals; the one cited here, for example, appeared in abridged form in *Kuo-ts'ui hsüeh-pao*, Vol. VII, No. 4, pp. 6–10.

[116] "P'ai-Man p'ing-i," *Min-pao*, No. 21, p. 1.

in the theory of evolution, that was applicable to modern China; Buddhism and the philosophies of Chou and Ch'in, on the other hand, were unscientific and had no relevance to present conditions.[117]

Chang's reply has a familiar ring:

> What he [Wu] refers to as science is the investigation of things to unify and systematize them. But the disorder of all things is not for science to rationalize completely. . . . Right and wrong, being and non-being and such concepts do not reveal their character in matter, but rather are categories that are worked out in the mind. . . .[118]

The senses are dubious guides to reality, Chang asserted, and moreover there were problems within science's own sphere of competence to which the senses could not provide answers, such as whether atoms or electrons really exist. Thus even science involved speculation, and there were scientific theories based not upon the investigation of things but upon imagination and inference. One example Chang cited was Haeckel's view that there are countless other worlds besides our own.[119]

Chang then turned to the question of science and human affairs. Anarchism, he wrote, concerned human affairs but tried to make use of science to develop its theory. A careful comparison between science and human affairs, however, would reveal

> the difference between observing things and understanding feelings. Human affairs derive from an amalgamation of feelings and knowledge, the form of which is subject to unpredictable change. [Men] are not like plants and animals which fulfill their inherent natures, or inanimate matter which moves mechanically. Their future cannot be known and their past reveals few patterns; thus to draw parallels between such vastly different things will lead to endless errors. Anarchism, then, is basically different from both science and philosophy, and it should not falsely assume their names in order to enhance itself.[120]

Western thought, Chang continued, was strongest in the sciences, and particularly in mathematics and physics. However it was deficient in "the study of social relationships." [121]

---

[117] Wu Chih-hui, "Shu p'ai-Man p'ing-i hou" (After Reading "A Balanced Discussion about Expelling the Manchus"), *HSC*, No. 57, p. 2.

[118] "Kuei Hsin Shih-chi," *Min-pao*, No. 24, p. 43.

[119] *Ibid.*, p. 44–45.        [120] *Ibid.*, pp. 45–46.        [121] *Ibid.*, p. 65.

Finally, Chang argued that there is a difference between what is useful and what is valuable; only the Utilitarian school confounds the two. "But I say that even if they only have value but no utility, the profundities of philosophy have never been despised because they were not useful; whereas even if anarchism is applicable in the West, one does not treasure it simply because it is useful." He drew an analogy with the difference between paper money and precious metal. "Comparing them in this way, what is valuable takes its own intrinsic qualities as its standard, and what is useful takes fashionableness as its standard. The one comes from within itself, and the other depends upon others. Therefore value and utility are not the same thing." [122]

Chang's dispute with Wu Chih-hui was clearly on the weightiest of issues, questions that had been taking shape for decades in the West and that were to convulse the Chinese intellectual world in the years to come. The fundamental difference in outlook between the two men is perhaps best summed up in Chang's final gibe at the *New Century* writers for always talking about being scientific but not being very scientific themselves.[123] Chang did not deny the value of science but its universal applicability, and he decried the uncritical spirit in which men gathered themselves into a cult of science and attempted to extend their idol's powers into all areas of knowledge and action.

Is it possible that Wu and the Paris group posed a challenge which led Chang to undertake a complete re-examination of his own new ideas? Did his comrades' republicanism begin to seem at least potentially as rash or dogmatic as Wu's scientism? If Wu did plant seeds of doubt in Chang's mind, there were certainly other seeds, and fertile soil as well. All that can be said with certainty is that a great variety of forces and tensions were working on Chang's mind, and that their number and intensity seemed to exceed what was experienced by any other revolutionary we have studied. These produced in him flights of fancy and waves of despair that defy explanation, quirks and eccentricities that lead us to question whether his faculties were always under his control, but also startling flashes of imagination and insight.

[122] *Ibid.*, p. 47.
[123] *Ibid.*, p. 65.

Chang Ping-lin's place in the history of the Chinese revolution remains difficult to assess.[124] On some issues he shared the views of his comrades in the T'ung-meng-hui or at least managed temporarily to accommodate his thinking to the needs of the movement. Among the clearest examples of sharing and accommodation are his anti-Manchuism, anti-imperialism, and arguments in favor of socialism and, on occasion, even republicanism. In these respects Chang did further the revolution by adding to its intellectual content, by putting philosophy and history in the service of politics.[125] At the same time, however, even when in agreement with other revolutionaries he drew so heavily on different sources of inspiration that the flavor and texture of his writings vary markedly from theirs. His visions of religion and *kuo-ts'ui* are the most obvious examples; they colored his nationalism to a tone that no other T'ung-meng-hui writer approached. Finally, for carefully thought out reasons, Chang was in the end unable to accept republicanism.

Chang's life and thought had wider significance in many ways. The one that most directly concerns us is his place in China's twentieth-century intellectual revolution. Once again our conclusion must be twofold and ambivalent. On the one hand, Chang shared with many of his contemporaries some attitudes that I believe characterize the beginning of this revolution. He could say at times that enlightenment comes from struggle and, like Wang Ching-wei, Sun Yat-sen, and the anarchists, he could suggest that revolution was in itself at least a partial solution to China's problems because it somehow fostered wisdom. There were stages of development in history and a certain inevitability about progress. Even in moments of deepest pessimism he could speak of a "period of final perfection." Faith in progress and belief in ultimate perfection may be largely a psychological phenomenon with which historians should deal very cautiously if at all,[126] but it is an important political phenomenon as well. Even the

---

[124] Interestingly, Chang has proved to be a thorny problem for Communist historians, who have devoted more attention to him than to any other revolutionary leader except Sun Yat-sen. A convenient introduction to this literature is Ts'ai Shang-se (ssu), "Chang Ping-lin ssu-hsiang te chieh-chi hsing" (The Class Character of Chang Ping-lin's Thought), *Li-shih yen-chiu*, 1962, No. 1, pp. 58–70. Ts'ai summarizes eight interpretations of Chang that have appeared in Communist writings and offers a ninth of his own.

[125] See Hu Shen-wu and Chin Tson-qi, *op. cit.*, p. 20.

[126] For a more scientific treatment of this question in terms of psychology see

most pessimistic thinker of the time could not remain unaffected by the climate of optimism. It was an atmosphere described vividly years later by a scholar who was for a time a student of Chang Ping-lin. Ku Chieh-kang relates how his generation expected changes that would destroy the most basic institutions: "I fancied that there was nothing under the sun too difficult for men to accomplish; that the good, the true, and the beautiful need only to be advocated and they will become actualities." It was in this spirit that Ku became a socialist in 1912.[127] It was in this climate that China's intellectual revolution took on the attributes of "political Messianism" and forged its link with "totalitarian democracy." [128]

Although Chang shared much with other revolutionary intellectuals, an abiding traditionalism and conservatism made him partly an outsider. There were specific issues such as republicanism on which he at last parted company with the others, and he could not fully share their vision of the future. As his debate with Wu Chih-hui demonstrates, the scientism that was to win such wide adherence in only a few years was anathema to him. His own proposals for social change were sometimes more radical than any advanced even by the Paris anarchists, as his "five negations" show, but on the whole he stood for less change than other revolutionaries. He remained aloof from the doctrines of science and democracy that came to be the dominant trends in the Chinese intellectual revolution.

---

Ira Progoff, "The Dynamics of Hope and the Image of Utopia," in *Vom Sinn der Utopie*, pp. 89–145. Note especially pp. 98–105. I am grateful to Professor Hellmut Wilhelm for guiding me to Progoff's writings.

[127] *Autobiography of a Chinese Historian*, p. 28.

[128] See J. L. Talmon, *The Origins of Totalitarian Democracy* and *Political Messianism* for the development of these concepts in their Western setting. My concluding chapter touches upon their relevance to China.

# *Conclusion*

The role played by intellectuals in the revolution of 1911 cannot yet be spelled out clearly. Much remains to be learned about the intellectuals, especially after 1908, and we know even less about the 1911 revolution than we do about the intellectuals. There are many basic questions about 1911 that await answers, including the ultimate one: what in China was revolutionized and what was not? Increasingly we become aware that the simple answers — the Manchus fell, the Ch'ing dynasty fell, the imperial system was overturned — will not do, at least not as anything more than starting points. It remains to be known, for example, what shifts in power distribution took place and what changes occurred in social relationships.

The answers to such questions not only await study of 1911 itself and post-1911 events; they also await studies of pre-1911 China. To know whether the fall of the Ch'ing resulted in a decisive shift of power from Manchus to Chinese requires that we know how power was divided between Chinese and Manchus before 1911 as well as after. The same is true of the relationship between central government power and regional or provincial power. If the power of the central government declined as rapidly and extensively for some fifty years before the revolution, as is often thought, was a revolution accomplished when a new central government was founded? We need to know more about the distribution of power before as well as after

1911, and we need to know who in the provinces held power before and after 1911.

One could add many such questions. Their sum would be an immense unknown about how much and what kind of revolution there was in 1911. A subtotal might be the hypothesis that there was a partial collapse of some old institutions but not a revolutionizing of very many. It might even be wiser to ask why the Ch'ing dynasty lasted as long as it did rather than why there was a revolution. For a dynasty to be in decline for well over a century was nothing new, but for a dynasty in decline for so long to withstand blows of the kind administered to the Ch'ing concurrently by massive rebellions and foreign powers was new. Were the Manchus doing more constructive things than they are generally credited with having done, and did those things perpetuate their existence? Or were they able merely to manipulate their opponents in such a way that they survived chiefly by directing their foes' energies against each other? Perhaps they were so sluggish that they could not even fall quickly.

So much is unknown about the 1911 revolution that students of it do well to be cautious. Furthermore, since the forces that combined to bring down the Ch'ing dynasty included deep historical ones as well as many immediate ones, it seems obvious that the part played by the T'ung-meng-hui and other such revolutionary groups is still undetermined. It is entirely possible that the dynasty would have fallen when it did or soon thereafter even if there had been no T'ung-meng-hui; I am inclined to doubt this, but the point is that no one really knows how much the revolutionaries hastened a process of decline that had been going on and intensifying for about a century before the T'ung-meng-hui was founded.

If the nature and extent of the revolution are so uncertain, and if the role played by the T'ung-meng-hui in a still largely unexamined revolution is also highly problematic, how much can we say about the ideas of a small group within the T'ung-meng-hui? After all, the intellectuals studied in this book amount to only a few men, often at odds with each other, within a rather small and divided organization, which was in turn only one of many revolutionary groups, which even added together may not have contributed very much to a revolution that may not have accomplished very much.

The many good reasons that demand restraint in evaluating the

1911 revolution and the T'ung-meng-hui intellectuals' contribution to it are counterbalanced by one fact and several speculations. The fact, an effective counterweight in itself, is that China became a republic in 1912. When the Manchus fell, the Chinese did not found a new dynasty, a constitutional monarchy, or anything else to which the T'ung-meng-hui was opposed. They founded a republic. Whatever factors may have contributed to this outcome other than T'ung-meng-hui advocacy, it is reasonable to believe that that advocacy was more responsible than any other cause for China's adopting a republican form of government in 1912. Men such as Yüan Shih-k'ai and the gentry in the provinces had many other reasons for wanting to overthrow the Manchus, develop a representative system, and do many of the things they did after 1911,[1] but it is doubtful that anything counted as heavily in their decision to create a republic as did T'ung-meng-hui insistence on it.

The revolutionaries' demand for a republic in 1912 was of course backed by a certain amount of power, military and otherwise. I cannot explore here the many reasons why others acquiesced to the T'ung-meng-hui's demand, but it seems safe to say that ideas of republicanism had some power of their own in China by 1911–12. In the context of this book, perhaps, Liang Ch'i-ch'ao's acceptance of the republic and his ready and immediate participation in it are the best evidence for this claim; Liang, after all, lived not by instruments of power such as guns; he lived by ideas.

Thus even if the T'ung-meng-hui intellectuals' share in the 1911 revolution has to be subject to a high discount rate, it should not be wiped off the board. We have seen that their demand for a republic had an immediate impact in 1911–12; it is also likely that the revolutionaries' ideas affected the course of events of China for some years before 1911. For example, the Manchu government probably would have moved even more slowly toward constitutionalism than it did had it not been for the pressures exerted by the revolutionaries. Whether the revolutionaries' influence was for good or ill remains to be determined; for now I wish only to make it clear that Chinese in-

---

[1] Numerous aspects of these and related subjects are touched upon in the articles by Marie-Claire Bergere, Chang P'eng-yüan, John Fincher, Ichiko Chuzo, and Ernest P. Young in *China in Revolution: The First Phase, 1900–1913*, ed. Mary C. Wright.

tellectuals had a considerable effect on events in the decade before 1912. In view of the many gaps in our knowledge of this subject, I do not think I can say with any assurance more than I have said here and in the body of the book.

The significance of our story up to this point might be assessed somewhat as follows. First, the numerous pre-twentieth-century seeds of modern Chinese nationalism remained scattered and dormant until touched by Western and Japanese imperialism. The actions of Western countries and Japan nourished a feeling in nineteenth-century China that something "Chinese" was being threatened in an unprecedented way. The measures taken to meet that threat led to a deliberate inquiry to determine what was most distinctively and fundamentally Chinese. To preserve the Chinese "basis" (*t'i*) one had first to identify it. The earliest results of this investigation showed little that was new, but as it went on, hand in hand with the study of what was distinctively and fundamentally Western, some men (such as Yen Fu, Liang Ch'i-ch'ao, and Sun Yat-sen) discovered the concept of a nation-state. Their discovery roughly coincided with the high tide of imperialism in China and the failure of the 1898 reform, when the Manchu government seemed to them helpless to defend China and incapable of improving itself. Criticisms that had been made of specific shortcomings and failures of the regime now spread to its very legitimacy. Many critics became revolutionaries, having concluded either that China had failed to become a nation-state because she had been under alien and barbarian (Manchu) domination, or that a historic Chinese nationality had existed but had been suppressed by the Manchus. In reaction against the Manchus, to distinguish themselves from the barbarians and to deny the Manchus' right to rule, the Chinese revolutionaries defined what it meant to be Chinese in an entirely new way.

When anti-imperialism was supplemented by anti-Manchuism, when anti-Manchuism combined resentment against Ch'ing weakness vis-à-vis imperialism and contempt for the Manchus as foreign barbarians with the modern concepts of nation and sovereignty, and when these ideas were fused into the program of an armed and organized conspiracy that rang its message out to Chinese deep in China itself and from Japan to Hong Kong to Singapore to Burma and on to Africa, Europe, and the Western hemisphere, modern Chinese nationalism was born.[2]

Even the most negative feature of the revolutionaries' thinking had its positive side, or at least positive consequences. Anti-imperialism and anti-Manchuism helped to beget a more widely shared feeling that all Chinese were citizens, *min* of a *kuo*;[3] all Chinese had something in common because all shared the Chinese characteristics listed by Wang Ching-wei. For the first time in Chinese history these ideas of citizenship and nationhood received concrete and deliberate formulation and expression, were widely circulated, and became part of a broader political and social program that was vigorously advanced by serious contenders for power. From this time on nationalism was a powerful force in Chinese life.

Second, consonant with their remarkably determined effort to plan the future as well as explain their discontent with present and past, the revolutionaries spelled out a good many of their theoretical assumptions about republicanism and suggested ways in which their ideals of representative government might be realized. Their discussion underlines many of the difficulties of adapting a Western political concept to Chinese conditions. In particular, the ease with which the voices of postrevolutionary planning were virtually drowned out by thundering anti-Manchu choruses demonstrated anew the difficulty of planning constructively amidst violence and destruction. But the start that was made under immensely trying conditions remains impressive. Ideas about democracy, government by consent, shared power, and the role of law were taking shape rapidly enough to suggest that they may have an appeal that not only goes beyond class and social background[4] but even across wider seas than the Atlantic; indeed, the appeal may be universal.

In China these ideas were experimented with during a time and under circumstances which did not allow a very fair trial then and

[2] A vivid example of the revolution's penetration into China may be found in *A Chinese Testament* (The Autobiography of Tan Shih-hua as told to S. Tretiakov), pp. 47–57.

[3] See Joseph R. Levenson's discussion of *t'ien-hsia* and *kuo*, world and nation, in *Confucian China and Its Modern Fate*, I, 95–108.

[4] R. R. Palmer, "The Great Inversion: America and Europe in the Eighteenth-Century Revolution," *Ideas in History*, ed. Richard Herr and Harold T. Parker, pp. 18–19.

which are not conducive to predictions now about their possible success in other times, places, and circumstances. But the failure of the Chinese experiment with republicanism will not support the conclusion that transference of political ideas from one culture to another is doomed.

The same may be said of socialism. Like ideas about democracy and republicanism it reached China in somewhat garbled form, having passed through the hands of numerous translators and interpreters. These men, especially the German and Japanese scholars, imparted something of themselves to the ideas they transported, and the Chinese also to some extent transformed the ideas they received. Such handling of outside ideas is sometimes regarded too disdainfully by modern scholars. We go through a not dissimilar process when we attempt to master Chinese thought, and we do it without feeling the pressure to redirect our lives according to what we learn. The difference is of course very great, but we and our students often find ourselves interpreting a newly encountered idea by comparing it with those with which we are familiar, much as Chinese interpreted socialism by comparing it with the *chün-t'ien* system. Some such process is quite natural at an early stage of learning. More important, at this stage of China's intellectual history, tradition was a powerful enough force to make at least some new ideas unacceptable purely in their own terms. It is also premature to rule out the possibility that there were some points of contact between new ideas (such as socialism) to which Chinese were attracted and old ideas (such as *chün-t'ien*) that also attracted them.[5] It is not pathetic that they attempted to find such points of contact; rather, it is tragic that history did not allow them the time for this more leisurely and rational approach to intellectual borrowing.

Sympathy for the tragic plight of the Chinese intellectuals should not obscure the fundamental point. History simply did not wait. Is there a deeper significance in the way the Chinese approached Western ideas? The significance lies partly in what they selected. It is very

[5] On this point see Mary C. Wright, *The Last Stand of Chinese Conservatism*, pp. 224 ff., where the description of "The Chinese attempt to use . . . European counterparts of the Confucian ethic" as a basis for a new foreign policy suggests to me that such efforts were not total failures. See also Professor Wright's "A Review Article: The Pre-Revolutionary Intellectuals of China and Russia," *The China Quarterly*, No. 6, p. 179.

risky to generalize, because so many different new ideas found adherents for so many different reasons, but I remain impressed by the extent to which Chinese intellectuals chose democratic and humanitarian ideas. I do not wish to minimize the importance of their devotion to national power, their willingness to resort to violence, and their determination to strengthen the state even at the cost of curtailing individual liberty. These were extremely important and indeed probably dominant sentiments among the Chinese revolutionaries; the new ideas to which they gave allegiance had mainly to do with translating those sentiments into the new institutions of a wealthy and powerful China. But in view of the conditions of the times — the level of their dissatisfaction, the vehemence of their protest, the hatred and the desperate urgency they felt — it is altogether remarkable that they gave as much thought as they did to democratic processes and means of ensuring political rights, social justice, and equality.

The revolutionaries' interest in anarchism also illustrates how they nourished their humanitarian impulses and ideals even as those ideals were compromised. Often the revolutionaries turned to anarchism by embracing its ideals of brotherhood and "mutual aid" but then veered quickly toward the violent and conspiratorial features of anarchism. There were "assassination squads" and a good deal of glorification of political murder; Wu Yüeh and Hsü Hsi-lin were hailed as heroes.[6] Considering what the atmosphere in China was like at the outset of the twentieth century, these trends are not at all surprising; what seems more striking is that the fundamental theory of anarchism and its noblest principles received so much continuing attention. Many anarchist writers persisted in upholding the ideals of liberty, freedom from restraint and authority, social betterment, and equality. The explanation for this continuing idealism is not that it was confined to intellectuals who lived in an ivory tower; on the contrary, many intellectuals accepted with gusto the need for violence. For example, Wang Ching-wei, the respectable republican theorist, who also flirted with anarchism for a time, attempted an assassination in 1910. Still, even amid all the pressures, a number of men kept their

---

[6] Hsü assassinated En-ming, the governor of Anhwei, in 1907; Wu had attempted to murder the imperial commissioners in 1905. A lively memoir on this subject is Wu Yu-chang, *The Revolution of 1911*, pp. 97–102.

balance and many held to their ideals for decades after 1911. They were probably very far from being a majority, but it is clear that at least some of the revolutionaries held fast to values and long-range goals toward which a wealthy and powerful China might some day aim. And many of those values and goals came from the modern West.

Thus the major firm conclusions of this study have to do with the founding of the Chinese republic, the flowering of modern Chinese nationalism, and the introduction of new ideas about democracy (and socialism) which contributed to the growth of democratic socialist movements. Where does radicalism fit in?

The answer is twofold. Radicalism is first of all the widest net I can cast that will hold all the major thinkers of the time and still be conceptually useful. It was characteristic of more members of China's new intelligentsia than was any other general feature. Anti-Manchuism and modern Chinese nationalism were born in the period I have studied, but a considerable number of important intellectuals either remained aloof from these doctrines or actively opposed them. Liang Ch'i-ch'ao and the reformers were not anti-Manchu. The anarchists also were uncomfortable with anti-Manchuism and very critical of nationalism. Even among the nationalists there were substantial differences. Chang Ping-lin's anti-Manchuism, for example, was more deeply rooted in traditional Chinese culture than in twentieth-century China and nineteenth-century Europe; Chang was satisfied to regard Huang Ti as the founder of the Chinese nation, but most revolutionaries (since they shared with Liang Ch'i-ch'ao an esteem for Cavour, Bismarck, and Napoleon that was at least equal to the respect they had for Huang Ti) derived their sense of nationhood from more modern ideas.

Similarly, not all the new intellectuals and not even all the revolutionaries wanted a republic. Some wanted no representative system at all and some wanted no government at all. Liang, of course, wanted a constitutional monarchy. Not all approved of "westernization" or "modernization." Chang Ping-lin disapproved largely because modernization required departures from the "national essence," and some anarchists dreamed of an Arcadia more than a New Lanark.

All the men discussed in this book were radicals. They were radicals in that their discontent with the present far exceeded their satisfaction with it, so much so that they committed themselves to promoting changes that would go to the root of their dissatisfactions and change society in fundamental and extreme ways. This designation illuminates the most widely held beliefs and attitudes among Chinese intellectuals in the first decade of the twentieth century. It underlines the shared desires of men who in other ways, ways that were quite significant, differed markedly from each other. It helps us to identify some of the chief similarities as well as the differences within the new intelligentsia that emerged in the course of the revolutionary movement, and it helps us to see this generation of new intellectuals in comparison with other generations, especially later ones.

Radicalism, for example, links Liang Ch'i-ch'ao with the revolutionaries. Liang shared their goals of modernization and also their desire to modernize thoroughly. "All forms of radical politics make their appearance at moments of rapid and decisive change, moments when customary status is in doubt and character (or 'identity') is itself a problem. Before Puritans, Jacobins, or Bolsheviks attempt the creation of a new order, they must create new men." [7] Liang was no less dedicated to the creation of a new order than the revolutionaries, and no one did more than he to propagate the idea that the new order depended upon creating a "new people." Similarly, radicalism links Liang and the T'ung-meng-hui with Hu Shih and all others who fought for the creation of a new culture in the next decade.

On the other hand, since the differences between Liang and the revolutionaries were far more than personal, those differences reveal the issues that most troubled Chinese intellectuals before 1911. One issue was doubtless the form that democratic and constitutional government would take in China, whether it would be republican or monarchical, as in England; the issue was a real one, and the sentiment against even a figurehead monarch was widespread and passionate. Few would tolerate even this remnant of hereditary privilege.

Close to the surface of anti-monarchical feeling, indeed so close that one hesitates to separate them, was anti-Manchuism. There is no evidence that any significant number of revolutionaries clung to

[7] Michael Walzer, *The Revolution of the Saints*, p. 315.

a desire for a Chinese monarchy, but their arguments in favor of a republic stemmed largely from their anti-Manchu views. The debate with Liang made it clear that the attitudes the two sides held toward the Manchus divided them far more sharply than their views on the relative merits of constitutional monarchy and republicanism.

Finally, Liang and the revolutionaries were divided on the issues of violent revolution and the possibility and advisability of promoting *rapid* social change. These were the crucial questions that split the radical Chinese intelligentsia. It was a split that cut Liang Ch'i-ch'ao off from the mainstream of Chinese radicalism before 1911, much as Hu Shih was cut off during the New Culture Movement a decade later. Liang and Hu wanted thoroughgoing change, but they eschewed violence and were doubtful that change could be speeded. On these issues the leading T'ung-meng-hui ideologues such as Wang Ching-wei, Hu Han-min, Chu Chih-hsin, Ch'en T'ien-hua, Feng Tzu-yu, and even Sun Yat-sen found common ground with other revolutionaries in their own time and in the years to come. Unlike Liang Ch'i-ch'ao, the revolutionary radicals believed that an anti-Manchu revolution, despite the use of violence and the circulation of doctrines of racial hatred, could create a free, strong, prosperous, independent, and democratic China in which social justice and equality could be secured for all. This belief linked the T'ung-meng-hui with later radicals, and it brings us to the second and more speculative aspect of the birth of modern Chinese radicalism.

When people have been deeply dissatisfied with the conditions under which they live, they have created in their minds better conditions. In ancient times it required exceptional gifts of imagination and reasoning for men to create in their minds a very detailed picture of better conditions, particularly one that would differ drastically from familiar values and practices. It required further unusual talents for them to work out a plan to translate even small parts of that picture into reality. To plan the creation of conditions that would conform entirely to their ideals demanded still more gifts. Finally, to have their plans executed seemed to require abilities and good fortune that were unlikely to be granted to men even by the most generous God. The few who could not resist applying themselves to such tasks fell so far short that they described their aim as

Utopia, i.e., "nowhere." The pessimism implicit in the term suggests their failure.

Whether driven by hope, misery, or something else, these men continued their quest. Some believed that a past golden age might be recovered; others, particularly after the age of exploration began to reveal new worlds, sought a hidden Eldorado. Then something different happened. As the scientific and industrial revolutions advanced, man's power to control nature grew; concurrently, more men claimed the right to be educated, and modern technology — in printing, communication, and transportation especially — made it possible for them to have their claim satisfied. As the search for Eldorado failed, it began to seem possible to find Utopia in the future instead of in the past or in some other place. The pessimism of "nowhere" became, in the age of industrialization, evolution, and Progress, the optimism of tomorrow.[8] It was one of the most pregnant transformations in human history.

It is a commonplace that belief in the possibility of change contributes to change; in human affairs ranging from the stock market to politics to fashions in dress, undreamed-of things have come about as men dreamed and then thought and then acted. The very triteness of these remarks testifies to how common our assumption is that ideas have an effect on events. Hopes become desires, desires become expectations, expectations produce demands, and demands lead to action. Among the most important examples of this sequence are revolutions.

Considering how much human suffering there has been in history, there have not been many revolutions. They have been few partly because of the difficulty, even under favorable circumstances, of effecting very rapid and extreme changes, and partly because of the difficulty of arousing enough people to an awareness of the possibility of improving their lives. Even when many people are aware of this possibility, they will not necessarily agree on the desirability of improvement, since for religious, psychological, or other reasons some will prefer to remain as they are. But it seems clear that one of the principal barriers to change has often been the inability of people to appreciate the possibility of it. Now the modern world has

[8] See Leslie C. Tihany, "Utopia in Modern Western Thought," in Herr and Parker (eds.), *Ideas in History*, pp. 20–38.

raised the odds in favor of change and communicated to more people the news that a vastly different life is possible. The issues among men have tended to become questions of what kind of change, by what means, and in what sequence. As science and technology seem to shift the odds increasingly in favor of change, and as more men see more of the world where conditions seem better than their own, the expectation that faster and more extensive changes can be made leads to demands that such changes be made. The result is a proliferation of revolutionary movements.

In Western Europe these familiar developments had the time to stockpile for centuries. Scholars regard "modernization" as it took place in the West to have been a more "natural" or evolutionary or organic process than similar processes that have occurred elsewhere in the world. Still, the West has been convulsed in violence and social disruption ever since these developments reached a critical mass in the eighteenth century. Indeed, there was much violence and disruption in earlier times as well. Such periods of peace and stability as the West has had in the last two hundred years may be traced to its having undergone not merely a gradual and organic process of growth but a distinctive sequence of modernization; profound changes in trade, industry, finance, science, technology, and intellectual life went together and got well under way before modern political revolutions took place. Even as early as the English revolution of 1689 the economic and scientific revolutions were already far advanced; new classes took shape, and eventually political institutions began to be molded to fit new social and economic realities as well as changing conceptions of government. The length and sequence of this process permitted changes in various aspects of life to adjust to each other sufficiently to permit modernization to proceed constructively, but it cannot be overemphasized that even the many centuries Europe had in which to change piecemeal and gradually did not save it from immense upheaval.

History was generous with her gifts of time to Asia before about 1500, but since then it has been too sparing. In China when the warnings of the sixteenth, seventeenth, and eighteenth centuries went unheeded, the nineteenth turned increasingly harsh. In a society in which concepts of change and time had acquired their own character and very deep roots [9] and in which these concepts had been at peace with each other and with the dominant ideals of stability and harmony for centuries, there suddenly erupted the accumulated volcanic fires of revolutionary Europe.

China has a long history of utopian thought,[10] but before the full impact of the modern West was felt, it lacked the preconditions for full flowering. Both the desirability and possibility of changes were conceived of in very limited ways, ways that were suited only to traditional Chinese needs, possibilities, and visions of what was desirable and possible. In particular, of course, there was not the dimension provided by Western science and technology, with its potential for putting men's destiny in their own hands. This potential only began to be appreciated and valued by a sizable group of people in China, and concurrently made part of a program of rapid and thoroughgoing change, during the course of the revolutionary movement in the first decade of this century.

The new Chinese intelligentsia disagreed about many things, but they all shared a deep dissatisfaction with the present, an urgent sense that change was desperately needed and above all an optimism about the future. Some were less optimistic than others; Liang Ch'i-ch'ao and Chang Ping-lin were on the borderline. What is significant is that they were even on or close to the border of optimism. In some other crucial matters they were at odds with the main body of modern Chinese intellectuals, but even Chang, the least modern of them all, might differ enormously from the others about anti-Manchuism and republicanism but could not remain aloof from optimism. Liang was even closer to the optimism of the other revolutionaries. A highly contagious confidence in China's future filled the air.

Most revolutionaries, however, went beyond optimism to a special form of radicalism. It was a radicalism according to which the failure of a massive effort at reform was proof that a more massive effort was needed. Others might conclude that the 1898 reforms failed because too much was attempted too quickly and that therefore it would be wise to attempt a little less, or move a little more slowly or

[9] The best introduction to this subject is Hellmut Wilhelm, *Change: Eight Lectures on the "I Ching"*; also, see Joseph Needham, *Time and Eastern Man*.

[10] For a sampling see *Chung-kuo ta-t'ung ssu-hsiang tzu-liao* (Materials on Chinese Utopian Thought).

a little differently; thus Liang Ch'i-ch'ao, shortly after 1898, lowered his sights and reconciled himself to less radical change. Most revolutionaries concluded that the resisting wall had to be attacked harder and closer to its foundations; once it was smashed, the attackers could pour through in greater numbers and with fewer impediments than if they had chipped out only a small hole. The revolutionaries, in contrast to Liang, raised their sights to new and more distant possibilities. The trend is best illustrated by Sun Yatsen's locomotive analogy and his comment on the Hawaiians' "single leap," by Wang Ching-wei's argument that China could have democracy without going through all the stages of development the West had followed, and by the anarchists' and Chang Ping-lin's utopias.

There were of course differences among the revolutionaries; the optimistic spirit and the vision of rapid advance to a vastly better China did not uniformly affect the thoughts and actions of them all. But I believe that it was in the expression of this mood, this spirit, this attitude, and this vision that they functioned as revolutionary intellectuals and fulfilled a major historic role. The crucial elements in a revolution are not simply the presence of deep grievances, the breakdown of a social system or a community, or the inability of the existing authorities to relieve the grievances, repair the social system, or restore the community. Such conditions may exist for a century or more without a revolution taking place. For a revolution to occur, there must also be an expectation that a better alternative exists. A revolutionary situation is one where such expectations exceed the existing government's ability to satisfy them. The existing government may well be doing more to meet grievances and solve social problems than it or any other government has ever done before; it may not lack the ability to deal with society's problems. But if enough people are convinced that their government lacks this ability, that different leadership can do better, and that a different set of principles and institutions is needed to do better, a revolutionary situation exists. Much research needs to be done on the Ch'ing government between 1870 and 1911 before one can say with confidence that it was doing all that could have been done, but there can be little doubt that the T'ung-meng-hui intellectuals effectively propagated the idea that it was not. The revolutionaries accomplished this result chiefly by centering their attacks not on what the Manchus were doing but on who they were, and also by predicting vast improvements under a Chinese republic. Thus the revolutionary radicals expressed the yearning of many for a better life, described something of what the better life would look like, and by articulating these scarcely imagined possibilities, aroused new hopes and expectations.

Many of those hopes were dashed shortly after 1911. Within only a few years many T'ung-meng-hui men were so discouraged by all that their revolution had not accomplished that they either abandoned politics altogether or cynically went along with China's new rulers. Still others confronted China's problems once again and, inevitably, found many different answers. Some, such as Sun Yat-sen, returned to the old form of revolutionary conspiracy. Others, joined by newer members of the new intelligentsia, re-examined what had been done and tried to explain what had gone wrong. Of these, the group that turned out to be most historically significant came to conclusions resembling both the ones Liang Ch'i-ch'ao had come to around 1903–5 (that China was not ready for republican government) and those the revolutionaries came to about the 1898 reforms. They decided that the old culture had posed too many obstacles to success. More had to be done, and faster. They resolved to root out the old culture and create something entirely new, a culture in which democracy could flourish. In brief, the revolutionary movement produced the next generation of Chinese leadership.[11]

The revolution of 1911 generated not only China's new leaders but also a mood and an attitude. Like their predecessors who concluded that the antidote to the Manchus' failure was to strike harder and deeper, the leaders of the New Culture Movement decided that the antidote to the failure of 1911 was to strike still harder and deeper.

[11] In Chow Tse-tsung's words, the students who had been in Japan "provided much of the leadership of the May Fourth Movement; they furnished, in the main, the militant elements, most of the leading creative writers of the new literature, and many of the revolutionary extremists including nationalists, socialists, and anarchists." Interestingly enough, Chow finds that "they also included many of the military and civil officials who opposed the movement." *The May Fourth Movement*, p. 31. It cannot yet be established with certainty, but it seems a reasonable hypothesis that the great majority of returned students later supported the May Fourth Movement. In any case, it is not numbers that are most important here.

What impressed them was not that 1911 had accomplished much more than any earlier attempt at modernization but that it had accomplished much less than the revolutionaries had expected. Before long, others were to draw similar conclusions about the New Culture Movement. In this sense the Communists may be regarded as the third wave of a radicalism that with each wave resembled more closely a radicalism of impotence, a radicalism whose intensity is inversely proportionate to its practical possibilities.

Chinese Communist history then went on to produce several more waves of this sort. One was the Great Leap Forward of 1958, which also combined a sense of desperate urgency with the pursuit of optimistic goals, such as matching British industrial production within fifteen years, "going all out, aiming high and achieving greater, faster, better, and more economical results in building socialism," and indeed reaching communism before the Soviet Union.[12] Like earlier failures in twentieth-century China, the collapse of the Great Leap Forward followed by the "three bad years" persuaded some to shorten their sights. But these same failures have only convinced others that still more drastic steps are needed and still greater things are possible, that armed with Mao's thought, it is possible to work miracles.

Thus each spurt toward modernization has had the way paved for it by a preceding one whose accomplishments were not insignificant but still were insufficient to meet rising expectations and frustrations. Much as the Manchus' reforms paved the way for the republican revolutionaries, the T'ung-meng-hui prepared the ground for the New Culture Movement, which in turn did the same for the Communist revolution. The growing emphasis on leaps and short cuts shows "the peculiar blend of rationalism and passion" that revolutionaries were long ago seen to possess,[13] but it shows also how the blend becomes heated with a larger proportion of passion. As one student said, years later,

> While we got our mental food from Liang Ch'i-ch'ao, we drew our emotional nourishment from Dr. Sun Yat-sen and his sympa-

[12] See Franz Schurmann, *Ideology and Organization in Communist China*, pp. 71, 296, 387, 397, 480, 490.

[13] See Sheldon S. Wolin's "Foreword" to Chalmers Johnson, *Revolutionary Change*, p. viii.

thizers. Generally speaking, it is emotion that leads to action when a decisive hour comes; when that hour came in China Dr. Sun, both dreamer and man of action, won a decisive victory over the new literati who stood for constitutionalism.[14]

This suggests why Liang is one of the most tragic figures in modern Chinese history, but it suggests something more. Liang has been almost universally acclaimed by modern Chinese intellectuals, usually as being the one who "opened my eyes" or who "first introduced the new thought to me." Nearly all of them read him in their teens but forgot him in their twenties. He was admired by all but followed by only a few. One reason is surely that Liang's ideas shifted too frequently for others to follow, but perhaps a more fundamental reason is that he was radical enough to capture the imaginations of young Chinese intellectuals but not radical enough to hold them. No moderate solutions to China's problems, not even moderately radical ones, received much of a hearing in the twentieth century. There was too much to do, too little time to do it, and it appeared more and more possible (as Japan seemed to prove) to do almost anything. It is ironic that as intellectuals became increasingly prominent in the Chinese revolutionary movement, the movement became increasingly dominated by emotions more than intellect, by passions more than rational thought.

China's new intelligentsia sought a grander vision than Liang painted for them in 1905–8, and they wanted it realized sooner than he would promise. They wanted something so different from the oddly traditional Chang Ping-lin's vision that they could not take him very seriously, except as an antidote to the even more oddly traditional K'ang Yu-wei and as a spokesman for their anti-Manchuism in terms they would not or could not use. They wanted something closer to the rapid progress Sun and perhaps even the anarchists promised, combined with the sense of nationhood, political fulfillment, and social justice that Wang Ching-wei, Hu Han-min, and the other *Min-pao* writers promised would be achieved once the Manchus were overthrown and a republic established.

From this point of view the debate between reformers and revolutionaries served China both well and ill. It helped to spell out the

14 Chiang Monlin, *Tides from the West*, p. 53.

revolutionaries' ideas about their nation and their future government and society. It also distracted intellectuals' attention from problems that were deeper than the nature of the Manchus and the relative merits of constitutional monarchy and republican *forms* of government. The latter were discussed in an abstract fashion that had little if any relevance to China's political problems, and anti-Manchuism so inflamed the atmosphere that little could be discussed apart from questions of race. At the same time the revolutionaries propagated the idea that the abolition of Manchu rule and the establishment of a republic would go very far toward solving China's problems; indeed, a reader of *Min-pao* could easily have concluded that those two steps alone would bring China close to perfection. Expectations of this sort led inevitably to rising frustrations and even greater desperation. After 1911, ideas such as anarchism that had been on the fringes of the movement until it failed then moved to the center of the next revolutionary wave. Much of the anarchists' spirit and thinking was at the core of the New Culture Movement.

The history of the process by which radical ideas so swiftly gained ascendancy in twentieth-century Chinese thought and politics raises questions about the relationships between revolution and democracy and between revolution and modernization. One begins to wonder whether the needs of revolution and the needs of democracy are so incongruent as to be incompatible, at least in societies whose leaders promote revolutions of vast proportions. When the changes sought are so great and the hatred generated so intense, and when violence is relied upon as the chief agent of political change by the very same leaders who preach democratic ideals, it proves impossible simultaneously to create a belief in orderly processes, the rule of law, a legal and loyal opposition, peaceful transference of power, and similar accoutrements of popular rule. Furthermore, violent revolutions attract men with very different motives and aspirations, not only men whose long-range goals preclude postrevolutionary cooperation but men who seek only personal aggrandizement and adventure. The Chinese revolution attracted many who subverted its principles, and even among its most prominent leaders the disagreements were substantial enough to interfere with the revolution itself, to say nothing of the republic. But perhaps the fatal weakness was to allow differences like those between the reformers and the T'ung-meng-hui to overshadow the common purposes. The enduring puzzle is why Liang Ch'i-ch'ao chose to cooperate with the Manchus (while prodding them to quicken their reforms) rather than cooperate with (and perhaps slow down) the revolutionaries, while Sun Yat-sen and Wang Ching-wei could more easily cooperate with Chang Ping-lin than with Liang. When men who shared a similar vision of an independent, strong, democratic, and prosperous China allowed those common purposes to be overshadowed by their differences about the Manchus' incorrigibility, the speed of social and political change, and the *form* of Chinese democracy, it is clear that there were passions at work which made democratic revolution highly unlikely. The very effort the Chinese made confirms this, for it would be unreasonable to expect during the course of a violent revolution a more noble or more determined and conscious effort than they made to understand the principles of democracy and plan a transition to a democratic form of government.

Successful modernization by means of revolution may be unlikely for similar reasons. This proposition seems even more speculative, but one crucial point is that to the Chinese modernization included democracy. The two do not necessarily go together, but the Chinese revolutionaries believed that they did. Not all modern societies are democratic, of course, but the Chinese intelligentsia of 1903–11 would not have considered an undemocratic China a truly modern China. Second, although modernization is inevitably a disruptive process because changes in different sectors of society proceed at uneven speeds, it is likely to be more successful if disruption is minimized enough to permit institutionalization of whatever is newly introduced.[15] Two points are particularly important here. One is that the more new ideas outrace society's capacity to absorb new institutions, the greater the gap will be between the desirable and the possible, and the greater the resulting frustration. The other is that a society such as China's finds it more difficult to modernize because of the strength of its tradition and finds it a unique problem because of the uniqueness of its tradition. The very strength of Chinese tradition dictates that modernizers compromise with it. China is probably

[15] This idea is developed in Samuel P. Huntington, "Political Development and Political Decay," *World Politics*, XVII, 386–93.

destined to profit from foreign models less than countries with less deeply rooted traditions. Even more than most other societies, China will have to find her own way to modernization.

The remarks above might seem to imply that men ought not to dream or otherwise indulge in extravagant visions. No advice would be more foolish or more useless. Men will dream, and their dreams will release imaginative energies and perhaps help men to realize their highest aspirations.[16] But the art of being a successful revolutionary leader is to paint a future that will be close enough to men's own desires to catch their eye, exciting enough to quicken their pulses and goad them to action, far enough beyond them to raise their sights and hopes and stretch their abilities, but not so far beyond their reach that falling short brings them to frustration and despair.

The Chinese revolutionary movement between 1903 and 1908 saw the beginnings of modern Chinese nationalism, democracy, and socialism. But although these doctrines provided the revolutionaries with a substantial body of common beliefs, those beliefs were far from being unanimously held. What united all the new intellectuals, what encompassed nationalism, democracy, and socialism, what linked the T'ung-meng-hui revolutionaries with some nonrevolutionary intellectuals in their own time and with revolutionaries of later times was radicalism. This radicalism did not consist merely of certain ideas that grew out of the revolution of 1911; it was a mood, an attitude, a way of approaching social and political problems.

The specific doctrines changed a great deal, but they too paved the way for those that followed. For example, socialism in China after 1917, and especially after the establishment of the Chinese Communist Party in 1921, was very different from what it had been in the T'ung-meng-hui period. The precise relationship between T'ung-meng-hui socialism and post-1917 Chinese socialism cannot be examined here. But socialism was widely acclaimed by T'ung-meng-hui writers, and they regarded it as a doctrine whose central feature was its emphasis upon social and economic equality and justice; these facts have important implications for socialism's subsequent popularity in China and for its relationship to the later nationalist move-

[16] Frank E. Manuel, "Toward a Psychological History of Utopias," in Manuel (ed.), *Utopias and Utopian Thought*, p. 95.

ment. Chinese intellectuals who heard the news of the Russian Revolution were already attuned to the ideals the Bolsheviks professed and were waiting to hear how these ideals could be wedded to national power and sovereignty.[17]

The development of Marxism in China, its connections with the May Fourth Movement, and related questions such as the Kuomintang-Communist alliance are of course too complex for simple explanations in a discussion as brief as this. But the course of China's intellectual revolution, allied from the first with revolutionary nationalism and socialism, created an outlook that was peculiarly receptive to the message from Russia. The growth of Marxism-Leninism in China, and indeed all Chinese intellectual and political history in the twentieth century, have been affected by the fact that the new intelligentsia was radical from its very beginning: willing to use force, amenable to departing from tradition, dedicated to building a strong China, receptive to new ideas, confident in its ability to lead and indeed determined to exert leadership, and above all convinced that a vastly better world was almost within its grasp. These characteristics did not determine that modern Chinese intellectuals would be Marxist, but they did mean that a revolutionary socialism which allied itself with nationalism would compete powerfully for their allegiance. In twentieth-century China "radicalism was trumps."[18]

China's new intelligentsia posed for itself nothing less than the task of defining China's role in the modern world and remodeling her whole intellectual, political, social, and economic fabric to fit that role. The intellectuals also posed narrower questions concerning the character of the Chinese nation and the virtues of various new political ideas that came under the heading of republicanism; they raised questions about the efficacy of representative government and the institutional patterns through which equality and justice might be realized. Some even debated whether and how the principles of science could be applied to social problems. These issues and others were posed, and answers began to be formulated. But before solutions could be devised, and indeed before many issues could even be

---

[17] I am presently engaged in a study of Chinese reactions to the Russian Revolution, and I hope to develop these points in more detail in a later publication.

[18] This term was first applied to post-World War One Germany. See R. G. L. Waite, *Vanguard of Nazism*, p. 42.

raised, the revolution came and went, leaving behind it shattered visions of the long-awaited republic. As China yielded to warlord-ism, even the visions became blurred. When China's intelligentsia next came to the fore, it was once again to release forces far stronger than itself; this time the visions were even more grandiose — science, democracy, a new culture — and their shattering even more complete, with a significance for China and the world the dimensions of which we are still only beginning to realize.

# Glossary

| | |
|---|---|
| Ai-kuo hsüeh-she | 愛國學社 |
| Ai-kuo-hui | 愛國會 |
| Aisin Gioro | 愛新覺羅 |
| an-sha t'uan | 暗殺團 |
| Chan-kuo | 戰國 |
| Ch'an | 禪 |
| Chang Chi | 張繼 |
| Chang Chih-tung | 張之洞 |
| Chang Ching-chiang | 張靜江 |
| Chang Jen-chieh | 張人傑 |
| Chang Ping-lin | 章炳麟 |
| Chekiang-ch'ao | 浙江潮 |
| chen-ch'a wu-hsing | 診察物形 |
| chen-li chin-hua p'ai | 真理進化派 |
| Ch'en T'ien-hua | 陳天華 |
| Ch'en Tu-hsiu | 陳獨秀 |
| Cheng Ch'eng-kung | 鄭成功 |
| Cheng-ch'i-hui | 正氣會 |
| cheng-chih ke-ming | 政治革命 |
| cheng-ch'üan | 政權 |
| Cheng Kuan-ying | 鄭觀應 |
| Ch'eng-Chu | 程朱 |
| Chi | 姬 |
| chi-chin chu-i | 急進主義 |
| ch'i-wu | 齊物 |
| Ch'i-wu lun | 齊物論 |

| | |
|---|---|
| Chia-ch'ing | 嘉慶 |
| Chiang | 姜 |
| ch'iang-ch'üan | 強權 |
| Ch'iang-hsüeh-hui | 強學會 |
| chieh-chi | 階級 |
| chieh-lü | 戒律 |
| chien-chin chu-i | 漸進主義 |
| Chin | 晉 |
| chin-ch'en | 近臣 |
| chin-t'ieh chu-i shuo | 金鐵主義説 |
| Ching-chung jih-pao | 警鐘日報 |
| ching-t'ien | 井田 |
| ch'ing-i | 清議 |
| Ch'ing-nien-hui | 青年會 |
| Ch'ing-tai hsüeh-shu kai-lun | 清代學術概論 |
| Chiu-kuo shih-pa-yu | 救國十八友 |
| Chu Chih-hsin | 朱執信 |
| Chu Ho-chung | 朱和中 |
| Chu I-hsin | 朱一新 |
| Chu-shih | 主事 |
| chu-t'i | 主體 |
| Chu Yüan-chang | 朱元章 |
| Ch'u Min-i | 褚民誼 |
| chuan-ch'üan | 專權 |
| Chuang-tzu | 莊子 |
| Ch'un-ch'iu | 春秋 |
| Chung-ho-t'ang | 中和堂 |
| Chung-Hsi t'i-yung p'ai | 中西體用派 |
| Chung-hsing jih-pao | 中興日報 |
| Chung-kuo chiao-yü hui | 中國教育會 |
| Chung-kuo hua-le | 中國化了 |
| Chung-kuo jih-pao | 中國日報 |
| Chung-kuo ku-tai hsien-i chün-ch'üan chih fa | 中國古代限抑君權之法 |
| chung-tsu | 種族 |
| chü-jen | 舉人 |
| Chü O I-yung-tui | 拒俄義勇隊 |
| Ch'üan Tsu-wang | 全祖望 |
| Chün-kuo-min chiao-yü hui | 軍國民教育會 |
| chün-t'ien | 均田 |
| Erh-shih shih-chi chih Chih-na | 二十世紀之支那 |
| fa | 法 |
| Fa-hsiang | 法相 |

| | |
|---|---|
| fang-jen | 放任 |
| fei kuo-chia chu-i | 非國家主義 |
| Feng Kuei-fen | 馮桂芬 |
| Feng Tzu-yu | 馮自由 |
| Fu-pao | 復報 |
| Han-chih | 漢幟 |
| Han Shan-t'ung | 韓山童 |
| Han-sheng | 漢聲 |
| Ho Chen | 何震 |
| ho-ch'eng i-li | 合成意力 |
| ho-ch'eng jen-ke | 合成人格 |
| Ho Ch'i (Kai) | 何啟 |
| Ho Chih-ts'ai | 賀之才 |
| ho yü k'e-hsüeh | 合於科學 |
| Hozumi Yatsuka | 穗積八束 |
| Hsia Tseng-yu | 夏曾佑 |
| hsiao-ch'ou | 小醜 |
| Hsiao Kung-ch'üan | 蕭公權 |
| Hsiao Wen Ti | 孝文帝 |
| hsien | 縣 |
| Hsin ch'ing-nien | 新青年 |
| hsin-hsin | 信心 |
| Hsin-hunan | 新湖南 |
| Hsin-min shu | 新民説 |
| Hsin shih-chi | 新世紀 |
| Hsin shih-chi ts'ung-shu | 新世紀叢書 |
| Hsing-Chung-hui | 興中會 |
| hsiu-ts'ai | 秀才 |
| Hsü Hsing | 許行 |
| Hsü Shou-shang | 許壽裳 |
| hsü-wei | 虛偽 |
| Hsüeh Fu-ch'eng | 薛福成 |
| Hsün-tzu | 荀子 |
| Hu Han-min | 胡漢民 |
| Hu Li-yüan | 胡禮垣 |
| Hu Lin-i | 胡林翼 |
| Hua-hsing-hui | 華興會 |
| Huang-ch'ao t'ung-tien | 皇朝通典 |
| Huang Hsing | 黃興 |
| Huang K'an | 黃侃 |
| Huang Ti | 黃帝 |
| Hung-lu-ssu | 鴻臚寺 |

| | |
|---|---|
| Hupei hsüeh-sheng chieh | 湖北學生界 |
| i-tsu | 異族 |
| i-tzu pu i-t'a | 依自不依他 |
| jen | 仁 |
| jen-tao | 人道 |
| jen-ts'ai | 人才 |
| Juan Yüan | 阮元 |
| Jung | 戎 |
| Jung Hung (Yung Wing) | 容閎 |
| kai-liang | 改良 |
| k'ai-kuo chih jih | 開國之日 |
| kan-ch'ing | 感情 |
| kan-she | 干涉 |
| K'ang-hsi | 康熙 |
| K'ang Yu-wei | 康有為 |
| Kayano Nagatomo (Chōchi) | 萱野長知 |
| ke-hsin | 革新 |
| ke-jen chu-i | 個人主義 |
| ke-ming | 革命 |
| ke-ming chün | 革命軍 |
| k'e-t'i | 客體 |
| ken-pen | 根本 |
| Keng Ching-chung | 耿精忠 |
| Ko-lao-hui | 哥老會 |
| Ku-ching ching-she | 詁經精舍 |
| Ku-tai chih i-hui kuan-nien | 古代之議會觀念 |
| Ku Yen-wu | 顧炎武 |
| Kuang-fu | 光復 |
| Kuang-fu-hui | 光復會 |
| Kuang-hsü | 光緒 |
| Kuang-lu-ssu | 光禄寺 |
| kuei-tsu cheng-chih | 貴族政治 |
| kung-ch'an | 共産 |
| kung-ch'an chu-i | 共産主義 |
| kung-ch'üan | 公權 |
| kung-ho | 公和 |
| kung-ho li-hsien | 共和立憲 |
| kung-li | 公理 |
| Kung-yang | 公羊 |
| kuo-chia | 國家 |
| kuo-chia chu-i | 國家主義 |
| kuo-ch'üan | 國權 |

| | |
|---|---|
| kuo-min | 國民 |
| kuo-min cheng-fu | 國民政府 |
| kuo-min chu-i | 國民主義 |
| kuo-min ke-ming | 國民革命 |
| kuo-min shih-shih-shang chih ch'üan-li | 國民事實上之權力 |
| kuo-t'i | 國體 |
| kuo-ts'ui | 國粹 |
| Kuo-ts'ui hsüeh-pao | 國粹學報 |
| Kuo-tzu chien | 國子監 |
| Lao-tzu | 老子 |
| Lei Chao-hsing | 雷照性 |
| li (p. 211, n. 74) | 禮 |
| li (p. 180) | 里 |
| li (p. 211) | 理 |
| Li-chih-hui | 勵志會 |
| Li-fan yüan | 理蕃院 |
| Li Hung-chang | 李鴻章 |
| Li Hung-tsao | 李鴻藻 |
| Li Shih-tseng | 李石曾 |
| Li Tzu-ch'eng | 李自成 |
| Liang Ch'i-ch'ao | 梁啟超 |
| liang-chih | 良知 |
| Liao Chung-k'ai | 廖仲愷 |
| likin | 釐金 |
| Lin Tse-hsü | 林則徐 |
| Liu Ch'eng-yü | 劉成禹 |
| Liu Feng-lu | 劉逢祿 |
| Liu K'uei-i | 劉揆一 |
| Liu Shih-p'ei | 劉師培 |
| Liu Yü | 劉裕 |
| Lu Hao-tung | 陸皓東 |
| Lu-Wang | 陸王 |
| Lung-chi pao | 隆記報 |
| Lü Liu-liang | 呂留良 |
| lü-ying | 綠營 |
| Ma Chün-wu | 馬君武 |
| Man-hua [T'ang Tseng-pi] | 曼華 |
| mei-ch'eng | 美稱 |
| mei-ming | 美名 |
| min-chu | 民主 |
| min-chu li-hsien cheng-t'i | 民主立憲政體 |
| min-ch'üan | 民權 |

| | |
|---|---|
| min-ch'üan li-hsien | 民權立憲 |
| min-kuo | 民國 |
| Min-pao | 民報 |
| min-sheng | 民生 |
| min-tsu | 民族 |
| min-tsu chu-i | 民族主義 |
| min-tsu chu-i ta wei-jen | 民族主義大偉人 |
| min-tsu ke-ming | 民族革命 |
| min-tsu ti-kuo chu-i | 民族帝國主義 |
| Mo Ti | 墨翟 |
| Nü-tzu fu-ch'üan hui | 女子復權會 |
| O-shih ching-wen | 俄事警聞 |
| Ou-Mei | 歐美 |
| Ou-Mei cheng-chih yao-i | 歐美政治要義 |
| Pai Yü-huan | 白逾桓 |
| p'ai-Han | 排漢 |
| p'ai-Han cheng-ts'e | 排漢政策 |
| p'ai-Man chu-i | 排滿主義 |
| Pao-huang-hui | 保皇會 |
| Pao-kuo-hui | 保國會 |
| Pi Yung-nien | 畢永年 |
| p'ing-chün ti-ch'üan | 平均地權 |
| p'ing-min ke-ming | 平民革命 |
| p'ing-teng tzu-yu p'ai | 平等自由派 |
| po-ai | 博愛 |
| po-hsüeh hung-ju | 博學宏儒 |
| p'o-huai chu-i | 破壞主義 |
| pu | 部 |
| pu-lo chu-i | 部落主義 |
| San-fan (Rebellion) | 三藩 |
| san-kang wu-ch'ang p'ai | 三綱五常派 |
| Shang Chih-hsin | 尚之信 |
| she-chiao chih hsüeh | 社交之學 |
| Shen Nung | 神農 |
| Shen Yen-kuo | 沈延國 |
| sheng-wu chi | 聖武記 |
| Shih-chieh ch'i-ko wu-cheng-fu chu-i chia | 世界七個無政府主義家 |
| Shih-chieh-she | 世界社 |
| Shih Chien-ju | 史堅如 |
| shih-fei yu-wu | 是非有無 |
| Shih-wu pao | 時務報 |
| Shun | 舜 |

| | |
|---|---|
| ssu-ch'üan | 私權 |
| ssu fan-nao | 四煩惱 |
| Su-pao | 蘇報 |
| Su-pao an chi-shih | 蘇報案紀事 |
| Sui | 隋 |
| Sun Yat-sen | 孫逸仙 |
| Sung Chiao-jen | 宗教仁 |
| Ta Ch'ing hui-tien | 大清會典 |
| Ta-hsueh | 大學 |
| Ta hsüeh-shih | 大學士 |
| Ta-li ssu | 大理寺 |
| ta-t'ung | 大同 |
| Ta-t'ung jih-pao | 大同日報 |
| ta t'ung-ling | 大統領 |
| Ta t'ung-shu | 大同書 |
| Tai Chen | 戴震 |
| Tai Hung-tz'u | 戴鴻慈 |
| T'ai-ch'ang-ssu | 太常寺 |
| t'ai-hsü | 太虛 |
| T'ai-p'u-ssu | 太僕寺 |
| T'an Jen-feng | 譚人鳳 |
| T'an Ssu-t'ung | 譚嗣同 |
| T'ang Chen | 湯震 |
| T'ang Ts'ai-ch'ang | 唐才常 |
| T'ang Tseng-pi | 湯增璧 |
| T'ao Ch'eng-chang | 陶成章 |
| Teih (Ti) | 狄 |
| t'i | 體 |
| t'i-yung | 體用 |
| t'ien-fu chih jen-ch'üan | 天賦之人權 |
| t'ien-hsing | 天性 |
| T'ien-i pao | 天義報 |
| t'ien-jan chih p'ing-teng | 天然之平等 |
| t'ien-li | 天理 |
| Tsai-feng | 載灃 |
| Ts'ai Yüan-p'ei | 蔡元培 |
| ts'e-yin chih hsin | 惻隱之心 |
| Tseng Ching | 曾静 |
| Tseng Kuo-fan | 曾國藩 |
| Tso-chuan | 左傳 |
| Tsou Jung | 鄒容 |
| tsu-lei | 族類 |

| | |
|---|---|
| tsui-kao chi-kuan | 最高機關 |
| Tsung-hui pao | 總匯報 |
| tsung-i | 總意 |
| tsung-lang chi-kuan | 總攬機關 |
| Tsung-li | 總理 |
| Tsungli Yamen | 總理衙門 |
| Tu-ch'a-yüan | 都察院 |
| t'u-ti kuo-yu | 土地國有 |
| t'u-ti wei kuo-min so kung-yu | 土地為國民所公有 |
| Tuan-fang | 端方 |
| t'uan-t'i chu-i | 團體主義 |
| T'ung-cheng-ssu | 通政司 |
| t'ung-lei | 同類 |
| t'ung-ling | 統領 |
| t'ung-meng | 同盟 |
| T'ung-meng-hui | 同盟會 |
| tzu-chüeh | 自覺 |
| tzu-hsing | 自性 |
| Tzu-li-hui | 自立會 |
| Wang An-shih | 王安石 |
| Wang Ching-wei | 汪精衛 |
| Wang Fu-chih | 王夫之 |
| Wang Hsien-ch'ien | 王先謙 |
| Wang Kung-ch'üan | 汪公權 |
| Wang Mang | 王莽 |
| Wang Tung | 汪東 |
| Wang Yang-ming (Shou-jen) | 王陽明（守仁） |
| Wei Ch'en-tsu | 魏宸組 |
| wei-jen | 委任 |
| wei-so | 衛所 |
| wei tao-te | 偽道德 |
| wei wen-ming | 偽文明 |
| Wei Yüan | 魏源 |
| wen-hua hsiang-t'ung | 文化相同 |
| Wen T'ing-shih | 文廷式 |
| Wen Wang | 文王 |
| wo-chien | 我見 |
| wo Chung-kuo k'ai-kuo | 我中國開國 |
| Wo-jen | 倭仁 |
| wo-so | 我所 |
| wu-cheng-fu | 無政府 |
| wu-chi | 無記 |

| | |
|---|---|
| Wu Chih-hui | 吳稚暉 |
| wu-chü-lo | 無聚落 |
| wu-chung-sheng | 無衆生 |
| Wu-neng-tzu | 无能子 |
| Wu San-kuei | 吳三桂 |
| wu-sheng | 無生 |
| wu-shih-chieh | 無世界 |
| wu-tuan | 武斷 |
| wu-wo | 無我 |
| Yang Ch'ü-yün | 楊衢雲 |
| Yang Tu | 楊度 |
| Yao | 堯 |
| Yen Fu | 嚴復 |
| ying-hsiung ke-ming | 英雄革命 |
| Yu-hsüeh i-pien | 游學譯編 |
| Yü Yüeh | 俞樾 |
| Yüan | 元 |
| Yüeh Fei | 岳飛 |
| yung | 用 |
| Yung-cheng | 雍正 |

# ABBREVIATIONS

| | |
|---|---|
| *50th Anniversary Documents* | *Chung-hua min-kuo k'ai-kuo wu-shih-nien wen-hsien*, Section (*Pien*) One, *Ke-ming yüan-liu yü ke-ming yün-tung* |
| *HHKM* | *Hsin-hai ke-ming* |
| *HSC* | *Hsin shih-chi* |
| *HSCTS* | *Hsin shih-chi ts'ung-shu* |

# Selected Bibliography

The Chinese characters for entries marked with an asterisk (*) may be found in the Glossary.

Abosch, David. "Katō Hiroyuki and the Introduction of German Political Thought in Modern Japan: 1868–1883." Unpublished Ph.D. dissertation, University of California, Berkeley, 1964.

"L'Anarchisme," trans. Li Shih-tseng* ("Shih-chieh ch'i-ko wu-cheng-fu chu-i chia"*), *HSCTS*, pp. 33–50.

Arendt, Hannah. *On Revolution*. New York: Viking Press, Compass Books ed., 1965.

Avineri, Shlomo. "Marx and the Intellectuals," *Journal of the History of Ideas*, XXVIII, 269–78.

Baldwin, Roger N. (ed.). *Kropotkin's Revolutionary Pamphlets*. With Introduction, Biographical Sketch, and Notes. New York: Vanguard Press, 1927.

Banno, Masataka. *China and the West, 1858–1861*. Cambridge, Mass.: Harvard University Press, 1964.

Bernal, Martin. "The Triumph of Anarchism over Marxism, 1906–1907," *China in Revolution: The First Phase, 1900–1913*, edited with an introduction by Mary C. Wright (New Haven: Yale University Press, 1968), pp. 97–142.

Biggerstaff, Knight. *The Earliest Modern Government Schools in China*. Ithaca, N.Y.: Cornell University Press, 1961.

Black, C. E. *The Dynamics of Modernization: A Study in Comparative History*. New York: Harper & Row, 1966.

Bodde, Derk. *China's Cultural Tradition*. New York: Rinehart, 1957.

Boorman, Howard L. "Wang Ching-wei: China's Romantic Radical," *Political Science Quarterly*, LXXIX (1964), 504–25.

—— (ed.). *Men and Politics in Modern China, Preliminary Fifty Biographies*, Part I. New York: Columbia University, 1960.

——, and Richard C. Howard (eds.). *Biographical Dictionary of Republican China*, Vol. I. New York: Columbia University Press, 1967.

Borton, Hugh. *Japan's Modern Century*. New York: Ronald Press, 1955.

Brinton, Crane. *The Anatomy of Revolution*. Rev. ed. New York: Vintage Books, 1957.

Britton, Roswell S. *The Chinese Periodical Press, 1800–1912*. Shanghai: Kelly and Walsh, 1933.

Cameron, Meribeth E. *The Reform Movement in China, 1898–1912*. Stanford: Stanford University Press, 1931.

Chang Chi.* *Chang P'u-ch'üan hsien-sheng ch'üan-chi* 張溥全先生全集 (Complete Works of Mr. Chang P'u-ch'üan [Chang Chi]). Compiled and edited by the Kuomintang Historical Commission. Taipei:Chung-yang wen-wu kung-ying she 中央文物供應社, 1951.

Chang Chiang-ts'ai 張江裁. *Wang Ching-wei hsien-sheng hsing-shih hsü-lu* 汪精衛先生行實續録 (A Record of the Activities of Mr. Wang Ching-wei), Peking, 1943.

Chang, Chung-li. *The Chinese Gentry*. Seattle: University of Washington Press, 1955.

Chang Hsing-yen 章行嚴 (Chang Shih-chao 章士釗). "Su Pao an shih-mo chi" 蘇報案始末記 (A Complete Record of the Su-pao Case), *HHKM*, I, 387–90.

Chang Huang-chi 張篁溪. "Chang T'ai-yen hsien-sheng tsai yü i-wen lu" 章太炎先生在獄佚聞録 (A Casually Heard Account of Mr. Chang T'ai-yen's Stay in Jail), *HHKM*, I, 394–97.

——. "Kuang-fu-hui ling-hsiu T'ao Ch'eng-chang ke-ming shih" 光復會領袖陶成章革命史 (The Career of Restoration Society Leader T'ao Ch'eng-chang in the Revolution), *HHKM*, I, 521–29.

——. "Su-pao-an shih-lu" 蘇報案實録 (A True Account of the Su-pao Case), *HHKM*, I, 367–86.

Chang Nan 張枬 and Wang Jen-chih 王忍之 (eds.). *Hsin-hai ke-ming ch'ien shih-nien-chien shih-lun hsüan-chi* 辛亥革命前十年間時論選集 (Selected Essays from the Decade Preceding the 1911 Revolution). 2 vols., each in 2 parts. Peking: San-lien Shu-tien, 1960 and 1963.

Chang P'eng-yüan 張朋園. *Liang Ch'i-ch'ao yü Ch'ing-chi ke-ming* 梁啓超與清季革命 (Liang Ch'i-ch'ao and the Revolution in the Late Ch'ing Period). Taipei: Academia Sinica, Institute of Modern History, 1964.

Chang Ping-lin.* "Chang hsü" 章序 (Preface), to Lien Heng 連橫, *T'ai-wan t'ung-shih* 臺灣通史 (A General History of Taiwan). Taipei, 1955. I, 1.

——. *Chang-shih ts'ung-shu* 章氏叢書 (Complete Works of Mr. Chang [Ping-lin]). 24 *ts'e*, 4 *han*. Chengtu, 1943.

——. "Cheng-wen she-yüan ta-hui p'o-huai chuang" 政聞社員大會破壞狀 (How We Broke up the Cheng-wen-she Meeting), *Min-pao*, No. 17 (Oct. 25, 1907), pp. 109–15. The pages of this article are numbered 1–7, and the one that follows begins on a page incorrectly numbered 109. This article, however, begins on the page following p. 108.

——. "Chi Yin-tu Hsi-p'o-ch'i Wang chi-nien-hui shih" 記印度西婆耆王紀念會事 (Report of a Meeting Held in Commemoration of King Sivaji of India), *Min-pao*, No. 13 (May 5, 1907), pp. 93–97.

——. "Chien-li tsung-chiao lun" 建立宗教論 (On the Establishment of Religion), *Min-pao*, No. 9 (Nov. 15, 1906), pp. 1–26.

——. *Ch'iu-shu* 訄書 (Book of Raillery). Shanghai: Ku-t'ien wen-hsüeh Publishing Co., 1958.

——. "Chung-hua min-kuo chieh" 中華民國解 (An Explanation of the [Term] Republic of China), *Min-pao*, No. 15 (July 5, 1907), pp. 1–17.

——. "Fa-k'an hsü 發刊序 (Preface to Inaugurate the Journal), *Han Chih* 漢幟 (The Chinese Banner), Jan. 19, 1907, p. 1.

——. "Ke-ming chih tao-te" 革命之道德 (The Morality of Revolution), *Min-pao*, No. 8 (Oct. 25, 1906), pp. 13–31.

——. "Kuan-chih so-yin" 官制索隱 (A Guide to Bureaucracy), *Min-pao*, No. 14 (June 8, 1907), pp. 1–21.

——. "Kuei Hsin shih-chi" 規新世紀 (Setting *Hsin shih-chi* Straight), *Min-pao*, No. 24 (Oct. 10, 1908), pp. 41–65.

——. "Kuo-chia lun" 國家論 (On the State), *Min-pao*, No. 17 (Oct. 25, 1907), pp. 1–14.

——. "Man-chou tsung-tu ch'in-t'un chen-k'uan chuang" 滿洲總督侵吞賑欵狀 (The Embezzlement of Relief Funds by Manchu Governors-general), *Min-pao*, No. 22 (July 10, 1908), pp. 35–39.

——. "P'ai-Man p'ing-i" 排滿平議 (A Balanced Discussion about Expelling the Manchus), *Min-pao*, No. 21 (June 10, 1908), pp. 1–12.

——. "Po Chung-kuo yung wan-kuo hsin-yü shuo" 駁中國用萬國新語説 (Refuting the Idea of China Using the New International Language), *Min-pao*, No. 21 (June 10, 1908), pp. 49–72.

——. "Po K'ang Yu-wei lun ke-ming shu" 駁康有為論革命書 (In Refutation of K'ang Yu-wei's Essay on Revolution), *Chung-kuo chin-tai ssu-hsiang shih ts'an-k'ao tzu-liao chien-pien* 中國近代思想史參考資料簡編 (Source Materials on the History of Modern Chinese Thought) (Peking: San-lien Shu-tien 三聯書店, 1957), pp. 598–611.

——. "She-hui t'ung-ch'üan shang-tui" 社會通詮商兑 (A Discussion of *A History of Politics* [by Edward Jenks], *Min-pao*, No. 12 (Mar. 6, 1907), pp. 1–24.

——. "Ssu-huo lun" 四惑論 (The Four Delusions), *Min-pao*, No. 22 (July 10, 1908), pp. 1–22.

——. "Ta T'ieh Cheng" 答鐵錚 (In Reply to T'ieh Cheng), *Min-pao*, No. 14 (June 8, 1907), pp. 113–22.

——. "Tai-i jan-fou lun" 代議然否論 (On Whether or Not to Have Representative Parliamentary Government), *Min-pao*, No. 24 (Aug. 10, 1908), pp. 1–27.

——. *T'ai-yen hsien-sheng tzu-ting nien-p'u* 太炎先生自定年譜 (Mr. [Chang] T'ai-yen's Chronological Autobiography). Hong Kong: Lung Men Book Store, 1965.

——. "Wu-wu lun" 五無論 (Essay on the Five Negations), *Min-pao*, No. 16 (Sept. 25, 1907), pp. 1–22.

——. "Yen-shuo lu" 演説録 (Speech Transcript), *Min-pao*, No. 6 (July 25, 1906), pp. 1–15.

Ch'en, Jerome. *Mao and the Chinese Revolution*. London: Oxford University Press, 1965.

Ch'en Shao-pai 陳少白. *Hsing-Chung-hui ke-ming shih-yao* 興中會革命史要 (An Outline History of the Hsing-Chung-hui Revolution). Taipei, 1956.

Ch'en T'ien-hua.* "Lun Chung-kuo i kai-ch'uang min-chu cheng-t'i" 論中國宜改創民主政體 (China Ought to Change to a Democratic Form of Government), *Min-pao*, No. 1 (Nov. 26, 1905), pp. 41–50.

Cheng, Shelley Hsien. "The T'ung-meng-hui: Its Organization, Leadership and Finances, 1905–1912." Unpublished Ph.D. dissertation, University of Washington, 1962.

Ch'i Ping-feng 亓冰峯. *Ch'ing-mo ke-ming yü chün-hsien ti lun-cheng* 清末革命與君憲的論爭 (Controversies between the Revolutionists and Constitutional Monarchists in the Late Ch'ing Period). Taipei: Academia Sinica, Institute of Modern History, Monograph Series No. 19, 1966.

Chiang Fu-sen 姜馥森. "Chang T'ai-yen yü Liang Jen-kung" 章太炎與梁任公 (Chang Ping-lin and Liang Ch'i-ch'ao), *Ta-feng* 大風 ("The 'Typhoon' Magazine"), Vol. LXXIX (Nov. 20, 1940), pp. 2561–62.

Chiang, Monlin. *Tides from the West*. Taiwan: China Culture Publishing Foundation Reprint, 1957.

Chiang Wei-ch'iao 蔣維喬. "Chung-kuo chiao-yü hui chih hui-i" 中國教育會之回憶 (Reminiscences of the Chinese Education Society), *HHKM*, I, 485–96.

"Chih-ta" 志達 [Identity unknown]. "Pao-Man yü p'ai-Man" 保滿與排滿 (Protect the Manchus, Expel the Manchus), *T'ien-i pao*, No. 3 (July 10, 1907), Chang Nan and Wang Jen-chih, *Selected Essays*, II, 915–16.

*The Chinese Classics*. Translated by James Legge. 2nd ed. Hong Kong: Hong Kong University Press, 1960. 5 vols.

*Ching-chung jih-pao* 警鐘日報 (The Warning Bell Daily). Shanghai, Feb. 27, 1904–Jan. 30, 1905.

Chow, Tse-tsung. *The May Fourth Movement*. Cambridge, Mass.: Harvard University Press, 1960.

Chu Chih-hsin.* "Hsin-li ti kuo-chia chu-i" 心理的國家主義 (Psychological Nationalism), *Min-pao*, No. 21 (June 10, 1908), pp. 13–35.

——. "Lun Man-chou sui yü li-hsien erh pu-neng" 論滿洲雖欲立憲而不能 (On the Manchus' Inability to Establish a Constitution Even If They Wish To), *Min-pao*, No. 1 (Nov. 26, 1905), pp. 31–41.

——. "Lun she-hui ke-ming tang yü cheng-chih ke-ming ping-hsing" 論社會革命當與政治革命並行 (The Social Revolution Should Proceed Simultaneously with the Political Revolution), *Min-pao*, No. 5 (June 26, 1906), pp. 43–66.

Chu Ho-chung.* "Ou-chou T'ung-meng-hui chi-shih" 歐洲同盟會紀實 (An Account of the T'ung-meng-hui in Europe), *Ke-ming wen-hsien*, II, 251–70.

Chu, Samuel C. *Reformer in Modern China: Chang Chien, 1853-1926*. New York and London: Columbia University Press, 1965.

Ch'u Min-i.* "Hao ku" 好古 (Loving Antiquity), *HSC*, No. 24 (Nov. 30, 1907), p. 2.

——. "Hsü wu-cheng-fu shuo" 續無政府說 (Anarchism, continued), *HSC*, No. 60 (Aug. 15, 1908), pp. 5–9.

Ch'ü, T'ung-tsu. *Local Government in China under the Ch'ing*. Cambridge, Mass.: Harvard University Press, 1962.

"Ch'üan, ch'üan, ch'üan" 勸勸勸 (Take Heed, Hear Me, Take Heed), *HSC*, No. 115 (Nov. 13, 1909), pp. 4–11, and No. 116 (Dec. 18, 1909), pp. 9–13.

Chung-hua min-kuo k'ai-kuo wu-shih-nien wen-hsien pien-tsuan wei-yüan-hui 中華民國開國五十年文獻編纂委員會 (Committee to Edit Documentary Collections for the 50th Anniversary of the Founding of the Chinese Republic), *Chung-hua min-kuo k'ai-kuo wu-shih-nien wen-hsien* 中華民國開國五十年文獻 (Documents on the 50th Anniversary of the Founding of the Chinese Republic). Two Sections *(Pien)*, Section One (16 vols.), *Ke-ming yüan-liu yü ke-ming yün-tung* 革命源流與革命運動 (Origins of the Revolution and the Revolutionary Movement). Taipei: Cheng-chung Book Co., 1963–64. Volumes *(ts'e)* X–XVI, "Ke-ming chih ch'ang-tao yü fa-chan" 革命之倡導與發展 (Promotion and Development of the Revolution).

*Chung-kuo ta-t'ung ssu-hsiang tzu-liao* 中國大同思想資料 (Materials on Chinese Utopian Thought). Edited by Department of the History of Philosophy, Research Institute of Philosophy, Chinese Academy of Sciences. Peking: Chung-hua Book Co., 1959.

Coker, Francis W. *Recent Political Thought.* New York: Appleton-Century, 1934.

Cole, G. D. H. *A History of Socialist Thought.* 4 vols. London: Macmillan, 1956.

deBary, William Theodore, Wing-tsit Chan, and Burton Watson (eds). *Sources of Chinese Tradition.* New York: Columbia University Press, 1960.

deBary, William Theodore, Stephen Hay, Royal Weiler, and Andrew Yarrow (eds.). *Sources of Indian Tradition.* New York: Columbia University Press, 1958.

Eastman, Lloyd E. "Political Reformism in China before the Sino-Japanese War." Unpublished manuscript. The article has since been published in *The Journal of Asian Studies,* XXVII, 695–710.

Emerson, Rupert. *State and Sovereignty in Modern Germany.* New Haven: Yale University Press, 1928.

*Encyclopedia of the Social Sciences.* 15 vols. New York: Macmillan, 1930.

Engels, Friedrich. *The Condition of the Working Class in England.* Translated and edited by W. O. Henderson and W. H. Chaloner. New York, 1958.

*Erh-shih shih-chi chih Chih-na* 二十世紀之支那 (Twentieth-Century China), No. 1. Tokyo, June 24, 1905.

Fairbank, John K. *Trade and Diplomacy on the China Coast.* Cambridge, Mass.: Harvard University Press, 1953.

Fass, Josef. "A Few Notes on the Birth of Nationalism in China," *Archiv Orientalni,* XXXII (1964), 376–82.

——. "Revolutionary Activity in the Province Hu-pei and the Wu-ch'ang Uprising of 1911," *Archiv Orientalni,* XXVIII (1960), 127–49.

——. "The Role of the New Style Army in the 1911 Revolution in China," *Archiv Orientalni* (Prague), XXX (1962), 183–91.

Fellman, David. "Racism," *Twentieth Century Political Thought,* ed. Joseph S. Roucek (New York: Philosophical Library, 1946), pp. 105–31.

Feng Tzu-yu.* "Chi Chung-kuo T'ung-meng-hui" 記中國同盟會 (Remembering the China T'ung-meng-hui), *Ta-feng pan-yüeh k'an* 大風半月刊, Vols. LX and LXI (Jan. 20 and 25, 1940). Reprinted in *Chung-kuo chintai shih lun-ts'ung* 中國近代史論叢 (Essays on Modern Chinese History). Taipei: Cheng-chung shu-chü 正中書局, 1959. First Collection, Vol. VIII, "Chung-hua Min-kuo chih chien-li" 中華民國之建立 (The Establishment of the Republic of China), pp. 31–42.

——. *Chung-hua min-kuo k'ai-kuo ch'ien ke-ming shih* 中華民國開國前革命史 (A History of the Revolution before the Founding of the Republic

of China). 2 vols. Taipei: World Book Co. (Shih-chieh shu-chü 世界
書局), 1954.

——. *Chung-kuo ke-ming yün-tung erh-shih-liu nien tsu-chih shih* 中國革命
運動二十六年組織史 (A History of Organizations in the Twenty-six
Years of the Chinese Revolutionary Movement). Shanghai: Commercial
Press, 1948.

——. *Ke-ming i-shih* 革命逸史 (An Informal History of the Revolution).
2 vols. Taipei: Commercial Press, 1953.

——. "Kuang-fu-hui"* (The Restoration Society), *HHKM,* I, 515–20.

——. "Min-sheng chu-i yü Chung-kuo cheng-chih ke-ming chih ch'ien-t'u"
民生主義與中國政治革命之前途 (The Principle of People's Livelihood
and the Future of the Chinese Political Revolution), *Min-pao,* No. 4
(May 1, 1906), pp. 97–122.

Feuerwerker, Albert, Rhoads Murphey, and Mary C. Wright (eds.). *Approaches to Modern Chinese History.* Berkeley and Los Angeles: University of California Press, 1967.

Feuerwerker, Albert. *China's Early Industrialization.* Cambridge, Mass.:
Harvard University Press, 1958.

Franke, Wolfgang. *The Reform and Abolition of the Traditional Chinese
Examination System.* Cambridge, Mass.: Harvard University Press,
1963.

Friedrich, Carl J. *Constitutional Government and Democracy.* Boston, 1941.

Fung, Yu-lan. *Chuang Tzu, A New Selected Translation with an Exposition
of the Philosophy of Kuo Hsiang.* Shanghai: Commercial Press, 1933.

——. *A History of Chinese Philosophy.* Translated by Derk Bodde. 2 vols.
Princeton: Princeton University Press, 1953.

Galt, Howard S. "Oriental and Occidental Elements in China's Modern
Education System," *Chinese Social and Political Science Review,* Vol.
XII, No. 3 (July, 1928), pp. 405–25; No. 4 (Oct., 1928), pp. 624–47; Vol.
XIII, No. 1 (Jan., 1929), pp. 12–29.

George, Henry, Jr. *The Life of Henry George.* New York: Doubleday, Page,
1904.

Gide, Charles, and Charles Rist. *A History of Economic Doctrines,* trans.
R. Richards. 2nd ed. Boston, Mass.: D. C. Heath, 1948.

Goodrich, L. Carrington. *The Literary Inquisition of Ch'ien-lung.* Baltimore: Waverly Press, 1935.

Gray, J. "Historical Writing in Twentieth Century China," *Historians of
China and Japan,* ed. W. G. Beasley and E. G. Pulleyblank (London:
Oxford University Press, 1961), pp. 186–212.

Hackett, Roger F. "Chinese Students in Japan, 1900–1910," *Papers on
China* (Harvard University, East Asian Research Center), III (May,
1949), 134–69.

*Han Chih* 漢幟 (The China Banner). Tokyo, Jan. 19, 1907.

*Han min-tsu hsing-ch'eng wen-t'i t'ao-lun chi* 漢民族形成問題討論集 (Collected Discussions of the Problem of the Formation of the Chinese Nation [Han Race]). Peking, 1957.

*Han-sheng* 漢聲 (The Voice of China). Nos. 1–3. Tokyo, 1903.

Hankins, Frank H. "Race as a Factor in Political Theory," *A History of Political Theories: Recent Times,* ed. Charles Edward Merriam and Harry Elmer Barnes (New York: Macmillan, 1924), pp. 508–48.

Hao, Yen-p'ing. "The Abortive Cooperation between Reformers and Revolutionaries (1895–1900)," *Papers on China* (Harvard University, East Asian Research Center), XV (Dec., 1961), pp. 91–114.

Heilbroner, Robert L. *The Worldly Philosophers.* New York, 1953.

Herr, Richard, and Harold T. Parker. *Ideas in History.* Durham, N.C.: Duke University Press, 1965.

Hirth, Friedrich. *The Ancient History of China.* New York: Columbia University Press, 1923.

Ho Chen* and Liu Shih-p'ei.* "Lun chung-tsu ke-ming yü wu-cheng-fu ke-ming chih te-shih" 論種族革命與無政府革命之得失 (On the Advantages and Disadvantages of Racial Revolution and Anarchist Revolution), *T'ien-i pao,* Nos. 6 and 7 (Sept. 1 and Sept. 15, 1907), Chang and Wang, *Selected Essays,* II, 947–59.

Ho, Ping-ti. *The Ladder of Success in Imperial China: Aspects of Social Mobility, 1368–1911.* New York: Science Editions, John Wiley & Sons, 1964.

——. *Studies on the Population of China, 1368–1953.* Cambridge, Mass.: Harvard University Press, 1959.

Howard, Richard C. "The Concept of Parliamentary Government in 19th Century China: A Preliminary Survey." Unpublished paper presented to the University Seminar on Modern East Asia—China and Japan, Columbia University, Jan. 9, 1963.

Hsiao, Kung-ch'üan.* "Anarchism in Chinese Political Thought," *T'ien Hsia Monthly,* Vol. III, No. 3 (Oct., 1936), pp. 249–63.

——. "The Case for Constitutional Monarchy: K'ang Yu-wei's Plan for the Democratization of China," *Monumenta Serica,* XXIV (1965), 1–83.

——. *Chung-kuo cheng-chih ssu-hsiang shih* 中國政治思想史 (A History of Chinese Political Thought). 6 vols. Taipei: Chung-hua wen-hua ch'u-pan shih-yeh wei-yüan-hui 中華文化出版事業委員會, 1954.

——. "K'ang Yu-wei and Confucianism," *Monumenta Serica,* XVIII (1959), 96–212.

——. "Li Chih: An Iconoclast of the Sixteenth Century," *T'ien Hsia Monthly,* Vol. VI, No. 4 (Apr., 1938), pp. 317–41.

——. "The Philosophical Thought of K'ang Yu-wei," *Monumenta Serica,* XXI (1962), 129–93.

——. "Weng T'ung-ho and the Reform Movement of 1898," *Tsinghua Journal of Chinese Studies,* N. S. I, No. 2 (Apr., 1957), 111–245.

Hsieh, Pao Chao. *The Government of China (1644–1911).* Baltimore: The Johns Hopkins University, 1925.

*Hsin-hai ke-ming* 辛亥革命 (The Revolution of 1911). 8 vols. Compiled and edited by the Chung-kuo shih-hsüeh-hui 中國史學會. Shanghai: Jen-min ch'u-pan she 人民出版社, 1957.

*Hsin-hai ke-ming hui-i-lu* 辛亥革命回憶錄 (Recollections of the 1911 Revolution). Edited by the Chung-kuo jen-min cheng-chih hsieh-shang hui-i ch'üan-kuo wei-yüan-hui wen-shih tzu-liao yen-chiu wei-yüan-hui (Committee on Written Historical Materials of the National Committee of the Chinese People's Political Consultative Conference). Peking, 1961——, I——.

"Hsin-hai ke-ming shih-ch'i chung-yao pao-k'an tso-che pi-ming lu" 辛亥革命時期重要報刊作者筆名錄 (Table of Pen-Names Used by Writers in Newspapers and Magazines during the Period of the 1911 Revolution), *Ssu yü yen* 思與言 (Thought and Word), Vol. IV, No. 5 (Jan. 15, 1967), pp. 1059–68.

*Hsin Hunan* 新湖南 (The New Hunan). 1 issue, no date or number. (1903?).

*Hsin-min ts'ung-pao* 新民叢報 (The New People's Fortnightly). Nos. 1–96. Yokohama, Feb. 8, 1902–Nov. 20, 1907.

*Hsin shih-chi* 新世紀 (The New Century). Nos. 1–121. Paris, June 22, 1907– May 21, 1910. Photolithograph reprint, Shanghai, 1947, with *HSCTS* (next).

*Hsin shih-chi ts'ung-shu* 新世紀叢書 (A Collection of Reprinted Works from *Hsin shih-chi*). Photolithograph edition, Shanghai, 1947.

Hsü Shou-shang.* *Chang Ping-lin.** Nanking: Sheng-li ch'u-pan kung-ssu 勝利出版公司, 1946.

Hsüeh, Chün-tu. *Huang Hsing and the Chinese Revolution.* Stanford: Stanford University Press, 1961.

Hu Han-min.* "Ch'ih Hsin-min ts'ung-pao chih miu-wang" 斥新民叢報 之謬妄 (Exposing the Falsehoods of the *Hsin-min ts'ung-pao*), Min-pao, No. 5 (June 26, 1906), pp. 67–78.

——. "Min-pao chih liu ta chu-i" 民報之六大主義 (The Six Great Principles of the *Min-pao*), *Min-pao,* No. 3 (Apr. 5, 1906), pp. 1–22.

——. "P'ai-wai yü kuo-chi-fa" 排外與國際法 (Anti-foreignism and International Law), *Min-pao,* No. 4 (May 1, 1906), pp. 57–79; continued in Nos. 6, 7, 8, 9, 10, and 13.

——. "Shu Hou-kuan Yen-shih tsui-chin cheng-chien" 述侯官嚴氏最近政見 (The Most Recent Political Views of Yen Fu), *Min-pao,* No. 2 (Jan.

22, 1906), pp. 1–17 [Pages in this issue not numbered consecutively; each article begins with page no. 1].

——. "Tzu-chuan" 自傳 (Autobiography), *Ke-ming wen-hsien,* III, 373–442.

——. "Wu-hu! Man-chou so-wei Hsien-fa Ta-kang" 嗚呼！滿洲所謂憲法大綱 (Alas, the Manchus' So-called Outlines of the Constitution), *Chung-hsing jih-pao* 中興日報 (Restoration Daily), Sept. 24–Oct. 9, 1908. A substantial portion of it has been reprinted in *50th Anniversary Documents,* XV, 229–59.

——. "Yü *Kokumin shimbun* lun Chih-na ke-ming-tang shu" 與國民新聞論支那革命黨書 (Letter to *Kokumin Shimbun* Discussing the Chinese Revolutionary Party), *Min-pao,* No. 11 (Jan. 25, 1907), pp. 113–35.

Huang, Philip Chung-chih, "A Confucian Liberal: Liang Ch'i-ch'ao in Action and Thought." Unpublished Ph.D. dissertation, University of Washington, 1966.

Hummel, Arthur W. (ed.). *Eminent Chinese of the Ch'ing Period.* 2 vols. Washington, D.C.: United States Government Printing Office, 1944.

Huntington, Samuel P. "Political Development and Political Decay," *World Politics,* XVII (1965), 386–430.

*Hupei hsüeh-sheng chieh* 湖北學生界 (The Hupei Student World). Nos. 1–4. Tokyo, 1903.

Ike, Nobutaka. *The Beginnings of Political Democracy in Japan.* Baltimore: The Johns Hopkins Press, 1950.

Jansen, Marius B. *The Japanese and Sun Yat-sen.* Cambridge: Harvard University Press, 1954.

Jenks, Edward. *A History of Politics.* London: J. M. Dent & Co., 1900.

Johnson, Chalmers A. *Revolution and the Social System.* (Hoover Institution Studies, No. 3.) Stanford, 1964.

——. *Revolutionary Change.* Boston and Toronto: Little, Brown & Co., 1966.

Joll, James. *The Anarchists.* London: Eyre & Spottiswoode, 1964.

K'ang, Yu-wei. *Ta T'ung Shu: The One-World Philosophy of K'ang Yu-wei.* Translated with Introduction and Notes by Laurence G. Thompson. London: George Allen and Unwin, 1958.

Kao Liang-tso 高良佐. "K'ai-kuo ch'ien ke-ming yü chün-hsien chih lun-chan" 開國前革命與君憲之論戰 (The Debate on Revolution and Constitutional Monarchy before the Founding of the Republic), *Chien-kuo yüeh-k'an* 建國月刊 (The Nation-Building Monthly), Vol. VII, Nos. 3–6 (1932), and Vol. VIII, Nos. 5 and 6 (1933).

*Ke-ming hsien-lieh chuan-chi* 革命先烈傳記 (Biographies of Revolutionary Torchbearers). N.p., Kuomintang Historical Commission, 1941.

*Ke-ming wen-hsien* 革命文獻 (Documents of the Revolution). Edited by Lo

Chia-lun and compiled by the Kuomintang Historical Commission. Vols. I-IV. Taipei, 1953.

King, Frank H. H. *Money and Monetary Policy in China, 1845–1895.* Cambridge, Mass.: Harvard University Press, 1965.

Ko Kung-chen 戈公振. *Chung-kuo pao-hsüeh shih* 中國報學史 (A History of Chinese Journalism). Shanghai: Commercial Press, 1935.

Kosaka, Masata. "Ch'ing Policy Over Manchuria (1900–1903)," *Papers on China* (Harvard University, East Asian Research Center), XVI (Dec., 1962), 126–53.

Krabbe, H. *The Modern Idea of the State.* Translated with an Introduction by George H. Sabine and Walter J. Shepard. New York and London: D. Appleton & Co., 1930.

Kropotkin, Petr. *Mutual Aid, A Factor of Evolution.* Boston: Extending Horizons Books, 1955.

*Kuo-ts'ui hsüeh-pao* 國粹學報 (The National Essence Journal). Shanghai, 1905–11.

Kwok, D. W. Y. *Scientism in Chinese Thought, 1900–1950.* New Haven: Yale University Press, 1965.

——. "The Ta-t'ung Thought of Wu Chih-hui." Paper presented at the International Conference on Asian History, Aug., 1964, Hong Kong.

Lei Chao-hsing 雷照性. "Cheng-fu shuo" 政府説 (On Government), *Min-pao,* No. 17 (Oct. 25, 1907), pp. 87–97.

Levenson, Joseph R. *Confucian China and Its Modern Fate.* Berkeley and Los Angeles: University of California Press, 1958. 3 vols.

——. *Liang Ch'i-ch'ao and the Mind of Modern China.* Cambridge, Mass.: Harvard University Press, 1959.

Li Chien-nung 李劍農. *Chung-kuo chin pai-nien cheng-chih shih* 中國近百年政治史. 2 vols. Taiwan: Commercial Press, 1957. [See next entry for the abridged English translation.]

——. *The Political History of China, 1840–1928.* Edited and translated by Ssu-yü Teng and Jeremy Ingalls. Princeton: Van Nostrand, 1956.

Li, Dun J. *The Essence of Chinese Civilization.* Princeton, N.J.: Van Nostrand, 1967.

Li Shih-tseng.* "Chin-hua yü ke-ming" 進化與革命 (Evolution and Revolution), *HSC,* No. 20 (Nov. 2, 1907), pp. 1–3.

——. "Ke-ming" 革命 (Revolution), *HSCTS,* pp. 5–8.

——. "Lai-shu fu-ta" 來書附答 (Replies to Incoming Letters), *HSC,* No. 6 (July 27, 1907), p. 1.

——. "T'an hsüeh" 談學 (Talking about Learning), *HSC,* No. 7 (Aug. 3, 1907), p. 2.

——. "Wu-cheng-fu chu-i k'e-i chien-chüeh ke-ming-tang chih tse-jen hsin" 無政府主義可以堅決革命黨之責任心 (Anarchism can Solidify the

Revolutionary Party's Sense of Responsibility), *HSC,* No. 58 (Aug. 1, 1908), pp. 10–13.

Li Shu-hua 李書華. "Wu Chih-hui hsien-sheng sheng-p'ing lüeh-shu" 吳稚暉先生生平略述 (A Biographical Sketch of Mr. Wu Chih-hui), *Wu Chih-hui hsien-sheng ti sheng-p'ing* 吳稚暉先生的生平 (The Life of Mr. Wu Chih-hui), edited by Taiwan sheng kuo-yü t'ui-hsing wei-yuan-hui 臺灣省國語推行委員會 (Taipei: Taiwan Kuo-yü Promotion Committee, 1951), pp. 47–66.

Liang Ch'i-ch'ao.\* "Cheng-chih-hsüeh ta-chia Po-lun-chih-li chih hsüeh-shuo" 政治學大家伯倫知理之學説 (The Thought of the Great Political Theorist Bluntschli), *Yin-ping-shih wen-chi* 飲冰室文集 (Collected Essays of the Ice-drinkers' Studio), XIII, 83–86.

———. *Intellectual Trends in the Ch'ing Period.* Translated with Introduction and Notes by Immanuel C. Y. Hsü. Cambridge, Mass.: Harvard University Press, 1959.

———. "K'ai-ming chuan-chih lun" 開明專制論 (On Enlightened Absolutism), *Hsin-min ts'ung-pao,* No. 73, pp. 1–24; No. 74, pp. 1–15; No. 75, pp. 1–50; No. 77, pp. 1–10.

———. "Lu-sou hsüeh-an" 盧梭學案 (Rousseau's Works), *Yin-ping-shih wen-chi* 飲冰室文集 (Shanghai: Chung-hua Book Co., 1926), *chüan* 9, pp. 1–15.

Liao Chung-k'ai.\* "She-hui chu-i shih ta-kang" 社會主義史大綱 (An Outline of the History of Socialism), *Min-pao,* No. 7 (Sept. 5, 1906), pp. 101–11.

———. "Wu-cheng-fu chu-i chih erh-p'ai" 無政府主義之二派 (Two Branches of Anarchism), *Min-pao,* No. 8 (Oct. 8, 1906), pp. 131–38.

———. "Wu-cheng-fu chu-i yü she-hui chu-i" 無政府主義與社會主義 (Anarchism and Socialism), *Min-pao,* No. 9 (Nov. 15, 1906), pp. 1–7 (last section; consecutive pagination in this issue stopped at p. 120; this article is actually on pp. 145–51 of the magazine).

Lin Kuang-hao 林光灝. "Chang T'ai-yen yü Taiwan hsin-wen chieh" 章太炎與臺灣新聞界 (Chang T'ai-yen and the Newspaper World of Taiwan)- *Ch'ang-liu* 暢流, Vol. XXXIV, No. 8 (Dec. 1, 1966), pp. 9–10.

Lin Yao-hua 林耀華. "Kuan-yü min-tsu i-tz'u ti shih-yung ho i-ming ti wen-t'i" 關於民族一詞的使用和譯名的問題 (Concerning the Problem of the Usage and Translation of the Term *min-tsu*), *Li-shih yen-chiu* (Historical Research), II (1963), 171–90.

Lin, Yu-t'ang. *A History of the Press and Public Opinion in China.* Chicago: University of Chicago Press, 1936.

Liu Shih-p'ei.\* "Fei-ping fei-ts'ai lun" 廢兵廢財論 (Away with Soldiers and Property), *T'ien-i pao,* No. 2 (June 25, 1907), reprinted in Chang Nan and Wang Jen-chih, *Selected Essays,* II, 900–904.

——. "Jen-lei chün-li shuo" 人類均力説 (Equal Powers for All Humanity), *T'ien-i pao,* No. 3 (July 10, 1907), Chang and Wang, *Selected Essays,* II, 907–13.

——. "Lun hsin-cheng wei ping-min chih ken" 論新政為病民之根 (Modern Government Is the Root Cause of What Ails the People), *T'ien-i pao,* Nos. 8–10 (combined issue, Oct. 30, 1907), Chang and Wang, *Selected Essays,* II, 968–75.

——. "Pien Man-jen [in the last two parts, Man-chou] fei Chung-kuo chih ch'en-min" 辨滿人[洲]非中國之臣民 (Distinguishing the Manchus as non-Chinese), *Min-pao,* No. 14 (June 8, 1907), pp. 39–111; No. 15 (July 5, 1907), pp. 35–62; No. 18 (Dec. 25, 1907), pp. 1–25.

——. "Wu-cheng-fu chu-i chih p'ing-teng kuan" 無政府主義之平等觀 (Anarchism's Concept of Equality), *T'ien-i pao,* Nos. 4, 5, and 7 (July 25, Aug. 10, and Sept. 15, 1907), Chang and Wang, *Selected Essays,* II, pp. 918–32.

Lo Chia-lun 羅家倫 (ed.). *Kuo-fu nien-p'u ch'u-kao* 國父年譜初稿 (A Chronological Biography of Sun Yat-sen, First Draft). 2 vols. Taipei: Kuomintang Historical Commission, 1959.

Lo, Jung-pang (ed.). *K'ang Yu-wei: A Biography and a Symposium.* Tucson: University of Arizona Press, 1967.

Ma, Feng-ch'en. "Manchu Chinese Social and Economic Conflicts in Early Ch'ing," in *Chinese Social History,* ed. E-tu Zen Sun and John de Francis (Washington, D.C.: American Council of Learned Societies, 1956), pp. 333–51.

Malozemoff, Andrew. *Russian Far Eastern Policy, 1881–1904.* Berkeley and Los Angeles: University of California Press, 1958.

"Man-hua" 曼華 [T'ang Tseng-pi 湯增璧]. "Tung-meng-hui shih-tai Min-pao shih-mo chi" 同盟會時代民報始末記 (A Complete Record of *Min-pao* during the T'ung-meng-hui Period), *Ke-ming wen-hsien,* II, 218–38. This article may also be found in *HHKM,* II, 438–59. "Man-hua" has been identified as a pseudonym of T'ang Tseng-pi by Chün-tu Hsüeh, *Huang Hsing and the Chinese Revolution,* p. 236.

Manuel, Frank E. "Toward a Psychological History of Utopias," *Utopias and Utopian Thought,* ed. Frank E. Manuel (Boston: Houghton-Mifflin, 1966).

Maximoff, G. P. (ed.). *The Political Philosophy of Bakunin: Scientific Anarchism.* Glencoe, Ill.: The Free Press, 1953.

Maybon, Albert. *La Politique Chinoise, 1898–1908.* Paris: V. Giard and E. Briere, 1908.

McNeil, Gordon H. "Robespierre, Rousseau, and Representation," *Ideas in History,* ed. Richard Herr and Harold T. Parker (Durham, N.C.: Duke University Press, 1965), pp. 135–56.

Michael, Franz. "The Military Organization and Power Structure of China during the Taiping Rebellion," *Pacific Historical Review,* XVIII (1949), 469–83.

———. *The Origin of Manchu Rule in China.* Baltimore: Johns Hopkins University Press, 1942.

———. "Regionalism in Nineteenth-Century China," Introduction to Stanley Spector, *Li Hung-chang and the Huai Army* (Seattle: University of Washington Press, 1964), pp. xxi-xliii.

Miller, Frank O. *Minobe Tatsukichi: Interpreter of Constitutionalism in Japan.* Berkeley and Los Angeles: University of California Press, 1965.

*Min Pao* 民報. Nos. 1–26. Tokyo, Nov. 26, 1905–Feb. 1, 1910. Reprinted by Chinese Academy of Sciences. 4 vols. Peking: K'e-hsüeh ch'u-pan she, 1957.

Montagu, Ashley. *Man's Most Dangerous Myth: The Fallacy of Race.* 3rd ed. New York: Harper, 1952.

Moore, Wilbert E. "The Utility of Utopias," *American Sociological Review,* XXXI (1966), 765–72.

Morrison, Esther. "The Modernization of the Confucian Bureaucracy." Unpublished Ph.D. dissertation, Radcliffe College, 1959.

Muramatsu, Yuji. "Some Themes in Chinese Rebel Ideologies," *The Confucian Persuasion,* ed. Arthur F. Wright (Stanford: Stanford University Press, 1960), pp. 241–67.

Needham, Joseph. *Time and Eastern Man.* London: Royal Anthropological Institute of Great Britain and Northern Ireland, 1965.

*O-shih ching-wen* 俄事警聞. Nos. 1–73. Shanghai, Dec. 15, 1903–Feb. 25, 1904.

Oakeshott, Michael. *Rationalism in Politics.* London: Methuen, 1962.

Onogawa, Hidemi 小野川秀美. "Liu Shih-p'ei and Anarchism," *Acta Asiatica,* No. 12, 1967, pp. 70–99.

Palmer, Robert R. *The Age of the Democratic Revolution.* 2 vols. Princeton, N.J.: Princeton University Press, 1959 and 1964.

———. "The Great Inversion: America and Europe in the Eighteenth-Century Revolution," *Ideas in History,* ed. Richard Herr and Harold T. Parker (Durham, N.C.: Duke University Press, 1965), pp. 3–19.

———. "The National Idea in France before the Revolution," *Journal of the History of Ideas,* I (1940), 95–111.

Powell, Ralph L. *The Rise of Chinese Military Power, 1895–1912.* Princeton, N.J.: Princeton University Press, 1955.

Pyle, Kenneth B. "The New Generation: Young Japanese in Search of National Identity." Unpublished Ph.D. dissertation, Johns Hopkins University, 1965.

Rawlinson, John L. *China's Struggle for Naval Development, 1839–1895.* Cambridge, Mass.: Harvard University Press, 1967.

Reeves, *(Captain)* James H. *Notes on the Chinese Revolution of 1911–1912.* War Department, General Staff, No. 6790–6842 (dated 1912).

Reischauer, Edwin O., and John K. Fairbank. *East Asia: The Great Tradition.* Boston: Houghton Mifflin Co., 1958.

Rhoads, Edward J. M. "Nationalism and Xenophobia in Kwangtung (1905–1906): The Canton Anti-American Boycott and the Lienchow Anti-Missionary Uprising," *Papers on China* (Harvard University, East Asian Research Center), XVI (Dec., 1962), 154–97.

Roll, Eric. *A History of Economic Thought.* New York: Prentice-Hall, 1942.

Sabine, George H. *A History of Political Theory.* Rev. ed. New York: Henry Holt, 1955.

Sansom, G. B. *The Western World and Japan.* New York: Alfred A. Knopf, 1951.

Scalapino, Robert A., and Harold Schiffrin. "Early Socialist Currents in the Chinese Revolutionary Movement," *The Journal of Asian Studies,* XVIII (1959), 321–42.

———, and George T. Yu. *The Chinese Anarchist Movement.* Berkeley: Center for Chinese Studies, University of California, 1961.

Schiffrin, Harold. "Sun Yat-sen's Early Land Policy: The Origin and Meaning of 'Equalization of Land Rights,' " *The Journal of Asian Studies,* XVI (1957), 549–64.

———, and Sohn, Pow-key. "Henry George on Two Continents: A Comparative Study in the Diffusion of Ideas," *Comparative Studies in Society and History,* Vol. II, No. 1 (Oct., 1959), pp. 85–109.

Schumpeter, Joseph A. *Capitalism, Socialism, and Democracy.* 2nd ed. New York and London: Harper, 1957.

Schurmann, Franz. *Ideology and Organization in Communist China.* Berkeley and Los Angeles: University of California Press, 1966.

Schwartz, Benjamin. "Ch'en Tu-hsiu and the Acceptance of the Modern West," *Journal of the History of Ideas,* XII (1951), 61–74.

———. *In Search of Wealth and Power. Yen Fu and the West.* Cambridge, Mass.: Belknap Press, 1964.

Sharman, Lyon. *Sun Yat-sen: His Life and Its Meaning.* New York: John Day, 1934.

Shen Yen-kuo.* *Chi Chang T'ai-yen hsien-sheng* 記章太炎先生 (Remembering Mr. Chang T'ai-yen [Ping-lin]). Shanghai: Yung-hsiang t'u-shu-kuan 永祥圖書館, 1946.

Shih, Vincent Y. C. "The Ideology of the Taiping T'ien Kuo," *Sinologica,* Vol. III, No. 1 (1951), pp. 1–15.

——. "Some Chinese Rebel Ideologies," *T'oung Pao,* XLIV (1956), 150–226.

Smythe, E. Joan. "The Tzu-li Hui," *Papers on China* (Harvard University East Asian Research Center), XII (Dec., 1958), 51–68.

Soothill, William Edward, and Lewis Hodous (eds.). *A Dictionary of Chinese Buddhist Terms.* London: Kegan Paul, Trench, Trubner & Co., Ltd., n.d.

Spector, Stanley. *Li Hung-chang and the Huai Army.* Seattle: University of Washington Press, 1964.

*Su Pao* 蘇報. Shanghai, Jan. 24, 1900—July 7, 1903.

Sun, E-tu Zen. "The Chinese Constitutional Missions of 1905–1906," *Journal of Modern History,* Vol. XXIV, No. 3 (Sept., 1952), pp. 251–68.

Sun Yat-sen.* "Chih Wu Ching-heng ch'ing yü Hsin shih-chi p'ing-lun Jih-Hua hsin-pao p'o-huai tang-shih miu-lun ko-han" 致吳敬恒請於新世紀評論日華新報破壞黨事謬論各函 (Letters to Wu Chih-hui asking that he criticize in *Hsin Shih-chi* the false accusations in *Jih-Hua hsin-pao* which are destroying party operations), *Kuo-fu ch'üan-chi,* V, 89–91.

——. "Chung-kuo wen-t'i chih chen chieh-chüeh" 中國問題之真解決 (The True Solution of the Chinese Question), *Kuo-fu ch'üan-chi,* VI, 220–26.

——. "Chung-kuo ying chien-she kung-ho-kuo" 中國應建設共和國 (China Should Establish a Republic), *Kuo-fu ch'üan-chi,* III, 1–6.

——. *Kuo-fu ch'üan-chi* 國父全集 (Complete Works of Sun Yat-sen). Compiled and edited by the Kuomintang Historical Commission. 6 vols. Taipei: Chung-yang wen-wu kung-ying she 中央文物供應社, 1957.

——. "Po Pao-huang pao" 駁保皇報 (Refuting the Emperor-Protection Newspaper [i.e., the reformist *Lung-chi pao* of Honolulu]), *Kuo-fu ch'üan-chi,* VI, 226–32.

——. *San Min Chu I: The Three Principles of the People.* Translated by Frank W. Price. Shanghai: Commercial Press, 1930.

——. "San Min Chu I yü Chung-kuo min-tsu chih ch'ien-t'u" 三民主義與中國民族之前途 (The Three People's Principles and the Future of the Chinese Nation), *Kuo-fu ch'üan-chi,* III, 8–16.

——. "Shang Li Hung-chang t'ung-ch'en chiu-kuo ta-chi shu" 上李鴻章痛陳救國大計書 (A Letter to Li Hung-chang, Painfully Presenting a Great Plan to Save the Country), *Kuo-fu ch'üan-chi,* V, 1–12.

——. "Tsai Ou chiang ch'ü Mei-kuo shih chih Lun-tun Wu Ching-heng han" 在歐將去美國時至倫敦吳敬恒函 (Letter to Wu Ching-heng [Chih-hui] in London, Written in Europe as I Was about to Go to America), *Kuo-fu ch'üan-chi,* V, 82–85.

Sung Chiao-jen.* *Wo chih li-shih* 我之歷史 (My History). Taipei, 1952.

Talmon, J. L. *The Origins of Totalitarian Democracy.* New York: Praeger, 1960.

——. *Political Messianism: The Romantic Phase.* New York: Praeger, 1960.

T'an Pi-an 譚彼岸. "O-kuo min-ts'ui chu-i tui T'ung-meng-hui ti ying-hsiang" 俄國民粹主義對同盟會的影響 (Influence of Russian Populism on the T'ung-meng-hui), *Li-shih yen-chiu* (Historical Research), 1959, No. 1, pp. 35–44.

T'ang, Leang-li. *Wang Ching-wei: A Political Biography.* London: N. Douglas, 1931.

T'ao Ch'eng-chang.* "Che-an chi-lüeh" 浙案紀略 (A Sketch of Affairs in Chekiang), *HHKM,* III, 3–111.

Teng, Ssu-yü, and John K. Fairbank. *China's Response to the West.* Cambridge: Harvard University Press, 1954.

*T'ien-i* 天義 (Heaven's Righteousness). Nos. 4 and 5. Tokyo, July 25—Aug. 10, 1907.

Tihany, Leslie C. "Utopia in Modern Western Thought: The Metamorphosis of an Idea," *Ideas in History,* ed. Richard Herr and Harold T. Parker (Durham, N.C.: Duke University Press, 1965), pp. 20–38.

Ting Wen-chiang 丁文江 (ed.). *Liang Jen-kung hsien-sheng nien-p'u ch'ang-pien ch'u-kao* 梁任公先生年譜長編初稿 (First Draft of a Chronological Biography of Liang Ch'i-ch'ao). 3 vols. Taipei: World Book Co., 1958.

Tsien, Tsuen-hsuin. "Western Impact on China through Translation," *Far Eastern Quarterly,* XIII (1954), 305–27.

Tso Shun-sheng 左舜生. "Huang Hsing p'ing-chuan" 黃興評傳 (A Critical Biography of Huang Hsing), *Chuan-chi wen-hsüeh* 傳記文學 (Biographical Literature), Vol. X, No. 3 (Mar., 1967), pp. 6–15.

Tsou Jung.* "Ke-ming chün" 革命軍 (The Revolutionary Army), *HHKM,* I, 331–64.

Tsou Lu 鄒魯. *Chung-kuo Kuo-min-tang shih-kao* 中國國民黨史稿 (A Draft History of the Kuomintang). Changsha: Commercial Press, 1938.

Tu Ch'eng-hsiang 杜呈祥. *Tsou Jung chuan* 鄒容傳 (Biography of Tsou Jung). Taipei: Pamir Book Co., 1952.

Waite, R. G. L. *Vanguard of Nazism.* Cambridge, Mass.: Harvard University Press, 1952.

Wakeman, Frederic, Jr. *Strangers at the Gate: Social Disorder in South China, 1839–1861.* Berkeley and Los Angeles: University of California Press, 1966.

Walsh, Chad. *From Utopia to Nightmare.* London: G. Bles, 1962.

Walzer, Michael. *The Revolution of the Saints: A Study in the Origins of Radical Politics.* Cambridge, Mass.: Harvard University Press, 1965.

Wang Ching-wei.* "Hsi-wang Man-chou li-hsien che ho t'ing chu" 希望

滿洲立憲者盍聽諸 (Why don't those who hope for the Manchus to establish a constitution listen to this?), *Min-pao,* No. 3 (Apr. 5, 1906), pp. 23–39 [but numbered 1–17, since in this issue pagination of each article began with no. 1], and No. 5 (June 26, 1906), pp. 1–41.

———. "Ke-ming chih chüeh-hsin" 革命之決心 (Revolutionary Determination), *Min-pao,* No. 26 (Feb. 1, 1910), pp. 21–28.

———. "Lun ke-ming chih ch'ü-shih" 論革命之趨勢 (On Trends in the Revolution), *Min-pao,* No. 25 (Jan. 1, 1910), pp. 1–19; and No. 26 (Feb. 1, 1910), pp. 1–20.

———. "Man-chou li-hsien yü kuo-min ke-ming" 滿洲立憲與國民革命 (Manchu Constitutionalism and the National Revolution), *Min-pao,* No. 8 (Oct. 25, 1906), pp. 33–54.

———. "Min-tsu ti kuo-min" 民族的國民 (A Nationalistic Citizenry), *Min-pao,* No. 1 (Nov. 26, 1905), pp. 1–30; and No. 2 (Jan. 22, 1906), pp. 1–23.

———. "Po Hsin-min ts'ung-pao tsui-chin chih fei ke-ming lun" 駁新民叢報最近之非革命論 (Refuting *Hsin-min ts'ung pao*'s Most Recent Anti-revolutionary Article), *Min-pao,* No. 4 (May 1, 1906), pp. 1–43.

———. "Po ke-ming k'e-i chao kua-fen shuo" 駁革命可以召瓜分說 (To Refute the View That Revolution May Invite Partition), *Min-pao,* No. 6 (July 25, 1906), pp. 17–39.

———. "Po ke-ming k'e-i sheng nei-luan shuo" 駁革命可以生內亂說 (Refuting the View That Revolution May Beget Internal Disorder), *Min-pao,* No. 9 (Nov. 15, 1906), pp. 27–50.

———. "Tsa-po Hsin-min ts'ung-pao" 雜駁新民叢報 (Miscellaneous Refutations of *Hsin-min ts'ung-pao*), *Min-pao,* No. 10 (Dec. 20, 1906), pp. 43–56; No. 11 (Jan. 25, 1907), pp. 25–37; and No. 12 (Mar. 6, 1907), pp. 25–43.

———. "Tsai po Hsin-min ts'ung-pao chih cheng-chih ke-ming lun" 再駁新民叢報之政治革命論 (In Further Refutation of *Hsin-min ts'ung-pao*'s Article on Political Revolution), *Min-pao,* No. 6, pp. 79–98; and No.7, pp. 33–62.

———. "Tzu-shu" 自述 (Autobiography). Hsin-lü wen-hsüeh she 新綠文學社 (ed.), *Ming-chia chuan-chi* 名家傳記 (Biographies of Famous People) (Shanghai: Wen-i shu-chü 文藝書局, 1934), pp. 45–50.

———. "Yen-chiu min-tsu yü cheng-chih kuan-hsi chih tzu-liao" 研究民族與政治關係之資料 (Materials for Studying the Relationship between Race and Politics), *Min-pao,* No. 13 (May 5, 1907), pp. 17–37.

Wang Kung-ch'üan.* "She-hui chu-i chiang-hsi hui ti-i-tz'u k'ai-hui chi-shih" 社會主義講習會第一次開會記事 (A Record of the First Meeting of the Society for the Study of Socialism), *T'ien-i pao,* No. 6 (Sept. 1, 1907); reprinted in Chang Nan and Wang Jen-chih, *Selected Essays* (see entry under Chang Nan), pp. 944–47. This article may also be found in *HSC,*

No. 22 (Nov. 16, 1907), p. 4; No. 25 (Dec. 7, 1907), pp. 3–4; No. 26 (Dec. 14, 1907), p. 4.

"Wang-kuo?" 亡國 (Destroying the Country?), *HSC,* No. 48 (May 23, 1908), pp. 1–2.

Wang Te-chao 王德昭. "T'ung-meng-hui shih-ch'i Sun Chung-shan hsien-sheng ke-ming ssu-hsiang ti fen-hsi yen-chiu" 同盟會時期孫中山先生革命思想的分析研究 (An Analytical Study of Sun Yat-sen's Revolutionary Thought in the T'ung-meng-hui Period), *Chung-kuo hsien-tai shih ts'ung-k'an* 中國現代史叢刊 (Anthology on Recent Chinese History), Vol. I, ed. Wu Hsiang-hsiang 吳相湘. Taipei: Cheng-chung Book Co., 1960.

Wang Tung.* "Ke-ming chin-shih lun" 革命今勢論 (On Current Conditions in the Revolution), *Min-pao,* No. 17 (Oct. 25, 1907), pp. 33–60.

Wang, Y. C. *Chinese Intellectuals and the West, 1872–1949.* Chapel Hill: University of North Carolina Press, 1966.

Ward, Robert E. "Political Modernization and Political Culture in Japan," *World Politics,* XV (1963), 588–96.

Wilhelm, Hellmut. *Change: Eight Lectures on the I Ching.* New York: Pantheon Books, 1960.

——. "The Po-hsüeh hung-ju Examination of 1679," *Journal of the American Oriental Society,* LXXI (1951), 60–66.

Wong, Frank F. "Liang Ch'i-ch'ao and the Conflict of Confucian and Constitutional Politics." Unpublished Ph.D. dissertation, University of Wisconsin, 1965.

Woodcock, George. *Anarchism: A History of Libertarian Ideas and Movements.* Cleveland: Meridian Books, 1962.

Wright, Arthur F. (ed.). *The Confucian Persuasion.* Stanford: Stanford University Press, 1960.

Wright, Mary Clabaugh (ed.). *China in Revolution: The First Phase, 1900–1913.* New Haven: Yale University Press, 1968.

Wright, Mary Clabaugh. *The Last Stand of Chinese Conservatism: The T'ung-Chih Restoration, 1862–1874.* Stanford: Stanford University Press, 1957.

——. "A Review Article: The Pre-Revolutionary Intellectuals of China and Russia," *The China Quarterly,* No. 6 (Apr.–June, 1961), pp. 175–79.

"Wu-cheng-fu chu-i yü kung-ch'an chu-i" 無政府主義與共産主義 (Anarchism and Communism), trans. Li Shih-tseng,* *HSCTS,* pp. 41–55.

Wu Chih-hui.* "Shu tzu-yu ying-yeh kuan-chien hou" 書自由營業管見後 (After Writing My Humble Opinion of Free Enterprise), Wu, *Learned Essays,* pp. 19–21 (dated May, 1909).

——. "T'an wu-cheng-fu chih hsien-t'ien" 談無政府之閒天 (An Anarchist Elysium), in Wu, *Learned Essays,* pp. 253–57; also *HSC,* No. 49 (May 30, 1908).

——. "Tang-jen" 黨人 (Party People), *HSC,* No. 117 (Jan. 22, 1910), pp. 1–10.

——. "Tsung-chiao tao-te yü she-hui chu-i" 宗教道德與社會主義 (Religion, Morality, and Socialism), Wu, *Complete Works,* VI, 1–6; also, *HSC,* No. 42 (Apr. 11, 1908).

——. "Tsung-chiao wen-t'i" 宗教問題 (The Problem of Religion), Wu, *Complete Works,* VI, 6–26; also, *HSC,* No. 54 (July 4, 1908), and No. 55 (July 11, 1908).

——. "Yü-lun" 輿論 (Public Opinion), Wu, *Learned Essays,* pp. 135–42 (dated May, 1908).

*Wu Chih-hui hsien-sheng ch'üan-chi* 吳稚暉先生全集 (Complete Works of Mr. Wu Chih-hui). 10 vols. Shanghai: Ch'ün-chung t'u-shu kung-ssu 群衆圖書公司, 1927.

*Wu Chih-hui hsüeh-shu lun-chu ti-san-pien* 吳稚暉學術論著第三編 (Learned Essays of Wu Chih-hui, Third Series). Shanghai: Ch'u-pan ho-tso she 出版合作社, 1927.

Wu Hsiang-hsiang. "K'uang-tai i-ts'ai Yang Tu" 曠代逸才楊度 (Yang Tu, An Unconventional Man of His Time), in *Min-kuo cheng-chih jen-wu* 民國政治人物 (Political Personalities of the Republic), *Wen-hsing ts'ung-k'an,* Vol. XIII, No. 1 (1964), pp. 69–85.

——. *Sung Chiao-jen, Chung-kuo min-chu hsien-cheng ti hsien-ch'ü* 宗教仁 中國民主憲政的先驅 (Sung Chiao-jen, The Forerunner of Chinese Democratic Constitutional Government). Taipei, 1964.

Wu Yu-chang. *The Revolution of 1911.* 3rd ed. Peking: Foreign Languages Press, 1964.

Yao Yü-hsiang 姚漁湘. *Hu Han-min hsien-sheng chuan* 胡漢民先生傳 (A Biography of Hu Han-min). Taipei: Chung-yang wen-wu kung-ying-she, 1954.

Young, Ernest P. "Ch'en T'ien-hua (1875–1905): A Chinese Nationalist," *Papers on China* (Harvard University, East Asian Research Center), XIII (Dec., 1959), 113–62.

*Yu-hsüeh i-pien* 遊學譯編 (Overseas Students Translations). Tokyo, 1902–1903.

# Index

*Ai-kuo hsüeh-she* (Patriotism Academy), 37, 42
*Ai-kuo-hui* (Patriotic Society), 33–34
Aisin Gioro, 205
Anti-Manchuism: of Liang Ch'i-ch'ao, 24; first expressions among students in Japan, 32–36, 39–41, 42–43, 61–62; of Tsou Jung, 39–41; in T'ung-meng-hui oath, 48; pre-modern, 65–67; revolutionaries' emphasis on, 65–105 *passim*; explained by T'ung-meng-hui, 66–67; and modern nationalism, 67–68, 70, 90–91, 99–105, 168, 231–32, 235; overshadows anti-imperialism, 68–70; as a propaganda tactic, 83–84, 85; divisiveness of, 134–35, 237; comment by anarchists, 166–67. *See also* Chang Ping-lin, Ch'en T'ien-hua, Chu Chih-hsin, Hu Han-min, Sun Yat-sen, and Wang Ching-wei
Aquinas, Thomas, 104
Arcadia, 235
Aristotle, 34

Bakunin, Michael (1814–76), 156, 158–60, 161, 163, 164, 165, 182
Bentham, Jeremy (1748–1832), 199
Bible, 151
Bismarck, Otto von (1815–98), 235
Bluntschli, Johann Kaspar (1808–81), German jurist, 109
Bornhak, Conrad (1861–1944), German jurist, 109–12
Boxer movement, 6, 194
Buddhism: Chang Ping-lin on, 197–98, 199–200, 207–10

Canton uprising (1895), 29
Carbonari, 101
Cavour, Camillo Benso di (1810–61), 235
Centralization: Manchus' policy debated, 86–90
Chang Chi (1882–1947), 38, 62, 166, 191, 212
Chang Chien (1853–1926), reformer, 173
Chang Chih-tung (1837–1909), 7, 8, 15
Chang Ching-chiang (Jen-chieh, 1877–1950), 155n, 155–56, 167n

Chang Hsing-yen. *See* Chang Shih-chao
Chang Ping-lin (Chang T'ai-yen, 1868–1922): relationship to other revolutionaries, xxii, 190–91, 201–5, 226–27; activities in revolutionary career, 32, 37, 42, 44, 57, 191–94, 197–98; and Tsou Jung, 37–38; imprisoned, 42, 197–98; and Kuang-fu-hui, 44, 212; and Sun Yat-sen, 47, 55–56, 94, 182–86, 192–93, 212–13; as traditionalist, 51–52, 192, 193, 196, 199–202, 203, 213, 222–23, 227, 235; pessimism, 190, 210–13, 221–22; anti-Manchuism, 191–92, 193–94, 195–96, 201, 202, 203–10, 226; criticizes K'ang Yu-wei, 192, 193–94, 195–97, 199n, 202–3, 204–5; on democracy, 197, 199, 213–19; five negations, 210–13, 214, 221; individualism, 219–22; feud with Wu Chih-hui, 222–25; on science, 224–25; on utilitarianism, 225; mentioned, 36, 81n, 82n, 98, 124, 125, 137, 171, 179, 180, 235, 240, 241, 244, 246
Chang Shih-chao (T. Hsing-yen, 1881——), 38
Cheng Ch'eng-kung (Koxinga, 1624–62), 191, 192
Ch'eng Chia-ch'eng, 50
*Cheng-wen-she* (Political Information Club), 94
Ch'en T'ien-hua (1875–1905): attacks Manchus, 77, 86, 116, 138–39; on freedom, 116; on Japan as a model, 140–41; mentioned, 50, 51, 78n, 79, 101–2, 237
Ch'en Tu-hsiu (1879–1942), 33–34, 157
Chia-ch'ing emperor (r. 1796–1820), 73
Chiang, Monlin (Chiang Meng-lin, 1886–1964), educator: recalls feelings around 1904, 35–36
*Ch'iang-hsüeh-hui* (Society for the Study of Self-strengthening), 192, 204
China Arise Society. *See* Hua-hsing-hui
*China News*, 97
Chinese Education Society. *See* Chung-kuo chiao-yü-hui
Ch'ing dynasty (1644–1912). *See* Manchus
*Ch'ing-nien-hui* (Youth Society), 32–33, 44

# FAR EASTERN AND RUSSIAN INSTITUTE
# PUBLICATIONS ON ASIA

1. Compton, Boyd (trans. and ed.). *Mao's China: Party Reform Documents, 1942–44.* 1952. Reissued 1966. Washington Paperback-4, 1966. 330 pp., map.
2. Chiang, Siang-tseh. *The Nien Rebellion.* 1954. 177 pp., bibliog., index, maps.
3. Chang, Chung-li. *The Chinese Gentry: Studies on Their Role in Nineteenth-Century Chinese Society.* Introduction by Franz Michael. 1955. Reissued 1967. Washington Paperback on Russia and Asia-4. 277 pp., bibliog., index, tables.
4. *Guide to the Memorials of Seven Leading Officials of Nineteenth-Century China.* Summaries and indexes of memorials to Hu Lin-i, Tseng Kuo-fan, Tso Tsung-tang, Kuo Sung-tao, Tseng Kuo-ch'üan, Li Hung-chang, Chang Chih-tung, 1955. 457 pp., mimeographed. Out of print.
5. Raeff, Marc. *Siberia and the Reforms of 1822.* 1956. 228 pp., maps, bibliog., index. Out of print.
6. Li Chi. *The Beginnings of Chinese Civilization: Three Lectures Illustrated with Finds at Anyang.* 1957. Reissued 1968. Washington Paperback on Russia and Asia-6. 141 pp., illus., bibliog., index.
7. Carrasco, Pedro. *Land and Polity in Tibet.* 1959. 318 pp., maps, bibliog., index.
8. Hsiao, Kung-chuan. *Rural China: Imperial Control in the Nineteenth Century.* 1960. Reissued 1967. Washington Paperback on Russia and Asia-3. 797 pp., illus., bibliog., index.
9. Hsiao, Tso-liang. *Power Relations within the Chinese Communist Movement, 1930–1934.* Vol. I: *A Study of Documents.* 1961. 416 pp., bibliog., index, glossary. Vol. II: *The Chinese Documents.* 1967. 856 pp.
10. Chang, Chung-li. *The Income of the Chinese Gentry.* Introduction by Franz Michael. 1962. 387 pp., tables, bibliog., index.
11. Maki, John M. *Court and Constitution in Japan: Selected Supreme Court Decisions, 1948–60.* 1964. 491 pp., bibliog., index.
12. Poppe, Nicholas, Leon Hurvitz, and Hidehiro Okada. *Catalogue of the Manchu-Mongol Section of the Toyo Bunko.* 1964. 391 pp., index.

13. Spector, Stanley. *Li Hung-chang and the Huai Army: A Study in Nineteenth-Century Chinese Regionalism.* Introduction by Franz Michael. 1964. 399 pp., maps, tables, bibliog., glossary, index.

14. Michael, Franz, and Chung-li Chang. *The Taiping Rebellion: History and Documents.* Vol. I: *History.* 1966. 256 pp., maps, index. Vols. II and III: *Documents and Comments.* In press 1969.

15. Shih, Vincent Y. C. *The Taiping Ideology: Its Sources, Interpretations, and Influences.* 1967. 576 pp., bibliog., index.

16. Poppe, Nicholas. *The Twelve Deeds of Buddha: A Mongolian Version of the Lalitavistara; Mongolian Text, Notes, and English Translation.* 1967. 241 pp., illus. Paper.

17. Hsia, Tsi-an. *The Gate of Darkness: Studies on the Leftist Literary Movement in China.* Preface by Franz Michael. Introduction by C. T. Hsia. 1968. 298 pp., index.

18. Hsiao, Tso-liang. *The Land Revolution in China, 1930–1934: A Study of Documents.* 1969. 376 pp., tables, glossary, bibliog., index.

19. Gasster, Michael. *Chinese Intellectuals and the Revolution of 1911: The Birth of Modern Chinese Radicalism.* 1969. 320 pp., glossary, bibliog., index.